Lebanon

Ann Jousiffe

Lebanon

1st edition

Published by
Lonely Planet Publications
Head Office: PO Box 617, Hawthorn, Vic 3122, Australia
Branches: 155 Filbert St, Suite 251, Oakland, CA 94607, USA
10 Barley Mow Passage, Chiswick, London W4 4PH, UK
71 bis rue du Cardinal Lemoine, 75005 Paris, France

Printed by
SNP Printing Pte Ltd, Singapore

Photographs by
Paul Doyle   Andy Ferguson   Ann Jousiffe   Peter Jousiffe   Diana Saad

Front cover: Cornice detail from the Temple of Jupiter at Baalbek (Ann Jousiffe)

First Published
February 1998

Although the authors and publisher have tried to make the information as accurate as possible, they accept no responsibility for any loss, injury or inconvenience sustained by any person using this book.

National Library of Australia Cataloguing in Publication Data

Jousiffe, Ann.
Lebanon.

1st ed.
Includes index.
ISBN 0 86442 350 0.

1. Lebanon – Guidebooks. I. Title.

915.6920444

text & maps © Lonely Planet 1998
photos © photographers as indicated 1998
climate chart of Baalbek compiled from information supplied by Patrick J Tyson, © Patrick J Tyson, 1998

Ann Jousiffe

Ann Jousiffe is a travel writer, journalist and photographer who lives and works in London. Her work has appeared in many UK and international magazines and newspapers. She has specialised in North Africa and the Middle East for many years and has acted as consultant and researcher for several TV documentaries.

Ann has contributed to other Lonely Planet guides, including the Libya chapters for *North Africa* and *Africa on a shoestring*, the Lebanon chapter in *Middle East on a shoestring* and the *Jordan, Syria & Lebanon travel atlas*. Her great passion is Islamic architecture and the Sahara Desert, and when not working, she likes to relax in her London flat with a glass or two of red wine.

From the Author

I would like to thank the many people who have made the writing of this book possible, especially those people in Lebanon who helped so much with the research. Bassam Lahoud, François and Pascal Matta, and Munzer and Renee Awaida have my heartfelt thanks for their valuable support.

Between the commissioning of this book and its publication, I was diagnosed with breast cancer and saw more of the inside of a hospital than I ever wanted or planned to. I would like to thank my friends and family who gave me their love and support and who propped me back in front of the computer and got me going again workwise and lifewise. I couldn't have done it without them.

To Peter, my husband, and Sheila, my mother, to Corinne Simcock and Mick Williams, to Judith Hampson, Lindsay Fulcher, Chris Hooke and Angela Fairchild, to Adam and Caroline Krajweski and all my other good friends who were around when I needed them – a big thank you. I would also like to thank senior editor Sam Carew who stood by me patiently when things got tough.

This Book

This guide grew out of the Lebanon chapter in Lonely Planet's *Middle East on a shoestring*. Diana Saad researched and wrote the original Lebanon chapter. Ann Jousiffe researched and wrote this book.

From the Publisher

This first edition of *Lebanon* was edited and proofed by Katrina Browning with assistance from Michelle Glynn, Diana Saad and Isabelle Young. The mapping was done by Indra Kilfoyle, Sally Gerdan, Mark Germanchis, Rachael Scott and Trudi Canavan. Trudi was responsible for the design and layout and many of the illustrations. Additional illustrations were drawn by Indra, David Andrew, Verity Campbell and Graham Imeson. Adam McCrow designed the front cover and did the back cover cartography.

Thanks to Samar Kadi, from the *Daily Star* newspaper in Beirut, for updating the manuscript at short notice. Thanks also to Christine Niven who researched and wrote The Architecture of Lebanon section; Katrina for the additional boxed stories;

Helen Castle for the recipes in A Guide to Lebanese Cuisine; Joumana Faddoul and the staff at the Lebanese consulate in Melbourne and to the staff at the Lebanese embassy in Canberra; Cleopatra's restaurant in Melbourne for the yummy Lebanese food; Paul Piaia for creating the climate charts; Peter Ward of Peter Ward Book Exports for his help with the bookshops section; Michelle for useful insights into the Middle East; and Sam Carew, Cathy Lanigan and Greg Herriman for their advice and support.

Thanks

Many thanks to the following travellers who used *Middle East on a shoestring* and wrote to us with helpful hints, useful advice and interesting anecdotes about travelling in Lebanon:

Ayad Abou-Chakra, Philip Anthony, Scotty Boothey, Lucinda Coates, CarolAnne Duncan, Mary Findell, Steve Harrison, Simone Hoppler, Graham Jones, Mark Korenhof, Gabriel Kuhn, W Stöckl-Manger & B Manger, Kjetil Nørvåg, Alexander Styhre, Kevin Troy and Paul Werne.

Warning & Request

Things change – prices go up, schedules change, good places go bad and bad places go bankrupt – nothing stays the same. So, if you find things better or worse, recently opened or long since closed, please tell us and help make the next edition even more accurate and useful.

We value all of the feedback we receive from travellers. Julie Young coordinates a small team who read and acknowledge every letter, postcard and email, and ensure that every morsel of information finds its way to the appropriate authors, editors and publishers.

Everyone who writes to us will find their name in the next edition of the appropriate guide and will also receive a free subscription to our quarterly newsletter, *Planet Talk*. The very best contributions will be rewarded with a free Lonely Planet guide.

Excerpts from your correspondence may appear in new editions of this guide; in our newsletter, *Planet Talk*; or in updates on our Web site – so please let us know if you don't want your letter published or your name acknowledged.

Contents

INTRODUCTION..**9**

FACTS ABOUT LEBANON... **11**

History 11
Geography 30
Climate 31
Ecology & Environment 32
Flora & Fauna........................ 32

Government & Politics 33
Economy 34
Population & People................ 34
Education 35
Arts.. 35

Society & Conduct................... 38
Religion..................................39
**The Architecture of
Lebanon 43**
Language...................................50

FACTS FOR THE VISITOR **56**

Planning 56
Suggested Itineraries 57
Tourist Offices......................... 57
Visas & Documents 57
Highlights 58
Embassies 61
Customs.................................... 63
Money....................................... 63
Post & Communications 65
Books....................................... 66
Online Services........................ 67
Films... 68
Newspapers & Magazines....... 68

Radio & TV 68
Video Systems 69
Photography & Video 69
Time 70
Electricity.............................. 70
Weights & Measures 70
Laundry.................................... 70
Health....................................... 70
Toilets....................................... 79
Women Travellers................... 79
Gay & Lesbian Travellers 80
Disabled Travellers.................. 80
Senior Travellers...................... 80

Travel with Children................ 80
Useful Organisations............... 80
Dangers & Annoyances 80
Business Hours 81
Public Holidays........................ 81
Activities.................................. 82
Work... 83
Accommodation....................... 84
Entertainment.......................... 84
Spectator Sport......................... 85
Things to Buy........................... 85
**A Guide to Lebanese
Cuisine 87**

GETTING THERE & AWAY **96**

Air.. 96
Land 101

Sea 102
Departure Tax 102

Organised Tours 102
Warning.................................... 103

GETTING AROUND...**104**

Bus... 104
Train... 104
Taxi & Service Taxi................. 104

Car & Motorcycle 105
Bicycle 106
Hitching 106

Walking................................... 106
Local Transport....................... 106
Organised Tours 106

BEIRUT **108**

History 109
Orientation............................. 111
The Rebuilding of Beirut 112
Information 113
The Corniche Walk................. 117

Museums............................. 118
Things to See & Do 120
Activities.............................. 124
Organised Tours..................... 125
Places to Stay......................... 125

Places to Eat............................ 129
Entertainment......................... 133
Things to Buy.......................... 134
Getting There & Away 135
Getting Around 135

AROUND BEIRUT **137**

Beit Meri.............................. 137
Broummana 139
Bikfaya 140
Jebel Sannine........................ 140

Nahr al-Kalb 141
Jeita Grotto 142
Jounieh 143
Harissa 146

Faraya.....................................147
Faqra 148
Rachana................................. 149

NORTH OF BEIRUT **150**

Byblos (Jbail) 150
Amchit 158
Qartaba 160

Afqa Grotto.......................... 160
Laklouk 161
Douma................................... 161

Batroun.................................... 162
Moussalayha Castle 163
Qubba..................................... 163

TRIPOLI & THE CEDARS 164

Tripoli (Trablous).............. 164	Chekka 172	Bcharré 173
Around Tripoli 171	Qalamoun.................................173	The Cedars 175
Qubbet al-Beddawi................ 171	Balamand 173	The Kadisha Valley 176
Enfe..172	**Bcharré & The Cedars..... 173**	**Akkar 179**

THE BEKAA VALLEY 181

Chtaura 181	Aanjar 185	Baalbek 187
Zahlé 183	Lake Qaraoun & the Litani	Hermel......................................193
Around Zahlé.......................... 185	Dam..187	Around Hermel 194

SOUTH OF BEIRUT 195

The Chouf Mountains 195	Around the Chouf.................. 200	Around Sidon 205
Deir al-Qamar........................ 196	**The South 200**	Tyre (Sour) 209
Beiteddine.............................. 197	Sidon (Saida) 200	Around Tyre 214

GLOSSARY 216

INDEX 219

Maps 219	Boxed Stories.......................... 219	Text... 219

Map Legend

BOUNDARIES

.... International Boundary
.... Provincial Boundary
.... Disputed Boundary

ROUTES

..... Freeway, with Route Number [A25]
.... Major Road
.... Minor Road
.... Minor Road - Unsealed
.... City Road
.... City Street
.... City Lane
.... Train Route, with Station
.... Cable Car or Chairlift
.... Ferry Route
.... Walking Track

AREA FEATURES

.... Building
.... Christian Cemetery
.... Non-Christian Cemetery
.... Beach
.... Market
.... Park, Gardens
.... Pedestrian Mall
.... Urban Area

HYDROGRAPHIC FEATURES

.... Canal
.... Coastline
.... Creek, River
.... Lake, Intermittent Lake
.... Rapids, Waterfalls
.... Swamp

SYMBOLS

✈	.... Airport	血 .... Museum
🌑 CAPITAL .... National Capital	.... Ancient or City Wall	← .... One Way Street
◉ CAPITAL .... Provincial Capital	⊖ .... Bank	)(....................... Pass
● CITY .... City	🏛 .... Castle	⛽ .... Petrol Station
● Town .... Town	⌂ .... Cave	★ .... Police Station
● Village .... Village	Cathedral, Church	✉ .... Post Office
■ .... Place to Stay	Cliff or Escarpment	∴ .... Ruins
Å .... Camping Ground	○ .... Embassy	⛷ .... Ski Field
🚐 .... Caravan Park	✿ .... Garden	◎ . ... Spring
⌂ .... Hut or Chalet	⊕ .... Hammam	⛱ .... Surf Beach
	⊕ .... Hospital	▭ .... Swimming Pool
▼ .... Place to Eat	👗 .... Lighthouse	☎ .... Telephone
☕ .... Pub or Bar	▣ .... Monastery	血 ..... Temple (Classical)
☕ .... Cafe	♠ .... Monument	▣ .... Tomb
	◖ .... Mosque	❶ ..... Tourist Information
	▲ .... Mountain or Hill	⊖ .... Transport

Note: not all symbols displayed above appear in this book

Introduction

Lebanon has been off the agenda for tourists for so long, due to 17 years of civil war, that six years after the cease-fire there is still only a trickle of visitors. The world at large seems unaware that Beirut is no longer war-torn and that the international press have long ago sent their war correspondents on to another trouble spot.

The calm that has followed the storm is a surprise to foreigners who probably expect a country full of tension. Travellers today can see many Lebanese people rediscovering their own country, visiting areas which were denied to them during the effective partition of the Christian and Muslim communities during the conflict, and enjoying what is widely thought of as the most beautiful of the Middle Eastern countries.

It would be naive to think that all the problems and complexities which caused the conflict have been solved, or that Lebanon will automatically resume its prewar position as the Switzerland of the Middle East,

but there is a level of optimism about Lebanon's future which has been missing for decades. To re-establish tourism is one of the aims. The word is slowly getting round that travel to, and around, Lebanon is not only possible but surprisingly free of hassles.

Geographically, Lebanon is as diverse as it is possible to imagine in a country so small. In a very compact space there is a coastal plain with ancient historical cities strung along its length, a soaring mountain range with popular ski resorts, and an agricultural plain bound in by a second mountain range. Culturally too, there is diversity: the ancient Christian heritage and the Islamic architecture mix throughout the country with the classical remains of earlier civilisations.

The Lebanese are proud of their heritage which stretches back to the Phoenician civilisation. All the great conquering peoples of antiquity have left signs of their presence in Lebanon – many of these monuments are well preserved. Apart from the Phoenicians,

9

there are relics from the Egyptians, Greeks, Romans, Byzantines, Arabs, Ottoman Turks, Crusaders and latterly the French, who had a mandate over Lebanon until independence in 1946.

The civil war has left huge amounts of damage, and the Lebanese have a long way to go before everything is restored. This is clearly going to involve more than just repairing buildings and roads. After two decades of intense media coverage of the war, the hostage crisis and large-scale human tragedy, the indelible impression to outsiders is that Lebanon is a trouble spot to be avoided. The reality is that Lebanon is now at peace and a visitor can travel safely throughout the country, except for the extreme south which is under United Nations (UN) and Israeli control.

The handful of foreign visitors who are now finding their way back to Lebanon are nearly all well-heeled package tourists and consequently have little contact with Lebanese people. Independent travellers are a bit of a rarity but are made to feel very welcome. The Lebanese are not shy about inviting you into their homes, and offers of help are genuine manifestations of their hospitality and friendliness towards strangers. Now is a perfect time to visit – before the country becomes too popular, as it surely will in the years to come.

Facts about Lebanon

HISTORY

The history of Lebanon has been eventful and complex. Its unique geography in the Middle East has often been a factor in the events which have shaped its history. The region was known in the Bible as 'the land of milk and honey', and conquerors have always been attracted to Lebanon by the abundant natural resources, the safe anchorages on the coastline and the defensive possibilities of the high mountains. The mountains also played a role later in Lebanese history by providing a refuge for persecuted religious minorities. Many people have taken refuge there and then put down roots in their strongholds. Much of the characteristic division of areas into Christian and Muslim communities today is a result of these earlier struggles.

The shores of Lebanon attracted settlers from about 10,000 BC onwards. These simple, early settlements evolved into more complex villages over time and eventually, around 3000 BC, into prototype cities. (The layers of development can be seen most clearly in the modern excavations at Byblos.) By 4000 BC these settlements had started to use copper, although only in a decorative way, and ceramics had become quite sophisticated. By around 2500 BC the coast had been colonised by the people who later became known as the Phoenicians. From this point onwards, the culture of the region and the trading skills of its people developed rapidly.

These times were far from peaceful as wave after wave of warlike tribes conquered and reconquered various parts of the Middle East. The Akkadians from the Euphrates Valley in Mesopotamia were the first people to control an empire in the modern sense. In a burst of expansionism, the Akkadian army thrust towards the Mediterranean under the leadership of Sargon of Akkad, who reigned from 2334 to 2279 BC. He became the world's first known empire-builder. The coastal cities prospered from the increased demand for raw materials, such as the cedar wood of Lebanon.

Around 2100 BC the Amorites conquered Phoenicia, followed about 300 years later by the Hyksos and then the Egyptians. During the 14th century BC the Hittites (from Anatolia) invaded from the north, gradually breaking Egypt's control of the region. By 1100 BC, Phoenicia was independent once more.

Phoenicians

One of the greatest early civilisations of the Mediterranean came out of the tiny strip of land known as Phoenicia, most of which is in modern Lebanon. The Phoenicians (a Semitic race, probably related to the Canaanites who had settled in the coastal lowlands from about 3000 BC), became one of the most influential cultures of the region. They dominated the sea with their superior vessels and navigational skills and created the first real alphabet – a remarkable breakthrough which paved the way for the great works of literature of the early Greeks and subsequently the rest of the classical civilisations.

Despite their great innovations and skills as artisans and traders, the Phoenicians never became unified politically, remaining instead as independent city-states along the Lebanese shore. Gebal (Byblos, later Jbail) and Tyre (Sour) were the most important of these cities, followed by Sidon (Saida) and Berytus (Beirut). The Phoenicians' success is all the more remarkable because it was not the result of conquest and war, but of enterprise and intellectual endeavour.

The Phoenicians had absorbed various cultural and religious influences from the peoples with whom they had come into contact. For example, their pantheon of gods greatly resembled that of the Semitic peoples of Mesopotamia. They worshipped Baal, 'the Lord of Heaven', who represented the sun, and Ashtoreth, the Assyrian Astarte,

Time Line

BC

c3000 Bronze Age; Byblos develops from a village into an urban settlement

c3000-2500 Phoenicians colonise Lebanon's coastline

c2100 Amorites conquer Phoenicia

c1800-1200 Hyksos, Egyptians and Hittites control Phoenicia

c1200-1150 Sea Peoples attack Phoenician cities, destroying Aradus and Sidon

1100-c868 Phoenicia's golden age of independence; growth of Tyre under King Hiram

c868-612 Assyrians rule Phoenicia

c612-539 Neo-Babylonians take over Assyrian Empire

539 Persians conquer Babylonian Empire

346 King Tennes of Sidon leads failed rebellion against Persians

333 Alexander the Great defeats Persians at the Battle of Issus; all Phoenician cities except Tyre submit to the Greeks

332 Tyre falls to Alexander the Great after lengthy siege

323 Alexander the Great dies; Greek empire divided between Ptolemy, Seleucus and Antigonus; Ptolemy I rules Phoenicia

198 Seleucids, under Antiochus III, conquer Phoenicia

64 Romans, under Pompey the Great, take over Phoenicia, which becomes part of the Roman province of Syria

40-4 Herod the Great is governor of Syria; Berytus (Beirut) becomes an important centre

AD

68 Baalbek's Temple of Jupiter is completed

306-37 Constantine reigns as emperor and moves capital to Byzantium (Anatolia), which he renames Constantinople (modern Istanbul)

394 Christianity made the official religion of the Roman Empire

395 Roman Empire split into east and west; Lebanon becomes part of eastern Byzantine Empire

c570 Birth of Mohammed in Mecca

608 Persian king Khosrau II overruns Lebanon

c625 Byzantine troops retake Lebanon

632 Mohammed dies at Medina

636 Arabs defeat Byzantine army at the Battle of Yarmouk; Byzantine army retreats towards Anatolia (modern Turkey)

661 Mu'awiyah establishes Umayyad dynasty

750 Umayyads fall to Abbasid dynasty

759-60 Christian peasants revolt against Muslims in the Bekaa Valley

969 Fatimids establish own caliphate in Cairo and take over Lebanon

1095 Pope Urban II launches Crusades

1099 Crusaders take Jerusalem

1171 Fatimid dynasty abolished

1176 Saladin establishes Ayyubid dynasty

1258 Osman, the founder of the Ottoman Empire, is born

c1260 Mamelukes overthrow Ayyubids and establish control over Lebanon

1291 Last Crusaders forced out of Acre

1453 Ottoman Turks under Sultan Mehmed II take Constantinople, bringing an end to the Byzantine Empire

1516-17 Ottoman Sultan Selim I conquers Lebanon

1586 Fakhr ad-Din establishes control over Lebanon and parts of northern Palestine

1633 Fakhr ad-Din captured by the Ottomans, taken to Constantinople and executed in 1635

1667 Fakhr ad-Din's nephew, Ahmad Ma'an, establishes emirate

1711 Shihab family takes over reins of power after death of Ahmad Ma'an; Shihab emirs rule the country until 1841

1842 Ottomans return to govern Lebanon

1914-19 World War I; French and British troops occupy Lebanon after Allied victory in 1918

1923 Lebanon comes under French Mandate

1926 Greater Lebanon renamed the Lebanese Republic

1943 French ousted by British-led troops; independence promised; unratified National Pact agreement reached

1946 Lebanese independence declared

1958 Muslims launch insurrection; civil war averted with aid from US troops

1975-92 Civil war

1996 Israel launches 'Operation Grapes of Wrath'; UN base in Qana shelled

their 'Great Mother'. Ashtoreth originally represented the moon, but later became the goddess of nature, and was worshipped with orgiastic rites. Melkart, the god of the cities (later called Heracles by the Greeks), and Dagon, god of the fishes, were also worshipped. The legend of Adonis, or Tammuz, flourished in Phoenicia, and has a potent resonance throughout all the subsequent religions of the area, even to this day. It is a classic tale of life, death and rebirth symbolised by the passing seasons (see the

Mythology boxed story in The Architecture of Lebanon section later in this chapter).

Later the Phoenicians also adopted some of the Egyptian gods and rites but they apparently did not believe in an afterlife, expecting to live on only in the memories of their families and friends.

From the 16th century BC the land of Phoenicia was ruled by Egypt, a rule which lasted for the next four centuries and is clearly visible in the architecture and religious artefacts which remain from the period. The invasion by the 'peoples of the sea' around 1200 BC had a direct effect on some of the coastal cities: Aradus (north of Tripoli) was destroyed as was Sidon, according to historical sources. These invaders are thought to have been the Philistines, a people of possible Aegean origin who settled on the southern coast between Joppa (modern Tel Aviv) and Gaza.

It was not until after this invasion that the Phoenicians enjoyed the period of independence which was to be their golden age of sea trading, exploration and colonisation on which their fame rested. From Tyre, Sidon and the other Phoenician cities, sailors went forth into the Mediterranean and spread both their cultural ideas and their goods.

It was also during this time that the alphabet gradually came to be used, most likely as an aid to international commerce. There is some question as to whether the Phoenicians actually invented the alphabet themselves or adapted the concept from an earlier source. In any case the idea was revolutionary. Up until that time, writing had consisted of pictograms, which involved many hundreds of different symbols. The complexity of early written languages meant that only learned scribes could use the system. With the advent of a modern-style alphabet, writing became vastly more accessible for ordinary people. It was an idea which had enormous impact on the literature which was developing in early Greece and gradually became the basis for all writing in the western world. (See the Phoenician Alphabet boxed story on the next page for more details.)

Apart from their trading skills, the Phoenicians were also talented manufacturers. They produced some of the finest metalwork, glass and textiles in the world at the time. Sidon, in particular, was famed for the

The Phoenician World

0   500   1000 km

Phoenician Alphabet

The Phoenicians were crucially important to the development of the alphabet. Their language, a variant of 'north-west' Semitic, was very close to Hebrew and Moabite. The earliest Phoenician inscription that has survived is on King Hiram's sarcophagus found at Byblos, dating from the 11th century BC.

Until the alphabet was invented, writing was restricted to scribes who could learn the complicated hieroglyphic and cuneiform scripts. Hieroglyphs were pictorial representations of whole words or ideas in quite involved symbols. Cuneiform script was made up of wedge-shaped characters from which this writing system was named – the Latin word *cuneus* means 'wedge'.

Trade was no doubt the 'mother of invention' that saw the development of the much simpler 22-letter alphabet. It was a writing system that was less complicated and quicker to write than the hieroglyphic and cuneiform scripts. The Phoenicians took this alphabet with them throughout the Mediterranean. The Greeks soon adopted the system and it is from Greek that Latin and subsequently all European written language is descended.

Herodotus, the 5th-century BC Greek historian and the 'father of history', wrote that the alphabet was introduced into Greece by Cadmus and his Phoenician followers. The Greeks did not, according to Herodotus, call the new letters 'alphabet' but 'phoinikia grammata' – 'Phoenician letters'. The modern term 'phonetic' comes from this revolutionary idea of assigning symbols to corresponding sounds. ■

Latin Script	Early Phoenician (12th c BC)	Late Phoenician (9th c BC)	Early Greek (7th c BC)	Aramaic	Hebrew	Punic (Carthage)	Modern Arabic
a							
b							
g							
d							
h							
w							
z							
ḥ							
ṭ							
e							
k							
l							
m							
n							
s							
o							
f							
ṣ							
q							
r							
sh							
t							

Front and back of an arrow head from around 1100 BC, with Phoenician script translated as 'Arrow of X son of Y'.

quality of its goods. In the *Iliad*, which is set several centuries earlier, Homer describes how, at the funeral of Patroclus, Achilles offered as a prize to the swiftest runner the most perfectly shaped bowl in the world. It was one made in Sidon. The silver bowl with a golden rim that Menelaus gave to Telemachus was also from Phoenicia. The beautiful robe offered by Hecaba to the goddess Athene, a robe stiff with embroidery and 'shining with the brightness of a star', was the work of Phoenician women.

Despite the obvious talents of the Phoenicians they remained a trading rather than a military force, and were always vulnerable to invasion and conquest. Their success in exploration and navigation involved a large amount of secrecy. There was a good deal of what today would be called industrial espionage. New routes and safe harbours were anxiously sought. If a Phoenician captain thought his ship was being followed, he would risk being shipwrecked rather than reveal a secret anchorage. These safe havens were dotted around the coast and provided safe overnight camps and supplies of food and water for the ships. The vessels themselves had improved greatly during the Phoenician era, relying on sail power rather than teams of oarsmen, which left more room on board for cargo.

By the latter part of the 11th century BC, Tyre had become the most important of the Phoenician cities and much of the exploration of the time emanated from its port. Jezebel, a princess of Tyre, married King Ahab strengthening political ties with the early state of Israel.

Much of Tyre's wealth came from the manufacture of Tyrian purple, a dye produced from the murex shell. The process was a closely guarded secret and involved harvesting the molluscs from deep water breeding grounds. Their dye sacs were extracted and mixed in various proportions with that of another mollusc, the buccinum, producing many shades of pink and mauve. Huge mounds of murex shells have been uncovered both at Tyre and Sidon and, the trade of this dye outlasted the Phoenician

A Shipwreck at Cape Gelidonya

In the early 1960s archaeologists excavated one of the oldest shipwrecks in the world in the waters around Cape Gelidonya (the 'Cape of the Swallows') off the coast of Turkey near Bodrum. The ship, lying in approximately 30m of water, turned out to be a Phoenician trader that had sunk around 1200 BC as it carried a cargo of bronze and copper ingots to Greek metalworkers. The ingots, cast in the four-handled 'oxhide' shape common to the period, had been loaded on board at Cyprus, ancient Alashiya, probably the ship's last major port of call.

As it was navigating a stretch of water described by the Roman writer Pliny as 'extremely dangerous to mariners', the ship's 9 to 12m hull struck a reef of jagged rocks. Thanks to its cargo, it sank like a stone. ∎

culture and continued on into the Middle Ages. (See the Murex boxed story in the South of Beirut chapter.)

Cedar wood was also a source of wealth. During the reign of Solomon in Israel (around 961-922 BC), King Hiram of Tyre supplied him with materials and artisans to build his temple and palace in Jerusalem. It was not only cedar but also gold and silver, which adorned these buildings and the King of Tyre was amply rewarded with a yearly payment of oil and wheat.

King Hiram enlarged the city of Tyre by building protective walls and dikes, and embellished the city with new temples dedicated to Ashtoreth and Melkart. He also

Hiram versus Solomon

Relations between King Hiram of Tyre and King Solomon of Israel were cordial but competitive. According to the annals of Tyre, there was a contest of wisdom between the two kings. They would each set riddles for the other. Whoever failed to guess correctly had to pay a fine. Wrong answers cost Hiram a fortune, but he eventually sharpened his wits and turned the tables on Solomon, winning back all he had lost and more. ∎

erected a great golden column in the temple of Baal Shamem (Zeus).

Phoenician colonies spread throughout the Mediterranean from Utica and Carthage in North Africa to Gades (Cadiz) in southern Spain. The Phoenicians' navigational skills were unsurpassed – they discovered the use of the north star as an important navigational point. Voyages of exploration took them as far south as India where their cultural influence has been identified. It is thought that some traders made it as far north as Cornwall in southern England to buy tin.

It is believed that the Phoenicians may have managed to carry out the first circumnavigation of Africa, leaving via the ancient canal connecting the Nile to the Red Sea and returning via the Mediterranean. The expedition, under the patronage of Pharaoh Necho, apparently took four years to complete as nothing was known about the size of Africa and the voyage was punctuated with stops to grow grain crops in order to continue. An account of this voyage is reported in the writings of Herodotus, a 5th-century BC Greek historian. Even though he was sceptical of the whole account, his remark about the sun setting in a different direction is correct for the southern hemisphere and supports the story.

Some sources have also suggested that the Phoenicians sailed across the Atlantic and made contact with several cultures in South America. The basis for this idea is the discovery of some bearded sculptures in South America which bear a strong resemblance to the Semitic Phoenicians. It is a romantic idea but unlikely, as the Phoenicians relied on frequent anchorages for their long voyages and were unable to negotiate a long ocean crossing without landfall.

In the 9th century BC Phoenicia came under the conquering boot of the Assyrian king Ashurnasirpal II, and was forced to pay heavy tributes. Byblos was not annexed and was left in a state of relative autonomy, as was the island of Tyre, but the other cities and their surrounding areas suffered. The Phoenicians' exclusive hold on trade in the Mediterranean had been broken. Following

Stone relief of a Phoenician trading ship with single mast, carved on a sarcophagus found at Sidon in the 2nd century AD

the fall of Nineveh in 612 BC, the Assyrian rule was replaced by that of the Neo-Babylonians. Attempts at rebellion failed and it was only the conquest of Babylonia by the Persians in 539 BC that rid Phoenicia of the Babylonian yoke. The Phoenicians regarded the Persians as liberators at the time and Phoenicia became temporarily one of the most prosperous provinces in the Persian empire.

Moves towards independence during the next couple of hundred years were fruitless. The most serious rebellion took place in 346 BC, led by King Tennes of Sidon, who destroyed the provincial governor's palace and sacked the royal park. Artaxerxes Ochus brutally put down the rebellion and burnt Sidon to the ground, killing 40,000 people in the process including King Tennes. Shortly afterwards Persian rule came to an end in Phoenicia, when Alexander the Great swept through the Middle East in a sequence of brilliant military triumphs. (See the Alexander the Great boxed story in the South of Beirut chapter for more details.)

It is difficult to pinpoint the end of Phoenician history. Following Alexander the Great's conquest, the city-states of Phoenicia declined very gradually, absorbing more and more Greek culture and language as the whole of the eastern Mediterranean became Hellenised.

Lebanon's diverse geography ranges from an extensive coastal plain strung with ancient cities and beach resorts (top) to the soaring Mount Lebanon range complete with impressive ruins such as those at Faqra (middle) to the agricultural plain of the Bekaa Valley bounded by the Anti-Lebanon range and dotted with the remains of past civilisations (bottom).

Greeks & Romans

After the Battle of Issus in 333 BC in which the Greeks defeated the Persians decisively, the main cities of Phoenicia (Aradus, Byblos and Sidon) submitted immediately, opening their gates to the conquering hero. Tyre chose to resist. The reigning king, Azemilkos, was still in the pay of the Persians and chose to send a princess to represent him and pay homage on the mainland. Alexander wanted to enter the island-city of Tyre and make a sacrifice in the shrine of Melkart. The princess tried to persuade him to make his sacrifice in the more ancient temple on the mainland, but Alexander wanted the city of Tyre for its strategic importance and refused to go along with these tactics. He prepared to lay siege to the city.

The process was a lengthy one. First he had to build a causeway to the island to carry across his troops. He engaged the services of the fleets from other Phoenician cities to protect him during the operation. (Practically the whole of the Phoenician fleet was moored at nearby Sidon.) Tyre's request for assistance from Carthage failed to materialise – the Carthaginians were engaged in other wars. Tyre finally fell in 332 BC after several months of battle. The city was rebuilt as a Macedonian fortress and colonised by the Greeks.

From this time the dominant culture of the region was Greek. The essence of Phoenicia slipped away, giving way to new customs, laws and religious practices. After the death of Alexander in 323 BC, his empire was parcelled up among his generals, with the three strongest, Ptolemy, Seleucus and Antigonus, taking the main prizes. Phoenicia came under the dominance of Ptolemy I along with Egypt and part of Palestine, while Seleucus took Babylonia and Antigonus took Asia Minor and Macedonia. The next century saw much squabbling between the Seleucids and the Ptolemies about control of Palestine and Phoenicia. On several occasions the Seleucids tried to force their claim unsuccessfully. In 198 BC they finally succeeded under Antiochus III.

Antiochus III tried to spread his influence westwards into the Mediterranean, but was held in check by the emerging new power emanating from Rome. The immense empire of Alexander the Great had fragmented and although Greek thought and culture was a great civilising force in the world, the Romans were gaining the upper hand as a military force.

In 188 BC Antiochus' army was decisively beaten after a three-year campaign by the Romans and he was forced to concede all his territories in Asia Minor. In 64 BC Pompey the Great conquered Phoenicia. The country was stripped of her name and, along with Palestine, became part of the Roman province of Syria. Berytus (Beirut) became an important new centre of power under Herod the Great, who was appointed governor and ruled from 40 to 4 BC. Despite his reputation as a tyrant, who during his later life was reputed to be mentally unstable, this was a rare period of peace and prosperity referred to as the *Pax Romana*.

Baalbek became an important centre for worship during this time. It was known as 'Heliopolis', a Greek word meaning 'City of the Sun'. The great temples were built or enlarged from the earlier buildings and displayed all the splendour and might of the Roman Empire. Both Heliopolis and Berytus were made official colonies by the first emperor of Rome, Augustus.

Culturally the people began to merge more with their Syrian neighbours, adopting Aramaic as their everyday language. The Romanisation of the temples saw the decline of the Phoenician and Greek pantheon and the corresponding rise of their Roman counterparts.

The splendour of the Roman Empire was not to last. By 250 AD the Goths began to invade Europe; the first of successive waves of tribes which would ultimately destroy Rome and split the empire. From the east, the Sassanians from Persia attacked Syria, putting further pressure on the Roman administration. The temples of Baalbek were barely finished before they became redundant as the Roman Empire fell apart and the old religion with it.

Christianity & Byzantium

Meanwhile Christianity was the new rising religious force in the region. St Paul passed through Lebanon on one of his journeys in the 1st century, but it is thought to have been the apostle St Peter who began to sow the seeds of Christianity in the Phoenicians. These early Christians were affiliated to the Patriarch of Antioch (modern Antakya in southern Turkey). A legend from these early days is that one of the first pontiffs to the see of Rome was Lebanese. His name was Anicetus and he became Pope around 157 AD. He was martyred between 161 and 168 AD and later canonised.

The new religion gathered momentum, despite being severely repressed by the pagan emperors of Rome who saw the Christians as anarchists and traitors. However, eventually the Roman emperors themselves adopted Christianity. In 324 AD Emperor Constantine, who was himself a Christian convert, moved the capital of the empire to Byzantium on the shores of the Bosphorus. The city was renamed Constantinople (modern Istanbul). This shifted the focus away from Italy, which was in turmoil, and by the end of the 4th century, the Roman Empire was officially split into west and east. The area of modern Lebanon became part of the eastern Byzantine Empire, which gathered in strength and importance as Rome withered and declined.

The Byzantine Empire was to long outlive the western empire, surviving until the Turks captured Constantinople in 1453. Blending the refined influences of Hellenistic culture with that of Christianity, the Byzantines adopted a strict orthodoxy. In 394 Emperor Theodosius made Christianity the official religion of the empire, outlawing all forms of pagan worship. The orthodox form of Christianity imposed on the people of Lebanon and Syria caused many tensions. There were frequent raids from the east, and in 608 the Persian king Khosrau II overran Lebanon and Syria. The Byzantine emperor Heraclius liberated the country in the early 620s and forced the Persians into a peace agreement. But the peace was not to last; Arab invaders were attacking the borders to the south of the country and internal fighting frequently broke out.

By the 7th century the Maronites, a Syrian sect adhering to the 'heretical' idea of monothelitism (that Christ was both human and divine but with only one will), took refuge in the north of Mount Lebanon to escape persecution. They built numerous monasteries and gathered around the holy monk St John Maron, who was the founder of the Maronite church. St John Maron became their patriarch-elect from 685 to 707, and during his reign defended his community against the nonstop fighting that was taking place between the Greeks and the Arab tribes. Neither side cared much for the Maronites, and in 694 the Greeks sacked the monastery of St Maron and killed about 500 monks who lived in the settlement. The Arabs later finished the job and totally destroyed the monastery. St John Maron took his people and entrenched them in the rugged Kadisha Valley, where they remained cut off from outside influences until the Crusades.

During this time, throughout the rest of Lebanon and Syria, the Byzantines built many magnificent churches and established a large Christian community of the orthodox rites. But their position of power had become weakened through military conflict with the Persians and dissent from religious groups at odds with their form of Christianity. Just around the corner was a new conqueror, coming this time from the south, that would change the face of the Middle East forever.

The Arabs & the Crusaders

Arabia had not been a major player in the classical world. Skirmishes on the borders of the Byzantine Empire had failed to make a lasting impression. However, during the 7th century a new religion swept through Arabia – Islam. The prophet Mohammed was born in about 570 in Mecca, in western Arabia. In the year 610 he began to receive a series of divine revelations from God. These lengthy revelations were committed to memory and subsequently written down to form the holy book of Islam, the *Qur'an*, known as the Koran. Mohammed gathered a huge following and, after his death in Medina in 632, his followers formed a conquering force the like of which had not been seen since Alexander the Great.

In 636 this formidable army won a decisive victory at the Battle of Yarmouk, which marks the modern border between Jordan and Syria. Conquest of most of Syria followed and the Byzantine forces retreated towards Anatolia. Within 20 years of Mohammed's death, Muslim Arab armies had taken Palestine, Syria, Egypt, Persia and parts of what is now Afghanistan. Within a century they controlled an empire which stretched from the Atlantic to India. In Lebanon they faced little resistance; many local people regarded themselves as being liberated from the Byzantine tyranny and welcomed the newcomers.

Under Mohammed's successors, the focus of power quickly shifted from Medina to Damascus in Syria, partly because of its position at the hub of pilgrim and trade routes to and from Arabia. In 658 Mu'awiyah, the military governor of Syria and a distant relation of the Prophet, established the first of the great Muslim dynasties, the Umayyads, or Omayyads, who would reign for about a century. The name Umayyad is derived from Mu'awiyah's clan, the Bani Umayyah, part of the Prophet's tribe, the Quraysh.

The Umayyads were ambitious; they embarked on a building spree which has left some of the finest examples of Islamic architecture ever constructed, including the Umayyad Mosque in Damascus, the Dome of the Rock in Jerusalem and the city of Aanjar in Lebanon's Bekaa Valley. The famous Desert Castles in Jordan are also theirs. They never lost their love of the desert and the court would retire there to hunt and to relax. However, by the end of their reign the Umayyads had lost their simple piety and had gained a reputation for decadence, corruption and tyranny. There were almost constant plots, insurrections and rebellions which the Umayyads put down ruthlessly, including revolts in Iraq and Arabia itself.

The indigenous Christian and Jewish populations were left pretty much alone under the early Muslim rulers and were allowed to retain their religion, although they were subjected to discriminatory taxes and laws. Initially the persecuted Christian minorities had welcomed the Muslim invaders, but trouble inevitably erupted between them. The last Umayyad caliph, Marwan II, appointed a puppet Patriarch of Antioch, Theophylactus, who persecuted the Maronites with the help of Muslim soldiers. In 759 and 760 a revolt of the Christian peasants spread from the mountains to the Bekaa Valley. The Lebanese mountain people were spurred into revolt by the temporary appearance of Byzantine troops in the area. The revolt came to nothing, but the Maronites were forging their own cultural and national identity despite the pressures of Arabisation around them.

The Umayyads finally fell to a new dynasty, the Abbasids, in 750 and the seat of power moved once more – this time to Baghdad. The coup was carried out by a former slave, Abu Muslim, who accused the Umayyads of impiety and rallied the Shiites of Persia to support him. With this shift of power, Syria, Lebanon and Palestine went into a decline. They became a backwater of the Abbasid Empire which took on a distinctly Persian flavour. The new capital was far from the Levantine (and therefore Byzantine) influences. The cultural pool from which the Abbasids drank was far more eastern.

The most famous Abbasid caliph was Harun ar-Rashid who reigned from 786 to 809. His reign saw extraordinary advances in art, science and literature. Harun's son, Al-Ma'mun founded the Beit al-Hikmah, or 'House of Wisdom', which dedicated its efforts to translating the classics of Greece and Rome into Arabic. It was due to these translations that many important works were saved for posterity.

After the death of Harun, the empire was split between two rival sons and heirs. Al-Ma'mun won the civil conflict that followed and ruled for the next 20 years. He made the fatal mistake, though, of moving his capital from Baghdad to Samarra, the old Persian capital 100km to the north. He hired Turkish mercenaries to protect him, and as a result, his successors found themselves increasingly in the power of these Turks who ran the empire themselves while hiding behind puppet caliphs.

The empire was now so vast that the central power began to break up into new dynasties to rival Baghdad. Spain was lost to a remaining Umayyad leader. North Africa also slipped away at the end of the 8th century, and in the early 9th century, the eastern provinces followed suit. Egypt eventually broke away under the Fatimids, a Shiite dynasty from North Africa, in 969. The Fatimids made Cairo their capital and took most of Syria, Lebanon and eastern Arabia, including the holy cities of Mecca and Medina. Being ruled from Cairo brought Lebanon and the rest of the Levant closer to the ruling power. Cairo became an important seat of learning with the foundation of the Al-Azhar – the oldest mosque and university in the world. Al-Azhar remains one of the leading centres of Islamic studies.

The Fatimid dynasty regarded itself as the true heir to the caliphate and rejected the authority of the Abbasids in Baghdad. Once established, the Fatimids sought to subvert the remaining power of the Abbasids and their supporters by a system of state missionaries. In 1016 the sixth Fatimid caliph, Al-Hakim bi-Amrillah, announced that he was the earthly incarnation of God. Under his vizier, Hamzah ibn Ali ibn Ahmad, his following developed into the Druze sect which today occupies the southern part of Mount Lebanon and constitutes a powerful political force in modern Lebanon (see the Religion section later in this chapter for more information).

The Fatimids soon began to weaken. Feuding between different ethnic groups undermined the Fatimid armies. By the second half of the 11th century, the government in Egypt was crumbling. In 1073 the general Badr al-Jamali seized power and took control of all state departments, but his efforts to reassert Fatimid control over Syria,

Lebanon and the Arabian peninsula ended in failure. His successors kept the caliphs as puppet figureheads. During a succession struggle in 1094, Fatimid unity was finally destroyed. Syria and Yemen broke away from Cairo's control and a Syrian sect, known as the Assassins, waged a campaign of terrorism against the Egyptian caliphs. The Fatimids struggled on until 1171. On the death of the last caliph, his vizier, Salah ad-Din, known in the west as Saladin, took power as Sultan of Egypt. See the Saladin boxed story in the South of Beirut chapter for more details.

It was into this fragmented political maelstrom that the Crusaders launched their bid to liberate the Holy Land – Jerusalem being the prime objective. In 1095 Pope Urban II called for a Christian force to fight this holy war. The Seljuk Turks had moved northwards and taken Armenia, Azerbaijan and part of Anatolia (Asia Minor). The Byzantine emperor, together with the Greek Orthodox Church, felt under such pressure that they appealed to the Pope for help. Urban saw an opportunity to establish Rome's primacy in the Holy Land.

The Crusaders linked forces with the Byzantine army and besieged Antioch, and then marched down the Syrian and Lebanese coast before turning towards Jerusalem. Jerusalem fell in 1099 after a six-week siege. The Crusaders massacred the local population – Muslims, Jews and Christians alike – and plundered all non-Christian religious sites, turning the Dome of the Rock into a church. They built massive fortifications all along the coast of the Levant and at strategic points inland. The success of the early Crusades depended largely on the disarray of their enemies. Within a short time, the Crusaders had established four states in the Middle East. Northern Lebanon came under the County of Tripoli and the southern area under the Kingdom of Jerusalem.

Up until that time the Maronites had lived an isolated existence. With the coming of the new Christian rulers, they were brought into contact with the nations of the west and the Church of Rome. From the beginning the

Maronites apparently welcomed the new-comers both as fellow Christians and as a respite from the ravages of some of their Muslim rulers. The Maronites proved useful to the Crusaders as they knew the mountain paths, valleys and gorges, and they became valuable guides. Later their archers served as an auxiliary force for the Crusaders.

Marriage between the Crusaders and the native Christians – many of whom were Leba-nese – produced a new mixed race known as the 'Pullani'.

The most significant change for the Maronites was the renewed link with the western church. According to the famous historian of the Crusades, Archbishop William of Tyre, some 40,000 Maronites came down from the mountain en masse and declared their allegiance to Rome, renounc-ing their heretical monothelitism. The clergy adopted some of the Latin rites, although the church was still essentially eastern.

During this period, the great fortified castles at Tripoli, Byblos and Sidon were built, using stones from the earlier temples. Despite their immensity, these Crusader strongholds were only effective against a divided and weakened Muslim force. Their hold on the coastal strip was tenuous and only lasted until the 12th century.

The Muslim reconquest began in 1144 when Zengi, the founder of a short-lived Kurdish dynasty from Mosul (in modern Iraq), wiped out the Crusader County of Edessa. Within a few years he and his suc-cessor, Nur ad-Din, had gone on to reduce the principality of Antioch to a sliver of land along the coast. The tide was turning for the Crusaders.

Nur ad-Din placed his general, Saladin, in the Fatimid court in Cairo. Saladin took control of Egypt in his own right in 1171 and went on to head the Muslim armies which reconquered Jerusalem in 1187, followed by Palestine and later Beirut. Over the next century, Saladin's dynasty, the Ayyubids, squeezed the Crusaders into a small corner. The Muslim army was held at bay by the Third Crusade, which clung on to the coastal strip for another century. But finally Antioch

and Jaffa fell in 1268, Tripoli in 1289, and Acre in 1291.

The Mamelukes & the Ottomans

The Ayyubids ruled Syria, Egypt, western Arabia and parts of Yemen until they were in turn overthrown. Power fell into the hands of the strange soldier-slave kings known as the Mamelukes, who ruled Lebanon from the end of the 13th century for the best part of 300 years.

The Mamelukes were of Turkish origin and evolved out of a liberated slave class. They ran what we would today call a military dictatorship, but the only way you could get into their army was to be press-ganged. Non-Muslim boys were captured or bought outside the empire (often in Europe or central Asia), made to convert to Islam and raised in the service of a single military commander. They were expected to give this commander their total loyalty, in exchange for which their fortunes would rise, or fall, with his. The children of Mameluke soldiers were free men and women and were not allowed to join the army. Sultans were chosen from among the most senior Mame-luke commanders.

By the 13th century the Mongol armies, united under Genghis Khan, were rampaging across Asia, destroying everything as they went. In 1258 they sacked Baghdad, under the leadership of Hulagu Khan (Genghis' grandson), killing 800,000 people in a week-long orgy of destruction. This was followed by another Mongol army – that of Tamer-lane, who in five short years, from 1399 to 1404, swept through to Syria sacking Aleppo and Damascus. Repelling the Mongol hordes left the Mamelukes severely weakened and they went into a slow decline over the next century.

In Lebanon the tribal leaders had con-tinued to practise their political manoeuvres, enabling them to maintain a considerable degree of autonomy. The Tanukhid *emirs* (rulers) of central Lebanon had long played off the Muslims and the Crusaders, and they now supported the Mamelukes. In northern Lebanon the Maronites maintained contacts with Rome and the newly emerged Italian republics. Less fortunate were the Druze who, during the end of the 13th century, took advantage of the Mameluke's preoccupation with the Mongol incursions and started a revolt, which led to widespread devastation in the Chouf area of central Lebanon.

In 1258, the same year as Hulagu Khan sacked Baghdad, a boy named Osman was born to the chief of a pagan Turkish tribe in western Anatolia. He was to become leader of what would eventually become the Ottoman Empire. He converted to Islam in his youth and embarked on a military career hiring out his tribe's army as mercenaries in the civil wars, besetting what was left of the

Süleyman the Magnificent
The Ottoman Empire reached its peak under Süleyman the Magnificent, who reigned from 1520 to 1566. He led the Ottoman armies west to the gates of Vienna, east into Persia and south through the holy cities of Mecca and Medina and into Yemen. His control also extended throughout North Africa. He cracked down on corruption, reformed the Ottoman legal system and was the patron of the great Ottoman architect Sinan, who designed the Süleymaniye Mosque in Constantinople and oversaw the reconstruction of the Grand Mosque in Mecca. This was the golden age for culture in the Middle East and many of the finest Islamic buildings still visible today come from this period. ■

Byzantine Empire. Payment came in the form of land.

By scooping up territories that Constantinople could no longer control, Osman's successors soon had an empire of their own. By the end of the 14th century, they had conquered Bulgaria, Serbia, Bosnia, Hungary and all of the territory that makes up modern Turkey. In 1453 Sultan Mehmed II took Constantinople, bringing to an end the era of the Byzantines once and for all.

In the early 16th century the Turcoman family of Assaf and after them, the Banu Saifa, rose to prominence in the area from Beirut to the north of Tripoli. Meanwhile, in the south of Lebanon, the Druze family of Ma'an took over as leaders from the Tanukhid emirs. After the conquest of the Lebanon in 1516-17, the ruling sultan, Selim I, endorsed their privileges and imposed only a small tribute. Despite this favour, fighting still broke out from time to time with the Ottomans. In 1584 a large tribute was hijacked from its convoy on its way from Egypt to Constantinople. Sultan Murad III sent a punitive expedition into Lebanon to ravage the lands of the Druze.

In the south of Lebanon the house of Ma'an reached its greatest influence under Fakhr ad-Din II (1586-1635). He had used every trick in the book to establish an independent power over the whole of Lebanon and parts of northern Palestine. He cultivated a close alliance with the Grand Duke of Tuscany with whom he formed a commercial treaty in 1608. This also included a secret military agreement directed against the sultan. In 1613 the sultan, concerned about Fakhr ad-Din's rising power, sent a naval and military expedition against him. Fakhr ad-Din was forced to flee to Tuscany, but, returning in 1618, he was soon the virtual ruler of an area stretching from Aleppo to the borders with Egypt.

The sultan, meanwhile, had his hands occupied with revolt in Anatolia and Persia and could not act against Fakhr ad-Din. Fakhr ad-Din then began an ambitious programme of development in Lebanon. He engaged Italian engineers and agricultural experts to increase the quality of silk and olive oil production. He encouraged the Christians from the north to migrate south and to promote silk production there. The political and economic cooperation that he fostered became the foundation of future Lebanese autonomy. Beirut and Sidon flourished as a result and religious missions from Europe – Capuchins, Jesuits and Carmelites – were allowed to settle in Lebanon and Syria. This was an important development for France, who had ambitions to form a protectorate over all the Christian areas of the Ottoman Empire.

Fakhr ad-Din's success aroused Ottoman hostility and he was defeated and captured in 1633. He was taken to Constantinople and executed in 1635. But by 1667 his grand-nephew, Ahmad Ma'an, had revived the family's power in southern Lebanon and the Kisrawan district in central Lebanon. The Lebanese emirate was established, forming the nucleus of the modern country. Unfortunately, Ahmad Ma'an died without an heir, and the reins of power passed to the Shihab family with the approval of the sultan.

By 1711 the Shihabs had completely reorganised the feudal system in their emirate to maintain their power, which they kept until 1840. In the late 18th century the ruling branch of the family embraced Christianity and became Maronites. Under Emir Yusuf (1770-1788) and Emir Bashir II (1788-1840), who is known to be a Christian, the influence of the Shihab dynasty extended north to embrace all of Mount Lebanon.

The Shihab emirs took great pains to stay on good terms with the Turkish *pashas* (provincial governors) in Tripoli, Sidon and Damascus. In return the pashas took every opportunity to stir up trouble and foment rivalries, which gave them an edge in the constant internal power struggles and religious differences which always dogged Lebanese politics.

Bashir II was the most distinguished of the Shihab emirs. In 1810 he helped the Ottomans to repel an invasion by the Wahabi tribe of Arabia, but in 1831 he allied himself politically to Muhammed Ali, Pasha of Egypt,

Bashir II, Emir of Lebanon from 1788 to 1840. He ruled from Tripoli to Tyre and from the Bekaa Valley to Wadi at-Taim.

when that ruler invaded Syria. Things went wrong though when, as a vassal of Egypt, Bashir II was forced to impose on his own people an unpopular policy of high taxes and conscription, enforced by Ibrahim Pasha, the son of Muhammed Ali. An internal revolt broke out in Lebanon and the Turks routed the Egyptian pasha with European help. Bashir II was deposed and sent into exile. His successor, Bashir III, was unable to control the Druze feudal chiefs and left office the following year.

The age of the Lebanese emirs was at an end. In 1842 Mount Lebanon was divided into two administrative regions, or *qa'im maqamiyats*. The Ottomans appointed two *qa'im maqams* – one Druze, the other Maronite – who ruled under the supervision of the pashas of Sidon and Beirut.

The Christians and the Druze became increasingly distrustful of one another. The Christians were agitating for a return of the Lebanese emirate. The southern area of the country was ruled by a Druze, and as southern Lebanon had a Christian majority at that time, the population opposed this arrangement. These arguments and tensions were encouraged and used by the Ottomans as a means of enacting a 'divide and rule' policy.

By 1845 there was open war between the Christian and Druze populations. The Ottoman government intervened and modified their administration in an attempt to appease the warring factions. They did not succeed in the long term. In 1858 Maronite peasants in the north revolted against their own Maronite aristocracy and destroyed the feudal system which had been in place since the Middle Ages. By 1860 the Christian peasants in the south were being encouraged to revolt against the Druze leadership. The Druze pre-empted the revolt by massacring more than 11,000 Christians.

The Ottomans came under pressure from the European powers to act and so they reformed Mount Lebanon into a single administrative unit under the new Organic Regulation for Mount Lebanon. This new move brought the whole of Lebanon under an Ottoman Christian governor, called a *mutasarrif*, who was appointed by the sultan and approved by the European powers. An elected council, representing the various Lebanese communities in proportion to their numbers, was appointed to advise and assist the governor. Feudalism was abolished and civil liberties guaranteed; justice and law enforcement were the responsibility of the governor.

The system worked. It produced stability and economic prosperity. The Lebanese ports expanded and the raw silk trade boomed. Beirut, in particular, became an important trading go-between for Europe and the Arab world. Foreign missions established a number of fine schools, including the American University of Beirut (AUB), and the country gained a reputation as an academic and cultural centre in the Ottoman Empire. The establishment of a publishing industry stimulated a revival in Arabic literature. Up to this point, the Turkish Ottomans had been accepted as guardians of Islamic culture and political dogma, but now there was a revival of Arab nationalism.

With the outbreak of WWI, Lebanon swiftly came under Turkish military rule. Turkey had allied herself to Germany and Austria, and the Organic Regulation for Mount Lebanon was suspended. The whole of the Levant became a theatre of war between the Turks and Germans on one side, and the British, French and Russians on the other. Lebanon was badly affected by the war, which caused serious famine.

Following the Allied victory in 1918, Beirut and Mount Lebanon, together with Syria, were occupied by French and British troops. The French High Commissioner in Beirut added together the coastal cities, Mount Lebanon and the Bekaa Valley and proclaimed the state of Greater Lebanon which was placed under the control of the French.

Colonial Rule

In 1923 Lebanon and Syria were placed under a mandate from the newly-formed League of Nations and administered by a French governor, who was advised by an elected representative council. In 1926 a new constitution was drawn up and passed, changing the state of Greater Lebanon into the Lebanese Republic. One feature of this new constitution was the formalising of the idea of power-sharing, based on the respective size of each religious group. This was no easy task; there was a mosaic of different sects and churches to be considered. A Lebanese president was elected to exercise office under French supervision.

The first president was Charles Debbas who was Christian Greek Orthodox, but after 1934 it became the tradition for the president to be Maronite and the prime minister, Sunni Muslim – a custom that survives today. It also became customary to allocate posts in the cabinet and state institutions to various religious communities in proportion to their number in the population. The speaker of the house is always Shiite, the commander of the army Maronite and the chief-of-staff Druze. There was also an agreement that all state bodies be staffed by a ratio of six Christians to five Muslims.

The French were ousted in 1943 by British-led troops, aided by the Free French, who had promised independence to both Lebanon and Syria after the fall of the French Vichy government. Lebanon was then granted full independence by the Free French commander, General Catroux. A new president, Bishara al-Khuri, took over and his Nationalist majority struggled with French authorities over the transfer of power. When, in November 1943, the Lebanese government passed legislation removing the French authority, the French retaliated by arresting the president and members of his cabinet, and suspending the constitution. Britain, the US and the Arab states supported the Lebanese cause for independence, and in 1944 the French began the transfer of all public services to Lebanese control, followed by the withdrawal of French troops. Independence was declared in 1946.

Independence

President al-Khuri was largely responsible for the internal agreement between the religious groups, known as the National Pact, although this was always a 'gentleman's agreement' and not ratified in law. Internally Lebanon was affected by the growth of the nationalist movement in Syria, some sections of which demanded the reduction of Lebanon to its prewar limits or even its abolition as an independent state altogether. Some Sunni areas of Lebanon, which had been added to the republic in 1920, supported this idea. During the Syrian revolt in 1925-26, the trouble spread to these parts of southern Lebanon.

The Maronites generally supported the idea of an independent Lebanon, but still suffered from internal political differences, mainly concerning Lebanon's relationships with Europe and the Arab world. Despite this, Lebanon entered a period of economic growth from the 1950s until the early 1970s. Free enterprise led the country to become the financial capital of the Middle East.

In the early 1950s Lebanon came under pressure from Syria to form a full economic union. Lebanon refused. This followed an awkward period when France devalued the franc and obliged Lebanon to sign a new economic agreement with France. Syria was in the same boat, but refused to sign an agreement with France. The result was a period of complicated wrangling between the two countries over the nature of their economic and financial arrangements.

It was always a difficult problem for Lebanon to maintain good relationships with both the east and the west. Lebanon had been technically at war with Israel since 1948, but had played no real part in the conflict apart from opening the border to tens of thousands of Palestinian refugees. During the Suez crisis in 1956 the government stayed neutral, but many Lebanese Muslims sided with Egypt while many Christians sided with the west. This crisis came to a head when President Camille Chamoun refused to support Egypt's anti-western policy. A state of emergency was declared and there was a threat of civil war; a situation only averted by the intervention of US marines who landed in Beirut.

The US began to take a great interest in the Middle East and offered financial and military aid to pretty well any country who would accept it. US concerns about the rise of communism in the region prompted this offer, which was favourably received by the Lebanese government. The Lebanese foreign minister stated that Lebanon would cooperate closely with the US on this programme. Financial assistance to the tune of US$20 million and support in developing the military was forthcoming.

Some political groups protested at this blatant pro-western alliance, arguing that it would isolate Lebanon from its Arab neighbours and impair Arab solidarity. Despite this, the Lebanese government stood firm in its commitment to the US. Military equipment had already begun to arrive in the summer of 1957 and the US pledged a further US$15 million for the following year.

There began a period of political unrest, mainly due to these pro-US policies, which erupted around the time of the elections in the summer of 1957. By winter feelings were still running high; bombings and assassinations followed. In an attempt to curtail these subversive activities, the government imposed a strict control over the Palestinian refugees. After an outbreak of violence in the north, the government declared it to be under military control.

Further tension arose when Lebanon refused to join the United Arab Republic (a union of Syria and Egypt) or the Arab Federation (with Iraq and Jordan) or anything that would impede its total independence. The Muslim population in Lebanon tended to be pro-Arab rather than pro-Lebanese. There were tensions also within the ranks of the government's supporters, some of whom only lent their support in order to maintain Lebanon's independence, but disliked the alliance with the west intensely. The seeds were sown for a full-blown conflict between Christians and Muslims.

One crisis followed another. In order to protect their interests and promote unity, the government removed from power those critical of its pro-western position. This did nothing to ease the tensions building up in the Muslim areas. The Druze were also involved in the conflict, being sharply divided into pro and anti-government factions. Hostile demonstrations led to the destruction of US Information Centres in Beirut and Tripoli. The US despatched support in the form of army and police equipment, and decided at the same time to re-enforce their sixth fleet stationed in the Mediterranean. The Soviet Union accused the US of interfering in Lebanese internal affairs and appealed to the Arab League (a league of independent Arab states formed in 1945) for their ruling on the matter. They failed to do so and the problem came before the United Nations (UN), which decided to send an observer corps into Lebanon.

The Lebanese government was, by this time, facing widespread insurrection, in which the Muslim groups were ranged against the Christian groups. Beirut, Tripoli, Sidon and some areas of the extreme north of the country were controlled by anti-government forces. There were abortive attempts to negotiate a settlement, but concerns arose that President Chamoun was going to try and reform the constitution in order to allow himself to run for a second term in office in the autumn of 1958. The prime minister gave his assurances that this was not the case, but the leaders of the insurrection demanded Chamoun's immediate resignation. The president refused and requested US troops to enter Lebanon to maintain security. About 10,000 troops were deployed in the Beirut area, creating an uproar from the Soviet Union and China. To avoid further complications, the UN adopted a resolution which provided for an evacuation of US troops from Lebanon under the auspices of the UN and the Arab League.

The elections saw a new president sworn into office, Fouad Chehab, who appointed Rachid Karami, the leader of the insurrectionists in Tripoli, to the post of prime minister. An agreement was reached that the US forces would leave Lebanon by the end of October. A more serious crisis was averted in the short term, and by 1960 the economy had more or less recovered from the troubles of 1958.

The 1960s were characterised by frequent changes of cabinet, both in number and in personnel. Fouad Chehab was succeeded as president by Charles Helou in 1964 and by Suleiman Franjieh in 1970. The successive governments were still committed to free trade and private enterprise, but a financial crisis in 1966, in which a major bank closed due to a run on withdrawals, caused a curb on commercial banking. Until then there had been a free-for-all in the banking sector, based on the flow into Lebanon of vast amounts of oil money from Saudi Arabia and the Gulf States.

Lebanon had managed to avoid direct involvement in the Arab-Israeli wars of 1967 and 1973, but after 1967 Palestinian guerrillas started to mount attacks on Israel from their camps in southern Lebanon. The Israeli forces retaliated with attacks across the border in May 1968 and the Lebanese government tried to restrict Palestinian guerrilla activity, without much success. Events escalated in December of the same year when an Israeli airliner was machine-gunned at Athens airport. Two days later the Israelis launched an attack on Beirut airport and destroyed 13 Lebanese passenger aircraft. The message was clearly a warning not to allow any further attacks from Lebanese soil. Israel was heavily criticised for the attacks; international sympathy went to Lebanon who, it was felt, did not deserve the blame for the actions of the Palestinians living within its borders. This did not prevent the fall of the government for its lack of response.

In 1969 Lebanese forces clashed violently with Palestinians, who demanded to be independent in the matter of camp security and to be free to launch attacks across the border into Israel. Under pressure from the Lebanese Muslim supporters, the Lebanese government was forced to sign the Cairo Agreement with the Palestine Liberation Organization (PLO), in which most of the Palestinians' demands were met and the camps were moved away from civilian towns to protect civilians from injury during reprisal raids. The agreement also stated that military training in refugee camps was to cease and that guerrillas must enter Israel before launching attacks.

Although the Lebanese army was not involved, fighting broke out in the streets of Beirut between Palestinian guerrillas and right-wing Christian Phalangist groups. In May the Israelis launched a major attack on southern Lebanon, occupying a large area for a couple of days. Friction in the region increased considerably after the events of 'Black September' in 1970, when Palestinian guerrillas were heavily defeated in Jordan by the Jordanian army. Following this defeat, Palestinians flocked into Lebanon in great numbers.

The increased power of the Palestinians, coupled with the shift in relative numbers of the Muslim and Christian populations in Lebanon, brought the balance of power, carefully maintained since the National Pact was drawn up under President al-Khuri, into question. Lebanon was becoming increasingly factionalised; groups were arming

themselves and forming private militias. The control of the government forces was slipping away. Clashes between the Palestinian and Lebanese forces continued, culminating in a heavy round of fighting in 1973. The frequent Israeli raids in southern Lebanon drove the mainly Shiite populations to the cities in great numbers, often to the poor districts next to the Palestinian refugee camps.

By the mid-70s this cocktail of pressures led the Christian Maronites to boost their own power, which was coming increasingly under threat. The left-Muslim alliance, which supported the Palestinians, pushed for constitutional reforms, which would break the existing guarantees of Maronite power. The Maronites gambled on receiving support from Israel and the west if they took a stand against the PLO. What happened next plunged Lebanon into 17 years of misery, civil war and foreign occupation.

The Civil War

In 1975 fighting broke out between the Lebanese Muslims and the Maronite-dominated Phalangist militias. The government had ceased to function and power fell more and more into the hands of the various armed factions. Lebanon was effectively in a state of anarchy. The PLO joined the Muslim side early in 1976. This caused Syria to intervene against the PLO, being wary of Israeli reaction to events.

Beirut soon became partitioned along the infamous 'Green Line'. East Beirut was Christian and West Beirut, Muslim. The rest of the country, likewise, was controlled area by area along lines marked out by the various religious sects. This state of affairs would last throughout the 17-year civil war, although loyalties would change and sides would reform many times.

In June of 1976 the Arab League brokered a truce, creating a peacekeeping force led by the Syrians. Fighting continued in spite of this, and in 1978 Israel invaded southern Lebanon in an all-out attack on the Palestinian bases. Israeli forces withdrew and were replaced by a UN peacekeeping force, but

Bashir Gemayel, president in 1982, was killed after less than month in office when a bomb exploded at the Christian-militia headquarters.

this did not stop the Israelis using the Maronite militias as a 'cat's paw' to continue to strike at PLO targets.

In June 1982 Israel invaded once again, this time overrunning the PLO and reaching the Beirut guerillas. By mid-August the PLO agreed to leave Beirut after a deal was brokered by the US. Many Palestinian fighters were evacuated to other countries in the Middle East and North Africa.

During the same summer, elections, held under Israeli occupation, voted in a new president, Christian-militia leader Bashir Gemayel. His term of office was brief; in September he was assassinated and his brother, Amin Gemayel, was elected to take his place. Revenge for the assassination was horrific. Up to 1000 Palestinian civilians in the Sabra and Chatila refugee camps in Israeli-occupied west Beirut were slaughtered by the Phalangist militia. The massacre took place under the eyes of Israeli troops who did nothing to intervene. Reports of the massacre shocked the outside world, and subsequently the Israelis withdrew from Beirut to southern Lebanon. An international peacekeeping force was moved into Beirut, but these mainly western forces were viewed as pro-Christian, causing friction with the Muslim side. The peacekeeping force became the target of terrorist attacks and when over 300 US and French troops were killed in October 1983, the western forces pulled out.

By 1985 the Israelis also pulled out of southern Lebanon, taking hundreds of prisoners into Israel. They left a 'Security Zone' under the control of the pro-Israeli South Lebanese Army (SLA). In June of that year, a US airliner was hijacked by a Shiite group, the Amal, who demanded the release of the prisoners. A US navy man was killed and 39 other passengers were held in Beirut for 2½ weeks by the Amal militia, lead by Nabih Berri. The passengers were eventually released, after lengthy negotiations, and the Israelis began to release some of the Lebanese prisoners.

Another group was to emerge and wage war on the SLA for control of the south; the Hezbollah or 'Party of God', a radical Shiite group backed by Iran. At the same time, Israel continued to attack PLO positions and conditions deteriorated rapidly. The radical Shiites started to target western civilians and a wave of kidnappings took place. Many foreigners who had stayed during most of the hostilities packed up and left in the face of the kidnapping threat. The unlucky handful who were taken hostage spent many months and often years in captivity, pawns in a no-win political game. But it was not only foreigners who were kidnapped; many Lebanese were taken by opposing factions and were ransomed (often for money) or 'disappeared' permanently.

In 1987 the Syrian army entered Beirut in a bid to end the fighting between the Lebanese and Palestinian Muslims. Syria was the most influential foreign power in Lebanon and was perhaps the only force in the region with enough muscle to influence events. Technically there was still a government and the institutions set up at independence remained precariously intact. But the real military and administrative power lay in the hands of the sectarian militias. The Shiites had become the largest group, but they were relatively weak. The Amal had a mass following politically, but little military muscle. The Amal was challenged by the Hezbollah, a more religious and fundamentalist group. The Maronites were still a fairly cohesive group despite internal rifts in 1985, and enjoyed economic self-sufficiency. The Druze, headed by Walid Joumblatt, were small in number, but strong in solidarity.

The longer the war went on, the more fragmented the main groups became. Political power reverted to smaller and smaller units and the credibility of Lebanon as an independent country eroded. One proposed solution was to partition the country along sectarian lines, but the scheme would only have succeeded with the cooperation of all sides.

When Amin Gemayel's presidential term of office expired in September 1988, he named General Michel Aoun, a Christian and commander in chief of the army, to head an interim government. The various Lebanese leaders established their own administrations as no one could agree on a new president. Aoun attempted to re-establish the authority of the Lebanese army and aimed to expel all Syrian troops from Lebanon; a failed enterprise. A serious attempt to negotiate a peace settlement came in October 1989. A meeting in Taif, Saudi Arabia, proposed a new constitution giving more power to the Muslims. This idea was scuppered by General Aoun and the threat of permanent partition loomed.

A new charter, known as the Taif Agreement, was ratified by all the legislators on 5 November. René Moawwad was elected president, but he was assassinated 17 days later. Parliament chose another candidate, Elias Hrawi, who is still in office. In October 1990 Syrian forces set about suppressing and disarming the Christian forces (who were loyal to Aoun) in east Beirut. Subsequently the Syrian army and the Lebanese army jointly regained control of most of the country.

After considerable international pressure was applied and after some reluctance on the part of the militias, a process of disarmament

took place. The Palestinians announced that they would not disarm, as Palestinian militias were a regional and not a domestic Lebanese matter.

There was understandable apprehension about the remaining armed groups. These included the PLO's 6000 troops, the Iranian Revolutionary Guards in Baalbek, the Hezbollah in the Bekaa Valley and southern Lebanon, and the Israeli-backed SLA. Yasser Arafat's al-Fatah group, based in Sidon, refused to disband on the grounds that it was not a militia but a resistance movement. The SLA also refused to disarm or comply with the UN Security Council's Resolution 425 which asked for the unconditional withdrawal of Israeli troops from Lebanon.

According to the programme of reconciliation, Lebanon would have far greater ties with Syria culminating in the signing, in 1991, of a treaty which linked the two countries on a range of issues including military, economic and security affairs. This received a mixed reception, and the Phalangist and other Christian elements abstained from voting in the cabinet session which approved the treaty.

In August 1991 John McCarthy, a British journalist, was released from his captivity. He had been held hostage since 1986 by the Islamic Jihad, an extremist group. This prompted a flurry of diplomatic activity by the UN and other parties to secure the release of the other hostages. There was an exchange of hostages, some of whom were held by Israel and some by various groups in Lebanon. By June 1992 all of the western hostages held in Lebanon had been released.

All these positive steps on the road to peace did not prevent the Israelis from launching another heavy attack on southern Lebanon in July 1992. The Israelis still wanted to eradicate the Hezbollah and Palestinian guerrillas. The effect was to displace as many as 300,000 Lebanese civilians who fled north to escape the shelling, causing further chaos in the cities.

In October 1992 Rafiq Hariri, a Lebanese-born Saudi entrepreneur, became the new prime minister of Lebanon with a newly

Rafiq Hariri, the prime minister of Lebanon since 1992

elected 30-member cabinet. His appointment was made on the basis of his ability to oversee the vast amount of reconstruction needed. A US$13 billion recovery plan was unveiled in March 1993.

The long war was over. It had cost some 150,000 Lebanese lives since 1975 and left the country in a ruinous state. The public services were nonexistent and war damage to buildings and roads ran into many tens of billion dollars.

The Reconstruction of Lebanon

In January 1994 the Lebanese government issued shares in Solidere, the company formed to carry out the reconstruction of central Beirut which had suffered the most damage during the long conflict. Much of the former commercial district was beyond repair and an ambitious clearance and rebuilding scheme was launched (for further details, see the Rebuilding of Beirut section in the Beirut chapter). Meanwhile there was widespread poverty caused by the direct effects of the war and the disastrous devaluation of the Lebanese pound (*lira*). Many

dangerously damaged buildings were being inhabited by squatters.

The south of the country still suffered from periodic attacks from Israel. In March 1995 a senior Hezbollah official was assassinated by a rocket attack on his car near Tyre. Retaliations were inevitable, and in response to counter attacks from the Hezbollah, Israel launched another campaign – 'Operation Grapes of Wrath' in April 1996. This was a combined land-sea-air offensive, ostensibly aimed at Hezbollah positions, but it extended far beyond the south and involved attacks on Beirut, knocking out the power station. The attack was clearly intended to pressurise the Lebanese government to act against the Hezbollah themselves. Civilians once again fled from the area of attack. Some sought refuge at a UN base at Qana which was shelled by Israel, killing over 100 civilians and UN personnel. International response condemned Israel and a cease-fire was achieved by the end of April. A UN report concluded the base at Qana was deliberately targeted.

Since Operation Grapes of Wrath, Israel seems to be soft-pedalling in its approach to southern Lebanon, but there are still shells being fired in both directions from time to time – Israel particularly targeting the Hezbollah strongholds in the Nabatiyeh area and in the southern Bekaa Valley. Casualties have occurred on both sides. The fight has reached a standoff where the conflict is far from over, but neither side is gaining or losing ground.

Internally, Lebanon is on a rapid ride to recovery; building is widespread, institutions are being reopened and the economy is slowly recovering. Pope John Paul visited the country on a peace mission in May 1997 which signalled a breakthrough in the attitude of the outside world to Lebanon.

GEOGRAPHY

Lebanon is one of the world's smallest countries with an area of only 10,452 sq km, but within its borders are several completely diverse geographical regions. There is a very narrow, broken, coastal strip on which the major cities are situated. This stretches 225km from the Israeli border in the south at Naqoura to the Nahr al-Kabir at the northern border with Syria. There are many rivers which flow into the Mediterranean along the Lebanese coast.

Inland the Mount Lebanon range rises steeply with a dramatic set of peaks and ridges – the highest, Qornet as-Sawda, reaches over 3000m south-east of Tripoli. Near Beirut, Jebel Sannine reaches 2628m. The unusual feature of this mountain range is its non-porous layer of rock which forces water to the surface at a high altitude and in large enough quantities to produce great springs at up to 1500m. This means that, apart from an abundance of picturesque waterfalls, cultivation can take place at unusual heights.

The Mount Lebanon range gives way steeply to the Bekaa Valley, 150km from end to end, which, although low in comparison to the mountain peaks, is still 1000m above sea level. Flanked on both sides by mountains, the Bekaa Valley lies in a rain shadow and is considerably more arid than the rest of the country. The Bekaa is the major wine producing area of the country, and was also a major producer of cannabis until quite recently.

The Anti-Lebanon range to the east of the Bekaa Valley forms a natural border with Syria and rises in a sheer arid massif from the plain. The highest peak in the range is Jebel ash-Sheikh (Mt Hermon) at 2814m.

CLIMATE

With such a diverse topography, it is not surprising that the weather varies quite considerably from region to region. Broadly speaking, Lebanon has three different climate zones – the coastal strip, the mountains and the Bekaa Valley.

The coastal strip has cool, rainy winters and hot Mediterranean summers. The Mount Lebanon range can concentrate the summer heat and humidity on the coast to a stifling degree. During the spring and autumn the weather on the coast is warm and dry with the occasional shower. October and April can

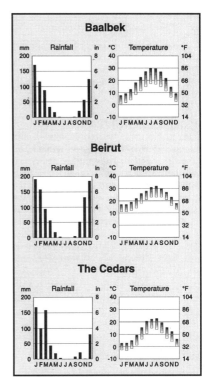

see very heavy rainfall (Beirut has more rainfall than Manchester in the UK, but only half the number of rainy days).

The mountains have a typical alpine climate. Fresh breezes keep the summer heat comfortable – which is why many people head there to escape the oppressive heat of Beirut during the summer months. There is heavy winter snow, which lasts from December to May on the higher peaks. At certain times of year you can stand on the warm coast and look inland at snow-covered peaks. The brochure clichés are true: it is indeed possible to go skiing in the morning and swimming in the afternoon, although I have yet to meet anyone who has actually done it. The main roads and those up to the ski stations are kept open during the winter months, but some of the minor roads are closed until the thaw.

The Bekaa Valley has hot, dry summers and cold, dry winters with snow and frost. The valley is set between two parallel mountain ranges and the wind can blow quite fiercely, especially in the winter.

ECOLOGY & ENVIRONMENT

The environment suffered considerable damage during the war; pollutants and rubbish were dumped in the sea and rivers, and unplanned buildings sprang up everywhere. There are still problems, but the Lebanese government and various conservation organisations are attempting to rectify the damage and protect the natural environment with legislation. See also Nature Reserves under the Flora & Fauna section.

FLORA & FAUNA
Flora

The most famous flora in Lebanon – the cedar tree – is now found on only a few mountaintop sites, notably at Bcharré and near Barouk in the Chouf Mountains. These lonely groves are all that remain of Lebanon's great cedar forests which in biblical times once covered vast areas of the country. There are some sites where new trees are being planted, but given that some of the surviving mature trees are over 1000 years old, we certainly shan't see the results of the replanting in this lifetime. (For more information, see the Cedar Tree boxed story in the Tripoli & The Cedars chapter.)

Apart from the cedars, Lebanon is still the most densely wooded of all the Middle Eastern countries. Many varieties of pine, including Aleppo pine, flourish on the mountains. In spring there is an abundance of wild flowers on the hills and mountains, which makes these areas well worth visiting in May.

Much of the coastal land is cultivated with fruit trees, such as oranges, lemons, medlars, bananas and olives. In the Bekaa Valley most of the arable land is given over to wine producing and vines stretch across the valley. Cannabis, once the main crop of the Bekaa,

The hoopoe, which rejoices under the Latin name of *Upupa epops*, is related to the kingfisher. It can be seen in the Palm Islands Park, a protected wildlife sanctuary, during the summer.

is now only found in the far-flung corners of the valley.

In Beirut many of the magnificent, mature palm trees, which lined the Corniche, were blown up during the civil war. Replanting schemes are taking place, but it will be 20 years or more before tall palms sway in the Beirut breeze again.

Fauna

There doesn't seem to be much in the way of wild animals in Lebanon. You may come across the odd tortoise or hedgehog, but more exotic animals are hard to spot. Not so the sheep and goats which are everywhere, grazing by the road side in the rural areas. The only camels you are likely to see are in the Bekaa Valley, giving rides to tourists at Baalbek. The camel caravans have now given way to trucks and pickups.

Bird-watchers may have a more rewarding time of it. The mountain areas have many birds of prey and the nature reserve near

Ehden (see Nature Reserves, following) lists an impressive array of bird life including golden and imperial eagles, buzzard, red kite, Bonelli's eagle, Sardinian warbler and Scop's owl.

The Palm Islands Park has a variety of marine wildlife, both on the islands and beneath the waves. The park is a protected wildlife sanctuary. Marine birds nest there and, away from disturbance and pollution, it is hoped that the populations of the bird colonies will increase now that their environment is protected. Some of the bird species which nest here in summer include the lesser crested tern, hoopoe, sand martin, little ringed plover and crag martin. Various other birds visit the island on their migratory routes, such as a variety of terns, the broad-billed sandpiper and osprey. Resident birds can be seen year-round, including the kingfisher, rock dove, barbary falcon and little owl. The waters surrounding the islands are home to the green turtle and the Mediterranean monk seal.

Nature Reserves

Lebanon's ecology has been under a lot of pressure due to the civil war and increasing industrialisation. The lack of government control has meant that unlawful quarrying and logging has gone on unchecked in many mountain areas, not to mention wholesale dumping of rubbish in mountain streams. Recently the Friends of Nature – a green organisation in Lebanon – has secured an area of primary forest, which is now protected by law as a nature reserve.

The Horsh Ehden Forest Nature Reserve is 35km from Tripoli and 100km from Beirut in the northern stretch of the Mount Lebanon range, just 3km from the summer resort of Ehden. The reserve is a unique natural habitat supporting rare indigenous trees and plants, including the Cicilian fir, Lebanon violet, Ehden milk vetch, and dozens of other plants which are named after Lebanon and only found here. It also provides a habitat for many rare birds and butterflies. It is the last natural archetype of the ancient indigenous forests of Lebanon.

The same ecology group has also pressured the government into protecting some of the small islands off the shore of Al-Mina in Tripoli. These low-lying islands are now only visited with permission from the Friends of Nature office in Tripoli. The local tourism office can also issue permits for bona fide visitors; see the Tripoli & The Cedars chapter for more details. The three islands – Palm Island, Sanani Island and Ramkine Island – are now collectively called the Palm Islands Park.

GOVERNMENT & POLITICS

Lebanon has been an independent, sovereign republic since 1946. The head of state is an elected president with a nonrenewable term of six years. In 1990, as a result of the Taif Agreement, the executive power of the state was transferred from the president to the cabinet of ministers who are appointed by the president. There are currently 30 ministers, including the prime minister who is the head of government. The religions of the various ministers and the president are laid down in the constitution. According to this, the president has to be a Maronite Christian, the prime minister a Sunni Muslim, and the choice of other ministers must be in proportion to the size of the respective religious communities.

The constitution, which was first drawn up in 1926, also says that there is no state religion, and that personal freedom and freedom of the press are guaranteed and protected. Every Lebanese over the age of 21 has the right to vote.

The legislative power of the country lies in the National Assembly, which has 128 members and holds two three-month sessions a year. Elections to the National Assembly normally take place every four years. There is no secret voting in the Assembly chamber; all votes have to be public, either by show of hands or standing and sitting. Half the elected members are Christian and the other half are Muslim.

The most powerful figure in the present government is Rafiq Hariri, the Sunni prime minister, who is a Lebanese-born Saudi

Arabian entrepreneur. He is heavily involved, in both a political and business sense, in the rebuilding programme in Lebanon. His appointment in October 1992 was clearly designed to restore faith, both within Lebanon and abroad, in the economy. Following the cease-fire, he put together ambitious proposals for the rebuilding of Beirut and he also has interests in Solidere, the company responsible for the extensive redevelopment of central Beirut. For more details of Lebanon's political history, see the History section earlier in this chapter.

ECONOMY

The economy went into a dramatic nosedive during the civil war. The Lebanese pound went from a stable LL 2.50 to the US dollar in 1975 to the current value of LL 1536 to the US dollar. In real terms, wages have decreased as they have not kept pace with inflation. The loss of revenue from taxation during the war years means that the government is extremely cash-strapped, and many ministries are providing only skeletal or no public services. Priority has been given to restoring the public telephone, power and road systems and rebuilding the airport. Other sectors, such as education and health, are almost entirely in the private sector.

Agriculture plays an important role in the economy and accounts for 10% of the gross domestic product. About 19% of the workforce is employed in the agricultural sector. The most important crops are citrus and soft fruit, followed by olives and vegetables and, to a lesser extent, cereals. Quite a lot of these crops are exported, although Lebanon also needs to import food.

Tourism was also an important industry before the war, and now that the country is open for business again, there are many plans to woo tourists back. Hotel building seems to be almost an epidemic in some areas, so there clearly is confidence that the tourists will return. As things stand now, Lebanon is beginning to feature in some of the upmarket tour operator's brochures, often in conjunction with a tour to Syria and Jordan.

As far as other industry goes, there is a lot going on in the building trade, cement factories and so on. Other factories such as food processing plants, which had closed during the war, look set the reopen. Before the war, Lebanon was a major banking centre, both for the Middle East and for many western banks. After waiting cautiously to see if the peace would hold, some foreign banks are now planning to reopen branches in Beirut along with other international companies. Banking should become a major factor in the economy once more.

As Lebanon is poised for an economic recovery, which will still take some years, it is unlikely that the country will achieve the prewar high which some people were predicting. Private foreign investment has been less forthcoming than the government hoped, although the World Bank granted the country US$175 million to restore its infrastructure. Lebanon is now embarking on a series of trade fairs and promotions to encourage investment.

POPULATION & PEOPLE

There are no official government population figures and no census has been held since 1932, due to political sensitivity over the numbers belonging to various sects, but the population is estimated at three million. This makes Lebanon the most densely populated of the Middle Eastern countries with about 307 people per sq km.

It is generally acknowledged that Muslims these days account for more than 60% of the population. Many Lebanese, who left during the war, are now returning and the population is due to increase further. Sixty-five per cent of the total population lives in urban areas with about 1.5 million people living in Beirut. There are an estimated 400,000 Palestinian refugees and 300,000 other Arab nationalities, Kurds and Armenians.

Ethnically, the Lebanese are descended from Phoenicians, Arabs, Turks and Assyrians, with the addition of the various conquering peoples, such as the Greeks and Romans thrown in. Christian Lebanese tend to identify with their Phoenician past and

Muslim Lebanese lean towards their Arab roots, although this is a broad generalisation.

EDUCATION

Parents who can afford it send their children to private schools. Although there are some government schools available, they are usually of inferior quality. The civil war disrupted the education system and schools were often closed due to the fighting. Schools had to adapt by extending the school year and improvising classrooms. Education is highly regarded in Lebanon and the country has a 95% literacy rate. Children are encouraged to study at college and university; a degree is seen as the key to a better life. Since the early 1980s the UN Relief and Works Agency (UNRWA) has funded and run schools in the more deprived areas and the Palestinian refugee camps.

Lebanon has several highly regarded universities which have excellent international reputations. The best known of these is the American University of Beirut (AUB) which has pupils of all sects. The University of Balamand in the north is also regarded as a fine academic institution.

ARTS

Lebanon has a very lively arts scene, both traditional and contemporary. In the summer almost every village has a festival in which both traditional music and dance play a part.

The world renowned international festival held in Baalbek was relaunched in July 1997 after an absence of 22 years. The annual festival runs over four days and includes both international and national acts. The 1997 festival featured the local Caracalla Dance Theatre and the cello virtuoso Mstislav Rostropovitch. The organising committee can be contacted at (☎ (01) 373151/2; fax 373153; web site www2.baalbeck.org.lb; email info@baalbeck.org.lb) for future dates and programmes.

Dance

The national dance, the *dabke*, is an energetic folk dance that is performed all over the country. Dabke dancers wear the traditional

Oriental Dancing

This ancient form of dance, known in the east as *raks sharki* and to the world at large as belly dancing, sums up the eastern nightclub experience. The dance is characterised by its sensual hip movements and graceful arm movements – and also by the skimpy costumes worn by the practitioners. When westerners first saw this dance performed, they were struck by its erotic quality and this image has stayed with the dance ever since. Not surprisingly really – Europe of the 18th century had no equivalent dance and the degree of nudity involved in oriental dancing must have been shocking to Christian Europeans of that time.

Professional belly dancers can earn a fortune for a single performance. Others make do with large denomination notes tucked into their costume as a tribute from their appreciative audience. The top dancers are usually Egyptian, although you come across dancers from just about every country you can think of.

The origins of the dance are lost in history. Some scholars think it comes from the professional dancers of medieval Spain. Others think it has a connection with pagan fertility dances performed in temples. These days the dance is performed as entertainment in clubs and restaurants and still plays an important role at traditional weddings. The sensual belly dancer who performs at weddings represents the transition from virgin bride to sensual woman; significantly, belly dancers are only ever hired to dance at a woman's first wedding.

If you find yourself confronted by a gyrating torso at a club, etiquette requires that you place a rolled or folded banknote into the bra or waistband of the dancer without too much physical contact. The belly dancer will then move on to another table and repeat the performance. ∎

costume of the mountains and the dances portray aspects of village life.

There is a Dabke Club (☎ (01) 350000) at the AUB campus which holds performances on Tuesday and Thursday evenings during term time.

Music

The major music festival on the calendar is the Bustan Festival held at the Hotel Al Bustan in Beit Meri. An annual event held in the early spring, it concentrates on classical music; each year has a specific theme. The

Arabic Music

The traditions of Arabic music developed in the courts of the early Islamic empire from the 7th to the 13th centuries. The music is created using unharmonised melodies and rhythms. The structure is complex with the rhythmic cycles having up to 48 beats. In order to catch the rhythm, the listener must follow the long pattern. Set pieces are elaborated and improvised upon, in the style of Indian music or jazz performers.

Much of Arabic music is accompanied by singing. This can be long poetic recitations and even elaborate wordplay. The Arabic language lends itself to this kind of sophisticated, many layered word game – the greatest singers are masters of this art.

Apart from the human voice, the most important instruments are the various lutes, both long and short-necked, such as the *'ud*, the bowed lute or fiddle called the *rabab*, the oboe-style flute known as the *mijwiz* or *shawm* and the single-headed drum called the *tablah*. Various tambourines such as the *daff* (also called the *riqq* or *bandir*) are popular as is the double-headed drum and the *naker*, a small kettledrum.

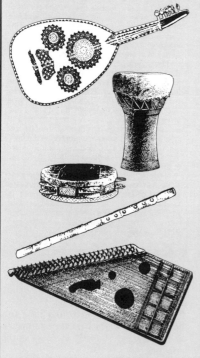

The 'ud has a deep, pear-shaped body, a fretless fingerboard, and between four and six strings. Body size, number of strings and tunings vary. The name 'ud, from the Arabic meaning 'wood', refers to the wood body of the instrument in contrast to the skin bellies of the earlier lutes.

The tablah is one of the most commonly played of the percussion instruments. It is usually made of clay, wood or metal with goat or fish skin stretched over its wide neck. It is held either under the arm, between the legs, or upright, upside down, and played by striking the edge or centre of the stretched skin.

Corresponding to the European tambourine, the daff consists of a round frame with a goat or fish skin stretched to cover one side. Pairs of metal discs, set into the frame, make the tinkling sound which sets the rhythm of Arabic music. It is usually associated with belly dancing.

The nay is a single reed, open-ended instrument which produces an extraordinary range of mellow sounds. It usually has six holes in the front for the fingers and one hole in the other side for the thumb. The sounds are produced by blowing from the pipe end and moving the fingers and thumbs over the holes.

The qanun is a trapezoid-shaped instrument with at least 81 strings stretched across its length. It is placed flat on the knees of the musician and the strings are plucked with the finger or two plectra attached to the forefingers of each hand. It has been an integral part of Arabic music since the 10th century.

Audiences applaud at the end of each section of the performance (as opposed to the western system of waiting until the end of all the movements of a piece before clapping). As well as clapping, audiences often exclaim out loud in appreciation of a performance and shouts of 'Allah!' can often be heard which urges the performer on to the next section. ■

1998 festival will be held from 18 February to 22 March, with the theme 'Paris'. For further details, contact ☎ (01) 425258/9. Tickets are available from major bookshops in Beirut, such as the Librairie Antoine in Hamra.

See also the Beiteddine Festival and the Tyre Festival in the South of Beirut chapter.

After WWII there was a major resurgence of Lebanese music, and with it, came an interest in Arabic as opposed to Turkish music. There are many contemporary singers and musicians – the most famous is Fairouz. She is practically a legend in Lebanon and throughout the Arab world for her long, soulful songs. She still performs occasionally and her son, Ziad, is a renowned experimental jazz performer. See the Fairouz boxed story later for more information.

Literature

Literature and poetry have always had an important place in Lebanese culture. This is reflected in the prolific publishing industry. One very popular form of poetry is the *zajal*, in which a group of poets enter into a witty dialogue by improvising verses. The verses are sung rather than recited. This is usually done over a meal and drinks of arak, the local spirit, and the poets are usually egged on by an enthusiastic audience.

The most famous Lebanese literary figure is Khalil Gibran, a 19th-century poet, writer and artist whose work explored Christian mysticism. His most famous work was *The Prophet*. (See the Khalil Gibran boxed story in the Tripoli & The Cedars chapter.)

There has recently been a revival of contemporary Lebanese writers, such as Hanan al-Shaykh, whose novels *The Story of Zahra* and *Beirut Blues* have given a powerful voice to a new generation of postwar Lebanese writers, who are attracting international acclaim. Other contemporary Lebanese writers include Amin Maalouf and Emily Nasrallah.

Architecture

There are still a few examples of traditional architecture in Beirut, but many of the old buildings have suffered the same redevelopment fate as in the rest of the Mediterranean. Old Beirut houses are usually large and airy with a courtyard garden, a terrace overgrown with vines and large, arched windows, often inset with coloured glass. The style is a mix of Italian influence and Arabic layout.

Most of the building since the 1960s is rather brutish concrete blocks. In the central district of Beirut, many of the buildings were too damaged by the war to be saved, but some are being restored and efforts are being made to rebuild in a sympathetic style.

In the regions, styles vary; some villages have red-tiled roofs, others a more Middle-Eastern style. In the north Tripoli has a wealth of medieval and Islamic architecture and a fine collection of 18th-century merchants houses can be seen in the small town of Amchit, north of Byblos.

For more information on Lebanese architectural styles, see The Architecture of Lebanon section later in this chapter.

Cinema

Cinema is very popular and often newly released western movies are shown (check whether the film has subtitles or is dubbed in Arabic though). Apart from Beirut, there are cinemas in most of the regional towns. The various cultural institutes also show films in their respective languages. See the Beirut chapter for a listing of cinemas and cultural institutes.

The Lebanese film industry suffered during the war and many film-makers (and other artists) left the country. There is now a small revival; some Lebanese films have been shown at the Africa Film Festival (held alternately in Carthage, Tunisia, and in Ougadougou, Burkina Faso) to critical acclaim. See also under Film in the Facts for the Visitor chapter.

Theatre

In Beirut there are quite a few theatres which show everything from serious drama to comedy revues, but performances are generally in Arabic only. The AUB campus has a theatre which sometimes performs plays in

Fairouz

Lebanon's number one superstar is the chanteuse Fairouz, famed throughout the Arab world since the early 1950s. She has a huge following and still plays to packed houses wherever she performs. Until Fairouz came on the scene, the undisputed queen diva was the Egyptian singer Umm Kalthoum, but even she was eclipsed by the haunting voice of Fairouz.

Fairouz was born Nohad Haddad in 1935 to a printer father. Her musical talent began to show at the age of 10 when her beautiful voice began to develop. Her stage name of Fairouz means turquoise and was given to her after Halim il-Roumi, father of Majida (another well-known singer), heard her sing. Her success really began when she formed a collaboration with the Rahbani Brothers, Mansour and Aassi, in 1952. Their first venture together *Itab* was recorded in Damascus and released in 1952. For the following 20 years, they held the top spot in Arabic popular music. Fairouz married Aassi Rahbani, sealing their partnership both professionally and personally. Aassi died in 1979, following a long illness caused by a stroke.

Instead of retiring, Fairouz developed a new sound, 'oriental jazz', with her son Ziad and reworked many of her old numbers in the new style. The result made her more popular than ever. She became an icon for Lebanon during, and after, the war. During the first concert in Beirut since the war broke out, 40,000 people crammed into the Place des Martyrs in the damaged Downtown district to hear her. As the strains of 'Ya Beirut' swept over the crowd, nothing could have better symbolised the reunification of the city.

All of Fairouz's albums are worth a listen, but the most popular ones include traditional music, such as *Andalousiat*, and the soundtracks of her operettas, such as *Biyaa al-Khawatem* (the seller of rings) and *Jbail al-Sawwan* (mountains of rocks). ■

English. Three well-known Lebanese playwrights are Roger Assaf, Jalal Khoury and Issam Mahfouz.

Other kinds of live entertainment abound. There has been a revival of the nightclub cabaret scene in a big way. It is probably flattering to include these shows under this heading, but if dancing girls and variety acts are your sort of thing, then there is no shortage of options.

Perhaps the most exciting theatre you may see in Lebanon is 'Caracalla', an amazing oriental ballet spectacular. The costumes and stagecraft are magnificent. It is a unique blend of east and west in terms of dance and music. They often tour the world, but if they are performing in Lebanon, don't miss them.

Painting & Sculpture

There are many artists in Lebanon and a lot of these have exhibited internationally. Private galleries, mainly in the capital, show modern sculpture, painting and photography. One of the most important venues for contemporary art is the Sursock Museum in Beirut, which holds several major exhibitions a year.

The Basbous brothers in Rachana village are all established sculptors and you can informally visit their workshops and galleries there. Their larger works line the streets nearby and attract quite a few visitors, especially at the weekend.

Beirut's most famous sculpture is the bronze monument in the Place des Martyrs. It suffered a lot of damage during the fighting, and although it was initially decided to leave the statue as a reminder of the destructiveness of the war, it is now being restored. The work is being carried out by students at the Holy Spirit University in Kaslik.

SOCIETY & CONDUCT
Traditional Culture

The Lebanese, in common with the rest of the Middle East, place a great importance on family life. In villages and small towns you often come across extended family networks where everyone seems to be related to everyone else. Most family occasions, such as weddings, funerals and christenings, are often large celebrations involving the whole community.

There is a disarming openness to strangers: you will often be invited into people's homes to sip a cup of coffee and when you ask for directions, people will often stop what they are doing and show you to the place you want to go – so don't be afraid to ask if you get lost.

Dos & Don'ts

The Lebanese are extremely liberal in matters of dress, especially in Beirut, where you often see women wearing the latest western fashions, including miniskirts. In the more remote areas and in the more conservative Muslim areas, it is more a matter of courtesy than necessity to cover up, but by doing so, you will avoid any unwelcome stares and unpleasantness. This applies to men as well as women. If you are visiting a mosque, it is necessary for women to wear a headscarf – some mosques even provide you with a hooded cloak. See also Women Travellers in the Facts for the Visitor chapter.

Given the complex loyalties and political affiliations of the various religious groups which culminated in the civil war, it would be unwise to get into any heavy political debates about the merits, or otherwise, of the various 'sides'. Although people from all the communities are very friendly towards foreigners, there is still a lot of resentment and prejudice lurking beneath the surface.

RELIGION

About 60% of Lebanon's population is Muslim and 40% is Christian. The largest Muslim group is the Shiite (Shia) sect, followed by the Sunni and the Druze. The largest Christian group is the Maronite sect, followed by the Greek Orthodox, the Greek Catholic, the Syrian Catholic, the Chaldean, the Protestant and the Orthodox churches.

Islam

Islam was founded in the early 7th century AD by the prophet Mohammed, who was born around 570 AD in Mecca. The basis of Islam is a series of divine revelations in which the voice of the archangel Gabriel revealed the word of God to Mohammed. His first revelation happened quite late in life at the age of 40. These revelations continued throughout his life and were originally committed to memory and then written down. This text forms the Qur'an (the name meaning literally 'recitation'), which also came to establish the form of written Arabic for centuries. Great care is taken not to change one single dot of the holy Qur'an – the speech of God – and foreign translations are never described as Qur'ans, only interpretations.

Mohammed's teachings were not an immediate success. He started preaching in 613, three years after the first revelation , but could only attract a few dozen followers. Having attacked the ways of Meccan life – especially the worship of idols – he also made many enemies. In 622 he and his followers retreated to Medina, an oasis town some 360km from Mecca. It is this *hijra*, or migration, which marks the beginning of the Muslim calendar.

In Medina Mohammed quickly became a successful religious, political and military leader. After several short clashes with the Meccans, he finally gathered 10,000 troops and conquered his home town, demolishing the idols worshipped by the population and establishing the worship of the one God.

Mohammed died in 632, but the new religion continued its rapid spread, reaching all of Arabia by 634, Egypt, Palestine, Syria, Lebanon and what is now Iraq and western Iran by 642, and most of Iran and Afghanistan by 656. This remarkable wave of conquests was achieved by Mohammed's successors, the caliphs (or Companions of Mohammed) of which there were four. By the end of the 7th century, the Muslims had reached across North Africa to the Atlantic, and having consolidated their power, invaded Spain in 710.

Sunnis & Shiites Not long after the death of Mohammed, Islam suffered a major schism that divided the faith into two main sects: the Sunnis and the Shiites. The split arose over disputes about who should succeed Mohammed, who had died without an heir. The main contenders were Abu Bakr, who was father of Mohammed's second wife Ayesha and the Prophet's closest companion, and Ali, who was Mohammed's cousin and husband to his daughter Fatima. They both had their supporters, but Abu Bakr was declared the first caliph, an Arabic word meaning 'successor' or 'lieutenant'.

Ali finally became the fourth caliph following the murder of Mohammed's third successor, Uthman. He in turn was assassinated in 661 after failing to bend to the military governor of Syria, Mu'awiyah. Mu'awiyah, a relative of Uthman who had revolted against Ali over the latter's alleged involvement in Uthman's killing, then set himself up as caliph.

Ali's supporters continued to hold fast to their belief in the legitimacy of his line and became known as the *shi'a* (Shiite) or '(partisans) of Ali'. They believe in 12 *imams* (spiritual leaders), the last of whom will one day appear to create an empire of the true faith.

The Sunnis are followers of the succession from the caliph.

The Faith A great number of people in the conquered countries converted to Islam. This is simply achieved by a profession of faith in front of two witnesses (the *shahada*). This is the first of the Five Pillars of Islam, the five tenets which guide Muslims in their daily life:

Shahada (the profession of faith) 'There is no God but Allah and Mohammed is his prophet'. This is the fundamental tenet of Islam and is often quoted at events such as births and deaths. The first part is used as an exclamation good for any time of life or situation.

Salat (the call to prayer) This is the obligation to pray in the direction of Mecca five times a day, when the *muezzins* call the faithful to prayer from the minarets. Prayers can be performed anywhere if a mosque is not available and Muslims often travel with a prayer mat and pray at the side of the road or anywhere else for that matter. The midday prayers on Friday are the most important of the week and are roughly equivalent to attending Sunday Mass for Catholics.

Zakat (the giving of alms to the poor) This was a fundamental part of the social teaching of Islam. It has become formalised in some states into a tax which is used to help the poor. In other countries it is a personal obligation to give and is a spiritual duty rather than the Christian idea of charity.

Sawm (fasting) Ramadan, the ninth month of the Islamic calendar, commemorates the month when the Qur'an was revealed to Mohammed. In a demonstration of Muslims' renewal of faith, they are asked to abstain from sex and from letting *anything* pass their lips from dawn to dusk for an entire month.

Hajj (pilgrimage) The pilgrimage to Mecca is the ultimate profession of faith for the devout Muslim. Ideally, the pilgrim should go to Mecca during the last month of the year, Zuul-Hijja, to join with Muslims from all over the world in the pilgrimage and subsequent feast. On the pilgrimage the pilgrim wears a white seamless robe and walks around the *Kaaba*, the black stone in the centre of the Grand Mosque, seven times. The returned pilgrim can be addressed as *hajji*.

To Muslims, Allah is the same God as the Christian and Jew worship. Adam, Abraham, Noah, Moses and Jesus are all recognised as prophets. Jesus is not recognised as the son of God. According to Islam, all these prophets partly received the word of God, but only Mohammed received the complete revelations.

Islamic Holidays The principal Islamic holidays are tied to the lunar hijra calendar. The word 'hijra' refers to the flight of the prophet Mohammed from Mecca to Medina in 622 AD, which marks the first year of the calendar (year 1 AH). The calendar is about 11 days shorter than the Gregorian (western) calendar, meaning that Islamic holidays fall 11 days earlier each year. See also the Islamic Holidays boxed story in the Facts for the Visitor chapter.

Ras as-Sana This means New Year's Day, and is celebrated on the first day of the Hijra calendar year, 1 Moharram.

Achoura This is the day of public mourning observed by the Shiites on 10 Moharram. It commemorates the assassination of Hussein ibn Ali, grandson of the prophet Mohammed and pretender to the caliphate, which led to the permanent schism between Sunnis and Shiites.

Mawlid an-Nabi This is a lesser feast celebrating the birth of the prophet Mohammed on 12 Rabi' al-Awal. For a long time this was not celebrated at all in the Arab world.

Ramadan & Eid al-Fitr Most Muslims take part in the fasting which characterises the holy month of Ramadan. It is a time when the faithful are called upon as a community to renew their relationship with God. Ramadan was the month in which the Qur'an was first revealed. From dawn until dusk the Muslims are expected to abstain from eating, drinking, smoking and sex. Those who are engaged in heavy physical work, or are travellers or nursing mothers are considered exempt, although they are expected to make up the slack at a later time. At sunset there is the *iftar*, or breaking of the fast. It is a time for prayers and both things often happen in the local mosque; praying followed by an animated picnic. Non-Muslims are not expected to observe the fast, but it is good manners not to eat and smoke in public during the fast. In any case most restaurants and cafés would be closed during the day.

The end of Ramadan is marked with *Eid al-Fitr*, the Festival of Breaking the Fast, which lasts for at least three days and often longer. Generally everything shuts down during this holiday.

Hajj & Eid al-Adha The hajj, or pilgrimage to Mecca, is the fifth pillar of Islam and it is the duty of all Muslims to perform at least one hajj in their lifetime. The traditional time for the hajj is during the month of Zuul-Hijja, the 12th month of the Muslim year.

The high point of the pilgrimage is the visit to the Kaaba, the construction housing the stone of Ibrahim in the centre of the *haram*, the sacred area into which non-Muslims are forbidden to enter. The pilgrims, dressed only in a plain white robe, circle the Kaaba seven times and kiss the black stone. This is only one of a series of acts of devotion carried out by pilgrims.

The hajj culminates in the ritual slaughter of a lamb (in commemoration of Ibrahim's sacrifice) at Mina. This marks the end of the pilgrimage and the beginning of *Eid al-Adha*, or Feast of Sacrifice. Throughout the Islamic world the act of sacrifice is repeated and the streets of towns and cities seem to run with the blood of slaughtered sheep. It is customary to give part of the sheep to the poor. The holiday runs from 10 to 13 Zuul-Hijja.

The Druze The Druze are one of the religious curiosities of the Middle East. Originally an offshoot of Islam, they have diversified so much from mainstream Islam that they are often considered to constitute a whole separate religion. The majority of Druze live in Lebanon, but there are also large numbers in Syria and a few in Israel.

Their origins stem from the Fatimid Ismailis, a branch of Shiite Islam. The Druze believe that God incarnated himself in men at various times and that his last, and final, incarnation was Al-Hakim bi Amrillah, the sixth Fatimid caliph who died in 1021 AD. Al-Hakim declared himself to be the incarnation of God in Cairo in 1016 AD and by 1017 the idea grew into a movement primarily due to the zeal of Hasan al-Akhram, an Ismaili missionary who proclaimed his divinity.

After the murder of al-Akhram in 1018, Hamzah ibn Ali ibn Ahmad became the leader and major founder of the new sect. He became *vizier* (minister) to Al-Hakim and made many converts, especially in Syria. The third founding member of the sect, from which its name derives, is Mohammed Ibn Ismail al-Darazi. He was an Ismaili teacher who went to Cairo around 1017. He taught that the divine spirit, embodied in Adam, passed down to Ali and from him through the imams to Al-Hakim. Al-Darazi disappeared – his followers say he withdrew secretly to Syria. In 1021 Al-Hakim also disappeared (possibly assassinated).

The laws laid down by Hamzah are still considered binding by the Druze today. Briefly they are as follows:

1. Veracity in dealing with each other.
2. Mutual protection and assistance.
3. Renunciation of other religions.
4. Belief in the divine incarnation of Al-Hakim.

5. Contentment with the works of God.
6. Submission to God's will.
7. Dissociation from unbelievers.

They believe in reincarnation and that there are a fixed number of souls in existence. Druze tenets also include the belief that Al-Hakim and Hamzah will reappear, conquer the world and establish justice.

The Druze gather for prayer meetings on Thursday evening, not in mosques, but in inconspicuous halls outside Druze villages. Outsiders are not permitted to attend and the rites remain highly secretive.

Christianity

Christianity accounts for about 40% of the population in Lebanon. There are many different churches and rites representing the three main branches of Christianity – Eastern Orthodox, Catholic and Protestant – but the main Christian sect in Lebanon is Maronite, a Roman Catholic church of eastern origin.

Maronite The Maronite church traces its origins back to the 4th century AD and to the monk, St Maro (also called St Maron), who chose a monastic life on the banks of the Orontes in Syria. It is said that 800 monks joined his community and began to preach the gospel in the surrounding countryside. After his death, his followers built a church over his tomb which was destined to become an important sanctuary. Later a monastery grew around the church. This became a centre from which early missionaries set out to convert the people.

The Byzantine emperor Heraclius visited the monastery in 628 to discuss his new ideas of mending the rifts in Christianity. His new doctrine was that of monothelitism, according to which the will of Jesus Christ, both divine and human, was defined as one and indivisible. The western orthodoxy later condemned this idea as heretical. But the Syrians of Lebanon remained attached to monothelitism which grew to be identified with their national and religious aspirations. This led to their isolation from both the orthodox and Jacobite sections of the Lebanese community.

Two major events charted the course of the Maronites. Firstly, the Arab conquest put an end to Christian persecutions of heretical groups. Secondly, serious differences led to the expulsion of the Patriarch of Antioch, and the Maronites elected their own national patriarch at the end of the 8th century who took the title Patriarch of Antioch and the East – a title still held today.

During the Crusades, the Maronites were brought back into contact with the Christian world and the Church of Rome. A gradual process of Romanisation took place, but the church still worshipped in Syriac (a dialect of Aramaic spoken in Syria) and maintained its own identity. Today the Maronite sect is considered a branch of Roman Catholicism.

Eastern Orthodox This branch of Christianity is well represented in Lebanon. There are many Greek and Armenian Orthodox churches as well as a small Syrian Orthodox community.

Greek Orthodox has its liturgy in Arabic and is the mother church of the Jacobites (or Syrian Orthodox), who broke away in the 6th century. Syrian Orthodox uses only Syriac, closely related to Aramaic, the language of Jesus. Armenian Orthodox (also known as the Armenian Apostolic Church) has its liturgy in classical Armenian and is seen by many to be the guardian of the national Armenian identity.

Catholic The Catholic churches come under the jurisdiction of Rome. The largest such group in Lebanon are the Maronites, but many other Catholic rites are represented. There are Greek Catholics (also know as Melchites) who come under the patriarch of Damascus, Syrian Catholics who still worship in Syriac, and Armenian Catholics whose patriarch lives in Beirut. There is also a small community of Catholics who worship in the Chaldean rite or the Latin rite. The Middle East-based patriarchs are often responsible for the worldwide members of their churches.

The
Architecture of Lebanon

The Architecture of Lebanon

Neolithic to Iron Age (5000-1200 BC)

Evidence at Byblos indicates that Stone Age villagers lived in round huts which had hard-packed, crushed limestone floors. Several settlements in the Byblos archaeological site reveal these types of floors which can still be seen today. With the advent of metal tools the villagers could better exploit the nearby forests and timber beams began to be used for roof construction. At first these timber-roofed rooms were long and narrow, a reflection of the fact that the people of the time didn't have the technology to cut the wood to size. Later, as this technology developed, the rooms became squarer.

The ramparts of Byblos, which date from the 3rd millennium BC, are one of the earliest examples of planning against invasions. Two gates were built in the ramparts: one led inland to escape invaders from the sea and the other led to the sea to escape invaders from the land.

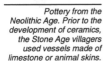

Pottery from the Neolithic Age. Prior to the development of ceramics, the Stone Age villagers used vessels made of limestone or animal skins.

Phoenician (1200-550 BC)

The typical Phoenician town was divided in two: a maritime town sited on a promontory with an island offshore; and an inland town separated from the maritime one by gardens. A good example of this is Sidon, which retains its Phoenician flavour to this day.

Phoenicians cities were quite compact, the houses were multistorey with small square windows and balustrades supported by miniature palm columns. The Greek historian and geographer Strabo has left a description of these houses, pointing out that the houses in Tyre were higher than those in Rome itself.

The Phoenicians laid out their cities in a grid pattern and surrounded them with defensive walls. They also took pains to ensure that their cities had access to more than one harbour. At Sidon this double harbour strategy (which pretty well guaranteed they had a wind to sail out on from one harbour or the other) is still evident.

Phoenician temples, where they exist, have been much modified over the centuries and even from earliest times displayed foreign influences, such as the Obelisk Temple at Byblos (obelisks were an Egyptian import) and the temple of Echmoun near Sidon whose Persian influence is evident in the setting – against a hill side – and in the manner of its inscriptions which are etched into the foundations.

The Phoenicians are credited with developing a new type of design for public buildings, a feature of which was the colonnaded porch. A famous example of this was the Temple of Solomon in Jerusalem which Phoenician artisans helped to construct.

Greeks & Romans (333 BC-300 AD)

The Greeks introduced three orders of architecture: the Doric, Ionic and Corinthian. The different orders are best distinguished by the temples and columns of this period.

Columns constructed in all three orders supported an upper section called an *entablature*. Colonnades around the outside of the *cella* (the hall containing the cult image) rested on a *stylobate*, the temple substructure or, more strictly speaking, the top stair of the temple. There are examples of Corinthian columns at the temple ruins in Faqra. Corinthian columns have also been incorporated into the design of the Great Mosque in Sidon.

Previous page:
Massive Roman columns of the Temple of Bacchus.
(Photo by Ann Jousiffe)

Mythology

Lebanon has temples and sanctuaries without number: some have been left to ruin, some have been turned into Christian churches, but very often there is still a resonance of their original purpose. The gods and goddesses of the ancient Middle East evolved into Greek, and later, Roman equivalents. Even the Christian holy family has some echo of the role played by older gods. To unravel some of the names of deities which crop up again and again in Lebanon, here is a brief guide.

Ashtoreth/Astarte/Ishtar Ashtoreth is the supreme female divinity of the Phoenicians, known by the Babylonians as Ishtar and the Greek and Romans as Astarte. They all symbolise the female principle in all her aspects, just as Baal symbolised maleness. She was the Great Mother, goddess of fertility and queen of heaven. Astarte was later identified with a number of Greek goddesses: Selene, the moon goddess, Artemis, the goddess of nature and Aphrodite, the goddess of love and beauty. Astarte is most famous for her love of the youth Tammuz. The story also features in Greek mythology as the story of Aphrodite and Adonis.

Bel/Baal Bel was the supreme god of the Babylonians and the name Bel is the Chaldean form of Baal. The name literally means 'lord' (as it still does in Hebrew). Bel presided over the air and was associated astrologically with the planet Jupiter, which, in astral mythology, is connected to the productive power of nature.

Dagon/Dagan Dagon is the second most important god after El, the supreme god. He is the recognised god of crop fertility and is also the legendary inventor of the plough. He is also known as the god of the fishes.

Echmoun/Asklepios/Aesculapius Echmoun is the principal god of the city of Sidon and is associated with healing. Echmoun began as a mortal youth from Berytus (Beirut). Astarte fell in love with him but to escape from her, he mutilated himself and died. She brought him back to life in the form of a god. He was still primarily a god of healing and is identified with the Greek Asklepios, the god of medicine, and the Roman god Aesculapius.

El El is the father of all gods except Baal. In Phoenician texts he is described as the creator of the earth. El is usually represented as an old man with a long beard and, often, two wings.

Melkart/Heracles Melkart, later called Heracles by the Greeks, is the god of the cities. He is specifically the patron god of Tyre.

Resheph/Reshef Resheph is the god of the plague, and of burning and destructive fire. Usually represented with a shield and lightning rod, he is also seen as a war god. He later became the Babylonian god Nergal.

Tammuz/Adonis Adonis was a beautiful youth loved by both Aphrodite and Persephone, queen of the underworld. When he was slain by a wild boar, Aphrodite pleaded with Zeus to restore him. Zeus agreed that Adonis should spend the winter months with Persephone in Hades and the summer months with Aphrodite. His story is the allegory of nature's death and rebirth every spring.

Zeus/Jupiter/Jove Zeus is the ruler of the gods and the son of Saturn (who he overthrew). Jupiter is identified with the Greek Zeus and was worshipped as the god of thunder and lightning. He was also guardian of law, defender of truth and protector of justice. ■

Stele of Baal, discovered at the Phoenician city of Ugarit.

Wooden figurine of Ashtoreth from Kamid el-Loz.

Roman temples differed from Greek ones in several respects: the stylobate was substituted with a podium; instead of stairs that ran around the temple, the Romans built just one flight, on the entrance facade; and the typically Greek colonnade became increasingly decorative and was sometimes set into the cella itself.

Like the Phoenicians, the Greeks designed their towns according to a grid system, orientating their temples on an east/west axis while other buildings were placed according to the lie of the land. The Romans were more concerned with imposing their style on the environment. As Lebanon experienced something of a building boom under the Romans, their vision of architectural ideals is much in evidence.

The Romans borrowed the Greek orders of architecture, adding two of their own, the Composite and the Tuscan. And, although they didn't invent it, they made good use of the arch as it suited their desire for space and monuments.

The Roman passion for order and harmony is reflected in their town planning. Two main roads, the *documanus maximus* (usually east/west) and the *cardo maximus* (usually north/south), intersected near the city centre, where the forum and amphitheatre could also usually be found. Important roads like these were invariably colonnaded. The layout divided the city into four quarters, the whole being enclosed within the city walls.

Excavations in the Downtown area of Beirut are revealing a distinct Roman heritage, including this Roman style of town planning. The Romans ensured the city was well endowed with temples and other public buildings, including a hippodrome and a monumental archway. Most have long since been lost, their existence known only from coins struck at the time and from descriptions in contemporary documents. Remains of Roman baths have, however, survived under the Grand Seraglio plateau.

Other historical sites in Lebanon have many examples of Roman architecture: a theatre in Batroun; a temple in Majdel Aanjar; and a necropolis in Dakweh.

List of details

1 Entablature
2 Column
3 Cornice
4 Frieze
5 Architrave
6 Capital
7 Shaft
8 Base
9 Plinth
10 Triglyph
11 Metope
12 Abacus
13 Echinus
14 Flute
15 Arris
16 Fascia
17 Volute
18 Fillet
19 Dentils

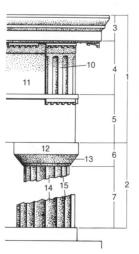

Doric

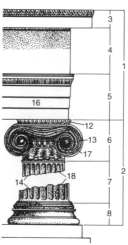

Ionic

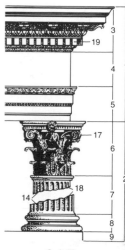

Corinthian

Sketches of Baalbek

We have the sketches and descriptions of some early travellers to Baalbek to help us understand what happened to the site. In 1759, Constantin-François Volney observed that the central lintel in the Temple of Bacchus had slipped down and hung suspended in the air as a result of the recent earthquake. (Around 1870 this was shored up by Richard Burton, the British consul in Damascus, who constructed a stone support.) He wrote that it was not only nature but humans who destroyed Baalbek. The stones were held with metal clamps and dowels which were greedily removed to make bullets. Once that was done the great stones were not secure and fell at the slightest tremor. Road building robbed the site of many cut stones. During the 19th century David Roberts, the famous artist, drew the temples at Baalbek but with more artistry than accuracy. ■

A sketch of the Temple of Bacchus with hanging keystone in 1839, by David Roberts.

A good example of a theatre that is still visible can be found in Byblos. Unlike the Greeks, who took advantage of natural slopes when building their theatres, the Romans didn't excavate but instead built on level ground. Walls formed a continuous barrier around the stage and seating. As they didn't use a chorus, the orchestra (reached through a series of vaulted passages) formed part of the auditorium.

Tyre has a typical example of a hippodrome that was lined with tiers of seats along each side. One end of the hippodrome was curved while the opposite end was squared off so the chariots could enter and draw up for the start.

Arguably the most important Roman remains are at Baalbek: the gigantic columns of the Temple of Jupiter; the well-preserved Temple of Bacchus (some claim it's the Roman world's finest example of a Corinthian building); and the circular Temple of Venus. Although their invention of concrete allowed the Romans to build gigantic structures elsewhere, at Baalbek they achieved the same effect using mortarless stone. These temples were built to last; the substructure at Baalbek contains some of the largest single blocks of stone to be found in the world.

Byzantines, Arabs & Crusaders (324-1300 AD)

The prime architectural legacy of the Byzantines is their churches. But here they owed a debt to the Romans before them, whose basilicas or halls of justice they copied. Byzantine churches were typically orientated on an east/west axis – a long hall terminated in an apse at the east end. Aisles on either side of the nave were separated from the nave itself by colonnades. The floors were covered with colourful mosaics (a feature also copied from the Romans). An example of such a mosaic, found by the British in Beirut in 1918, is now in the American University of Beirut Museum. More Byzantine remains are being uncovered as Beirut rebuilds. Already they include a mosaic from a Byzantine shopping colonnade on the northern side of the documanus maximus and a mosaic uncovered in the souks which features a musing (in Greek) on the nature of jealousy.

There are many examples of Byzantine churches in Lebanon, most notably in Sidon, Qartaba, Enfe and Beit Meri. In Tyre you can see a number of Byzantine buildings which have borrowed their style from the Romans.

Only one site, Aanjar, bears the imprint of the Damascus-based Umayyads whose influence waxed and waned between the 7th and 8th centuries. At first glance Aanjar seems almost Roman, laid out as it is in a square grid, with two 20m-wide thoroughfares (the cardo and the documanus), and enclosed within walls punctuated by four towers. Arcades of shops once lined the main roads; elsewhere are Roman-style baths, mosques and at least two palaces. The Umayyads made Beirut the centre of their caliphate in the 7th century, and current excavations there may yet reveal more evidence of their presence.

The Crusaders left behind their castles and their churches. At Byblos the Church of St John in Byblos (still in use, by the Maronites) was built in Romanesque style about 1116. Byblos' Crusader castle, built on the site of the old acropolis soon after the town was captured (in 1104), boasts some impressively large blocks of stone, although these were almost certainly liberated from more ancient structures nearby.

Here and elsewhere in Lebanon, the Crusaders used ancient temple columns in the walls to strengthen them and make undermining by enemies more difficult. Crusader castles were designed to withstand prolonged armed attacks and their architecture reflects their creators' attempts to meet the challenge of enemy tactics and weaponry.

ANN JOUSIFFE

The Obelisk Temple at Byblos has 26 sandstone or limestone obelisks, but only one has an inscription: a dedication in hieroglyphics to an Egyptian god.

ANDY FERGUSON

The Temple of Bacchus at Baalbek is one of the most magnificent and well-preserved Roman temples in the world. It has an interior span of 19m. The monumental gateway is 6.5m wide and nearly 13m high, yet it is more prized for its flamboyant decoration.

DIANA SAAD

The Umayyad ruins of Aanjar, comprising mosques, palaces, baths, shops and houses, were built in a symmetrical style reminiscent of Roman tradition. Little is known about the town's history, or why it was built in the Bekaa Valley.

The Crusader Castle at Byblos was built in the 12th century with stone taken from the ancient city's ruins. It has a square donjon (fortified tower) surrounded by an almost square bailey with towers at each corner.

PAUL DOYLE

The Palace of Beiteddine is an intriguing mixture of Arab and Italian architectural styles. The interior reveals intricate mosaics (right), rich wooden panelling, leadlight windows and ornate marble inlays. The exterior (far right) features charming fountains centred in courtyards, graceful arches, decorated facades and manicured gardens.

ANN JOUSIFFE

ANDY FERGUSON

The Taynal Mosque is one of the most outstanding examples of Islamic architecture in Tripoli. Built in 1336 this green-domed mosque merges the remains of a Christian church with 14th-century Islamic styles.

PAUL DOYLE

Typically 12th-century Crusader castles, such as the one at Byblos, featured a rectangular, two-storeyed donjon (the place of final retreat), which in the case of Byblos was accessed by a ladder to a 1st floor door. Staircases to the upper stories have been cut into the walls, which are 4m thick. The castle was defended from five towers (placed at the four corners of an almost square bailey), each with arrow slits to allow flanking fire.

The castle at Tripoli, built by Raymond de Saint-Gilles, was designed to put the local population under military and economic pressure. Like the castle in Byblos, it consisted of a rectangular, two-storeyed donjon; rectangular towers project gently from the outer walls. At Sidon the Crusaders built their castle on the small island just offshore from the promontory where the Phoenicians before them had built their city. The Mamelukes destroyed it. The Arabs rebuilt it. Unsurprisingly, it shows a mixture of styles and add-ons. In true Crusader fashion, ancient masonry was recycled by the Crusaders; the colonnades built into the outer walls are still in evidence.

1300 AD to the French Mandate

Just as temples were converted to churches by the Byzantines, so churches were converted to mosques by the Muslims – the 13th-century Great Mosque in Sidon was originally a church built by the Hospitallers of St John, for example.

A mosque, which is symmetrical and usually square or rectangular, is generally built around an open courtyard with one or more *iwan* (covered halls) leading from it. A mosque must also have a *mihrab* (a vaulted niche in a wall) which indicates the direction of prayer. Mihrabs can be simple or elaborate. On the right side of the mihrab is the *minbar* – a pulpit usually raised above a staircase. Most mosques also have a *kursi*, a wooden stand for holding the Qur'an.

The most visible, although not obligatory, element of a mosque is the *minaret* or tower from which the call to prayer is made. A minaret can be plain or ornate and it is this which usually distinguishes one mosque from another and from the other buildings in an Islamic town.

The Muslims also left a legacy of khans and caravanserais and other evidence of trade and commerce. Examples of khans, a cross between a market, an inn and a stable and usually two storeyed, can be found in the Old City in Tripoli and in Sidon. Earmarked for possible reconstruction is the khan that once stood in the souks of Beirut, until it was destroyed during the war.

The Palace of Beiteddine is a great example of early 19th-century Lebanese architecture. Conceived by Italian architects, it incorporates traditional Arab and Italian baroque architecture. All the buildings have arcades along their facades. The gate opens onto a vast 60m-long courtyard, walled on three sides only and a double staircase leads to an inner courtyard with a central fountain. The private *hammams* (bathing rooms) are intricately ornamented, and the reception rooms and inner court are decorated with rich wall panels, painted ceilings and mosaics.

In Beirut are the remnants of Ottoman rule (such as the Grand Seraglio, built in 1853 as the barracks for the Turkish army) and the imprint of the French Mandate. The French swept clear the medieval town plan and rearranged the streets in a star shape, placing the parliament building at its centre. The streets themselves were sometimes modelled on those in Paris; Maarad St, for example was modelled on Rue de Rivoli.

Christine Niven

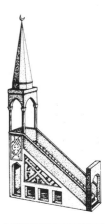

Minbar, the pulpit from which the sermon is delivered.

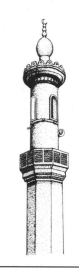

Minaret, the most dominant exterior feature, and one that is of the highest craftmanship.

LANGUAGE

Arabic is the official language of Lebanon. French is widely spoken in the area, but any effort to communicate with the locals in their own language will be well rewarded. No matter how far off the mark your pronunciation or grammar might be, you'll often get the response (usually with a big smile), 'Ah, you speak Arabic very well!'. These days English is also widely spoken in business circles, especially in Beirut.

Arabic

Learning the basics for day-to-day travelling doesn't take long at all, but to master the complexities of Arabic would take years of constant study. Western mispronunciation of place names seems to cause particular confusion to taxi drivers. The dialect of Arabic spoken in Lebanon is fairly close to Modern Standard Arabic, which is the language in use throughout the Arab world in the press and on television.

Street and town signs are in Arabic and Latin script, but use the French spelling and pronunciation. For example, 'ch' is always pronounced as in 'shoe' rather than as in 'cheese' and 'ou' is pronounced 'w'.

Difficult Consonants

Arabic pronunciation is not easy. Because Arabic uses sounds unknown in English, many westerners find these sounds hard to produce. We have used certain combinations of letters in the following transliteration system as a brief guide.

The sounds represented by the letters b, d, f, g, h, j, k, l, m, n, s, t, v, w, y, z are the same as their English counterparts.

sh represents the sound you find in 'shoot', slightly emphasised.

r is rolled slightly, as in French.

kh is like the final sound in Scottish 'lo**ch**' .

' indicates a glottal stop like the Cockney butter (bu'er), but this is a letter in its own right in Arabic, not an omission.

q is like a K but from further back in the throat. It is sometimes transliterated as

---

The Approximate Science of Transliteration

It is worth noting here that transliteration from the Arabic script into English – or any other language for that matter – is at best an approximate science. The presence of sounds unknown in European languages and the fact that most vowels are not written in the script combine to make it nearly impossible to settle on one method of transliteration. It is important to remember that there is no absolutely correct way of spelling an Arabic word in English; the best you can hope for is that the word reads as it is supposed to sound. So don't be surprised if you see the same place spelt two or three different ways, for example, Dawra, Daoura and Dora are all the same place. ■

'k', but 'k' actually represents another letter in Arabic.

h is a heavily aspirated 'h'. Try breathing the letter out very hard from the back of your throat.

gh The letter 'rayn' is a hard one for westerners. The sound is produced like a gargle from deep in the throat and rolled so it sounds a bit like the 'r' in Paris.

' The 'ayn' which is sometimes transliterated as '9', is produced in the same way as the 'rayn' but sort of swallowed again. A tough one, this.

Greetings & Civilities

Arabs place great importance on civility, and it's rare to see any interaction between people that doesn't begin with profuse greetings, enquiries into the other's health and other niceties.

Arabic greetings are more formal than greetings in English, and there is a reciprocal response to each. These sometimes vary slightly, depending on whether you're addressing a man or a woman. A simple encounter can become a drawn-out affair with neither side wanting to be the one to put a halt to the stream of greetings and well wishing. As an *ajnabi* (foreigner), you're not expected to know all the ins and outs, but if you make the effort to come up with the right xpression at the appropriate moment, ־ey'll love it.

The most common greeting is *salaam ־laykum* ('peace be upon you'), to which the ־orrect reply is *wa alaykum as-salaam* ('and ־pon you be peace'). If you get invited to a ־irthday celebration or are around for any of ־ıe big holidays, the common greeting is *kul ־ana wa intum bi-kheer* ('I wish you well for ־ıe coming year').

After having a bath or a haircut, you will ־ften hear people say to you *na'iman*, which ־oughly means 'heavenly' and boils down to ־n observation along the lines of 'nice and ־lean now, huh'.

Arrival in one piece is always something ־o be grateful for. Passengers will often be ־reeted with *al-hamdu lillah 'al as-salaama*, ־neaning 'Thank God for your safe arrival'.

־ıi.	*marhaba*
־ello. (literally 'welcome')	*ahlan wa sahlan/ahlan*
־ello. (response)	*ahlan beek*
־oodbye.	*ma'a salaama/ Allah ma'ak*
־ood morning.	*sabah al-khayr*
־ood morning. (response)	*sabah an-noor*
־ood evening.	*masa al-khayr*
־ood evening. (response)	*masa an-noor*
־ood night.	*tisbah 'ala khayr*
־ood night. (response)	*wa inta min ahalu*
־lease. (request)	*min fadlak* (m) *min fadlik* (f)
־lease. (formal, eg in restaurants)	*law samaht* (m) *law samahti* (f)
־lease. (come in/ go ahead)	*tafadal* (m) *tafadali* (f)
־hankyou.	*shukran*
־hanks a lot.	*shukran jazeelan*
־ou're welcome.	*'afwan or ahlan*
־ow are you?	*kayf haalak?* (m) *kayf haalik?* (f)
־ne. (literally 'thanks be to God')	*al-hamdu lillah*
־leased to meet you. (departing)	*fursa sa'ida*

Pardon/Excuse me.	*'afwan*
Sorry!	*'assif*
Congratulations!	*mabrouk*

Small Talk

What is your name?	*shu-ismak?* (m) *shu-ismik?* (f)
My name is ...	*ismi ...*
Where are you from?	*min wayn inta?*
Do you speak ...?	*btah-ki/hal tatakallam ...?*
I speak ...	*ana bah-ki/ana atakallam ...*
English	*ingleezi*
French	*faransi*
German	*almaani*
I understand.	*ana af-ham*
I don't understand.	*ma bif-ham/ la af-ham*
What does this mean?	*yaanee ay?*
I want an interpreter.	*ureed mutarjem*
I (don't) like ...	*ana (ma) bahib/ ana (la) uhib ...*
Yes.	*aiwa/na'am*
No.	*la*
No problem.	*mish mushkila*
Never mind.	*ma'lesh*
I am sick.	*ana mareed* (m) *ana mareeda* (f)

Questions like 'Is the bus coming?' or 'Will the bank be open later?' generally elicit the inevitable response *in sha' Allah* – God willing – an expression you'll hear over and over again. Another less common one is *ma sha'Allah* – God's will be done – sometimes a useful answer to probing questions about why you're not married yet!

Getting Around

How many km?	*kam kilometre?*
bus station	*mahattat al-baas*
railway station	*mahattat al-qitaar*
airport	*al-mataar*
car	*as-sayaara*
1st class	*daraja awla*
2nd class	*daraja thani*

here/there	*hena/henak*
left	*yasaar*
right	*shimal/yameen*
straight ahead	*'ala tuul*

Around Town

Where is (the) ...?	*wayn ...?*
bank	*al-masraf/al-bank*
hotel	*al-funduq*
market	*as-souq*
Mohammed St	*sharia Mohammed*
mosque	*al-jaame'/al-masjid*
museum	*al-mat'haf*
passport & immigration office	*maktab al-jawazaat wa al-hijra*
pharmacy	*as-saydaliyya*
police	*ash-shurta*
post office	*maktab al-bareed*
restaurant	*al-mat'am*
tourist office	*maktab as-siyaha*

Accommodation

Do you have ...?	*fi 'andakum ...?*
a room	*ghurfa*
a single room	*ghurfa mufrada*
a double room	*ghurfa bi sareerayn*
a shower	*doosh*
hot water	*mai harr*
a toilet	*twalet/mirhad / hammam*
soap	*saboon*
air-con	*kondishon/takyeef*
electricity	*kahraba*

Shopping

How much?	*qaddaysh/bikam?*
How many?	*kam wahid?*
How much money?	*kam fuloos?*
big	*kabeer*
small	*sagheer*
bad	*mish kwayyis/mu kwayyis*
good	*kwayyis*
cheap/expensive	*rakhees/ghaali*
cheaper	*arkhas*
closed	*maghlooq/musakkar*
open	*maftooh*

Time

When?	*mata/emta?*
yesterday	*imbaarih/'ams*
today	*al-yom*
tomorrow	*bukra/ghadan*
minute	*daqiqa*
hour	*sa'a*
day	*yom*
week	*usbu'*
month	*shaher*
year	*sana*
What is the time?	*as-sa'a kam?*
It's 5 o'clock.	*as-sa'a khamsa*

Days of the Week

Monday	*al-itneen*
Tuesday	*at-talata*
Wednesday	*al-arbi'a*
Thursday	*al-khamees*
Friday	*al-jum'a*
Saturday	*as-sabt*
Sunday	*al-ahad*

Numbers

Arabic numerals, unlike the written language, run from left to right.

0	•	*sifr*
1	١	*waahid*
2	٢	*itneen*
3	٣	*talaata*
4	٤	*arba'a*
5	٥	*khamsa*
6	٦	*sitta*
7	٧	*sab'a*
8	٨	*tamanya*
9	٩	*tis'a*
10	١٠	*'ashra*
11	١١	*hida'shar*
12	١٢	*itna'shar*
13	١٣	*talat-ashar*
14	١٤	*arba'at-ashar*
15	١٥	*khamas-ta'shar*
16	١٦	*sitta'shar*
17	١٧	*sabata'shar*
18	١٨	*tamanta'shar*
19	١٩	*tisata'shar*
20	٢٠	*'ishreen*
21	٢١	*wahid wa 'ishreen*
30	٣٠	*talateen*
40	٤٠	*arba'een*

50	٥٠	*khamseen*
60	٦٠	*sitteen*
70	٧٠	*sab'een*
80	٨٠	*tamaneen*
90	٩٠	*tis'een*
100	١٠٠	*miyya*
1000	١٠٠٠	*alf*

French

Although Arabic is the official language of Lebanon, French is widely spoken.

Grammar

An important distinction is made in French between *tu* and *vous*, which both mean 'you'. *Tu* is only used when addressing people you know well, children or animals. When addressing an adult who is not a personal friend, *vous* should be used unless the person invites you to use *tu*. In general, younger people insist less on this distinction, and they may use *tu* from the beginning of an acquaintance.

Basics

For more useful words and phrases than we have space for here, see Lonely Planet's *French phrasebook*.

Yes.	*Oui.*
No.	*Non.*
Maybe.	*Peut-être.*
Please.	*S'il vous plaît.*
Thank you.	*Merci.*
You're welcome.	*Je vous en prie.*
Excuse me.	*Excusez-moi.*
Sorry (Forgive me).	*Pardon.*

Greetings

Hello/Good morning.	*Bonjour.*
Good evening.	*Bonsoir.*
Goodbye.	*Au revoir.*

Small Talk

How are you? (formal)	*Comment allez-vous?*
How are you? (informal)	*Comment ça va?/ Ça va?*
Well, thanks.	*Bien, merci.*

What is your name?	*Comment vous appelez-vous?*
My name is ...	*Je m'appelle ...*
I'm pleased to meet you.	*Enchanté* (m)/ *Enchantée* (f).

Language Difficulties

I understand.	*Je comprends.*
I don't understand.	*Je ne comprends pas.*
Do you speak English?	*Parlez-vous anglais?*
Could you please write that down?	*Est-ce que vous pouvez l'écrire?*

Getting Around

I want to go to ...	*Je voudrais aller à ...*
I would like to book a seat to ...	*Je voudrais réserver une place pour ...*
What time does the ... leave/arrive?	*À quelle heure part/arrive ...?*
bus (city)	*(l'auto)bus*
bus (intercity)	*(l'auto)car*
boat	*le bateau*
ferry	*le ferry(-boat)*
aeroplane	*l'avion*
Where is (the) ...?	*Où est ...?*
bus stop?	*l'arrêt d'autobus*
ticket office	*le guichet*

Directions

How do I get to ...?	*Comment dois-je faire pour arriver à ...?*
Is it near/far from here?	*Est-ce près/loin d'ici?*
Can you show it to me (on the map)?	*Est-ce que vous pouvez me le montrer (sur la carte)?*
Go straight ahead.	*Continuez tout droit.*
Turn left.	*Tournez à gauche.*
Turn right.	*Tournez à droite.*
at the traffic lights	*aux feux*
at the next corner	*au prochain coin*

Around Town

| I'm looking for ... | *Je cherche ...* |
| a bank | *une banque* |

exchange office — *un bureau de change*

the ... embassy — *l'ambassade de ...*

my hotel — *mon hôtel*

the hospital — *l'hôpital*

the police — *la police*

the post office — *le bureau de poste / la poste*

the market — *le marché*

a public phone — *une cabine télé-phonique*

the tourist office — *l'office de tourisme*

Where is (the) ...? — *Où est ...?*

  main square — *la place centrale*

  mosque — *la mosquée*

  old city — *la vieille ville*

What time does it open/close? — *Quelle est l'heure de l'ouverture/ de fermeture?*

I'd like to make a telephone call. — *Je voudrais téléphoner.*

I'd like to change some money/ travellers'cheques. — *Je voudrais changer de l'argent/des chèques de voyage.*

Accommodation

I'm looking for ... — *Je cherche ...*

  the youth hostel — *l'auberge de jeunesse*

  the camping ground — *le camping*

  a hotel — *un hôtel*

I would like to book ... — *Je voudrais réserver ...*

  a bed — *un lit*

  a single room — *une chambre simple*

  a double room — *une chambre double*

  a room with a shower and toilet — *une chambre avec douche et WC*

  a bed in a dormitory — *un lit dans un dortoir*

How much is it per night/per person? — *Quel est le prix par nuit/par personne?*

Is breakfast included? — *Est-ce que le petit déjeuner est compris?*

Can I see the room? — *Est-ce que je peux voir la chambre?*

Where is the bath-room/shower? — *Où est la salle de bains/la douche?*

Where is the toilet? — *Où sont les toilettes?*

I'm going to stay ... — *Je resterai ...*

  one day — *un jour*

  a week — *une semaine*

Food

breakfast — *le petit déjeuner*

lunch — *le déjeuner*

dinner — *le dîner*

grocery store — *l'épicerie*

I would like the set lunch. — *Je prends le menu.*

I am a vegetarian. — *Je suis végétarien (m) / végétarienne (f).*

I don't eat meat. — *Je ne mange pas de viande.*

Shopping

How much is it? — *C'est combien?*

It's too expensive for me. — *C'est trop cher pour moi.*

Can I look at it? — *Est-ce que je peux le/la voir?*

I'm just looking. — *Je ne fais que regarder.*

chemist/pharmacy — *la pharmacie*

laundry — *la laverie*

market — *le marché*

Time & Dates

What time is it? — *Quelle heure est-il?*

When? — *Quand?*

today — *aujourd'hui*

tonight — *ce soir*

tomorrow — *demain*

yesterday — *hier*

Monday — *lundi*

Tuesday — *mardi*

Wednesday — *mercredi*

Thursday — *jeudi*

Friday — *vendredi*

Saturday — *samedi*

Sunday — *dimanche*

Numbers

1	*un*
2	*deux*
3	*trois*
4	*quatre*
5	*cinq*
6	*six*
7	*sept*
8	*huit*
9	*neuf*
10	*dix*
100	*cent*
1000	*mille*
one million	*un million*

Health

I need a doctor.	*Il me faut un médecin.*
Where is the hospital?	*Où est l'hôpital?*
I'm ...	*Je suis ...*
diabetic	*diabétique*
epileptic	*épileptique*
asthmatic	*asthmatique*
anaemic	*anémique*
I'm allergic to ...	*Je suis allergique ...*
antibiotics	*aux antibiotiques*
penicillin	*à la pénicilline*

bees	*aux abeilles*
I'm pregnant.	*Je suis enceinte.*
antiseptic	*antiseptique*
aspirin	*aspirine*
condoms	*préservatifs*
contraceptive	*contraceptif*
medicine	*médicament*
nausea	*nausée*
sun block cream	*crème (solaire) haute protection*
tampons	*tampons hygiéniques*
I am constipated.	*Je suis constipé* (m) / *constipée* (f).
I have diarrhoea.	*J'ai la diarrhée.*

Emergencies

Help!	*Au secours!*
Call the police!	*Appelez la police!*
Call a doctor/ ambulance!	*Appelez un médecin / une ambulance!*
Go away!	*Laissez-moi tranquille!*
I've been robbed.	*On m'a volé.*
I've been raped.	*On m'a violée.*
I'm lost.	*Je me suis égaré* (m) / *égarée* (f).

Facts for the Visitor

PLANNING
When to Go
Lebanon is a year-round destination depending on what activities you want to pursue. It is becoming increasingly popular as a winter sports destination. There are five ski resorts in the Mount Lebanon range and the ski season extends from December to May. The coast can be quite cold and rainy during the winter, though.

One of the most beautiful times of the year to visit Lebanon is spring. During May the weather is warm enough for swimming and the whole country is carpeted with flowers. If your time is just right, you can catch the end of the ski season and still sunbathe on the coast.

Autumn is also very scenic and the heat is less oppressive than the summer months. The end of September to the end of October is the best time to visit before the weather breaks. For real worshippers of the sun, the summer season from June to the middle of September is hot and dry, but be warned, the humidity on the coast can be very high.

What Kind of Trip?
Lebanon is ideally suited to an archaeological sightseeing tour. The country is small and easy to get around and has several outstanding sites. For the more adventurous, trekking or skiing is an option. The rugged mountains offer huge scope for an outdoors trip, although there is only one proper camp site in the country. Private camping is possible with permission from local landowners.

Maps
Lonely Planet's *Jordan, Syria & Lebanon travel atlas* has detailed coverage of the whole country. For Beirut the best map is by GEOprojects, which is available in most Lebanese bookshops. There is also a new map, published by the Ministry of Tourism, which is free if you go to the tourist information offices.

A good commercial map is published by All Prints of Beirut and is available for about US$3 in most of the bookshops. It is also available from Stanfords travel bookshop in London for UK£6.95. This is the most recent map of the country available and there is a good city map of Beirut on the reverse. English and French versions are available.

What to Bring
There is very little that you cannot buy in Beirut so don't laden yourself down with duty-free goods and toiletries – these things are cheaper in Beirut anyway. All toiletries are readily available in Beirut and the major towns.

As for clothing, this depends on the season in which you intend to travel. Even in May you will need a light jacket for the evenings or trips up to the mountains, but from June onwards you can travel much lighter. The heat can be quite intense in high summer and good sunglasses and a hat are essential to avoid sunstroke.

If you are visiting in winter, a waterproof coat is a good idea and you might even consider a pair of waterproof boots. You will certainly need a heavy sweater of some kind. The most useful thing you can pack at any time of the year is a sturdy pair of walking boots or, at the very least, a good pair of running shoes; you will almost certainly find yourself walking over some rugged terrain at some point in your trip.

Lebanon is riddled with caves, grottoes and dark churches, so a torch will be very useful on any number of occasions, including the occasional power cuts. If you are sleeping in Beirut, a pair of earplugs will help cut down the constant noise from traffic. Beirut is one big construction site at the moment, and will be for years to come. This has created a severe dust problem. If you are sensitive to dust, bring a good eye-drop solution with you and a pair of sunglasses. When the wind blows, the dust can become so much of a problem that you may need a protective face mask, or at least a scarf tied over your nose and mouth. For medical items, see the Health section later in this chapter.

SUGGESTED ITINERARIES
It is possible to see all the main sites in Lebanon in one week, but two would be better if you don't want to feel rushed. A good circuit (in the summer months) is to head north to Byblos (Jbail), a must see for its ruins and picturesque port, and then to Tripoli (Trablous), with its dramatic Crusader castle and fine Islamic monuments in the Old City district. Also in the north, near Jounieh, is Jeita Grotto – one of the most impressive of its kind anywhere and well worth a visit.

Then head across to Bcharré (don't miss the famous Cedars) and over the mountains to the Bekaa Valley and Baalbek, Lebanon's number one archaeological attraction. If you only have time to visit one place in Lebanon, then this should be it.

From there you can head south to Zahlé and back across Mount Lebanon to Beirut. From Beirut head south to the coastal towns of Sidon (Saida) and Tyre (Sour) which both have ancient ruins that should not be missed. Also to the south is the Palace of Beiteddine, a lavish Ottoman-style building set in a beautiful landscape.

TOURIST OFFICES
Local Tourist Offices
The main tourist information office (☎ (01) 343073; fax 340945, 343279) is at PO Box 11-5344, 550 Rue Banque du Liban, in the Hamra district of Beirut, in the same building as the Ministry of Tourism.

There are also tourist offices in Byblos (☎ (09) 540325), near the Crusader castle; in Zahlé's Chamber of Commerce building (☎ (08) 802566; fax 803595); and in Tripoli (☎ (06) 433590), on the roundabout with the large 'Allah' sign in Arabic. The tourist office in Jounieh is expected to reopen soon.

Tourist Offices Abroad
There are a number of Lebanese tourist offices in Europe and the Middle East. In addition to these, you can get brochures and information from the national airline, Middle East Airlines (MEA), offices and the Lebanese diplomatic missions. They both have a set of regional brochures of the main archaeological sites, many with useful maps of the ruins.

You can contact the tourist offices in the following countries:

Egypt
1 Sharia Talaat Harb (Midan Tahrir), Cairo (☎/fax (02) 393 7529)
France
124 Rue Faubourg St-Honoré, Paris 75008 (☎ 01 43 59 10 36, 43 59 12 13/4; fax 43 59 11 99)
Germany
Wiesenhüttenplatz 26, 60320 Frankfurt/Main (☎/fax (069) 24 26 47)
Saudi Arabia
Borj Building, Rue Medina al-Nazel, Jeddah (☎ (02) 653 5030; fax 653 4813)
UK
90 Piccadilly, London W1V 9HB (☎ (0171) 409 2031; fax 493 4929)

If you are buying your ticket in London from Trailfinders (☎ (0171) 938 3366) 194 Kensington High St, London W8 7RG, they have a small research library in their basement which is open to clients to have a browse. If you wish to do some deeper research, you can visit the library at the School of Oriental & African Studies, Malet St, London WC1, where there is the definitive collection of books on the Middle East. You will need to provide some ID such as a passport to gain entrance, and you are not be allowed to borrow books. There are photocopiers available.

VISAS & DOCUMENTS
Passport
All nationalities must have a valid passport to enter Lebanon. It pays to be aware if your passport is about to expire or is nearly full. Most foreign embassies in Lebanon can issue replacement passports to their nationals, but it is better to get a new passport

HIGHLIGHTS

Archaeological

Aanjar   *Bekaa Valley p. 185*
Only well-preserved Umayyad city in the Middle East – the reconstructed great palace is a real delight.

Baalbek   *Bekaa Valley p. 187*
Also known as the 'Sun City' of the ancient world, this is the most impressive historical site in Lebanon. The sheer scale of the Temple of Jupiter and the preservation of the Temple of Bacchus puts Baalbek in a class of its own.

Byblos   *North of Beirut p. 150*
A scenic port city with a rich archaeological site – excavated remains date from the Stone Age through Phoenician times to the Crusader era. Believed to be the world's oldest occupied city.

Nahr al-Kalb   *Around Beirut p. 141*
A series of ancient inscriptions left by the conquering armies of Lebanon including Egyptian Pharaohs and Assyrian kings.

Palace of Beiteddine   *South of Beirut p. 198*
Lavish palace of Arab and Italian influences in the Chouf Mountains which also houses a museum of growing significance.

Sidon   *South of Beirut p. 200*
Once an important Phoenician city, its most impressive feature now is the Crusader Sea Castle. Don't leave without also visiting the Great Mosque and the Phoenician Temple of Echmoun.

Tripoli   *Tripoli & The Cedars p. 164*
Perfect examples of Crusader and later Mameluke monuments feature in this city. A wander through the Old City's maze of narrow alleyways is a must.

Tyre   *South of Beirut p. 209*
Famous in the past for its cedar, glass, murex dye and the siege against Alexander the Great; now visited for its extensive Roman and Greek ruins.

Museums

AUB Museum   *Beirut p. 120*
The only archaeological museum open in Beirut at present, with a good collection of Phoenician glassware and earlier artefacts.

Gibran Museum   *Tripoli & The Cedars p. 174*
A museum of Bcharré's most famous citizen, Khalil Gibran – poet, artist and philosopher.

National Museum of Beirut   *Beirut p. 118*
The home of Lebanon's archaeological finds including Byzantine mosaics, Phoenician writing tablets and a collection of sarcophagi.

Sursock Museum   *Beirut p. 120*
Houses a permanent display of Islamic art as well as temporary modern art exhibitions.

Activities

Hiking
A wealth of opportunities exists for hikers: from a moderately steep hike up Jebel Sannine to peaceful walks from the scorpion-shaped village of Douma to the paradise of the Kadisha Valley.

Skiing
Lebanon's extensive ski resorts, Faraya, Faqra, Laklouk, the Cedars, Bakish and Zaarour, offer a choice of slopes for all skiers.

Swimming
With 225km of coastline, the best swimming spots are in Jounieh, Beirut, Tripoli and near Amchit (great snorkelling too).

Festivals

Baalbek Arts Festival   *Bekaa Valley p. 35*
An annual international arts festival relaunched in 1997 after 22 years. Held in front of the Temple of Bacchus, it features song, dance and classical music.

Bustan Festival   *Around Beirut p. 138*
An annual international music festival in February and March held at the Hotel Al Bustan in Beit Meri. A mixture of classical recitals and traditional Lebanese music with a specific theme each year.

HIGHLIGHTS *cont*

Natural Landscapes

Afqa Grotto   *North of Beirut p. 160*
The legendary grotto where the god Adonis was
thought to have been killed by a wild boar. See
the river run red in the spring.

Bala Gorge   *North of Beirut p. 161*
This extraordinary rock formation near Laklouk
is well worth the effort to visit. Be warned: the
drops are sheer.

Cedars   *Tripoli & The Cedars p. 175*
Considered a miracle of nature, these famous
trees are the revered symbol of Lebanon. Another
larger grove is to be found near Barouk in the
south.

Faraya Natural Bridge   *Around Beirut p. 147*
One of the most famous natural features of the
mountainous Faraya region. Thought to be the
work of human hands, it is now believed to be a
freak of nature.

Jeita Grotto   *Around Beirut p. 142*
A stunning series of caves with an abundance of
stalactites and stalagmites. A boat ride takes you
to the more magnificent caverns and a sound and
light show illuminates the whole grotto. No
cameras allowed though.

Kadisha Valley   *Tripoli & The Cedars p. 176*
A rugged and remote mountain area with views
of incredible rock-cut Maronite monasteries and
deserted cave havens. The valley is even more
spectacular under snow.

Palm Islands   *Tripoli & The Cedars p. 169*
A protected wildlife sanctuary where many birds
and a variety of marine life are readily seen. One
of the few wildlife sanctuaries in the Middle East.

Pigeon Rocks   *Beirut p. 123*
The most famous natural feature in Beirut which
can be seen from the cliff-top Corniche walk.
Worth a visit at sunset.

Relaxation

Ain Fawar Hot Spring   *Around Beirut p. 140*
A hot spring in the summer resort village of
Bikfaya which is reputed to be good for liver
ailments.

Jounieh   *Around Beirut p. 143*
The place to spend a few days relaxing and swimming, although you won't be alone. The night life
here is the best in Lebanon.

Wineries   *Bekaa Valley p. 185.*
The Bekaa Valley is the place to go if you want
to spend a couple of days touring the wineries.
Check first for opening (and tasting) hours.

Sights & Villages

Castle of Akkar   *Tripoli & The Cedars p. 180*
A very remote castle in the far north which offers
views of the Crac des Chevaliers in Syria. Tricky
to reach.

Deir al-Qamar   *South of Beirut p. 196*
A Maronite village in the Chouf Mountains
which is preserved as a national monument.

Downtown Beirut   *Beirut p. 121*
The former heart of Beirut which is set to return
to its former glory with the current redevelopment by Solidere.

Hermel Pyramid   *Bekaa Valley p. 194*
An intriguing sight which can't be missed (literally) as it soars 27m into the sky in the middle of
nowhere.

Moussalayha Castle   *North of Beirut p. 163*
A fairytale castle off the Tripoli highway in one
of the country's most picturesque settings.

Rachana   *Around Beirut p. 149*
Known as the Museum Village and home to the
fabulous modern sculptures of the Basbous
brothers.

Zahlé   *Bekaa Valley p. 183*
A charming town nestled on the slopes in the
Bekaa Valley. Famous for its open-air restaurants
and the national drink – arak.

before you leave home if you think you are going to need one.

It is also a good idea to keep your passport on you at all times when travelling around Lebanon. There are still a lot of Lebanese and Syrian army checkpoints, although they rarely ask to see your ID these days. However, if you are stopped and you don't have any ID, it will create unnecessary delays and hassles.

Visas

All nationalities, except Gulf Cooperation Council (GCC) nationals, need a visa to enter Lebanon. GCC nationals are issued with a three-month tourist visa on arrival. Some nationalities, including Australian, Canadian, most EEC, New Zealand, UK and US passport holders, can also get a visa on arrival.

Tourist visas are now quite straightforward and can be obtained from any Lebanese embassy or consulate. When you apply, you need to take or send two passport photos and a letter of reference from your employer or tour operator. Visas are usually valid for six months and are good for a stay of up to three months.

Costs vary from country to country, but average out at about US$20 for a single-entry visa and US$40 for a multiple-entry visa (which is useful if you are planning an excursion to Syria and need to return to Lebanon). The situation may have changed by the time you read this but, as this book went to press, Lebanese visas were not available in Damascus. Also, you cannot get a visa to enter Syria from Lebanon. Australian, Canadian, most EEC, New Zealand, UK and US passport holders can get a Lebanese visa at the Syria-Lebanon border, but other nationalities should make sure they have a visa before they get to the border.

It is sometimes possible to get visas on the same day, but normally allow two to three days for processing. If you have an Israeli stamp in your passport, you will be refused entry into the country.

Re-Entry Visas If you have a single-entry visa and you wish to take a side trip to Syria, it is necessary to get another visa from the General Security office (see Visa Extensions) to re-enter Lebanon. The cost for this is about US$20. Allow a day or two for processing. If you know in advance that you are going to need a re-entry visa, it is a lot less hassle to ask for a multiple-entry visa in your country of origin.

Visa Extensions Visas can be extended for a further three months at no cost at the *amn al-aam*, or General Security office, which is about 200m south-west of the Place Palais de Justice. At the time of writing, you didn't need another passport photo and a second extension of three months was possible. The office is on the 2nd floor and is open from 8 am to 2 pm every day, except Sunday. The staff speak English.

Photocopies

It is good idea to always keep photocopies of your passport data pages, birth certificate, credit cards, airline tickets, other travel documents, employment documents, education qualifications and a list of the serial numbers of your travellers' cheques. Keep this in an envelope in a different part of your luggage to the originals. To be extra cautious, you could also leave duplicates with someone at home in case all is lost.

Travel Insurance

A travel insurance policy to cover theft, loss and medical problems is an absolute must when travelling and is especially important in Lebanon as the only medical aid available is private and very expensive. Even a minor accident could end up being very costly to treat. Your property also needs to be insured; getting stranded without luggage is no joke.

There are scores of different insurance policies to choose from but the thing to remember is that the cheapest isn't always the best. Your travel agent will be able to advise you. Student travel organisations usually have good value policies, and agents such as STA Travel and Trailfinders offer competitively priced policies. Before handng over your cash, do check that you will be getting the cover that you need. Some policies are still not valid for Lebanon, even though it is no longer a war zone. Bearing in mind that medical costs in Lebanon are high, be sure to have sufficient cover for this. Check the small print:

1. Some policies specifically exclude 'dangerous activities' which can include scuba diving, motorcycling, even trekking. If such activities are on your agenda, you don't want that sort of policy. A locally acquired motorcycle licence may not be valid under your policy.
2. You may prefer a policy which pays doctors or hospitals direct rather than you having to pay on the spot and claim later. In the case of potentially expensive treatment this is obviously a desirable feature. If you have to pay and make a claim later, make sure you keep all documentation, including police reports in the case of theft. Some policies ask you to call on a toll-free number to a centre in your home country where an immediate assessment of your problem can be made. It is a good idea to keep this number on you at all times when travelling around or, even better, memorise it.
3. Check if the policy covers ambulances or an emergency flight home. If you have to stretch out, you will need two seats and somebody has to pay for them!

Other Documents

If you intend to drive in Lebanon, you should obtain an International Driving Permit (IDP) from your local automobile association before you leave home – you'll need a passport photo and a valid licence. Third-party insurance is not mandatory, but strongly recommended for your own protection. For information on driving in Lebanon, see the Getting Around chapter.

EMBASSIES

As a tourist, it's important to realise what your own embassy – the embassy of the country of which you are a citizen – can and can't do. Generally speaking, they won't help much in emergencies if the trouble you're in is even remotely your own fault. Remember that you are bound by the laws of the country you're in. Embassies will not be sympathetic if you end up in jail after committing a crime locally, even if such actions are legal in your own country. In genuine emergencies you might get some assistance, but only if other channels have been exhausted. For example, if you need to get home urgently, a free ticket home is exceedingly unlikely – the embassy would expect you to have insurance. If you have all your money and documents stolen, they might assist with getting a new passport, but a loan for onward travel is out of the question.

Embassies used to keep letters for travellers or have a small reading room with home newspapers, but these days the mail-holding service has been stopped, and even their newspapers tend to be out of date.

On the more positive side, if you are heading into very remote or politically volatile areas, you might consider registering with your embassy so they know where you are, but make sure you tell them when you come back too. Some embassies post useful warning notices about local dangers or potential problems. The US embassies are particularly good for providing this information and it's worth scanning their notice boards for 'travellers advisories' about security, local epidemics, and dangers to lone travellers.

Lebanese Embassies

Visas are available at all Lebanese foreign missions, including the following:

Australia
    Embassy: 27 Endeavour St, Red Hill, ACT 2603 (☎ (02) 6295 7378; fax 6239 7024)
    Consulate: Level 5, 70 William St, Sydney NSW 2000 (☎ (02) 9361 5449; fax 9360 7657). Issues visas to NSW residents only.
    Consulate: 117 Wellington St, Windsor, Vic 3181 (☎ (03) 9529 4588). Issues visas to Victorian residents only.
Belgium
    2 Rue Guillaume Stocq, Brussels 1050 (☎ (02) 649 94 60; fax 649 90 02)
Canada
    Embassy: 640 Lyon St, KIS 3Z5 Ottawa, Ontario (☎ (613) 236 5825; fax 232 1609)
    Consulate: 40 Chemin Côte Ste Catherine, H2V-2A2-PQ, Montreal 153 (☎ (514) 276 2638; fax 276 0090)

Egypt
> Embassy: 5 Rue Ahmed Nassim, Giza, Cairo (☎ (02) 361 0623, fax 361 0463)
> Consulate: 64 Rue de la Liberté, Alexandria (☎ (03) 482 6589)

France
> Embassy: 3 Villa Copernic, Paris 75016 (☎ 01 40 67 75 75; fax 01 40 67 16 42)
> Consulate: 424 Rue Paradis, Marseille 13008 (☎ 04 91 71 50 60; fax 04 91 77 26 75)

Germany
> Rheinallee 27, Bad Godesberg, 53173 Bonn (☎ (0228) 95 68 00)

Italy
> Embassy: Via Giacomo Carissimi 38, Rome 00198 (☎ (06) 844 0521; fax 841 1794)
> Consulate: 26 Via Larga, Milan 20122 (☎ (02) 86 45 45 40; fax 72 00 04 68)

Jordan
> 2nd Circle, Jebel Amman (☎ (06) 641381, 641751; fax 647818)

Netherlands
> 2 Frederick St, The Hague 2514 (☎ (070) 365 89 06; fax 362 07 79)

South Africa
> 7 16th Ave, Lower Houghton 2198, Johannesburg (☎ (11) 483 1106/7)

Spain
> 178 Paseo de la Castellana, Madrid 16 (☎ (91) 345 1370; fax 345 5631)

Switzerland
> 10 Thunstrasse, Berne (☎ (31) 95 12 972; fax 95 18 119)

Turkey
> 44 Kizculesi Sokak, Çankaya, Ankara (☎ (312) 4467487; fax 4461033). The office is open from 9 am to 3 pm.

UK
> 21 Kensington Palace Gardens, London W8 4QM (☎ (0171) 229 7265/6; fax 243 1699). The visa section is open weekdays from 9.30 am to noon.

USA
> Embassy: 2560 28th St NW, Washington DC 20008 (☎ (202) 939 6300; fax 939 6324)
> Consulate: Suite 510, 7060 Hollywood Blvd, Los Angeles, CA 90028 (☎ (213) 467 1253; fax 467 2935)
> Consulate: 9 East 76th St, NYC, NY 10021 (☎ (212) 744 7905/6; fax 794 1510)

Foreign Embassies in Lebanon

Many of the foreign embassies closed during the war or relocated to temporary offices in different parts of Beirut, even to Damascus in Syria. Some of these have returned to their former premises, or are planning to, so some addresses and telephone numbers may be subject to change.

Australia
> Farra Building, Rue Bliss, Ras Beirut (☎ 789010 18/30). It is open from 9 am to 1 pm.

Austria
> Sammakieh Building, Rue Madame Curie (☎ 354238; fax 602220)

Belgium
> Elie Helou Building, Baabda (☎ 468487 425083)

Canada
> Coolrite Building, Jal el-Dib (☎ 521163/4/5)

Czech Republic
> Near Presidential Palace, Baabda (☎ 468763 920501, 968763). The nearest Slovak embassy is in Damascus.

Denmark
> Duraffourd Building, Ave de Paris, Ain al-Mreisse (☎ 364264)

Egypt
> Rue Thomas Edison, Ramlet el-Bayda (☎ 863751, 867917)

Finland
> Sadat Tower, Rue Sadat, Hamra (☎ 802275/6)

France
> Mar Takla, Hazmieh (☎ 451611, 429629)

Germany
> Mataileb, Rabieh (☎ 406950/1, 405310)

Greece
> Antoine Boukhater Building, Rue des Ambassades, Naccache (☎ 521700, 418772)

Ireland
> Sadat Tower, Rue Sadat, Hamra (☎ 862966)

Italy
> Cosmides Building, Rue Makdissi, Hamra (☎ 340225/6/7)

Japan
> Mountain Building, Rue Club des Officiers, Baabda (☎ 922001/2/3)

Jordan
> Rue Elias Helou, Baabda (☎ 922500/1)

Netherlands
> Dawra (☎ 890671)

Norway
> Taher & Fakri Building, Rue Bliss (☎ 353731/2)

Spain
> Palace Chehab, Hadath (☎ 464120/1; fax 352448)

Switzerland
> Centre Debs, Kaslik (☎ 916279, 938894)

Turkey
> Tobi Building, Rue 3, Zone II, Rabieh (☎ 412118)

UK
> Villa Tohmeh, Rue no 8, Rabieh (☎ 417007, 405070, 403640)

USA
  Antelias (☎ 417774, 403300; fax 407112)

CUSTOMS

There is no problem bringing most items into Lebanon, such as camera equipment, videos or computers, and there is no censorship of books and magazines. Duty-free allowances are 400 cigarettes and one bottle of spirits or 200 cigarettes and two bottles of spirits, although there is little point as local prices for alcohol and tobacco are very low.

MONEY
Costs

Lebanon is quite expensive by Mediterranean and Middle East standards. If you are on a seriously low budget, you may find it a bit limited in choice. It is possible though, with careful spending, to live on US$25 to US$30 per day. To spend less than that, you would be talking about a very spartan existence indeed. Hotel costs are cheaper outside Beirut – at least there is a greater choice of budget accommodation available – but the cost of meals is pretty standardised throughout Lebanon.

The main item of expense is accommodation. There are very few hotels in the budget range and they are all extremely basic. Even these will set you back from US$15 to US$20 per night. Many of the hotels do not make a reduction for singles, so it is much cheaper if you are travelling with a friend. One thing to look out for is the service charge, which is often 16%, and can bump up your hotel bill. It is best to ask beforehand whether 'service' is included.

Cheap food is not so much of a problem. There are sandwich and snack bars all over Lebanon. They all serve the same repertoire of fillings and are usually substantial and very tasty. A sandwich will cost from LL 750 to LL 2000 and some places serve Lebanese 'pizzas' for about LL 1000. Sit down restaurants are more expensive, but the cheaper variety often serve a simple lunch or dinner for around US$7. Some restaurants offer a fixed-price menu for lunch or dinner which can be a good deal. Always ask if a place does a 'tourist menu' as they are not usually listed on the menu.

Sightseeing costs depend on the luxury of the transport and whether lunch or dinner is included or not. The price also depends on how many people book at once; the more, the cheaper. On average a one-day coach tour with lunch should cost US$35.

Transport around the city and to other parts of the country is cheap, especially if you use the service taxis. Fares within the centre of Beirut are only LL 1000 and to the regions from LL 1500 to LL 10,000, depending on the distance. There are a few bus routes (very few) around Beirut, which cost only LL 500 a trip.

Carrying Money

Although Lebanon is not a major crime area, it still pays to be circumspect when carrying money around with you. If you are carrying cash around, it is always a good idea to use a money belt or one of those inside-the-shirt fabric wallets that hang around your neck. Always buy these in a flesh colour so they don't show through your clothing. As for travellers' cheques, always keep your receipt for these in a separate part of your luggage.

It also pays to keep an emergency stash of money hidden away – say US$100 – to help you out of dire straights. Under the innersole of your shoe or in a plastic film container in your toiletries bag are a couple of ideas.

The best currency to bring into Lebanon is US dollars, either in cash or travellers' cheques. US dollars are universally accepted in shops, restaurants and hotels, even in taxis. Avoid bringing US$100 bills – because there are so many forgeries, people are unwilling to take them. Stick to US$50 and US$20, and single-dollar bills for tipping and small items. For safety, you should have some of your money in travellers' cheques.

If you don't like to carry cash, you can use most major credit cards in Lebanon (American Express, Visa etc). You can pay with a credit card in larger restaurants and many hotels or you can get a cash advance on Visa and Amex cards from many banks, but the commission is high.

Automatic teller machines (ATMs) are becoming more popular in Lebanon. You can find them near many banks in Beirut and also in the regional towns. Visitors can withdraw either US dollars or Lebanese pounds with a Visa card.

Currency

The currency in Lebanon is the Lebanese lira (LL), known locally as the Lebanese pound. The currency suffered from galloping inflation during the war and low denomination coins (piastres) are now virtually worthless. There are LL 250 and LL 500 coins still in circulation.

The notes are of the following denominations: 50,100, 250, 500,1000, 5000, 10,000, 20,000, 50,000 and 100,000, but you will rarely need anything smaller than 1000. Because of the lira's constant devaluation, US dollars are accepted virtually everywhere. There is a standard rate of exchange in shops etc between the US dollar and the lira, and often shops display prices only in dollars and will give you your change in either LL or US dollars. If it is a large amount, you can ask for your change in dollars.

Currency Exchange

Exchange rates are subject to frequent change, although the fluctuations are less extreme than they used to be. At the time of writing, the exchange rates were:

Australia	A$1	=	LL 1106
Canada	C$1	=	LL 1109
France	FF1	=	LL 260
Germany	DM1	=	LL 872
Japan	¥100	=	LL 1267
Jordan	JD1	=	LL 2168
Syria	Sr10	=	LL 367
Turkey	TL100,000	=	LL 887
UK	UK£1	=	LL 2474
USA	US$1	=	LL 1536

Changing Money

It is simple to change money in cash, or to a lesser extent, travellers' cheques, if they are in British pounds or US dollars. There are many banks in the capital and all but the smallest village has at least one bank.

If you are changing other currencies, you will need to go to one of the private exchange shops. There are many of these on and around Rue Hamra in Beirut, and all the smaller towns have at least one exchange shop. You may find it a problem changing money in some of the smaller, out of the way places.

Before using moneychangers try to find out what the current exchange rates are. Either ask at a bank or check the previous day's closing exchange rates in the local newspapers. The rate you'll be offered will never be the same as the published rate, as it includes the moneychanger's commission, but you can always bargain with them to bring the rate closer to it. If you're not happy with the rate offered by one moneychanger, try another one.

The commission varies from 3 to 5% for changing currency; for travellers' cheques, the fees are US$1 per US$50, US$2 per US$100 and US$3 per US$1000 and so on.

You can pay for goods in the larger establishments by travellers' cheques or major credit cards. Amex, Visa, Diner's Club and Eurocard are all widely accepted.

Tipping & Bargaining

Tipping is considered normal for service in Lebanon, even though most restaurants add a service charge to the bill (often 16%). Even so it is expected that you leave a tip of 5 to 10% on top of that. Wages for workers are very low and, in real terms, getting lower all the time with the devaluation of the lira. Therefore waiters rely on tips to supplement their incomes.

It is often possible to negotiate a better price at hotels, restaurants and in shops. This especially applies to the more expensive establishments, particularly in low season. Prices in shops can sometimes seem exorbitant, so it is always worth haggling, or making an offer, to bring the price down. If you are not happy, you will probably find the same thing at a better price elsewhere.

The same thing applies to the taxis. The

service routes have set prices, but the moment you try to hire a private taxi, the price quoted (in dollars) is often astronomical. The solution is to ask the price before getting in the taxi and if you are not happy, then find another taxi.

POST & COMMUNICATIONS

There are no public post boxes in Lebanon, and you have to go to a post office to buy stamps or mail anything. Mail delivery services have vastly improved and regional post offices are starting to reopen. It is still recommended that you send your mail from Beirut to avoid delays. There are now a few public telephone boxes on certain streets in Beirut such as Rue Bliss.

Postal Rates

The postal service has now resumed most of its services and is slow but quite reliable. Cards and letters to Europe take about 10 to 14 days and to the rest of the world two to three weeks. Parcel post has resumed, but there is a maximum weight allowance of 1kg, except to the US where the maximum weight is 500g. All parcels must go by registered post and delivery takes two to three weeks.

The postal service has recently introduced a 'one size fits all' postal charge for letters and cards, which is quite expensive. A postcard to any destination costs LL 1500 and a letter LL 3000.

If you are in a hurry, there is a DHL courier service which has its office one block south of the tourist information office in Beirut.

Receiving Mail

There are no poste restante services at the time of writing. If you know the hotel in which you will be staying, they will keep your incoming mail for you, but it is best to let them know that you are expecting letters. Delivery times from Europe are about a week and from the rest of the world 10 to 14 days.

Amex card holders can have their mail kept for them at the Amex office on the 1st floor, Gefinor Centre, Beirut.

Telephone

Although a lot of work is currently being carried out on the telephone system, there are only a few public phone boxes in Beirut. Most people will have to go to the main post offices in Beirut or the regional towns to use the telephone. To make a call, you have to fill out a slip of paper with the number(s) you require and wait until you are called. You pay at the desk when your calls are complete. The minimum charge for an international call is for three minutes. From the post office, calls cost LL 3400 to the UK and Europe, LL 7000 to the US and LL 4100 to Australia per minute.

There are also private companies providing local and international telephones on a meter. They are often in shops – look out for a sign, or ask where the nearest *bureau de téléphone* is. These are slightly more expensive than the post office telephones.

The cost for local calls from a public phone box would be either LL 250 or LL 500 depending on the length of the call. Local calls from a private phone within the same area code cost LL 30 for the first minute and then LL 20 per minute. Calls from one area code to another cost LL 50 for the first minute and then LL 40 per minute. Mobile phone calls cost US$0.06 and then LL 10 per minute. This is the same rate for calling a mobile number or calling from a mobile phone. The area code when dialling a mobile is 03. Local telephone area codes are:

Byblos (Jbail)	09
Greater Beirut	01
Lebanon North	06
Lebanon South	07
Mount Lebanon North	04
Mount Lebanon South	05
Zahlé	08

To dial into Lebanon, dial the international access code, followed by Lebanon's country code, 961, the area code (minus the zero) and the telephone number.

Fax & Email

Fax machines are widely used and most of the hotels, except for the very smallest, seem to have a fax machine. Many of the private bureaux also have fax machines. You can often get a hotel to send a fax for you even if you are not staying there. They charge commercial rates but they are not usually too exorbitant. The three-minute minimum call applies. From a hotel, faxes are charged at the same rate as phone calls.

There are no places in Lebanon as yet where you can send or receive emails except from private offices and companies. There is one place where you can access the Internet in Beirut. See under Information in the Beirut chapter for more details.

BOOKS

Most books are published in different editions by different publishers in different countries. As a result, a book might be a hardcover rarity in one country while it's readily available in paperback in another. Fortunately, bookshops and libraries search by title or author, so your local bookshop or library is best placed to advise you on the availability of the following recommendations. See also Literature under Arts in the Facts about Lebanon chapter.

Lonely Planet

Lonely Planet also publishes *Middle East on a shoestring* with chapters on all the Middle Eastern countries, including Lebanon. Lonely Planet's *Jordan, Syria & Lebanon travel atlas* is a great companion to this travel guide.

The Gates of Damascus by Lieve Joris, is one of many titles in Lonely Planet's new travel literature series. It paints an intimate portrait of contemporary Arab society, and offers a unique insight into the complexities of Middle Eastern politics.

Guidebooks

Not surprisingly the travel guide market dried up during the war and there are very few up-to-date guides to refer to. Some bookshops in Beirut still have a supply of a guide published in 1967, *The Middle East*, part of a series by Hachette, which has an interesting section on Lebanon. It is particularly detailed on the ancient sites, but of

course, the practical information is way out of date. It is also a little pricey at US$20. There are some locally published free guides which are little more than advertisements for businesses which have paid to be included, but the listings for hotels and restaurants are occasionally useful.

Travel

There have been many travellers to Lebanon who have written about their impressions of the country and have left a vivid record of Lebanese society at various points in her history. Some 19th-century travellers were sufficiently interesting (or notorious) that they themselves became the subject of books. Lady Hester Stanhope was one such person. She travelled to the Middle East and stayed for the rest of her life, dying alone in Lebanon and almost forgotten by the outside world. An interesting book concerning her travels and life in Lebanon is *The Nun of Lebanon – The Love Affair of Lady Hester Stanhope & Michael Bruce*, a collection of their letters edited by Ian Bruce. A biography worth reading if you can get hold of a copy is *Lady Hester Stanhope* by Frank Hamel. See also the boxed story on Lady Hester Stanhope in the South of Beirut chapter.

Another celebrated traveller to Lebanon was David Roberts, the artist, whose drawings and etchings of the Levant depicted a highly romanticised view of the country in the 19th century. *David Roberts R.A. 1796-1864: A Biography* is an interesting account of the artist's life and travels in the Middle East.

A more recent publication is *Freya Stark in the Levant* by Malise Ruthven. This book charts the travels of this well known Middle Eastern explorer with reproductions of many of her black-and-white photographs from the 1930s to the 1950s.

One of the best travel books is *The Hills of Adonis* by Colin Thubron. He gives a lucid and insightful account of his travels just before the civil war, weaving ancient religious beliefs and modern politics into a fascinating tale. Also well worth reading, if you can find a copy, is *Touring Lebanon* by

Philip Ward and published in 1971. Other old travel books worth tracking down include *Baalbek Caravans* by Charis Waddy (this can be found in some Beirut bookshops) and *Smelling the Breezes: A Journey Through High Lebanon* by Ralph & Molly Izzard.

History & Politics

A good general history of the region is *A History of the Arab Peoples* by Albert Hourani, which gives the reader some good background knowledge of the history, religion and culture of the Middle East. The same author also wrote *Syria & Lebanon* published in London in 1946, but this book is now out of print. Another history of Lebanon which is worth tracking down is *Lebanon in History* by Philip K Hitti. More recently there is *A House of Many Mansions – The History of Lebanon Reconsidered*, by Kamal Salibi, which looks at the root causes of the civil war in the light of a re-examination of Lebanese history.

A great deal of the recently published books on Lebanon concentrate, not surprisingly, on the civil war. There are some excellent accounts of these tragic events and the circumstances which led up to them. Much of this is harrowing reading, but I urge anyone visiting Lebanon to read at least one book about the civil war, as understanding at least the major forces at play in the country during the last two decades will greatly contribute to your understanding of the people and culture.

One of the most outstanding books on the Lebanese war is Robert Fisk's *Pity the Nation: Lebanon at War*, in which this respected Middle East correspondent for *The Times* recounts his experiences in Lebanon. It chronicles the events of the war from its beginning in 1975 and explains the different factions and parties involved.

Another book from a British correspondent is Charles Glass' *Tribes With Flags: A Journey Curtailed*, which describes the author's kidnapping and subsequent release. A sensitive and literate account of a Beirut kidnapping is *An Evil Cradling* by Irish teacher and former captive, Brian Keenan.

Sandra Mackey's *Lebanon – Death of a Nation* is another account of the war and its causes. It also elaborates on the misunderstanding between the Middle East and the western nations.

Other recommended books include John Bulloch's *Death of a Country: The Civil War in Lebanon* and *Lebanon: The Fractured Country* by David Gilmour. A drier account of Lebanon in the 20th century is *The Formation of Modern Lebanon* by Meir Zamir. This is a detailed look at how the independent state of Lebanon was formed in the wake of the disintegration of the Ottoman Empire after WWI. It shows how the creation of Greater Lebanon was bound to lead the country into a civil war.

For ancient history, *The Phoenicians*, by Donald Harden, is comprehensive and authoritative.

And for a postwar look at the redevelopment of Beirut, read Angus Gavin's *Beirut Reborn: The Restoration & Development of the Central District*.

General

There are many coffee-table books about Lebanon. One of the better ones is Fluvio Roiter's *Lebanon*. It has exquisite colour plates of prewar Lebanon, its heritage and people, but it is rather expensive at US$75.

ONLINE SERVICES

There are lots of web sites about Lebanon which are useful if you want to check out a few things before you go. Some have information specific to visitors and others have more general cultural notes. Here are just a few of the more interesting ones:

http://www.lonelyplanet.com.au This is Lonely Planet's award-winning site, containing destination updates, recent travellers' letters and a useful travellers' bulletin board.

http://www.embofleb.org The official home page for the Lebanon Embassy in the US. It has useful visa and travel news.

http://www.lebanon-directory.com This is Lebanon's official Ministry of Tourism home page. It has facts about the country, history, accommodation and travel information.

http://www.bookinn.com This is an online booking service for hotels, restaurants and car hire in Lebanon. This site caters mainly for business and upmarket travellers.

http://www.lebanon-online.com This informative site has news, culture, business and a chat room, and also links to other Middle East pages.

http://www.geocities.com/athens/acropolis/5347 Abdul's home page, which has links to all things Lebanese including news services, history, music and Islam.

http://www.geocities.com/vienna/4320 This is a Lebanon-based home page including the Lebanon white pages, the republic's national anthem, cultural groups, radio and TV services.

http://www2.patbaba.com.lb The site for one of Lebanon's oldest sweet shops. Try before you get to Lebanon with the shop's order service and worldwide delivery.

http://www2.inco.com.lb Has links to a wide range of sites – from the home page of the Ministry of Tourism to the Casino de Liban home page.

http://www.arab.net/lebanon-contents.html Has general information on the country.

http://www.beiruttimes.com Weekly news from Lebanon and also the Middle East each week. The newspaper is published in the US.

http://www.liii.com/~hajeri/arab.html General information about Lebanon, including travel agencies and hotels.

FILMS

Lebanon has begun to produce some notable postwar films, many of which have been shown at several international festivals. Most film-makers during the war were working outside of the country and their work was seldom shown in Lebanon. Some of the well-known film-makers include Maroun Baghdadi (who won an award at the Cannes Film Festival), Samir Nasri and Mohammed Sweid.

One of the rising stars of the Lebanese film community is Jocelyn Saab who lives in Paris. During the war she made 15 documentaries which were shot in Lebanon, but backed with European finance and only seen in the west or Japan. Her latest feature-length film, *Once Upon a Time Beirut*, uses a montage of footage from prewar Beirut to further the plot. The footage dates from 1914 to 1975 and comes from over 300 different films. It is being shown in Beirut cinemas.

Lebanon has four film schools and 36 TV stations, but it is early days for there to be a truly home-grown film industry. Before the war Lebanon was second only to Egypt in terms of film output in the Arab world.

NEWSPAPERS & MAGAZINES

Lebanon has two English-language daily newspapers, the *Daily Star* and the *Beirut Times*, and also a weekly colour magazine, *Monday Morning*, which reviews the week's local news and social events. There is a daily French-language newspaper, *L'Orient-Le Jour*, which is not bad and is useful for listings of local cinema and theatre performances. There are also the French-language weeklies *Magazine* and *La Revue du Liban*.

For those interested in green issues, there is a free paper, *Eco News*, which is published in English.

Published quarterly in English is the rather literary *Beirut Review*. There are a couple of glossy French-language monthlies, *Femme* for women and the excellent *Prestige*, which is a mixture of personality profiles and in-depth travel features with glossy photo spreads.

Imported newspapers and magazines are easily available from the major bookshops. European papers arrive about one day late and publications from further afield a couple of days late. The most popular and easily obtainable are: the *Independent*, the *Guardian*, *The Times*, *Le Monde*, *Le Figaro* and the *International Herald Tribune*. Of the international news weeklies, *Time*, *Newsweek*, the *Economist*, *Le Point*, *Paris Match* and *Der Spiegel* are all on sale at most bookstalls.

RADIO & TV

There are an abundance of commercial radio and TV stations in Lebanon. This is just a selection of what is on offer. On the radio, Switch FM (100 mHz) plays dance music and Hit FM (100.5 mHz) pop and rock, as does Radio One (105.5 mHz). For oriental music, tune to Delta (102.4 mHz) or Radio Rama (96.9 mHz). La Une (92.4) and France FM (92.7 mHz) broadcast in French, and Nostalgie (88 kHz) goes for golden oldies.

You can pick up BBC World Service on

1323 kHz or 720 kHz medium wave, which is a round-the-clock station.

You can go seriously crazy channel surfing Lebanese TV. There is everything from a station which seems to broadcast nothing but biblical epic movies to the indestructible MTV. Most half-decent hotels have satellite which means that you can watch the news in Arabic, English, Italian, French or Dutch. Euronews is popular with expats trying to keep up with the outside world. Also there is Superchannel, CNN (sometimes) and a host of others – many broadcasting in French. Most of the non-English channels show English language films with subtitles. *L'Orient-Le Jour* carries TV listings for the major stations.

VIDEO SYSTEMS

If you want to watch a video, Lebanon uses the PAL system. The various systems in use worldwide (PAL, NTSC and SECAM) are incompatible with each other. Tapes from one system will not play on another without a costly conversion.

PHOTOGRAPHY & VIDEO
Film & Equipment

Unless you want an obscure brand, you won't have any trouble buying film or video tapes in Lebanon; Kodak, Agfa and Fuji are the most widely available brands. Good quality colour transparency films are available in Beirut and the larger towns. It is sometimes available in tourist shops at historical sites, but watch the expiry date. Processing is widely available for colour negative films (C41 process) both in Beirut and around the country in fast turnover labs. There are also a few E6 labs which process colour transparencies. The overall quality is quite good. The cost of processing in Lebanon is about LL 4000 for negative film and about LL 16,000 for transparency film.

The cost of film and video tape is reasonable. A regular 36-exposure print film costs from LL 6500 to LL 8500, a slide film LL 15,000 (which sometimes includes processing). Black and white film is harder to find and to process, so it is better to bring your

own and have it processed when you return home. A VHS tape costs LL 10,000, Super VHS costs LL 25,000 and Hi-8 LL 30,000.

Many camera shops have a one-hour or same-day processing and printing service – LL 10,000 for a 36-exposure film – and they can be found in the main towns. You also shouldn't have too much trouble finding spare parts for the main makes of camera, such as Nikon, Pentax, Olympus and Canon. Check out Kamera (for Olympus and Canon) and Lord Camera Shop in Rue Hamra, next door to the Horseshoe Restaurant in Beirut. Other towns usually have at least one camera shop. There is no problem getting even unusual batteries for cameras in most places.

Photography

Lebanon is very photogenic with its dramatic landscapes and clear Mediterranean light. Dust can be a problem when taking your camera around Beirut and it is a good idea to keep it wrapped in a plastic bag even inside a camera bag. Take a soft lens brush and some camera wipes with you to prevent grit and dust getting inside the works. A flash gun is useful if you want to photograph the interiors of dark churches and mosques.

You should have no problems taking photographs anywhere in Lebanon, but if you happen to be near an army checkpoint, go up to the soldiers first and explain to them what you want to photograph. They usually won't object. It is not a good idea however to try and grab shots of the soldiers themselves. If you are travelling in the extreme south, be more careful than usual about pointing your camera at anything military – this is still a high-security zone.

Video

Lebanon makes a very interesting subject for a travel video. The same general advice applies as with still photography, but with a video, you have to think ahead more in order to make a successful sequence of shots. If you are not very experienced in shooting a video, be very sparing with the zooms and pans – and make them at least twice as slow as you think they should be. Bear in mind that a series of static shots well executed is preferable to too much camera movement. Those with unsteady hands should seriously consider the use of a tripod for as many shots as possible. If you plan to edit your video, then remember to shoot plenty of 'cutaways' – shots of details or establishing shots – which make the finished video far more professional and kinder to viewers.

Two important tips are: first, when shooting a landscape, keep some foreground interest in shot; and second, when shooting people, especially if they are talking to the camera, get in close. If you want some background in the shot, position the person to one side of the frame.

The light in Lebanon at most times of the year is very clear and good. Best times to shoot are in the morning until 10 am and the afternoon between 4 pm and sunset. If you can't avoid midday use a warm filter, and avoid unflattering shadows by shooting people in the shade, perhaps with a white reflector (even a T-shirt will do) bouncing the light back onto their faces.

Airport Security

X-ray machines are generally safe to pass film through, but if you are going on a multi-flight trip, ask for film to be hand searched to avoid the accumulative effects of exposure. If you are worried about your film, invest in lead-lined film pouches which protect your film from any harmful rays.

TIME

Lebanon is two hours ahead of GMT/UTC during the winter (October to March) and three hours ahead during the summer (April to September) when daylight saving is used. When it is noon in Lebanon, it is 10 am in London; 5 am in New York and Montreal; 2 am in Los Angeles; 1 pm in Moscow; and 7 pm in Melbourne and Sydney.

ELECTRICITY

Lebanon has now standardised its electricity supplies to 220V and mains power has been restored. Two-pin plugs are used. There are still power cuts in Lebanon, but most hotels

and large buildings have back-up generators, so the inconvenience is minimal. Some hotels outside Beirut turn off the generator at midnight and on again in the morning, so, once again, a torch is a good idea.

WEIGHTS & MEASURES

Lebanon uses the metric system. See the conversion tables inside the back cover of this guide.

LAUNDRY

Most neighbourhoods in the capital and major towns have dry-cleaners which offer a one or two-day service. Some also offer a laundry service, but there are no laundromats. Most hotels have their own laundry service, and if not, they can direct you to the nearest one.

HEALTH

There are sophisticated medical facilities available in Lebanon. Most doctors have graduated overseas and speak English or French, but they are almost all private (and expensive). The most highly recommended hospital in the country is the American University of Beirut Hospital. See the Medical Services & Emergency section in the Beirut chapter for more details.

There are pharmacies in almost every town and they can prescribe most drugs over the counter. The cost of medications is generally the same as in Europe. Pharmacists are usually very helpful and knowledgeable about the drugs they sell and most speak English or French.

Travel health depends on your predeparture preparations, your daily health care while travelling and how you handle any medical problem that does develop. While the potential dangers can seem quite frightening, in reality few travellers experience anything more than upset stomachs.

Predeparture Planning

Immunisations There are no required vaccinations for entry into Lebanon, unless you're coming from a disease-affected area. However it's recommended to have preven-

Medical Kit Check List
Consider taking a basic medical kit including:

- ☐ **Aspirin** or paracetamol (acetaminophen in the US) – for pain or fever.
- ☐ **Antihistamine** (such as Benadryl) – useful as a decongestant for colds and allergies, to ease the itch from insect bites or stings, and to help prevent motion sickness. Antihistamines may cause sedation and interact with alcohol, so care should be taken when using them; take one you know and have used before, if possible.
- ☐ **Antibiotics** – useful if you're travelling well off the beaten track, but they must be prescribed; carry the prescription with you.
- ☐ **Loperamide** (eg Imodium) or Lomotil for diarrhoea; prochlorperazine (eg Stemetil) or metaclopramide (eg Maxalon) for nausea and vomiting.
- ☐ **Rehydration** mixture – for treatment of severe diarrhoea; particularly important for travelling with children.
- ☐ **Antiseptic** such as povidone-iodine (eg Betadine) – for cuts and grazes.
- ☐ **Multivitamins** – especially for long trips when dietary vitamin intake may be inadequate.
- ☐ **Calamine lotion** or **aluminium sulphate spray** (eg Stingose) – to ease irritation from bites or stings.
- ☐ **Bandages** and Band-aids.
- ☐ **Scissors, tweezers** and a **thermometer** (note that mercury thermometers are prohibited by airlines).
- ☐ **Cold and flu tablets** and **throat lozenges**. Pseudoephedrine hydrochloride (Sudafed) may be useful if flying with a cold to avoid ear damage.
- ☐ **Insect repellent, sunscreen, chap stick** and **water purification tablets**.
- ☐ **A couple of syringes**, in case you need injections in a country with medical hygiene problems. Ask your doctor for a note explaining why they have been prescribed.

tative shots for polio, tetanus and typhoid for your personal protection. Be aware that there is often a greater risk of disease with children and in pregnancy.

Plan ahead for getting your vaccinations: some of them require more than one injection, while some vaccinations should not be given together. It is recommended that you seek medical advice at least six weeks before travel.

Record all vaccinations on an International Health Certificate, available from your doctor or government health department.

Discuss your requirements with your doctor, but vaccinations you should consider for this trip include:

- **Hepatitis A** This, the most common travel-acquired illness after diarrhoea (which can put you out of action for weeks), exists in all Middle Eastern countries including Lebanon. Havrix 1440 is a vaccination which provides long-term immunity (possibly more than 10 years) after an initial injection and a booster at six to 12 months.
  Gamma globulin is not a vaccination but is ready-made antibody collected from blood donations. It should be given close to departure because, depending on the dose, it only protects for two to six months.
  A combined hepatitis A and hepatitis B vaccination, Twinrix, is also available. This combined vaccination is recommended for people wanting protection against both types of viral hepatitis. Three injections over a six-month period are required.
- **Typhoid** This is an important vaccination to have where hygiene is a problem. Available either as an injection or oral capsules.
- **Diphtheria & Tetanus** Diphtheria can be a fatal throat infection and tetanus can be a fatal wound infection. Everyone should have these vaccinations. After an initial course of three injections, boosters are necessary every 10 years.
- **Hepatitis B** This disease, which exists in Lebanon, is spread by blood or by sexual activity. Travellers should consider a hepatitis B vaccination, especially those who are visiting countries where blood transfusions may not be adequately screened or where sexual contact is a possibility. It involves three injections, the quickest course being over three weeks with a booster at 12 months.
- **Polio** Polio is a serious, easily transmitted disease, still prevalent in many developing countries. Everyone should keep up-to-date with this vaccination. A booster every 10 years maintains immunity. The risk of contracting polio in Lebanon is low.
- **Rabies** Vaccination should be considered by those who will spend a month or longer in Lebanon, especially if they are cycling, handling animals, caving, travelling to remote areas, or for children (who may not report a bite). Pretravel rabies vaccination involves having three injections over 21 to 28 days. If someone who has been vaccinated is bitten or scratched by an animal, they will require two booster injections of vaccine, those not vaccinated require more.

Health Insurance Make sure that you have adequate health insurance. See Travel Insurance under Documents earlier in this chapter for details.

Travel Health Guides If you are planning to be away or travelling in remote areas for a long period of time, you may like to consider taking a more detailed health guide.

Travellers' Health, Dr Richard Dawood, Oxford University Press, 1995. Comprehensive, easy to read, authoritative and highly recommended, although it's rather large to lug around.
Travel with Children, Maureen Wheeler, Lonely Planet Publications, 1995. Includes advice on travel health for younger children.

There are also a number of excellent travel health sites on the Internet. From the Lonely Planet home page there are links at (http://www.lonelyplanet.com/weblinks/wlprep.htm) to the World Health Organisation and the US Centers for Disease Control & Prevention.

Other Preparations Make sure you're healthy before you start travelling. If you wear glasses, take a spare pair and your prescription. Losing your glasses can be a real problem, although Lebanon has many opticians where you could get a pair made up quite quickly.

If you require a particular medication, take an adequate supply, as it may not be available locally. Take part of the packaging showing the generic name, rather than the brand, which will make getting replacements easier. It's a good idea to have a legible prescription or even a letter from your doctor to show that you legally use the medication to avoid any problems.

Basic Rules

Food There is an old colonial adage which says: 'If you can cook it, boil it or peel it, you can eat it ... otherwise forget it'. Vegetables and fruit should be washed with purified water or peeled where possible. Avoid eating salads in cheap snack bars. Beware of ice cream which is sold in the street or anywhere

it might have been melted and refrozen; if there's any doubt (eg a power cut in the last day or two) steer well clear. Shellfish such as mussels, oysters and clams should be avoided as well as undercooked meat, particularly in the form of mince. Steaming does not make shellfish safe for eating.

If a place looks clean and well run and the vendor also looks clean and healthy, then the food is probably safe. In general, places that are packed with travellers or locals will be fine, while empty restaurants are questionable. The food in busy restaurants is cooked and eaten quite quickly with little standing around and is probably not reheated.

Water The number one rule is *be careful of the water* and especially ice, which is always made from tap water and which in Lebanon is *not* drinkable. If you don't know for certain that the water is safe, assume the worst. Reputable brands of bottled water or soft drinks are generally fine, although in some places bottles may be refilled with tap water. Only use water from containers with a serrated seal – not tops or corks. Take care with fruit juice, particularly if water may have been added. Milk should be treated with suspicion as it is often unpasteurised, though boiled milk is fine if it is kept hygienically. Tea or coffee should also be OK, since the water should have been boiled.

Water Purification The simplest way of purifying water is to boil it thoroughly. In most cases vigorously boiling should be satisfactory; however, at high altitude water boils at a lower temperature, so germs are less likely to be killed. Boil it for longer in these environments.

Consider purchasing a water filter for a long trip. Chlorine tablets (Puritabs, Steritabs or other brand names) will kill many pathogens, but not some parasites like giardia and amoebic cysts. Iodine is more effective in purifying water and is available in tablet form (such as Potable Aqua). Follow the directions carefully and remember that too much iodine can be harmful.

Nutrition

If your food is poor or limited in availability, if you're travelling hard and fast and therefore missing meals, or if you simply lose your appetite, you can soon start to lose weight and place your health at risk.

Make sure your diet is well balanced. Cooked eggs, tofu, beans, lentils and nuts are all safe ways to get protein. Fruit you can peel (bananas, oranges or mandarins for example) is usually safe (melons can harbour bacteria in their flesh and are best avoided) and a good source of vitamins.

Try to eat plenty of grains (including rice) and bread. Remember that although food is generally safer if it is cooked well, overcooked food loses much of its nutritional value. If your diet isn't well balanced or if your food intake is insufficient, it's a good idea to take vitamin and iron pills.

In hot climates make sure you drink enough – don't rely on feeling thirsty to indicate when you should drink. Not needing to urinate or small amounts of very dark yellow urine is a danger sign. Always carry a water bottle with you on long trips. Excessive sweating can lead to loss of salt and therefore muscle cramping. Salt tablets are not a good idea as a preventative, but in places where salt is not used much, adding salt to food can help. ■

Medical Problems & Treatment

Self-diagnosis and treatment can be risky, so you should always seek medical help. Although we do give drug dosages in this section, they are for emergency use only. Correct diagnosis is vital.

An embassy, consulate or five-star hotel can usually recommend a good place to go for advice. Also see the Medical Services & Emergency section in the Beirut chapter. Antibiotics should ideally be administered only under medical supervision. Take only the recommended dose at the prescribed intervals and use the whole course, even if the illness seems to be cured earlier. Stop immediately if there are any serious reactions and don't use the antibiotic at all if you are unsure that you have the correct one. Some people are allergic to commonly prescribed antibiotics such as penicillin or sulpha drugs; carry this information when travelling eg on a bracelet.

Environmental Hazards

Fungal Infections Fungal infections occur more commonly in hot weather and are usually found on the scalp, between the toes or fingers, in the groin and on the body (ringworm). You get ringworm (which is a fungal infection, not a worm) from infected animals or other people. Moisture encourages these infections.

To prevent fungal infections wear loose, comfortable clothes, avoid artificial fibres, wash frequently and dry carefully. If you do get an infection, wash the infected area at least daily with a disinfectant or medicated soap and water, and rinse and dry well. Apply an antifungal cream or powder like tolnifate (Tinaderm). Try to expose the infected area to air or sunlight as much as possible and wash all towels and underwear in hot water, change them often and let them dry in the sun.

Heat Exhaustion Dehydration and salt deficiency can cause heat exhaustion. Take time to acclimatise to high temperatures, drink sufficient liquids and do not do anything too physically demanding.

Salt deficiency is characterised by fatigue, lethargy, headaches, giddiness and muscle cramps; salt tablets may help, but adding extra salt to your food is better.

Heatstroke This serious, and occasionally fatal, condition can occur if the body's heat-regulating mechanism breaks down and the body temperature rises to dangerous levels. Long, continuous periods of exposure to high temperatures and insufficient fluids can leave you vulnerable to heatstroke. In Lebanon you can go through rapid temperature changes very quickly, so make sure you have the appropriate clothing with you.

The symptoms are feeling unwell, not sweating very much (or even at all) and a high body temperature (39 to 41°C or 102 to 106°F). Where sweating has ceased the skin becomes flushed and red. Severe, throbbing headaches and lack of coordination will also occur, and the sufferer may be confused and even aggressive. Eventually the victim will become delirious or convulse. Hospitalisation is essential, but in the interim get victims out of the sun, remove their clothing, cover them with a wet sheet or towel and then fan continually. Give fluids if they are conscious.

Hypothermia Too much cold can be just as dangerous as too much heat. If you are trekking at high altitudes or simply taking a long bus trip over mountains, particularly at night, be prepared. You should always be prepared for cold, wet or windy conditions even if you're just out walking or hitching.

Hypothermia occurs when the body loses heat faster than it can produce it and the core temperature of the body falls. It is surprisingly easy to progress from very cold to dangerously cold due to a combination of wind, wet clothing, fatigue and hunger, even if the air temperature is above freezing. It is best to dress in layers; silk, wool and some of the new artificial fibres are all good insulating materials. A hat is important, as a lot of heat is lost through the head. A strong, waterproof outer layer (and a 'space' blanket for emergencies) are essential. Carry basic supplies, including food containing simple sugars to generate heat quickly and fluid to drink.

Symptoms of hypothermia are exhaustion, numb skin (particularly toes and fingers), shivering, slurred speech, irrational or violent behaviour, lethargy, stumbling, dizzy spells, muscle cramps and violent bursts of energy. Irrationality may take the form of sufferers claiming they are warm and trying to take off their clothes.

To treat mild hypothermia, first get the person out of the wind and/or rain, remove their clothing if it's wet and replace it with dry, warm clothing. Give them hot liquids – not alcohol – and some high-kilojoule, easily digestible food. Do not rub victims, instead allow them to slowly warm themselves. This should be enough to treat the early stages of hypothermia. The early recognition and treatment of mild hypothermia is the only way to prevent severe hypothermia, which is a critical condition.

Jet Lag Jet lag is experienced when a person travels by air across more than three time zones (each time zone usually represents a one-hour time difference). It occurs because many of the functions of the human body (such as temperature, pulse rate and emptying of the bladder and bowels) are regulated by internal 24-hour cycles. When we travel long distances rapidly, our bodies take time to adjust to the 'new time' of our destination, and we may experience fatigue, disorientation, insomnia, loss of appetite, anxiety and impaired concentration. These effects will usually be gone within three days of arrival, but to minimise the impact of jet lag:

- Rest for a couple of days prior to departure.
- Try to select flight schedules that minimise sleep deprivation; arriving late in the day means you can go to sleep soon after you arrive. For very long flights, try to organise a stopover.
- Avoid excessive eating (which bloats the stomach) and alcohol (which causes dehydration) during the flight. Instead, drink plenty of non-carbonated, non-alcoholic drinks such as fruit juice or water.
- Avoid smoking.
- Make yourself comfortable by wearing loose-fitting clothes and perhaps bringing an eye mask and ear plugs to help you sleep.
- Try to sleep at the appropriate time for the time zone you are travelling to.

Motion Sickness Eating lightly before and during a trip will reduce the chances of motion sickness. If you are prone to motion sickness, try to find a place that minimises movement – near the wing on aircraft, close to midships on boats, near the centre on buses. Fresh air usually helps; reading and cigarette smoke don't. Commercial motion-sickness preparations, which can cause drowsiness, have to be taken before the trip commences. Ginger (available in capsule form) and peppermint (including mint-flavoured sweets) are natural preventatives.

Prickly Heat Prickly heat is an itchy rash caused by excessive perspiration trapped under the skin. It usually strikes people who have just arrived in a hot climate. Keeping cool, bathing often, drying the skin and using

Everyday Health

Normal body temperature is up to 37°C or 98.6°F; more than 2°C (4°F) higher indicates a high fever. The normal adult pulse rate is 60 to 100 beats per minute (children 80 to 100, babies 100 to 140). As a general rule the pulse increases about 20 beats per minute for each 1°C (2°F) rise in fever.

Respiration (breathing) rate is also an indicator of illness. Count the number of breaths per minute: between 12 and 20 is normal for adults and older children (up to 30 for younger children, 40 for babies). People with a high fever or serious respiratory illness breathe more quickly than normal. More than 40 shallow breaths a minute may indicate pneumonia. ■

a mild talcum or prickly heat powder or resorting to air-conditioning may help.

Sunburn In the tropics, the desert or at high altitude you can get sunburnt surprisingly quickly, even through cloud. Use a sun block, hat, and barrier cream for your nose and lips. Calamine lotion or Stingose are good for mild sunburn, but I can recommend the local cure – chilled yoghurt spread over the affected area. Protect your eyes with good quality sunglasses.

Infectious Diseases

Diarrhoea Simple things like a change of water, food or climate can all cause a mild bout of diarrhoea, but a few rushed toilet trips with no other symptoms is not indicative of a major problem.

Dehydration is the main danger with any diarrhoea, particularly in children or the elderly as dehydration can occur quite quickly. Under all circumstances *fluid replacement* (at least equal to the volume being lost) is the most important thing to remember. Weak black tea with a little sugar, soda water, or soft drinks allowed to go flat and diluted 50% with clean water are all good. With severe diarrhoea a rehydrating solution is preferable to replace minerals and salts lost. Commercially available oral rehydration

salts (ORS) are very useful; add them to boiled or bottled water. In an emergency you can make up a solution of six teaspoons of sugar and a half teaspoon of salt to a litre of boiled or bottled water. You need to drink at least the same volume of fluid that you are losing in bowel movements and vomiting. Urine is the best guide to the adequacy of replacement – if you have small amounts of concentrated urine, you need to drink more. Keep drinking small amounts often. Stick to a bland diet as you recover.

Lomotil or Imodium can be used to bring relief from the symptoms, although they do not actually cure the problem. Only use these drugs if you do not have access to toilets eg if you *must* travel. For children under 12 years Lomotil and Imodium are not recommended. Do not use these drugs if the person has a high fever or is severely dehydrated.

In certain situations antibiotics may be required: diarrhoea with blood or mucous (dysentery), any fever, watery diarrhoea with fever and lethargy, persistent diarrhoea not improving after 48 hours and severe diarrhoea. In these situations gut-paralysing drugs like Imodium or Lomotil should be avoided.

A stool test is necessary to diagnose which kind of dysentery you have, so you should seek medical help urgently. Where this is not possible, the recommended drugs for dysentery are norfloxacin 400mg twice daily for three days or ciprofloxacin 500mg twice daily for five days. These are not recommended for children or pregnant women. The drug of choice for children would be co-trimoxazole (Bactrim, Septrin, Resprim) with dosage dependent on weight. A five-day course is given. Ampicillin or amoxycillin may be given in pregnancy, but medical care is necessary.

Amoebic dysentery is more gradual in the onset of symptoms, with cramping abdominal pain and vomiting less likely; fever may not be present. It will persist until treated and can recur and cause other health problems.

Giardiasis is another type of diarrhoea. The parasite causing this intestinal disorder is present in contaminated water and seems to be on the increase in the Middle East and North Africa. The symptoms are stomach cramps, nausea, a bloated stomach, watery, foul-smelling diarrhoea and frequent gas. Giardiasis can appear several weeks after you have been exposed to the parasite. The symptoms may disappear for a few days and then return; this can go on for several weeks. Tinidazole, known as Fasigyn, or metronidazole (Flagyl) are the recommended drugs. Treatment is a 2g single dose of Fasigyn or 250mg of Flagyl three times daily for five to 10 days.

Hepatitis Hepatitis is a general term for inflammation of the liver. It is a common disease worldwide. The symptoms are fever, chills, headache, fatigue, feelings of weakness and aches and pains, followed by loss of appetite, nausea, vomiting, abdominal pain, dark urine, light-coloured faeces, jaundiced (yellow) skin and the whites of the eyes may turn yellow. **Hepatitis A** is transmitted by contaminated food and drinking water. The disease poses a real threat to the western traveller. You should seek medical advice, but there is not much you can do apart from resting, drinking lots of fluids, eating lightly and avoiding fatty foods. People who have had hepatitis should avoid alcohol for some time after the illness, as the liver needs time to recover.

Hepatitis E is transmitted in the same way, and it can be very serious in pregnant women.

There are almost 300 million chronic carriers of **Hepatitis B** in the world. It is spread through contact with infected blood, blood products or body fluids, through for example sexual contact, unsterilised needles and blood transfusions, or contact with blood via small breaks in the skin. Other risk situations include having a shave, tattoo, or having your body pierced with contaminated equipment. The symptoms of type B may be more severe and may lead to long-term problems. **Hepatitis D** is spread in the same way, but the risk is mainly in shared needles.

Hepatitis C can lead to chronic liver disease. The virus is spread by contact with blood – usually via contaminated transfusions or shared needles. Avoiding these is the only means of prevention.

HIV & AIDS HIV, the Human Immunodeficiency Virus, develops into AIDS, Acquired Immune Deficiency Syndrome, which is a fatal disease. HIV is not a major problem in Lebanon, but this does not mean you should not take the usual precautions. Any exposure to blood, blood products or body fluids may put the individual at risk. The disease is often transmitted through sexual contact or dirty needles – vaccinations, acupuncture, tattooing and body piercing can be potentially as dangerous as intravenous drug use. HIV/AIDS can also be spread through infected blood transfusions; some developing countries cannot afford to screen blood used for transfusions.

If you do need an injection, ask to see the syringe unwrapped in front of you, or take a needle and syringe pack with you.

Fear of HIV infection should never preclude treatment for serious medical conditions.

Intestinal Worms These parasites are most common in rural areas. The different worms have different ways of infecting people. Some may be ingested in food including undercooked meat and some enter through your skin. Infestations may not show up for some time, and although they are generally not serious, if left untreated some can cause severe health problems later. Tapeworms are common in the Middle East, so consider having a stool test when you return home to check for these and determine the appropriate treatment.

Sexually Transmitted Diseases Gonorrhoea, herpes and syphilis are among these diseases; sores, blisters or rashes around the genitals, discharges or pain when urinating are common symptoms. In some STDs, such as wart virus or chlamydia, symptoms may be less marked or not observed at all especially in women. Syphilis symptoms will eventually disappear completely, but the disease continues and can cause severe problems in later years. While abstinence from sexual contact is the only 100% effective prevention, using condoms is also effective. The treatment of gonorrhoea and syphilis is with antibiotics. The different sexually transmitted diseases require specific antibiotics. There is no cure for herpes or AIDS.

Typhoid Typhoid fever is a dangerous gut infection caused by contaminated water and food. Medical help must be sought.

In its early stages sufferers may feel they have a bad cold or flu on the way, as early symptoms are headaches, body aches and a fever which rises a little each day until it is around 40°C (104°F) or more. The victim's pulse is often slow relative to the degree of fever present – unlike a normal fever where the pulse increases. There may also be vomiting, abdominal pain, constipation or diarrhoea.

In the second week the high fever and slow pulse continue and a few pink spots may appear on the body; trembling, delirium, weakness, weight loss and dehydration may occur. Complications such as pneumonia, perforated bowel or meningitis may occur.

The fever should be treated by keeping the victim cool and giving them fluids as dehydration should be watched for. Ciprofloxacin 750mg twice a day for 10 days is good for adults.

Chloramphenicol is recommended in many countries. The adult dosage is two 250mg capsules, four times a day. Children aged between eight and 12 years should have half the adult dose; and younger children one-third the adult dose.

Cuts, Bites & Stings

Rabies is passed through animal bites. See Less Common Diseases later for details of this disease.

Bedbugs & Lice Bedbugs live in various places, but particularly in dirty mattresses and bedding, evidenced by spots of blood on bedclothes or on the wall. Bedbugs leave itchy bites in neat rows. Calamine lotion or Stingose spray may help. All lice cause itching and discomfort. They make themselves at home in your hair (head lice), your clothing (body lice) or in your pubic hair (crabs). You catch lice through direct contact with infected people or by sharing combs, clothing and the like. Powder or shampoo treatment will kill the lice and infected clothing should then be washed in very hot, soapy water and left in the sun to dry.

Cuts & Scratches Wash well and treat any cut with an antiseptic such as povidone-iodine. Where possible avoid bandages and Band-aids, which can keep wounds wet.

Insect Bites & Stings Bee and wasp stings are usually painful rather than dangerous. However in people who are allergic to them, severe breathing difficulties may occur and require urgent medical care. Calamine lotion or Stingose spray will give relief and ice packs will reduce the pain and swelling. There are some spiders with dangerous bites but antivenenes are usually available.

There are various fish and other sea creatures which can sting or bite dangerously or which are dangerous to eat. Again, local advice is the best suggestion.

Jellyfish Local advice is the best way of avoiding contact with these sea creatures which have stinging tentacles. Dousing in vinegar will de-activate any stingers which have not 'fired'. Calamine lotion, antihistamines and analgesics may reduce the reaction and relieve the pain.

Scorpions Scorpion stings are a serious cause of illness and occasional deaths in the Middle East including Lebanon, although effective antivenenes are available. Shake shoes, clothing and towels before use. Inspect bedding and don't put hands or feet in crevices or in dwellings where they may be lurking.

A sting usually produces redness and swelling of the skin, but there may be no visible reaction. Pain is common, and tingling or numbness may occur. At this stage, cold compresses on the bite and pain relief (eg paracetamol) are called for. If the skin sensations start to spread from the sting site (eg along the arm), then immediate medical attention is required.

Snakes To minimise your chances of being bitten always wear boots, socks and long trousers when walking through undergrowth where snakes may be present. Don't put your hands into holes and crevices.

Snake bites do not cause instantaneous death and antivenenes are usually available. Immediately wrap the bitten limb tightly, as you would for a sprained ankle, and then attach a splint to immobilise it. Keep the victim still and seek medical help, if possible with the dead snake for identification. Don't attempt to catch the snake if there is a possibility of being bitten again. Tourniquets and sucking out the poison are now comprehensively discredited.

Ticks You should always check all over your body if you have been walking through a potentially tick-infested area as ticks can cause skin infections and other more serious diseases. If a tick is found attached, press down around the tick's head with tweezers, grab the head and gently pull upwards. Avoid pulling the rear of the body as this may squeeze the tick's gut contents through the attached mouth parts into the skin, increasing the risk of infection and disease. Smearing chemicals on the tick will not make it let go and is not recommended.

Women's Health
Gynaecological Problems Sexually transmitted diseases are a major cause of vaginal problems. Symptoms include a smelly discharge, painful intercourse and sometimes a burning sensation when urinating. Male sexual partners must also be treated. Medical attention should be sought and remember in addition to these diseases HIV or hepatitis B may also be acquired during exposure. Besides abstinence, the best thing is to practise safe sex using condoms.

Antibiotic use, sweating, synthetic underwear, and contraceptive pills can lead to fungal vaginal infections when travelling in hot climates. Maintaining good personal hygiene, and wearing loose-fitting clothes and cotton underwear will help to prevent these infections.

Fungal infections, characterised by a rash, itch and discharge, can be treated with a vinegar or lemon-juice douche, or with yoghurt. Nystatin, miconazole or clotrimazole pessaries or vaginal cream are the usual treatment.

Pregnancy It is not advisable to travel to some places while pregnant as some vaccinations normally used to prevent serious diseases are not advisable in pregnancy eg yellow fever. In addition, some diseases are much more serious for the mother (and may increase the risk of a stillborn child) in pregnancy eg malaria.

Most miscarriages occur during the first three months of pregnancy. Miscarriage is not uncommon, and can occasionally lead to severe bleeding. The last three months should also be spent within reasonable distance of good medical care. A baby born as early as 24 weeks stands a chance of survival, but only in a good, modern hospital. Pregnant women should avoid all unnecessary medication; vaccinations and malarial prophylactics should still be taken where needed. Additional care should be taken to prevent illness and particular attention should be paid to diet and nutrition. Alcohol and nicotine, for example, should be avoided.

Less Common Diseases
The following diseases pose a small risk to travellers, and so are only mentioned in passing. Seek medical advice if you think you may have any of these diseases.

Cholera This is the worst of the watery diarrhoeas and medical help should be sought. Outbreaks of cholera are generally widely reported, so you can avoid such problem areas. *Fluid replacement is the most vital treatment* – the risk of dehydration is severe as you may lose up to 20L a day. If there is a delay in getting to hospital, then begin taking tetracycline. The adult dose is 250mg four times daily. It is not recommended for children under nine years nor for pregnant women. Tetracycline may help shorten the illness, but adequate fluids are required to save lives.

Leishmaniasis This is a group of parasitic diseases transmitted by sandflies, which are found in many parts of the Middle East. Cutaneous leishmaniasis affects the skin tissue causing ulceration and disfigurement; visceral leishmaniasis affects the internal organs. Seek medical advice as laboratory testing is required for diagnosis and correct treatment. Avoiding sandfly bites is the best precaution. Bites are usually painless, itchy and are yet another reason to cover up and apply repellent.

Rabies Rabies is a fatal viral infection found in all Middle Eastern countries, including Lebanon. Many animals can be infected (such as dogs, cats, bats and monkeys) and it is their saliva which is infectious. Any bite, scratch or even lick from a warm-blooded, furry animal should be cleaned immediately and thoroughly. Scrub with soap and running water, and then apply alcohol or iodine solution. Medical help should be sought promptly to receive a course of injections which will help to prevent the onset of symptoms and death.

Tetanus Tetanus occurs when a wound becomes infected by a germ which lives in soil and in the faeces of horses and other animals. It enters the body via breaks in the skin. All wounds should be cleaned promptly and adequately and an antiseptic cream or solution applied. Use antibiotics if the wound becomes hot, throbs or pus is seen. The first symptom may be discomfort in swallowing, or stiffening of the jaw and neck; this is followed by painful convulsions of the jaw and whole body. The disease can be fatal.

TOILETS

Toilets in Lebanon are virtually nonexistent outside of hotels and restaurants. Where they exist, they are of the European variety. The standard is quite good, although you would be advised to take your own toilet paper.

WOMEN TRAVELLERS

Women travelling in Lebanon will notice a huge difference in the attitude towards them than that shown in most other parts of the Middle East. It has a much more relaxed attitude to women in matters of dress and behaviour than the more conservative Arab countries, largely because Lebanon, and Beirut in particular, has for a long time been a cosmopolitan centre with people of different religions and cultural backgrounds. This has created a more relaxed society for women who play a dynamic role in business, government and the arts. Education is of a good quality (although not free) and many women now go to university and pursue demanding careers.

For foreign women there are relatively few hassles so long as you are sensible. In Beirut it is common to see women in miniskirts, tight trousers and sleeveless tops and this is quite OK, although a bra is a good idea – or at least a top which conceals the outline of the breasts. In the coastal resorts the dress code is also pretty relaxed. Bikinis are OK on the beach, but going topless is a no-no.

Away from the cities it is sensible to adopt a more conservative style of dress to avoid unwelcome attention. Some parts of Lebanon are predominantly Muslim and it could cause offence to walk around in revealing clothing. If you are planning to visit any mosques, be sure that your arms and legs are covered and that you take a headscarf with you – some mosques even provide a black cloak at the door to women visitors.

You may occasionally find yourself the subject of unwanted leers or rude remarks in the street, or at worst, attempts at conversation. The best thing to do is ignore them. If some persist, ask them loudly to leave you alone and the chances are they'll be told off by other passers-by.

In the middle and top-end hotels the security is usually very good and women need not worry about being hassled. In the budget-end hotels it might be more of a problem. Do not open your hotel room door unless you know who is there, and when you are alone in your room keep the door locked. In seedy hotels look out for holes in the walls – stuffing tissues into the keyhole and other suspicious holes can thwart any would-be peeping toms.

Women should not get into an unlicensed service taxi if there are no other passengers, especially at night. If a car stops when you are waiting for a taxi and you do not like the look of it, just firmly wave the car away – don't feel pressured into getting in.

GAY & LESBIAN TRAVELLERS

The gay traveller will find Lebanon more relaxed in its attitude than many other Middle Eastern countries, at least in the capital, Beirut.

Homosexuality is still illegal under Lebanese law, so it would pay to be discrete when checking into a double hotel room, for example. It is common for even straight unmarried couples to be refused a double room in many hotels. As a guide, the Muslim areas are more conservative than the Christian ones.

DISABLED TRAVELLERS

Depending on your disability, Lebanon may test your resources considerably. The streets of Beirut are strewn with rubble and pot-holes, which would make it difficult to get around in a wheelchair. Buildings and archaeological sites do not have wheelchair ramps. To tour Lebanon, you would need an able-bodied person with you to help, and it would be a good idea to avoid Beirut.

SENIOR TRAVELLERS

The older traveller, who is reasonably fit, will have no trouble with Lebanon. The main historical sites are all quite accessible and can be seen without too much climbing and exertion. The exceptions are the Kadisha Valley, which is very strenuous, and some of the minor ruins in the Bekaa Valley. If you prefer peace and quiet, consider staying

outside Beirut – Byblos or Tripoli, for example – and touring from there. In the summer, it would be more comfortable to stay higher up in the mountain resorts above Beirut – advice that is good for any age.

TRAVEL WITH CHILDREN

The Lebanese love children and bringing along the kids will open doors and guarantee you make new friends. Children, who are old enough to appreciate nature, will love the scenery and the food won't be a problem. The Lebanese way of eating lots of small dishes should find approval, and children are welcome in restaurants. If they want a break from Lebanese food and crave fast food, there are plenty of choices. Also in many places you will find some kind of playground or funfair to amuse them.

All kind of nappies and baby foods are easily available, so shopping for the younger children won't be a problem either. The only thing you will have to watch is the heat in the summer months – maximum protection sun block is a must. See Lonely Planet's *Travel with Children* by Maureen Wheeler for more information.

USEFUL ORGANISATIONS

For those touring by car or motorcycle, there is an automobile club, the Automobile et Touring Club du Liban (☎ (01) 390645). If you are in difficulties, call the Tourist Police (☎ (01) 343209).

DANGERS & ANNOYANCES

The extreme south of Lebanon is still subject to the occasional cross-border shelling from Israel or even air raids in retaliation for any cross-border guerrilla operations. The most dangerous zones are off-limits to visitors so there is little cause for worry. The army patrols keep people away from any dangerous areas.

The rest of the country is now quite safe to travel around. Since the disarming and disbanding of the militias in the early 1990s, it has become possible to travel anywhere day or night without worries about security. There are frequent army checkpoints on the

PAUL DOYLE

PAUL DOYLE

ANDY FERGUSON

PAUL DOYLE

PETER JOUSIFFE

Travelling throughout Lebanon is made all the easier by the friendliness of the Lebanese people. Don't be surprised by the hospitable welcome you're likely to receive from a young girl in Beirut (top left), bikers in Jounieh (top right), a pickle seller in the Tripoli souks (middle left), a young Tripoli boy (bottom left) or a woman in Byblos (bottom right).

PAUL DOYLE

ANDY FERGUSON

PAUL DOYLE

Top: Lebanon's traditional dance, the dabke, is a dazzling whirl of colour and sound.
Middle: A typical Lebanese meal begins with a variety of mezze dishes, and with over 4
dishes to choose from, the mezze often becomes the entire meal.
Bottom: Handcrafted silver souvenirs and unique trinkets on offer outside the Baalbek ruins

Islamic Holidays

Because the Islamic, or Hjira, calendar is 11 days shorter than the Gregorian (western) calendar, Islamic holidays fall about 11 days earlier each year. The 11-day rule is not entirely strict – the holidays can fall from 10 to 12 days earlier. The precise dates are known only shortly before they fall, depending upon the sighting of the moon. The Hjira calendar has 12 lunar months, which are:

1st	Moharram	7th	Ragab
2nd	Safar	8th	Shaaban
3rd	Rabi' al-Awal	9th	Ramadan
4th	Rabi' ath-Thani	10th	Shawal
5th	Gamada al-Awal	11th	Zuul-Qe'da
6th	Gamada at-Taniyya	12th	Zuul-Hijja

The following are the expected dates for the specific Islamic holidays:

Hjira Year	New Year	Prophet's Birthday	Ramadan Begins	Eid al-Fitr	Eid al-Adha
1418	–	–	31.12.97	29.01.98	08.04.98
1419	28.04.98	06.07.98	19.12.98	18.01.99	28.03.99
1420	17.04.99	26.06.99	09.12.99	08.01.00	16.03.00
1421	06.04.00	14.06.00	27.11.00	27.12.00	06.03.01

roads (both Lebanese and Syrian) and occasionally you may be required to show your passport, but this is normal and no cause for concern.

In Beirut the streets are pretty well crime free; the main dangers to the unwary are, firstly, the horrendous traffic in the city (crossing the road can be a test of nerves) and, secondly, the dangerous state of some of the bomb-damaged buildings. In some streets the locals choose to walk in the middle of the road rather than risk being injured by falling masonry. You would be advised to follow suit. Walking in the road will become second nature anyway as there are few undamaged pavements to walk on and cars tend to park on the few pavements that do exist.

The bad state of the roads and pavements can be a bit of a hazard when out walking at night. The streets can be dark and it is easy to stumble into a hole or twist your ankle on rubble. It is a good idea to take a torch with you if you are walking around after dark.

Theft can be a bit of a worry, but no more than is common in many other parts of the world. As a general rule, never leave your belongings unattended or leave money and valuables in your hotel room. Most hotels have a strong box where you can safely park your money and valuables. Use money belts and avoid showing too much cash. It is a good idea to have a small amount of money in your pocket to pay for taxis and so on rather than pulling out your purse or wallet in public.

BUSINESS HOURS

Sunday is the end-of-week holiday in Lebanon. Government offices, including post offices, are open Monday to Saturday from 8 am to 2 pm, except Friday when the opening hours are from 8 to 11 am. However you'll rarely find anyone at work before 9.30 am. Banks are open Monday to Saturday from 8.30 am to 12.30 pm.

Shops and private businesses open from 9 am to 6 pm Monday to Saturday. Many grocery stores keep later hours and open on Sunday as well. In summer many places close around 3 pm.

PUBLIC HOLIDAYS

Most holidays are religious, and with so many different sects in Lebanon, there are quite a few events to celebrate:

1 January
New Year's Day
9 February
Mar Maroun – the patron saint of the Maronites
March-April
Good Friday & Easter Monday (Western churches)
Good Friday & Easter Monday (Eastern churches)
18 April
Qana Day
1 May
Labour Day
15 August
Assumption
1 November
All Saints Day
22 November
Independence Day
25 December
Christmas Day

Qana Day is the official day of mourning for the massacre at Qana in 1996 in which 107 Lebanese civilians were killed by Israeli shells at a UN camp.

Also observed are the Muslim holidays of Eid al-Fitr, Eid al-Adha, the Prophet's Birthday, Islamic New Year and Ashura. The Muslim calendar is lunar and therefore the dates are approximately 11 days earlier each year. See the Islamic Holidays boxed story for exact dates.

ACTIVITIES
Swimming
There are not very many sandy beaches on the Lebanese coast; much of the swimming is from rocks or artificial platforms built out on jetties. Of the sand beaches, the best can be found in the far south of the country, south of Tyre, near Byblos and at Chekka near Tripoli. There is also a public sandy beach in Beirut, but the cleanliness of the water is highly questionable.

The rocky bathing makes for good snorkelling and there are often water sports facilities at the private beach resorts. Water-skiing, windsurfing and sailing are all popular in the summer season. There is still a pollution problem along some parts of the coast so it is best to check with the locals first. If there is a problem with sea bathing, there are good swimming pools at almost all the larger hotels or resorts. The only snag is

that they can be rather expensive at US$6 to US$20 per person per day, depending on the level of luxury.

Skiing
There are six main ski resorts in Lebanon with varying degrees of difficulty. Many of the facilities are now being renovated and upgraded as Lebanon is seeking to attract more overseas visitors. From November to April, you can take a short package ski holiday from Beirut arranged by some of the local tour operators. These include transfers to and from Beirut and full board at one of the ski hotels. Depending on the package chosen, and the class of hotel, the average costs are around US$80 per day inclusive (although this does not include ski and lift passes). The cost of hiring ski equipment is very reasonable and available at all the resorts – a full kit will cost about US$10 per day.

The Ministry of Tourism publishes a very useful booklet called *Ski Lebanon*, which details all the ski resorts and facilities.

Trekking
Lebanon has fabulous trekking opportunities in the mountains and gorges. There are no recent publications about trekking in Lebanon, but *Smelling the Breezes: A Journey Through High Lebanon* by Ralph & Molly Izzard, which was published in the 1960s, may be helpful. It describes a journey on foot and by mule through the mountains of Lebanon.

It is a good idea to consult your map carefully to calculate the distances before setting out and to make sure there are suitable places to stop for the night. The good thing about trekking in Lebanon is the relatively short distance between villages. There have been some reports of certain areas being mined, so if you are planning a trek always seek local advice about the safety of your intended route.

Some things to remember when trekking in Lebanon:

Carry out all your rubbish. If you've carried it in, you can carry it out.

Don't rely on water in plastic bottles. Disposal of these bottles can cause a major problem. Use iodine drops or purification tablets instead.

Where there is a toilet, please use it. Where there is none, bury your waste in a small hole 15cm deep and at least 100m from any watercourse.

Don't use detergents and toothpaste in or near watercourses, even if they are biodegradable.

Stick to the existing tracks and avoid short cuts. Hill sides and mountain slopes, especially at high altitudes, are prone to erosion.

WORK

You need a work permit to take on any official employment in Lebanon, but if you can get one, there are certainly many opportunities open to foreigners with professional skills to offer. Needless to say, the construction industry is booming with Beirut's reconstruction programme and there is a demand for technicians and engineers. Anyone with trained medical skills would also have no difficulty getting a job as there

Ski Resorts at a Glance

There are six main ski resorts in Lebanon with various grades of difficulty. They all have ski equipment hire and instruction. Following is a summary of the slopes and prices.

Bakish (☎ (09) 915833) Bakish is 47km from Beirut, just north of Baskinta. The altitude is 1904 to 2250m. There are four slopes here ranging from 900 to 1200m and there is a skiing area of 1.8 million sq m. Ski rental costs US$3 per day. For information on road conditions, call ☎ (09) 988001.

Faqra (☎ (01) 200019) Faqra is close to Faraya and has an altitude of 1735 to 2001m. It is 45km from Beirut and has a skiing area of 300,000 sq m. There are four slopes: a baby slope of 150m, an intermediate slope of 450m, a steep slope of 450m and one of 1000m. Ski passes cost US$10 during the week and US$20 at the weekend and during holidays. Ski rental is US$10 per day or US$15 at the weekend. For information on road conditions, call ☎ (09) 720060.

Faraya (☎ (09) 710733, 720733) In Mount Lebanon at Keserwan, Faraya is 52km from Beirut. The altitude is 1874 to 2463m. This is one of the most popular ski resorts. It has 11 slopes ranging from two baby slopes of 100m and 150m to four advanced slopes of 1500 to 1750m, plus several intermediate slopes. Ski passes cost US$13 for a full day and US$7 for half a day, except at the weekend and during holidays when a full-day pass costs US$20 and a half-day US$9. Ski rental costs US$5. There is a car parking charge of US$2 per day. For information on road conditions, call ☎ (09) 720060.

Laklouk (☎ (01) 200019) Located 28km east of Byblos in Mount Lebanon, Laklouk has an altitude of 1751m. It is 69km from Beirut and has a ski area of 600,000 sq m. There are four slopes with five ski lifts: one baby slope and steeper slopes of 450m, 600m, 700m and 1200m. Ski passes cost US$10 per day and US$15 at the weekend and during holidays. Ski rental costs US$3 or US$5 at the weekend and during holidays. For information on road conditions, call ☎ (09) 904184.

The Cedars (☎ (06) 671072) Near Bcharré in northern Lebanon, the Cedars is the highest of the ski resorts at 2100 to 2900m and the season lasts a bit longer here due to the altitude. The distance from Beirut is 122km. There are four slopes with lifts: one baby (85m), one beginner (1600m), and two intermediate (1800m and 2100m). A ski pass costs US$10 per day (US$15 at the weekend and during holidays). Ski rental costs US$5. For information on road conditions, call ☎ (06) 678002. For further information, see the Bcharré section in the Tripoli & The Cedars chapter.

Zaarour (☎ (04) 271152/3) Zaarour, only 35km from Beirut, has an altitude of 1651 to 2001m and a skiing area of 600,000 sq m. There are four slopes: two baby slopes of 100m, one of 700m and one of 1200m. Ski passes cost US$10 per day (US$15 at the weekend and during holidays). Ski rental costs US$3. For road conditions, call ☎ (04) 995730. ■

are many new private clinics and hospitals opening.

If you are looking for something more casual and short-term, the hotel and tourism industry is expanding rapidly. It may be worth approaching hotels and resorts directly for seasonal work. In late summer there is an opportunity to harvest grapes in the Bekaa Valley, but this is obviously only a short-term job.

As long as excavations are being carried out in Lebanon, there will be teams of student archaeologists from different parts of the world taking part in the digs. If you fancy joining a dig, it would be worth your while contacting the Department of Antiquities and inquiring. They would probably want a reference from your university though. Be warned though – there is no money for these volunteers, just accommodation and food provided.

ACCOMMODATION

If you are on a tight budget, finding accommodation in Lebanon can be a bit of a headache. There are very few hotels at the cheap end – the war destroyed most of the smaller hotels – and no hostels. Consequently the few that are cheap tend to be full, especially in the summer. Even the cheapest hotel rooms cost about US$20. There is one good camping ground which is a good alternative to staying in a cheap room (even assuming you can find one).

If you have a larger budget, the world is your oyster; there are many good hotels at the upper end and be prepared to spend US$70 to US$100 for a double room.

Camping

There is only one camping site still up and running in Lebanon and, thank goodness, it is in one of the best locations and is extremely well run. It is *Camping Amchit*, also known as *Les Colombes*, just north of Byblos on a beautiful promontory overlooking the sea. Situated in the centre of the coast, it is a convenient base from which to explore the country.

Hotels

There is certainly no shortage of hotels, especially in Beirut, and new ones seem to be springing up all the time. The snag is that the old hotels, which were damaged during the war, are all being replaced with four and five-star hotels. As things are, there are only about four really cheap hotels in the capital and very few scattered about the country. In the cheapies that do exist, the room price is often the same for singles and doubles, but there is no service charge added.

The service charge is something to watch out for when checking into a hotel (even mid-range hotels tend to add this onto the basic room charge). The service charge is usually 15 or 16%, which can make quite a difference to the bill, so ask first.

Mid-range hotels tend to cost about US$50 for a double room with bath. There are several in the Hamra district of Beirut and in the regional towns. These are often really quite good hotels with room service and good bathrooms. If you go for the more expensive hotels, they are comparable with three and four-star hotels in Europe and are very comfortable indeed. Many in this class have swimming pools and health clubs.

Long-Term Stays

If you are planning a longer stay in Lebanon, it might be worth considering renting an apartment, although this would be an expensive option if you were travelling alone. In Beirut and Jounieh, there are dozens of rental apartment buildings catering for long-term seasonal visitors (Lebanese people living abroad often visit Lebanon for the summer). These can work out much cheaper than hotels. Many of these apartment buildings have all the facilities of a hotel (porterage, room service, pool etc), but are self-catering. A small apartment would cost (depending on the season) from US$200 to US$300 per week. If you are staying more than a few weeks, the price is always negotiable.

ENTERTAINMENT
Cinemas & Theatres

All the main towns seem to have at least one

cinema and Beirut has more than a dozen. These often show the latest western releases in their original form with Arabic subtitles. Occasionally they are dubbed into Arabic, so it is a good idea to check first. Cinema tickets cost LL 10,000 and only LL 5000 on Mondays. There are sometimes short seasons of films shown at the foreign cultural institutes. These mostly consist of art-house movies from the countries concerned and are in the language of that country.

There is a lively theatre scene in Lebanon, mostly in Beirut. Comedy reviews and contemporary plays seem to feature heavily, but all the theatre performances seem to be in Arabic only. For plays in English, it is worth checking out the AUB campus theatre which often has English-language productions.

There is a listing section for cinemas and theatres in the daily newspapers, *L'Orient-Le Jour* and the *Daily Star*.

Discos & Nightclubs

Beirut used to be the nightclub capital of the eastern Mediterranean and there are still a huge array of night spots open. Nearly all large hotels have a floor show of some kind and a disco at the weekend.

The place to go for end to end nightclubbing is Jounieh – the whole bay seems to be one big playground in the summer season. You will see signs everywhere advertising 'Super Night Club'. This is not so much a comment on the quality of the place as to advertise the fact that they serve supper.

Live music and dancing shows tend to start at around 10 pm and go on pretty late into the night. The entertainment on offer varies from traditional Lebanese music and belly dancing to imported cabaret acts (often from the former eastern bloc). You don't have to eat at the nightclubs, but if you are intending only to drink, there may be a cover charge (sometimes quite hefty). Drink prices vary from the moderately expensive to the outrageous.

Jazz clubs are quite popular and there are a couple in Beirut, near the AUB, which are reasonably priced.

Lebanon's Grand Prix Ambitions

Lebanon has formulated a plan to become the home of the first Middle East Formula One Grand Prix. Beirut would be the host city with the route starting on Ave Ramlet el-Baida, following the Corniche and ending on Ave du Général de Gaulle.

To qualify Lebanon must first stage a Formula Three race; preparations are underway for an early 1998 staging. If successful in its bid, Lebanon will join the ranks of celebrated motor race countries such as Argentina, Monaco, Italy, Austria, Brazil and Australia. During the season over 20 races are held; the first in Australia and the season finale in Spain. ■

SPECTATOR SPORT

There are quite a few events such as motor rallies and football, but you will only get to know about them if you scour the newspapers. The Lebanese like to play football (is there a nationality anywhere who doesn't?) and have a national team and local leagues.

Sunday is the day for horseracing at the Beirut Hippodrome (☎ (01) 632520), but it is not *every* Sunday. This is a very popular sport with the locals and is a great way to soak up the atmosphere. Again, check the paper for details. Admission is US$10 to the grandstand and US$3 to the 2nd-class stand. The entrance is on Ave Abdallah Yafi, not far from the National Museum.

Apart from that, there are car rallies held from time to time, often using road circuits up in the hills which are closed off for the duration of the race.

Privately, the Lebanese like to play tennis and badminton and water sports are extremely popular during the summer. There are sometimes sailing regattas or power boat races. In the winter skiing is popular and easily accessible.

THINGS TO BUY

Beirut is full of shops, stalls and markets where you can buy everything from locally woven rugs to electronic calculators and the latest designer wear, often at good prices. A number of shops in Beirut, such as the Artisans du Liban, specialise in traditional ethnic goods.

If you are looking for something original to buy, one of the best places to look is Tripoli, where the coppersmiths are still turning out traditional work. There are large numbers of workshops in the old souks (just follow the din) and the prices for even elaborate pieces are quite reasonable.

Other areas are known for their particular handicrafts: Beiteddine and Byblos – weaving and embroidery; the Chouf – embroidery, weaving and silk; Ehden – copper and metalwork; Jezzine – cutlery; Rachaiya – jewellery; and Sarafand – glass.

There are a lot of imported tourist 'gift' items in shops in the various mountain resorts and in Beirut, but much of this comes from Syria or even India. Even so it is decorative and some of it is a bargain, especially the inlaid wooden boxes and backgammon sets.

Antiques at the cheaper end of the scale are hard to find, but in Byblos and a few other places you can find small terracotta antiquities on sale quite cheaply. Another popular souvenir is a fish fossil set in stone which comes from a mountain site. These make interesting paperweights and are on sale in shops all around the country but especially in Byblos.

A guide to
Lebanese Cuisine

Lebanese Cuisine

Lebanese cooking is one of the great cuisines of the Middle East and encompasses a wide array of dishes and cooking styles. Using fresh and flavoursome ingredients and refined spicing, the Lebanese have taken the best aspects of Turkish and Arabic cooking and given them a French spin.

The good news is that eating out need not be expensive. A traditional Lebanese meal starts with *mezze* which is a selection of hot and cold starters. These can be simple or elaborate. Some are so filling that you could easily forego a main course altogether. There are enough meatless dishes to satisfy vegetarians as well. These are usually aubergine or cheese dishes and sometimes pulses or beans.

Main courses are usually chicken, lamb or fish grilled with rice and salad (or the ubiquitous French fries) served with Lebanese flat bread *khoubiz*. *Marqouk*, or mountain bread, is also found everywhere in Lebanon.

Kibbe, the national dish

The national dish is *kibbe* – a finely minced paste of lamb and bulgur wheat. This is sometimes served raw as in steak tartare or more often stuffed with meat and pine nuts and fried or baked into a pie.

Fish and seafood in Lebanon is good and some restaurants specialise in this. In common with the rest of the Mediterranean, fish restaurants are notoriously expensive and fish is priced on menus per kilogram.

It is worth asking, even in the more expensive restaurants, if they do a 'tourist menu' for lunch – these are set, three-course menus which are often excellent value.

Street food in Lebanon is very good indeed, and very cheap, with an abundance of snack bars selling chicken or meat *shawarma* (seasoned and spit-roasted meat) or *felafels* (fried chickpea balls) in delicious sandwiches. In fact you will find almost everything stuffed into a sandwich: roast chicken, spicy sausages, cheese, you name it.

If you fancy something different, there are a growing number of foreign restaurants particularly in and around Beirut and Jounieh. You can find Japanese, Chinese, Indian, Italian, Mexican, French and good old American burger bars. Italian pizzas are very popular and Pizza Hut has several branches in Beirut.

Restaurants

In a good restaurant, you may find over 40 mezze dishes on offer – some familiar, some not so – and that's just the first course!

When eating out in Lebanon, you may order as many or as few dishes as you choose. It is quite acceptable to just order a range of different mezze dishes. The more people ordering, the more variety you can experience. As a general rule, three or four mezze dishes per person should be plenty for a good lunch or dinner; two mezze dishes each is usually enough if you are ordering a main course as well.

Eating out in a Lebanese restaurant, you may come across some of the following:

Breads
Khoubiz flat unleavened bread
M'Naish bi Za'atar flat bread seasoned with thyme and *sumak* (a tangy herb)

Dips
Baba Ghanouj purée of grilled aubergines with tahini, olive oil and lemon juice
Hummus bi Tahini purée of chickpeas and tahini with garlic and olive oil

Hummus Kawarmah a delicious variation with grilled lamb on top
Labneh Maa Toum fresh yoghurt with garlic and olive oil
Taratour bi Tahini creamy dip or sauce made from tahini, lemon juice and garlic

Cold Starters

Fattoush toasted bread salad with tomatoes, onions and mint leaves
Kibbe Nayeh ground lamb and cracked wheat served raw like steak tartare
Loubieh french bean salad with tomatoes, onions and garlic
Moutabel grilled aubergine slices with tahini, olive oil and lemon juice
Shanklish mature goat's cheese with onions, oil and tomatoes
Tabouleh salad of parsley and cracked wheat with onions and tomatoes
Warak Inab stuffed vine leaves without meat

Fatayer

Hot Starters

Fatayer triangular pastries with minced lamb stuffing
Fatayer bi Sbanikh triangular pastries stuffed with spinach and pine nuts
Felafel croquettes made with chick peas and fava beans spiced with coriander
Kibbe Maklieh ground lamb and cracked wheat croquettes stuffed with a savoury meat filling
Kofta mixture of minced meat and spices that can be baked or grilled on skewers
Kousa Mishni courgette stuffed with minced lamb and pine nuts, served either *bi Laban* – with yoghurt or *bi Bandoura* – with tomato sauce
Makanek Lebanese lamb sausages
Soujuk spicy Armenian sausages

Main Courses

Kharouf Mihshi lamb stuffed with rice, meat and nuts
Kibosh bi Lana kibosh balls cooked in yoghurt sauce
Lahm Meshwi cubes of lamb grilled on skewers
Musakhan chicken casserole spiced with sumak
Ruz wi Djaj chicken with rice and nuts
Sayadieh fish, delicately spiced, served with rice in an onion and tahini sauce
Shawarma lamb or chicken grilled on a large spit and carved into slices
Shish Taouk pieces of chicken breast cooked on skewers

Desserts

Mahallabiye milk custard with pine nuts and almonds

Snacks

Snack bars tend to specialise in one kind of food. You often come across places selling only felafels – spicy, ground chickpeas formed into balls and deep-fried, and then served wrapped in a flat bread roll with salad and sauce. These are very tasty and filling and cost only LL 1500. *Fuul,* a paste made from fava beans, garlic and lemon and served with oil, is also a standard snack at any time of the day.

Another popular and cheap snack is the Lebanese pizza, which, unlike Italian pizzas, is very thin with a small amount of topping – either meat, cheese or *za'atar* (a mixture of thyme and sumak). The pizzas, which are folded into a triangle, contain a delicious spinach and lemon filling. These all cost from LL 1000 to LL 1500.

Of course the most common snacks are *kebabs* and shawarma, which again come wrapped in flat bread with salad and dressing. They usually cost about LL 2000 and are very substantial.

Felafels in khoubiz

A traditional coffee pot

Cafés & Bars

There are a lot of the 'coffee and *nargileh* (water pipe)' places all over Lebanon. They tend to be patronised by men only but sometimes you see women sitting together over a pipe. If you don't fancy the traditional cafés, there is no shortage of European-style cafés and bars to suit all tastes and pockets. There are some good places around the American University of Beirut which are quite reasonably priced and lively in the evenings.

Self-Catering

The shops and supermarkets in Lebanon are well stocked with Lebanese and imported food, so there is no problem if you want to buy and cook your own food. The prices are roughly the same as in Europe. The Lebanese like to buy their fruit and vegetables fresh every day and the greengrocers have a daily supply of seasonal produce. The tomatoes and salad produce are always good and there are always large, green bunches of flat-leafed parsley to make the ever popular tabouleh.

Pickled vegetables are also very popular and these are served as appetisers or chopped into sandwiches. Cheeses are also very good. One of the most popular is *halloumi* – a salty, rubbery cheese which is good raw or fried. Soft, white cheese is on sale in most shops and is good in sandwiches.

If your cooking facilities are limited, you can buy delicious spit-roast chickens from many takeaway restaurants. These cost about LL 8000 for a whole chicken with garlic sauce. Some butchers also sell ready-marinaded chicken pieces to grill on your barbecue or to fry in a pan.

If you are near a fish market, seafood is quite cheap to buy straight from the boat (as opposed to the fancy prices in fish restaurants) and is a very simple, delicious and healthy option.

Some of the following words may come in useful if you are buying things off the street or in markets:

Okra

Vegetables & Salad

cabbage	*kharoum*	okra	*baamiya*
carrot	*jazar*	onion	*basal*
cauliflower	*arnabeet*	peas	*biseela*
cucumber	*khiyaar*	potatoes	*batatas*
eggplant	*bazinjan*	salad	*salata*
garlic	*tum*	tomato	*banadura*
green beans	*fasooliya*	turnip	*lift*
lentils	*'adas*	vegetables	*khadrawat*
lettuce	*khass*		

Meats

camel	*lahm jamal*	lamb	*lahm*
chicken	*farooj*	liver	*kibda*
kidney	*kelaawi*	meat	*lahm*

Fruit

apple	*tufah*	lime	*limoon*
apricot	*mish-mish*	mango	*manga*
banana	*moz*	olive	*zeitoun*
date	*tamr*	orange	*burtuqaal*
fig	*teen*	pomegranate	*rumman*
fruit	*fawaka*	strawberry	*fraise*
grape	*'inab*	watermelon	*batteekh*

Miscellaneous

butter	*zibda*	salt	*milh*
cheese	*jibna*	sour yoghurt	*ayran*
eggs	*beid*	drink	
milk	*haleeb*	sugar	*sukar*
mineral water	*maya at-ta'abiyya*	water	*mayy*
pepper	*filfil*	yoghurt	*laban*

Pomegranate

Recipes of Lebanon

Starters

Spinach and Yoghurt Dip Dips are a ubiquitous part of the mezze.

Ingredients
5 tbs olive oil
1 onion, very finely chopped
2 cloves garlic, crushed
1 bunch fresh spinach, washed and trimmed
500g plain yoghurt
1 tbs salt
freshly ground black pepper

Method
Heat oil in a frypan, toss in onion and sauté until transparent. Turn down heat, stir through garlic and fry gently for one minute. Remove pan from heat and cool mixture.

Steam or boil the spinach for three minutes. Drain and squeeze out excess liquid. Cool, then finely chop. Place yoghurt, onion mixture and spinach in a bowl. Whisk until smooth. Stir through salt and black pepper to taste.

Serve chilled with khoubiz.

Mains

Fasooliya Green bean stew in its many variations is a staple accompaniment in the Middle East.

Ingredients
5 tbs olive oil
3-4 cloves garlic, coarsely chopped
2 onions, finely chopped
1 tbs ground coriander
3 large tomatoes, skinned and coarsely chopped
1kg green beans, washed and tailed
salt and freshly ground black pepper
juice of 1 lemon

Method
Heat oil in a large heavy-based saucepan, toss in garlic and fry gently for two minutes. Add onion and gently fry until transparent. Add coriander and stir through until the aroma is released. Add tomatoes and a little salt to help release their water and simmer for about 15 minutes, stirring occasionally.

Add beans, black pepper and lemon juice. Stir beans through the tomato sauce, cover saucepan and simmer until beans are cooked. Check seasoning.

Serve hot or cold.

Traditionally, the kibbe are hollowed out and stuffed with minced lamb and pine kernels.

Kibbe Served both raw and cooked, in myriad variations, these meat and bulgur wheat 'balls' are pretty much the national dish of Lebanon.

Traditionally, this dish is prepared entirely by hand, from the grinding of the wheat to the pounding of the lamb, and finally by thoroughly kneading the ingredients to ensure a fine consistency.

In *A New Book of Middle Eastern Food*, Claudia Roden points to the mystique surrounding the preparation of this dish and says that women are 'said to be favoured by the gods if one is born with a long finger', which ensures the easy shaping of kibbe.

The following recipe is a simpler version which can be fried or char-grilled; a mincer or food processor will make your job a lot easier.

Ingredients
1 small onion, finely chopped
salt and freshly ground black pepper
400g minced lamb
1-2 tbs water
250g fine bulgur wheat, washed and drained
oil for frying

To Serve
cos lettuce
olive oil
lemon juice

Method
Mince the onion with salt and pepper.

Pound (or grind) the meat, adding sufficient water until smooth and well blended. Add onion mixture and bulgur and knead (or blend) until combined into a smooth paste.

Mould into round flat discs (approximately 5cm by 1cm) and deep fry until golden. Alternatively char-grill until crisp.

Serve with lettuce drizzled with oil and lemon juice.

Desserts
Mahallabiye This incredibly sweet dessert is common throughout Lebanon.

Ingredients
6 tbs ground rice
1 litre milk
100g sugar
2 tbs rose water

Method
Make a smooth and runny paste with the ground rice and some of the cold milk.

Place the remaining milk and sugar in a heavy-based saucepan and bring to the boil. Gradually add the paste while stirring constantly with a wooden spoon. Reduce heat, simmer and continue to stir mixture until mixture begins to thicken.

Add rose water, cook for one minute, then pour into a serving bowl.

Serve chilled. ■

Patisseries

The cake shops in Lebanon look so tempting with their vast array of cookies and pastries. Most of the pastries are specialities of the region and are unfamiliar to many visitors. All of them are totally delicious and worth trying, even if you don't have a particularly sweet tooth.

To help you choose, here is a quick description, together with the Arabic name, of some of the most popular sweets and some of the lesser known regional specialities.

Asabeeh Rolled filo pastry filled with pistachio, pine and cashew nuts and honey. Otherwise known as 'Lady's Fingers'.

Baklawa Layers of flaky filo pastry with crushed nuts, or sometimes dried fruit, in the centre. Cut into diamonds and soaked with syrup.

Ballawryeh A square slab of chopped pistachio in syrup topped with a layer of 'shredded wheat'.

Barazak Flat, circular cookies sprinkled with sesame seeds. Very crisp and light.

Borma Crushed pine nuts or pistachios wrapped in a sticky coating of shredded pastry and sliced into rounds.

Faysalyeh A triangular-shaped sweet with a filling of pistachio nuts.

Halawet al-jibn A soft, white pancake wrapped around a filling of cream cheese with syrup poured over. A speciality of Tripoli.

Halva Fruit and nuts covered with a sweet sesame paste, made into a slab and cut into squares.

Hriset al-Fustuk Green diamond-shaped pieces of sweetened pistachio paste.

Kanafeh A sort of baked cheesecake served in flat squares with syrup poured over and sometimes cream on top. This is sometimes served in a bread roll and is then called *Kaake Kanafeh*.

Kol wa Shkor Crushed pine nuts or pistachios in syrup, wrapped in filo pastry and soaked in syrup.

Ktayef Small half-moon shaped pastries with a nut paste filling, or sometimes cream cheese.

Maamoul Crisp, white biscuits stuffed with a paste of either pistachio or walnut.

Lebanese sweets. Clockwise from top left: borma, baklawa, maamoul, asabeeh, oush al-bulbul, sewa.

Moon Small squares layered in green and white with ground pistachio and almond.

Nammoura Squares of sweet semolina cake topped with nuts.

Oush al-Bulbul A doughnut-shaped sweet of filo pastry stuffed with a sweet nut paste and topped with chopped pistachio. Also known as 'Bird's Nest'.

Sanioura Pale, crumbly biscuits in an oval shape. Very light and not too sweet. A speciality of Sidon.

Sewa Same as Maamoul but with a date stuffing.

Tamara Small sausage-shaped sweets. White, flecked with chopped nuts and fruit.

Drinks

Nonalcoholic Drinks Lebanese coffee is excellent and always popular. It is made in the Turkish way – strong and served in tiny cups. You can have it *sadah* (without sugar), *wassat* (medium sugar) or *hilweh* (sweet). Tea is not quite as popular and you will have to get used to drinking it without milk. Instant coffee is known by the generic name Nescafé, but is not recommended and it's also expensive.

Fresh fruit juice is excellent and often sold by the side of the road where the vendor will squeeze it to order. Orange juice is the most popular as Lebanon is a major orange growing area, but you can also come across lemon, mango, even strawberry juice drinks. Pomegranate juice is good when in season. Juice bars sometimes also have freshly squeezed vegetable juices such as carrot, which is very refreshing in the heat of summer (not to mention healthy).

Some areas have their own specialities. In Batroun they make the best traditional lemonade, *limonade*, and in Tripoli they have a drink made out of raisins called *jellab*. *Ayran*, a salty yoghurt drink, is sold just about everywhere and is a delicious way of taking extra salt if you are worried about dehydration.

All kinds of foreign-brand soft drinks are also widely available.

Tea and coffee are enjoyed in cafés throughout Lebanon (Photo by Olivier Cirendini)

Alcoholic Drinks All kinds of wines and spirits, both domestic and imported, are easily available throughout Lebanon. Alcohol is cheap – about US$8 for a bottle of whisky and US$5 for a bottle of mid-range domestic wine.

The national drink is *arak*, an aniseed-flavoured drink which is mixed with water and ice, much like the French Pernod or Greek ouzo. It is an acquired taste, and people either love it or loathe it. Either way it has the virtue of being quite cheap (about US$6 a bottle). Good local brands include Ksarak and Le Brun. See also the Arak boxed story in the Bekaa Valley chapter.

Lebanon produces its own wine. Some of the wines produced are very good indeed and all are drinkable. The Ksara and Kefraya wines are well known internationally.

Lebanese beer is quite pleasant. Local brands include Laziza and Almaza, both of which are quite good. There is also Amstel, a Dutch beer brewed locally under licence. All are lager type brews.

Lebanese Wine

In 1906 a cave system which had been used by the Romans was rediscovered by a pack of hounds chasing a fox. The caves are now used as natural wine cellars by the Ksara vineyard. Ksara produces many varieties of wine of which about 50% are red. These are based on the cinsaut and grenache grapes with some of the heavier reds coming from cabernet sauvignon and syrah (shiraz) grapes. The whites are light and fruity and based on sauvignon blanc and chardonnay grapes.

Kefraya is the largest producer of wine in Lebanon, turning out a million bottles a year. They produce an early drinking rosé and a red 'nouveau' – both are easy to drink. The Chateau vintages are far more complex. For example, the Blancs de Blancs with its St Émilion, clairette, bourboulenc and sauvignon grapes have great depth and character with the earthy tang of the Levant.

Chateau Musar is the smallest of the commercial producers with the greatest reputation for quality. Most of its wine is exported (mainly to England) where the owner, Serge Hochar, receives rave reviews. He managed to produce wines throughout the war, even though most of the 1984 harvest, ironically one of the best vintages on record, was destroyed. Even so, a few bottles survive.

Lebanese wine is on the verge of becoming well recognised in the wine markets of the world. The unique soil and climate mean that the wine has less chemicals and a high strength without adding sugar. ■

PETER JOUSIFFE

Getting There & Away

Travel to Lebanon could not be easier these days. There is a growing number of airlines serving Beirut from most parts of the world. Almost all visitors to Lebanon fly into Beirut. The exceptions are people touring more than one country in the region, in which case they often travel on the cheap and frequent buses or taxis from nearby Syria.

However you're travelling, it's worth taking out travel insurance. Work out what you need. You may not want to insure that grotty old army surplus backpack – but everyone should be covered for the worst possible case: an accident, for example, that will require hospital treatment and a flight home. It's a good idea to make a copy of your policy, in case the original is lost. If you are planning to travel for a long time, the insurance may seem very expensive – but if you can't afford it, you certainly won't be able to afford to deal with a medical emergency overseas.

AIR

Air tickets to Lebanon are more expensive in the high season (May to September) and from mid-December until Christmas. At other times of the year, you can make a saving on the price of your ticket.

Airports

Beirut has the only airport in Lebanon, although there is talk of building a second airport near Tripoli in the north of the country. The airport suffered some damage during the civil war, and although some repairs have been made, it badly needs cosmetic surgery. A new terminal is on the list of things to be done, but, in the meantime, facilities are just about OK. Immigration procedures are reasonably straightforward and fast. Customs can be slow if they are searching luggage, but the staff are polite.

The airport is 5km south of the city centre and the runway is alarmingly close to houses in the southern suburbs. For details on getting to and from the airport, see Getting Around in the Beirut chapter.

Airlines

Beirut is rapidly resuming its former standing as a transport hub for the Middle East. Connections to Europe, Africa and Asia are frequent and over 40 airlines now have routes to or via Beirut. The national carrier, Middle East Airlines (MEA), has an extensive network including direct flights to and from Australia, Europe and the Arab world. Many other major airlines service Beirut including Air France, Alitalia, British Airways, British Mediterranean Airways, Emirates, Gulf Air, KLM-Royal Dutch Airlines, Malaysia Airlines, Royal Jordanian Airlines and Turkish Airlines.

Buying Tickets

The air ticket will probably be the single most expensive item in your budget, and buying it can be an intimidating business. There is likely to be a multitude of airlines and travel agents hoping to separate you from your money, and it is always worth putting aside a few hours to research the current state of the market. Start early: some of the cheapest tickets have to be bought months in advance, and some popular flights sell out quickly. Talk to other recent travellers – they may be able to stop you making some of the old mistakes. Look at the ads in newspapers and magazines (not forgetting the press of the ethnic group whose country you plan to visit), consult reference books and watch for special offers. Then phone round some travel agents for the ticket that best suits you. (Airlines can supply information on routes and timetables; however, except at times of inter-airline war, they do not supply the cheapest tickets.) Find out the fare, the route, the duration of the journey and any restrictions on the ticket (see Restrictions in the Air Travel Glossary later in this chapter). Then sit back and decide what is best for you.

You may discover that those unbelievably cheap flights are 'fully booked, but we have another one that costs a bit more', or the flight is on an airline notorious for its poor safety standards and leaves you in the world's least favourite airport in mid-journey for 14 hours. Or the travel agent may claim to have the last two seats available for that country for the whole of July, which they will hold for you for a maximum of two hours. Don't panic – keep ringing around.

Use the fares quoted in this book as a guide only. They are approximate and based on the rates advertised by travel agents at the time of going to press. Quoted airfares do not necessarily constitute a recommendation for the carrier.

If you are travelling from the UK, the USA or Australia, you will probably find that the cheapest flights are being advertised by obscure bucket shops whose names haven't yet reached the telephone directory. Many such firms are honest and solvent, but there are a few rogues who will take your money and disappear, to reopen elsewhere a month or two later under a new name. If you feel suspicious about a firm, don't give them all the money at once – leave a deposit of 20% or so and pay the balance when you get the ticket. If they insist on cash in advance, go somewhere else. And once you have the ticket, ring the airline to confirm that you are actually booked onto the flight.

You may decide to pay more than the rock-bottom fare by opting for the safety of a better known travel agent. Firms such as STA, which has offices worldwide, Council Travel in the USA or Travel CUTS in Canada are not going to disappear overnight, leaving you clutching a receipt for a nonexistent ticket, and they do offer good prices to most destinations.

Once you have your ticket, write its number down, together with the flight number and any other details, and keep the information somewhere separate. If the ticket is lost or stolen, this will help you get a replacement.

It's sensible to buy travel insurance as early as possible. If you buy it the week before you fly, you may find, for example, that you're not covered for delays to your flight caused by industrial action.

Round-the-World Tickets & Circle Pacific Fares Round-the-world (RTW) tickets have become very popular in the last few years. The airline RTW tickets are often real bargains, and can work out to be no more expensive or even cheaper than an ordinary return ticket. Prices start at about UK£850, A$1800 or US$1300.

The official airline RTW tickets are usually put together by a combination of two airlines, and permit you to fly anywhere you want on their route systems so long as you do not backtrack. Other restrictions are that you (usually) must book the first sector in advance and cancellation penalties then apply. There may be restrictions on how many stops you are permitted, and usually the tickets are valid for 90 days up to a year. An alternative type of RTW ticket is one put together by a travel agent using a combination of discounted tickets.

Circle Pacific tickets use a combination of airlines to circle the Pacific – combining Australia, New Zealand, North America and Asia. As with RTW tickets, there are advance purchase restrictions and limits to how many stopovers you can make. These fares are likely to be around 15% cheaper than RTW tickets.

Travellers with Special Needs
If you have special needs of any sort – you've broken a leg, you're vegetarian, travelling in a wheelchair, taking the baby, terrified of flying – you should let the airline know as soon as possible so that they can make arrangements accordingly. You should remind them when you reconfirm your booking (at least 72 hours before departure) and again when you check in at the airport. It may also be worth ringing round the airlines before you make your booking to find out how they can handle your particular needs.

Air Travel Glossary

Apex Apex, or 'advance purchase excursion', is a discounted ticket which must be paid for in advance. There are penalties if you wish to change it.

Baggage Allowance This will be written on your ticket: usually one 20kg item to go in the hold, plus one item of hand luggage.

Bucket Shop An unbonded travel agency specialising in discounted airline tickets.

Bumped Just because you have a confirmed seat doesn't mean you're going to get on the plane – see Overbooking.

Cancellation Penalties If you have to cancel or change an Apex ticket, there are often heavy penalties involved. Insurance can sometimes be taken out against these penalties. Some airlines impose penalties on regular tickets as well, particularly against 'no-show' passengers.

Check-In Airlines ask you to check in a certain time ahead of the flight departure (usually 1½ hours on international flights). If you fail to check in on time and the flight is overbooked, the airline can cancel your booking and give your seat to somebody else.

Confirmation Having a ticket written out with the flight and date you want doesn't mean you have a seat until the agent has checked with the airline that your status is 'OK' or confirmed. Meanwhile you could just be 'on request'.

Discounted Tickets There are two types of discounted fares – officially discounted (see Promotional Fares) and unofficially discounted. The lowest prices often impose drawbacks like flying with unpopular airlines, inconvenient schedules, or unpleasant routes and connections. A discounted ticket can save you other things than money – you may be able to pay Apex prices without the associated Apex advance booking and other requirements. Discounted tickets only exist where there is fierce competition.

Full Fares Airlines traditionally offer 1st class (coded F), business class (coded J) and economy class (coded Y) tickets. These days there are so many promotional and discounted fares available from the regular economy class that few passengers pay full economy fare.

Lost Tickets If you lose your airline ticket, an airline will usually treat it like a travellers' cheque and, after enquiries, issue you with another one. Legally, however, an airline is entitled to treat it like cash and if you lose it, then it's gone forever. Take good care of your tickets.

No-Shows No-shows are passengers who fail to show up for their flight, sometimes due to unexpected delays or disasters, sometimes due to simply forgetting, sometimes because they made more than one booking and didn't bother to cancel the one they didn't want. Full-fare passengers who fail to turn up are sometimes entitled to travel on a later flight. The rest of us are penalised (see Cancellation Penalties).

On Request An unconfirmed booking for a flight, see Confirmation.

Open Jaws A return ticket where you fly out to one place but return from another. If available, this can save you backtracking to your arrival point.

Airports and airlines can be surprisingly helpful, but they do need advance warning. Most international airports will provide escorts from check-in desk to plane when needed, and there should be ramps, lifts, accessible toilets and reachable phones. Aircraft toilets, on the other hand, are likely to present a problem; travellers should discuss this with the airline at an early stage and, if necessary, with their doctor.

Guide dogs for the blind will often have to travel in specially pressurised baggage compartment with other animals, away from their owner; although smaller guide dogs may be admitted to the cabin. All guide dogs will be subject to the same quarantine laws (six months in isolation etc) as any other animal when entering or returning to countries currently free of rabies, such as Britain or Australia.

Deaf travellers can ask for airport and in-flight announcements to be written down for them.

Children under two travel for 10% of the standard fare (or free, on some airlines), as long as they don't occupy a seat. They don't get a baggage allowance either. 'Skycots' should be provided by the airline if requested in advance; these will take a child weighing up to about 10kg. Children aged between two and 12 can usually occupy a seat for half to two-thirds of the full fare, and do get a baggage allowance. Push chairs can often be taken as hand luggage.

Overbooking Airlines hate to fly empty seats and since every flight has some passengers who fail to show up (see No-Shows) airlines often book more passengers than they have seats. Usually the excess passengers balance those who fail to show up, but occasionally somebody gets bumped. If this happens, guess who it is most likely to be? The passengers who check in late.

Promotional Fares Officially discounted fares, like Apex fares, which are available from travel agents or direct from the airline.

Reconfirmation At least 72 hours prior to departure time of an onward or return flight you must contact the airline and 'reconfirm' that you intend to be on the flight. If you don't do this, the airline can delete your name from the passenger list and you could lose your seat. You don't have to reconfirm the first flight n your itinerary or if your stopover is less than 72 hours. It doesn't hurt to reconfirm more than once.

Restrictions Discounted tickets often have various restrictions on them – advance purchase is the most usual one (see Apex). Others are restrictions on the minimum and maximum period you must be away, such as a minimum of 14 days or a maximum of one year. See Cancellation Penalties.

Stand-by A discounted ticket where you only fly if there is a seat free at the last moment. Stand-by fares are usually only available on domestic routes.

Tickets Out An entry requirement for many countries is that you have an onward or return ticket, in other words, a ticket out of the country. If you're not sure what you intend to do next, the easiest solution is to buy the cheapest onward ticket to a neighbouring country or a ticket from a reliable airline which can later be refunded if you do not use it.

Transferred Tickets Airline tickets cannot be transferred from one person to another. Travellers sometimes try to sell the return half of their ticket, but officials can ask you to prove that you are the person named on the ticket. This is unlikely to happen on domestic flights, but on an international flight, tickets may be compared with passports.

Travel Agencies Travel agencies vary widely and you should ensure that you use one that suits your needs. Some simply handle tours while full-service agencies handle everything from tours and tickets to car rental and hotel bookings. A good one will do all these things and can save you a lot of money, but if all you want is a ticket at the lowest possible price, then you really need an agency specialising in discounted tickets. A discounted ticket agency, however, may not be useful for other things, like hotel bookings.

Travel Periods Some officially discounted fares, Apex fares in particular, vary with the time of year. There is often a low (off-peak) season and a high (peak) season. Sometimes there's an intermediate or shoulder season as well. At peak times, when everyone wants to fly, not only will the officially discounted fares be higher, but so will unofficially discounted fares or there may simply be no discounted tickets available. Usually the fare depends on your outward flight – if you depart in the high season and return in the low season, you pay the high-season fare. ■

The USA & Canada

The *New York Times*, the *LA Times*, the *Chicago Tribune* and the *San Francisco Examiner* all produce weekly travel sections in which you'll find any number of travel agents' ads. Council Travel (☎ 800 226 8624) and STA Travel (☎ 800 777 0112) have offices in major cities nationwide.

The magazine *Travel Unlimited* (PO Box 1058, Allston, Mass 02134) publishes details of the cheapest air fares and courier possibilities for destinations all over the world from the USA.

In Canada, Travel CUTS has offices in all major cities. The *Toronto Globe & Mail* and the *Vancouver Sun* carry travel agents' ads. The magazine *Great Expeditions* (PO Box 8000-411, Abbotsford BC V2S 6H1) is also useful.

MEA flies from Montreal in Canada to Beirut for about US$1300 in the low season and US$1430 in high season (return). There are also flights from Toronto.

There are no direct flights from the USA at the time of writing, although this situation is likely to change now the US travel ban imposed in the mid-1980s has been lifted. A recommended route is with Royal Jordanian Airlines to Amman, and then picking up any of the frequent connections to Beirut.

Alternatively travellers could take advantage of the ludicrously low transatlantic fares and pick up an onward ticket to Lebanon in London or Paris.

Australia & New Zealand

STA Travel and Flight Centres International are major dealers in cheap air fares from Australia and New Zealand. Check the travel agents' ads in the Yellow Pages and ring around.

Emirates, Gulf Air, Malaysia Airlines and MEA fly from Australia to Lebanon. The return fares direct from Sydney/Melbourne to Beirut are from A$1450/1800 in low/high season. Emirates and Gulf Air have three flights a week while MEA and Malaysia Airlines have one flight a week.

There are no direct flights from New Zealand to Beirut. Travellers would be advised to either connect from Australia or from one of the main Middle Eastern cities, such as Dubai.

The UK

There are three carriers which have direct flights from London to Beirut – British Mediterranean, MEA and, more recently, British Airways. It is difficult to track down really cheap discounted fares on these airlines; return fares start at around UK£249 in the low season and UK£429 in the high season (higher on British Airways). Lower fares are available if you don't fly direct. For example, Olympic Airways flies via Athens for about UK£321 return. Air France does a cheap fare via Paris for UK£269, but the dates are restricted. The best deal at the time of writing was with Turkish Airlines via Istanbul for the bargain price of UK£230. Sadly, stopovers and travel between 15 June and 15 August are not included.

One of the cheapest deals to Beirut (or anywhere else for that matter) is with the Romanian carrier, TAROM, flying via Bucharest. This is a notoriously shambolic airline when it comes to honouring reservations on the connecting flight and the waiting time at Bucharest can be lengthy and not very comfortable – so be warned!

The best way to check out all the possibilities is to consult a travel agent who specialises in discount tickets, such as STA Travel (☎ (0171) 937 9921) at 86 Old Brompton Rd, London SW7 3LQ and 117 Euston Rd, London NW1 2SX, or Trailfinders (☎ (0171) 938 3366) at 194 Kensington High St, London W8 7RG. Their staff are very helpful and can offer you all the possible routes and prices. Council Travel (☎ (0171) 437 7767) also has an office at 28a Poland St, London W1.

Other sources of flight information are the freebie magazines such as *Southern Cross* and *TNT* which carry lots of ads for bucket shops. Also it's worth looking at the travel ads in the Sunday broadsheets, *Time Out* and the *London Evening Standard*. The magazine *Business Traveller* also has good advice on air fare bargains.

The Globetrotters Club (BCM Roving, London WC1N 3XX) publishes a newsletter called *Globe*, which covers obscure destinations and can help in finding travelling companions.

Most British travel agents are registered with the Association of British Travel Agents (ABTA). If you have paid for your flight to an ABTA-registered agent who then goes out of business, ABTA will guarantee a refund or an alternative. Unregistered bucket shops are riskier, but sometimes cheaper.

Continental Europe

Virtually all the capitals of Europe have direct flights to Beirut, either with MEA or the country's own national carrier. If you have a choice of departure city, the cheapest deals can be found in Athens, Istanbul, Berlin and Amsterdam. The most frequent flights are from Paris where there are at least two flights on most days.

Air France flies once a day from Paris to Beirut with return fares from US$572/681 in the low/high season. From Amsterdam there are four services a week with return fares from US$478/529 (low/high season) flying KLM-Royal Dutch Airlines. MEA has four services a week from Frankfurt with return fares from US$551/609 (low/high season). Turkish Airlines and MEA both have three services a week from Istanbul with return fares from US$332/365 (low/high season). Alitalia has five services a week from Rome, and MEA has two, with return fares from US$623/690 (low/high season). The short hop from Larnaca in Cyprus with either MEA or Cyprus Airways (both have four services a week) will cost you from US$210 return.

If you shop around and check out the bucket shops, you will probably find a much better deal. Airlines often have seasonal special fares, but avoid the lead-up to Christmas as flights to Beirut are very full at this time and airlines tend to charge full fare.

Some of the best fares from Europe are offered by the student travel agencies, such as NBBS Reiswinkels (☎ (020) 624 09 89), Roskin 38, Amsterdam, and Acotra (☎ 5127078), Rue de la Madeleine 51, 1000 Brussels. Their fares are comparable with those from London bucket shops. Outlets in other main transport hubs include CTS Voyages (☎ 01 25 00 76), 20 Rue des Carmes, Paris; SRID Reisen (☎ (069) 430 191), Bergerstr 118, Frankfurt; and ISYTS (☎ 322 1267), 2nd Floor, 11 Odos Nikis, Syntagma, Athens.

The Middle East

Beirut is well connected to other Middle Eastern cities. Syrian Arab Airlines and MEA both have one service a week from Damascus to Beirut with a round trip costing from US$65. Both Royal Jordanian Airlines and MEA fly daily from Amman with return fares from US$162. EgyptAir and MEA both have six flights per week from Cairo with fares from US$226 return. If you are coming from the Gulf, Emirates, Gulf Air and MEA fly daily from Dubai or Abu Dhabi and fares are US$454 one way and US$629 return. Again, it pays to shop around the airlines as the prices can vary.

LAND

The only land borders open to Lebanon at the moment are those with Syria. The southern border with Israel has been closed for many years and will remain so until a peace accord is signed – a process which is set to take some time. You cannot get a visa to enter Lebanon in Syria nor in Lebanon to enter Syria, and only some nationalities can get one at the Syria-Lebanon border, so make sure you have a visa before you arrive at the border. For more details, see under Visas in the Facts for the Visitor chapter.

Syria

Bus There are buses running between Beirut and Damascus every day at roughly two hour intervals, except for the first bus which starts at 7.30 am. Buses to Aleppo (ask for Halab) leave at 1½ hour intervals, but begin at 8 am. The journey to Damascus takes three hours and to Aleppo, seven hours. These are the drive times and don't take into account the border crossings which can vary depending on how heavy the traffic is. Unless there is a horrendous queue at the frontier, expect the process to take half an hour. See the Getting There & Away section in the Beirut chapter for more information.

Other bus services and service taxis go from Tripoli to Lattakia and Homs and from Beirut to Damascus, Homs and Aleppo. You would need to change buses to get to Turkey or Jordan.

The buses are not super luxurious, but they are clean and have allocated (numbered) seats. It is a good idea to book your seat the day before, if possible, as the buses can be full.

The place to catch the buses in Beirut is at the Cola taxi stand on the east side of the overpass. There is a small office which sells tickets to Syria near the place where the buses are parked.

If you are coming from Syria, the main Karnak bus station is about a 15-minute walk to the west of Martyrs Square in Damascus, although not all the buses running this route are Karnak buses. These are the Syrian-owned (government) buses and are usually more comfortable than the privately run services, although the fares are higher. The prices quoted in the table are for the privately operated buses.

From Aleppo, the buses leave from the bus station tucked away just behind Baron St, not two minutes from the Baron Hotel. Again the services to Beirut are mainly privately operated buses.

Fares	
Bus	
Beirut – Aleppo	LL 12,000
Beirut – Damascus	LL 6500
Beirut – Lattakia	LL 9500
Tripoli – Homs	LL 4000
Beirut – Ankara	US$30
Beirut – Istanbul	US$35
Service Taxi	
Beirut – Aleppo	LL 20,000
Beirut – Damascus	LL 20,000
Baalbek – Damascus/Homs	LL 8000
Tripoli – Homs	LL 7000
Beirut – Amman	LL 35,000

Taxi If you prefer to take a taxi, either service or private, they all leave from the Cola taxi stand in Beirut. The fares are similar to the buses and service taxis leave when full. There is seldom a wait of more than 20 minutes for a taxi to fill up. Private and service taxis go to and from Damascus, where you can change to go on to Jordan. A private taxi from Beirut and Damascus costs about US$50.

Car If you are bringing a foreign-registered vehicle into Lebanon, there is a hefty charge levied at the border (refundable when you leave). This is calculated on a sliding scale depending on the value of the vehicle. Unless you have large amounts of cash to leave as a deposit, this ruling effectively makes it unfeasible to bring your own car into Lebanon. A better plan would be to arrive by bus or service taxi and then rent a car locally.

If you do decide to drive into Lebanon, you will need an International Driving Permit (IDP), the vehicle's registration papers and liability insurance. Take a good supply of spares with you, although it is possible to service most common makes of vehicle in Lebanon. Petrol is available in the usual range of octanes and lead-free is sold at most petrol stations. See the Car & Motorcycle section in the Getting Around chapter for details of driving in Lebanon.

Bicycle Cycling is a cheap, convenient, healthy, environmentally sound and, above all, fun way of travelling.

You can bring your bicycle by air. If you want to avoid the hassle of taking it to pieces and packing it in a bag, check with the airline first; often they allow bicycles to be checked in with just the pedals removed and the handlebar turned sideways. See also the Bicycle section in the Getting Around chapter.

SEA
Ferry
The once regular ferry service between Larnaca in Cyprus and the Jounieh port, just north of Beirut, has been suspended due to blockading by the Israeli navy. There are no immediate plans to resume the service. When operational the trip takes 10 hours and costs about US$180 return. Enquire at the main travel agencies in Beirut and Larnaca for up-to-date information.

Yacht
There are several marina developments along the coast of Lebanon, both in Beirut and north of the city, and it is possible to arrive by private yacht. It is not advisable to arrive without advice from an experienced sailor who has knowledge of Lebanese waters.

It is definitely not safe to attempt to navigate into the southern ports. People on boats sailing in and out of Tyre report being fired on by Israeli gunboats, so the area is definitely to be avoided.

DEPARTURE TAX
There is a three-tier departure tax when leaving from Beirut international airport; LL 50,000 for economy passengers, LL 75,000 for business and LL 100,000 for 1st-class passengers.

There is no departure tax at land borders.

ORGANISED TOURS
Lebanon is picking up as a package tour destination and a number of tour operators now run either combined Syria and Lebanon or Lebanon-only tours. These tend to be at the upper end of the price range and concen-

trate on the cultural aspects of the country. Generally speaking the itineraries are a bit rushed, not allowing much time in each place, but if your time is short and your purse long, then they may be what you're looking for. They will take in the main attractions of Baalbek and Byblos and tend to be based at hotels in Beirut. The following British tour operators run tours to Lebanon:

Voyages Jules Verne, 21 Dorset Square, London NW1 6QG (☎ (0171) 723 5066), is a top class (and top price) tour operator. It offers a short five-day tour called 'From Baalbeck to Byblos', which is based in Beirut and costs from UK£595.

Prospect Art & Music Tours, 454-458 Chiswick High Rd, London W4 5TT (☎ (0181) 995 2151), does a five-day tour of Lebanon from UK£850 and an eight-day tour for UK£1175.

Cox & Kings, St James Court, 45 Buckingham Gate, London SW1E 6AF (☎ (0171) 873 5003), is also at the upper end of the market. It offers a 15-day 'Grand Tour of the Middle East', which includes Jordan, Syria and Lebanon. Prices start at UK£1735. It also runs a short five-day tour of Lebanon from UK£695.

Jasmin Tours, High St, Cookham, Maidenhead, Berks SL6 9SQ (☎ (01628) 531121), has specialised in tours to the Middle East for a long time. It has a combined 10-day Lebanon/Syria tour for UK£1172 and a nine-day 'Lebanon Express' tour starting at UK£799.

Other tour operators who go to Lebanon include: Bales Tours (☎ (01306) 885923) at Bales House, Junction Rd, Dorking, Surrey RH4 3HL; Swan Hellenic Tours (☎ (0171) 800 2300) at 77 New Oxford St, London WC1A 1PP; and British Museum Tours (☎ (0171) 323 8895) at 46 Bloomsbury St, London WC1.

The following French tour operators run tours to Lebanon:

Clio, 34 Rue du Hameau, 75015 Paris (☎ 01 53 68 82 82), runs specialised cultural tours of Lebanon for groups of 15 and 23 people. It offers a seven-day tour of Lebanon's major cities and sights for 8450FF.

Djos' Air Voyages, Le Bonaparte 20, CAPN, 93153 Le Blanc Mesnil Cedex (☎ 0800 48 19 71, 01 48 67 15 60), has an eight-day tour to northern Lebanon for 8350FF.

Intermèdes Art et Voyages, 60 Rue La Boétie, 75008 Paris (☎ 01 45 61 90 90), offers combined tours to Lebanon, Syria and Jordan. A 14-day tour, with four days in Lebanon, costs from 15,800FF.

Voyageurs au Proche-Orient, 55 Rue Sainte-Anne, 75002 Paris (☎ 01 42 86 17 90), runs private tours to Lebanon for between 7800FF and 9270FF for seven days. The price includes a private car with driver (no guide) and breakfast only.

Clio also has offices at 128 Rue Bossuet, 69009 Lyon (☎ 04 78 52 61 42), 45 Rue de la Paix, 13001 Marseille (☎ 04 91 54 02 13) and at 11 Rue du Mont-Blanc, 1201 Geneva, Switzerland (☎ (022) 731 70 26).

There are no tour operators in Australia and New Zealand which offer tours to Lebanon. Some specialised travel agents can organise tours with Lebanese-based operators out of Beirut. If you want to book a tour when you arrive in Lebanon, there are a number of good local tour operators in Beirut who can arrange a variety of itineraries. See Organised Tours in the Getting Around chapter for further details.

WARNING

The information in this chapter is particularly vulnerable to change: prices for international travel are volatile, routes are introduced and cancelled, schedules change, special deals come and go, and rules and visa requirements are amended. Airlines and governments seem to take a perverse pleasure in making price structures and regulations as complicated as possible. You should check directly with the airline or a travel agent to make sure you understand how a fare (and ticket you may buy) works. In addition, the travel industry is highly competitive and there are many lurks and perks.

The upshot of this is that you should get opinions, quotes and advice from as many airlines and travel agents as possible before you part with your hard-earned cash. The details given in this chapter should be regarded as pointers and are not a substitute for your own careful, up-to-date research.

Getting Around

Lebanon is a tiny country, and although there are no internal air services, you don't really need them. You can drive from one end of the country to the other in about three hours. Most people use service taxis – a huge number of which run on set routes around the country – to get around. In addition, there are many 'pirate taxis' cruising for fares. It is easy to get around, although you may have to catch more than one 'servees' to get where you want to go.

There have been efforts recently to resume bus services in Lebanon. A private company runs a network of routes throughout Beirut and the outlying areas. There are a few buses which run to Tripoli and Sidon, but few other routes. There are plans to restore an inter-city bus service.

BUS

Buses travel between Beirut and the major towns in Lebanon, but they often have only one or two departures a day and there are no timetables. There are two makeshift bus stations in Beirut: one outside the National Museum for buses travelling to destinations north of Beirut; the other at the Cola taxi stand (sometimes called Mazraa) for destinations south of Beirut. You can also catch buses from Dawra, east of Beirut.

The buses usually have the destination displayed on the front window or above it in Arabic only. You pay the fare on board.

The buses are all run by private companies as the government has not yet restored a nationwide bus service.

TRAIN

Before the war there was a railway network in Lebanon, even though it was reported to be slow and inefficient. The tracks can still be seen here and there, but now it looks increasingly unlikely that the railway will be restored. After such a long time of disuse, some of the tracks have been pulled up or even built over (planning permission went

by the board during the war). The old rolling stock is rusting away in a siding in Tripoli.

Fares

Bus

Beirut – Sidon	LL 1750
Beirut – Tyre (change at Sidon)	LL 2500
Beirut – Tripoli	LL 2000
Beirut – Byblos	LL 500

Service Taxi

Around Beirut	LL 1000
Beirut – Baalbek	LL 8000
Beirut – Beiteddine	LL 4000
Beirut – Byblos	LL 4000
Beirut – Jounieh	LL 4000
Beirut – Sidon	LL 2500
Beirut – Tripoli	LL 5000
Beirut – Tyre	LL 5000
Sidon – Tyre	LL 3000
Tripoli – Bcharré	LL 6000
Tripoli – The Cedars	LL 10,000

TAXI & SERVICE TAXI

Virtually the entire road communications network of Lebanon relies on the vast numbers of Mercedes taxis working the city and long-distance routes. Taxis are recognisable by their red number plates and, on some cars, a white sign with 'TAXI' written on it in red letters. It is unusual to wait more than two minutes by any road before a taxi turns up. There are two systems; private taxis and service taxis. The snag is that they are one and the same animal. It is important to state that you want a service taxi when you get in (especially if there are no other passengers), otherwise the driver may assume you want a private taxi and charge you accordingly.

The rule of thumb is that a service taxi takes five passengers and if you want a private taxi, the fare should be five times the service fare. In central Beirut the fare for any route in a service taxi is LL 1000. A private taxi will charge from LL 5000 for a short journey to LL 10,000 for a long trip. Beware of taxi drivers who try to bump up the prices – some are honest, but others will try and charge you whatever they think they'll get away with. Taxis from the airport are notorious for this, often charging US$25 or US$30 for the 20-minute ride into town. You can stop or be let out at any point on a service taxi's preset route. Just say *indak* (here) to the driver.

If you have a lot of sightseeing to do in out of the way places, you can hire a taxi and driver by the day. Haggling skills come to the fore here, but expect to pay at least US$80 per day plus tip.

You can order taxis by telephone from a number of private companies; they will take you anywhere in Lebanon and some also have services to Syria and Jordan. See the Taxi section in the Beirut chapter for contact numbers.

CAR & MOTORCYCLE

If there are a few people travelling together, it might be a good idea to hire a car. It certainly gives you the freedom to travel at your own pace and explore out of the way places. A word of warning – driving in Lebanon is not for the novice or the faint-hearted. The coast and city roads are very busy and the mountain roads are hair-raising.

If you decide to drive, petrol and diesel fuel are easily available and quite cheap. You will need an International Driving Licence (IDP) and insurance can be arranged by the rental company. See also the Land section in the Getting There & Away chapter.

Road Rules

The road rules in Lebanon can be summed up in one word – anarchy. In theory, the driving is on the right-hand side of the road, but don't always bet on it. In Beirut the horn is used as substitute for the brake and parking on the pavements is mandatory. This causes another hazard – pedestrians who walk in the middle of the road. Luckily the traffic jams are so bad that at least the cars aren't usually speeding. You will have to learn to nose out

into a stream of oncoming traffic if you do not want to get stuck at an intersection all day. When driving in the mountains, there are many blind hairpin bends – use your horn and take it slowly. It is not unusual to see cars overtaking on these blind corners.

If you are determined to drive in Lebanon, take great care. There is no speed limit. Another thing to watch out for is military checkpoints which occur at frequent intervals. Keep your eyes open for them and *never* drive past without being waved on, even if the person on the checkpoint does not appear to be taking much notice of you.

Rental

Cars can easily be rented in Lebanon but the prices, like everything else in the country, are a bit on the steep side. If there are three or four of you, it becomes much more feasible. Most of the big rental agencies are in Beirut, although a few can be found in other cities. If you shop around, you can probably find a modest saloon car for between US$40 and US$50 per day with unlimited km. A more luxurious model (Mercedes, for example) will be more like US$200 per day. If you want a local driver, it will set you back an additional US$50 per day.

Following is a list of rental companies and a sample of their prices.

Avis (☎ (01) 398850, 861614). Its cheapest car is a Fiat Uno, which costs US$40 per day. A Jeep Cherokee 4WD costs US$180 per day. Both cars include unlimited mileage after one week rental.
Europcar (☎ (01) 480480, 363636). The cheapest car is a Hyundai which costs US$30 per day. After three days of rental or 150km the price includes unlimited mileage.
Hertz (☎ (01) 423244, 427283). The cheapest car is an Opel Corsa for US$40 per day. The price includes unlimited mileage after one day's rental.
Prestige (☎ (01) 866328). It charges US$19 per day for a Tico, US$25 for a Kia, US$35 for a Hyundai and US$45 for a Nissan Maxima. All prices include unlimited mileage.

All companies require a refundable deposit except from credit card holders, and offer free delivery and collection during working hours. The minimum age for drivers is 21 years. At the time of writing you could not take hire cars over the border into Syria.

BICYCLE

If you are bringing a bicycle to Lebanon, make sure it is suitable for the road conditions – and that you are fit enough to ride it! The terrain is extremely steep once you leave the coastal strip and really only a mountain bike would be feasible. The traffic problems described earlier will also present a hazard to the cyclist and extreme care should be taken when riding anywhere in Lebanon. With that said, the scenery is beautiful and the air in the mountains clear, although it would be best to avoid the very hot months which could cause heat exhaustion if you are not careful.

Be sure to service your bike thoroughly before you leave home. Always carry a repair kit and suitable spare parts with you as repair shops in Lebanon are extremely thin on the ground. See also under Bicycle in the Getting There & Away chapter.

HITCHING

Hitching is never entirely safe in any country in the world, and we don't recommend it. Travellers who decide to hitch should understand that they are taking a small but potentially serious risk. However many people do choose to hitch, and the advice that follows should help to make the journey as fast and as safe as possible.

Hitching is not very common in Lebanon – the tourists who are venturing back tend to be chauffeured around in air-conditioned buses. This may be to your advantage if you decide to try hitching a lift. The novelty of visiting foreigners increases your chances of a lift – it helps if you *look* foreign. Lebanese people are very sociable and love the chance to chat with foreign visitors. The usual precautions apply though; *never* hitch alone if you are a woman, and even two women travelling together could attract the wrong sort of attention.

With the habit of private cars turning into taxis at will, there is a chance that the driver will expect payment. There does not seem to be a very polite way out of this situation, except to ask first if the driver is going to charge you for the ride.

WALKING

Hiking can be very rewarding once you get slightly off the beaten track. The terrain varies from moderately easy to quite tough once you get up into the mountains. You will certainly need a good pair of boots if you are intending to do anything more adventurous than a Sunday stroll.

In the city exploring on foot is not only more interesting but, given the traffic jams, probably quicker as well. Because of the immense number of construction sites in Beirut, it is a good idea to wear an old sensible pair of shoes for walking around (they will get filthy) and a clean pair in your bag to change into if you are going anywhere remotely smart.

LOCAL TRANSPORT
Bus

Beirut now has a reasonable bus service operated by the Lebanese Commuting Company. It operates a hail and ride system. Short hops cost LL 250 and longer journeys LL 500. For route details, see the Getting Around section in the Beirut chapter.

Taxi

Apart from hailing a taxi on the street, you can telephone one of several private hire firms (see the Beirut chapter). It is a good idea to establish the price on the telephone beforehand.

ORGANISED TOURS

Local tour operators offer a variety of tours – mostly one-day excursions starting and ending in Beirut. The prices are reasonable and usually include lunch. There are some longer tours available which include Syria and/or Jordan. All tours are by air-conditioned coaches. The main tour operators include:

Nakhal & Cie

Ghorayeb Building, Rue Sami al-Solh (☎ (01) 389507/8; fax 422302).

Their local tours cover Aanjar, Baalbek, Beiteddine, Byblos, the Cedars, Sidon, Tripoli and Tyre. They also organise tours from Lebanon to different places of interest in Syria including Damascus, the Crac des Chevaliers, Palmyra, Aleppo, Hama and others.

Rida Travel

(☎ (01) 640903, 643341; fax 630537; email ridatour@bignet.com.lb).

Rida organises one-day tours to the Casino du Liban, the Chouf Mountains, Ksara Winery, Baalbek, the Cedars and Faraya ski resorts, Nahr al-Kalb, Jeita Grotto, Harissa, Byblos, Bcharré and Tripoli. Prices range from US$20 to US$60 per person. Meals and drinks are not included in the price.

Tania Travel

Rue Sidani, opposite Jeanne d'Arc theatre (☎ (01) 739679, 739682/3/4; fax 340473; email taniatv@dm.net.lb; web site http://members.aol.com/TaniaTravl/main.html).

They have tours to Aanjar, Baalbek, Bcharré, Beiteddine, Byblos, the Cedars, Deir al-Qamar, Sidon, Tyre and one-day trips to Damascus.

Tour Vacances

(☎ (01) 424509, 426672).

A consortium of four tour operators that, in addition to the local sightseeing trips and tours to Syria and Jordan, offers three-day package deals starting from US$118/173 per person in singles/doubles. The price includes transfer to and from the airport, two nights in a Beirut hotel with breakfast, transfer to/from the Faraya ski resort and four nights in a Faraya hotel with breakfast. Additional nights are available for a longer stay.

Beirut

Beirut is the vibrant, battered capital city of Lebanon. Once the Paris of the Middle East and a magnet for the jet set from both east and west, it is now in a recovery phase after the terrible damage inflicted during the long civil war.

During the war, the notorious 'Green Line' divided the east and the west of the city into the Christian and Muslim halves respectively, and even today, the division still unofficially stands. The centre of the city – the Downtown district – was almost totally destroyed, creating a further geographical division between east and west. Nearly all the tourist attractions, night life and cheaper hotels are in west Beirut, which is livelier than the east of the city. The overwhelming impression is one of traffic, noise, bustle and more traffic. Everywhere you look, there are buildings going up or coming down and car horns honking. Beirut is definitely not the place to go for a quiet rest.

If you are a first time visitor to Beirut, be prepared for a shock at the extent of the war damage. Buildings near the Green Line are so peppered with bullet holes that they look like old lace. Even more shocking is that people are often still living in these perilous buildings having made their own makeshift repairs.

In the absence of state assistance, people are having to be resourceful and self-sufficient. Renovation is going on at such a pace, though, that it's not unusual to see an exclusive designer boutique or an expensive restaurant in a street of otherwise bombed-out buildings. The architectural style is diverse with beautiful traditional buildings jostling for space with the kind of breeze-block horrors that pass for architecture in the Mediterranean.

Beirut today has grown from a small, walled city in the mid-19th century with less than 100,000 people to a sprawling metropolis of about 1.5 million people. Despite its recent hardships, the people of Beirut are

HIGHLIGHTS

ANN JOUSIFFE

- Wander along the Corniche road – a favourite fishing spot for many Beirutis (above)
- Grab a table, order a few mezze and wait for the sun to set over the Pigeon Rocks
- Explore the grounds of the AUB campus and visit the university's impressive archaeological museum
- Walk through the Hamra district and savour the cosmopolitan sights of this rapidly changing city
- See the extensive plans for the redevelopment of the Downtown area and watch the work progress
- Imagine Fairouz singing to 40,000 fans at the end of the civil war in the Place des Martyrs
- Soak up the local atmosphere, and maybe win some cash, at the city's racecourse
- Visit the east Beirut site where St George is supposed to have slain the dragon

friendly and outgoing. After the cease-fire in 1991, the mood of caution has given way to a spirit of enterprise and renewed optimism for the future. Tourism is very much seen as part of the recovery and foreign visitors are made to feel very welcome, although independent travellers are still a bit thin on the ground.

HISTORY

The earliest traces of habitation date from the Stone Age when the area, now occupied by the city, was in fact two islands in the delta of the Beirut River. Later, when the river silted up, the area became one landmass. It seems likely that the area has been continuously occupied throughout prehistory. Its location is favourable with fresh water and abundant fish from the sea.

According to tradition, the first city was founded by the people of Byblos. The first historical reference to Beirut dates from the 15th century BC, when it is mentioned in a tablet with cuneiform script discovered at Tell al-Amarna in Egypt – but the city is older than that. Between Martyrs Square and the sea port, a Canaanite site has been uncovered dating from 1900 BC. This Bronze Age city has an entrance gate of dressed stone. Nearby are the remains of Phoenician canals with sloping sides. The Phoenicians had reused the Canaanite stones as well as smooth, round stones brought from the Beirut River.

New light on the obscure origins of this city may be shed by the excavations now underway in the Downtown district – the site of the original city. Large areas have had to be bulldozed in order to redevelop the centre of the city, giving archaeologists a unique opportunity to dig beneath the accumulated strata. From finds already uncovered, it is clear that the city was larger and more significant than had been previously thought, but deep excavations may be hampered by the time limit set for the rebuilding of the area.

The original name of the city seems to have been variously Birut, Birrayyuna or Birrayat, which suggests that it was named after a well or wells (modern Arabic still uses

the word *bir* for well). On the other hand, according to Philo in his History, Birut was the first queen of the city – all of Beirut's records of this time are buried deep and may never see the light of day.

Beirut was conquered by Agrippa in 64 BC and the city was renamed in honour of the emperor's daughter, Julia – its full name became Colonia Julia Augusta Felix Berytus. The veterans of two Roman legions were established in the city: the 5th Macedonian and the 3rd Gallic. The city quickly became 'Romanised'; large public buildings and monuments were erected and Berytus enjoyed full status as a part of the empire.

In the 3rd century AD the city entered a period of fame and prestige founded on its School of Law which rivalled those in Athens, Alexandria and Caesarea. This fame lasted for about 200 years and, up until the end of the 4th century, it was still one of the most important cities in Phoenicia. In the middle of the 5th century, there was a series of devastating earthquakes and tidal waves, the last of which, in 551 AD, almost totally destroyed the city. The death toll was high: 30,000 were people killed in Berytus alone and, along the Phoenician coast, the total number of casualties was close to 250,000. The School of Law was evacuated and moved to Sidon in the south. This calamity marked the decline of the city for centuries to come.

When the Arabs came in 635 AD, they took the city without much of a struggle. Their rule was uninterrupted until the Crusaders brought Beirut briefly back into the history books.

In 1110 AD, after a siege, the city fell into the hands of Baldwin I of Boulogne and a Latin bishopric was established. It remained in Crusader hands for 77 years during which time the Crusaders built the church of St John the Baptist of the Knights Hospitallers on the site of an ancient temple. In 1187 Saladin managed to wrest the city back into Muslim hands. This state of affairs lasted only six years before Amoury, King of Cyprus, besieged the city once again and the Muslim forces fled.

Under the rule of Jean I of Ibelin, the city's influence grew and spread throughout the Latin East, but the Crusaders lost the city again, this time for good, in July 1291 when the Muslim Mamelukes took possession.

There were periodic attempts to invade the city during the following centuries. In the 14th century, the Franks made a number of assaults but without result. In the 15th century the Franks returned, peacefully this time, as traders.

Beirut continued under the Mamelukes until they were ousted from the city by the Ottoman army in 1516. Now part of the powerful Ottoman Empire, the city was granted semiautonomy in return for taxes paid to the sultan. The local emirs had free rein, so long as the money flowed into the coffers of the Sublime Porte. One of the emirs, Fakhr ad-Din, established what was in effect an independent kingdom for himself and made Beirut his favourite residence.

Fakhr ad-Din's keen business sense led him to trade with the European powers, most notably the Venetians. Beirut began to recover economically and regain some of its former prestige, although physically it remained a tiny city. The sultan, meanwhile, became alarmed over Beirut's growing power and confronted Fakhr ad-Din's army, defeating him at Safed. Fakhr ad-Din was captured and taken to Constantinople, where he was executed in 1635.

The 18th century saw mixed fortunes for the city, depending on the whims and preferences of the local rulers. One, Bashir II, injected new vigour into the city, renewing its prosperity and stability once again. These peaks and troughs formed the pattern of existence for Beirut until the mid-19th century brought about changes which led to dramatic growth. The civil war brought the whole growth process to a dramatic halt.

For a brief spell in the mid-19th century, Beirut came under the Egyptian domination of Mehmed Ali, but the city was bombarded and subsequently recaptured on 10 October 1840 by the combined Anglo-Austro-Turkish fleet. The population of Beirut at that time was only 45,000, but it doubled during the following 20 years. The booming silk trade attracted a lot of people to Beirut, and the massacres, which took place in Damascus and other parts of Lebanon in 1860, also brought thousands of Maronites fleeing from the mountains to the city. This was the start of the commercial boom which saw Beirut transformed from a backwater into a commercial powerhouse. It was in 1868 that Syrian and American missionaries founded the Syrian Protestant College (now known as the American University of Beirut), which has become one of the most prestigious universities in the Middle East, adding to the importance of the city.

During WWI, Beirut suffered a blockade by the Allies, which was intended to starve the Turks out. The effect was a famine, followed by plague, which killed more than a quarter of the population. A revolt against the Turks broke out which resulted in the mass hanging of the rebel leaders in what was renamed Place des Martyrs.

WWI brought an end to Turkish rule and on 8 October 1918, eight days after the capture of Damascus by the Allies, the British army (including a French detachment) arrived in Beirut. On 25 April 1920 the League of Nations granted a French mandate over Syria and Lebanon, and Beirut became the headquarters of the French High Commissioner as well as the capital of the state of Greater Lebanon.

During WWII the city was occupied by the Allies and, thanks to its port, became an important supply centre. In 1946 the French left the city, and subsequently Beirut became one of the main commercial and banking centres of the Middle East. The Arab-Israeli War of 1948 saw huge numbers of Palestinian refugees settle in the south of Beirut, where they still live today.

During the civil war from 1975 to 1991, anarchy reigned in Beirut. The city was ruled, area by area, by militias loyal to one or other factions. What with the continual inter-communal fighting and shelling from Israeli fighter planes, the city suffered significant damage. The human casualties were enormous and the effect on the economy catastrophic. Beirut is now in the process of recovery, but it will take many years to complete the rebuilding programme and fully restore the infrastructure of the city. Certainly the Beirut dubbed as 'the Paris of the Middle East' is gone for the moment. What re-emerges in its place will remain to be seen.

ORIENTATION

Beirut is a promontory bound by the Mediterranean Sea on the north and west coast. The headland of the promontory has dramatic cliffs falling away into the sea, while to the south, the coast gives way to a sandy beach. In the west of the city, the land is very hilly, flattening out as you travel east. The city centre is now a wasteland currently under redevelopment. Many of the shops, businesses and government offices have moved to the Hamra district in west Beirut. This is now the true heart of the city where people go for shopping and entertainment. It is also where you'll find the Ministry of Tourism, major banks, hotels, travel agents, airline offices and restaurants – all within walking distance of each other. For most tourists, it is the obvious place to stay and is convenient for travelling around the city.

North of Hamra is the large American University of Beirut (AUB) campus with lots of coffee bars and cheap restaurants catering for the students. Heading east from there, you come to the Downtown district which is being redeveloped and further on, the port and the Beirut River, which is disappointingly just a concrete canal surrounded by highways. To the south east of the port is the rather exclusive suburb of Achrafieh set on a hill. This area is one of designer clothes shops and exclusive restaurants, but has little in the way of ambience.

The Corniche (Ave de Paris and Ave Général de Gaulle) runs around the coast from Raouché in the south west to the St George Yacht Club, just before you come to the Downtown district. This is the area where Beirutis come to promenade, jog, fish and generally hang out. There are many restaurants, cafés and snack stalls lining the Corniche, with some of the most popular overlooking the famous Pigeon Rocks.

To the south of the city are the southern suburbs which are much poorer districts and predominantly Shiite. This is also where the Palestinian camps of Sabra-Chatila and Bourj al-Barajnah can be found. The main roads through the southern suburbs are lined with shops, which sell all kinds of household goods alongside workshops and many food markets.

Further south is the airport. There have been warnings from some of the western embassies about the risk of wandering around this part of town – whether they are exaggerated or not is hard to tell. There is, in any case, nothing really to interest the casual sightseer.

Navigating your way around town can initially seem tricky because, firstly, the city has quite a confusing layout and, secondly, the streets are often known locally by a different name than the one that appears on the signs. The street signs, when they exist, give the names in both Arabic and French. A few of the streets use house numbers, but the majority do not. Buildings are often known either by the name of their owner or by their function (eg the British Bank building). When directing you, people refer to landmarks and the names of specific commercial institutions rather than street names. It is not as difficult as it first seems and you soon get used to the system.

The best way to familiarise yourself with the city is to travel around on foot. You can get to almost any point in west Beirut on foot within 30 minutes. Remember to take a street map with you.

Maps

The best map of Beirut is on the reverse of the GEOprojects map of Lebanon, available from the major bookshops in Beirut. There is also a commercial map, published by All Prints of Beirut, which has a good city map of Beirut on the reverse. English and French versions are available. It is also stocked by Stanfords in London.

The Rebuilding of Beirut

Beirut's Downtown district lies at the geographic and historical heart o the modern city. Before the civil war, Downtown Beirut was the commer cial, financial and administrative centre of Lebanon. So when faced with the huge task of rebuilding confidence in the country, the Downtown area was one of the first to be considered for reconstruction – a chance to recreate a city that could once again be the 'Paris of the Middle East'.

In 1992 the Lebanese Parliament formed the Lebanese Company fo the Development and Reconstruction of Beirut Central District, known by its French acronym Solidere, to oversee the project. Much of the old Downtown district is to be totally redeveloped and decisions are being made about which buildings to save and which to demolish. In total abou 1.8 million sq m of the Downtown district will be restored, including some 60 hectares of reclaimed sea land.

The approved Master Plan aims to combine a range of land uses including government, commerce, residential, cultural and leisure facil ities. The new city centre will be much like the prewar city core and akir to the successful centres of many other historic cities. At least 40,000 people are expected to be housed in the new development.

Solidere is also working with teams of archaeologists who are exca vating the cleared sites – a unique opportunity in an occupied city. Traces of all the historical periods – Canaanite, Phoenician, Persian, Hellenistic Roman, Byzantine, Umayyad, Abbasid, Crusader, Mameluke, Ottoman and French Mandate – have been revealed through the archaeologica excavations of the district. Extensive finds, many of which have already been uncovered, are to be displayed in a special 'archaeological park' The finds include Canaanite burial jars, ramparts from Phoenician Beirut, Roman lamps, evidence of silk and glass industries and many square metres of mosaics from the Byzantine era. The archaeologists would like more time to uncover the remains of the ancient civilisations, but as with any development the bulldozers are impatient to start the rebuilding process. With a project of this scale, there are bound to be conflicts of interests.

Rebuilding Beirut is more than just a practical problem, it also involves hugely complex legal problems. Solidere is a joint stock company with a majority shareholding of pre-existing land and property owners with cash assets of US$650 million. Land ownership rights of the former occupants of Downtown Beirut mean that a system of reimbursement had to be thought out. Shares in Solidere were issued to property owners whose buildings will be redeveloped.

Money for the project is coming partly from the state (for basic infrastructure) and from private investors. Its capital comes from the value of the real estate (some 1650 real estate lots) which is worth around US$1,170,000,000.

The new plans are not to everyone's taste, but there is a commitment to building a new city centre for all of Beirut's population. One thing is for sure – the rebuilding of Downtown Beirut is going ahead at a terrific pace It could yet regain its reputation as the most sophisticated city in the Middle East.

This colourful postcard reveals the bustling Place des Martyrs in Beirut's Downtown area in 1973. Beirut was known then as the 'Paris of the Middle East'.

Three years later, in 1976, the civil war had taken its toll. By the end of the war, the Downtown area of Beirut was almost totally destroyed.

By 1994, with Solidere in charge of clearing the Downtown area for reconstruction following the end of the civil war, the Martyrs Statue was the only recognisable feature of the prewar days.

After consulting several times with the Beirut population, Solidere's plans for the redevelopment of the Downtown district are going ahead at full speed.

PETER JOUSIFFE

PETER JOUSIFFE

PETER JOUSIFFE

ANN JOUSIFFE

Top: The natural, rugged cliffs of the Raouché district surprise many visitors to the capital
Left: Beirut is moving towards recovery from the damage suffered in the civil war.
Middle Right: A cinema poster from the Hamra quarter of Beirut.
Bottom Right: A damaged, but still exquisite, Byzantine mosaic in the National Museum.

INFORMATION
Tourist Office
Beirut's tourist information office (☎ (01) 343073; fax 340945, 343279) is on the ground floor of the same building as the Ministry of Tourism, on the Rue Banque du Liban (an extension of Rue Hamra and Rue Rome). The entrance is through a covered arcade which runs underneath the block. This office has a series of up-to-date brochures on the main archaeological and tourist sites of Lebanon. It also has some country and city maps. The staff are helpful and friendly, and speak English and French. They have a comprehensive list of hotels and apartments and can advise you about accommodation options. The office is officially open from 8 am to 2 pm, although often there is no one there until after 9.30 am.

Foreign Consulates
Beirut has a large number of foreign embassies and consulates. Some of the western embassies in west Beirut moved temporarily to east Beirut during the war. Some of them are relocating back to west Beirut, either to their original buildings or to new addresses. If you are planning to visit an embassy, it would be a wise idea to telephone first to double check the address. See under Embassies in the Facts for the Visitor chapter for a list of embassies in Beirut.

Money
There seems to be a bank every 50m in the centre of Beirut, so finding a place to change money is never a problem. There are also numerous moneychangers, but not all of them will deal with travellers' cheques. The Beirut Finance & Exchange Company (☎ 864280), in the Abdel Baki building on Rue Hamra, changes both cash and travellers' cheques. Failing that, you can usually change money or travellers' cheques at many of the larger hotels with no problem, although the commission charges are often higher. The banks are open from 8.30 am to 12.30 pm daily except Sunday. The private moneychangers have more liberal business

hours and often stay open until the early evening.

The American Express Bank (☎ 360390) is on the 1st floor in the Gefinor Centre on Rue Maamari, Hamra. It is open from 8.30 am to 12.30 pm. This is the place to come if you lose your travellers' cheques. There is also an Amex cards office on the same floor where you should go if you need to draw cash on your Amex card or if you need a replacement card. The office is open weekdays from 8 am to 6 pm and to 1.30 pm on Saturday.

Post
The postal system is reviving after the war and a full range of services is more or less available. There are no public post boxes and you have to make a visit to the post office in order to mail letters or parcels. These are not very numerous, but the deliveries are pretty reliable. At the moment there is no poste restante service available.

The main post office is on Rue Riad al-Solh in the Downtown district, but it's a bit out of the way. In Hamra the most convenient post office is on Rue Makdissi, almost opposite the Embassy Hotel. It is on the 1st floor above the Star Stationers, but the entrance is not clearly signposted at all – it is the door to the left of the shop as you face it. The opening hours are from 8 am to 2 pm daily, except Sunday and public holidays.

Also nearby is the on-campus post office at the AUB which can be used by visitors. If you use the main entrance to the campus on Rue Bliss, turn left and it is down a flight of stairs in the same building as the canteen. It is also open from 8 am to 2 pm daily, except Sunday. It does not sell stamps so you have to leave your letters to be franked.

In west Beirut there is a post office in Raouché, near the end of Rue Chatilia near the Protestant College, which keeps the same hours.

Telephone
There are a few public telephone boxes in Beirut, in particular on Rue Bliss in Hamra. If you want to make a call, you will most probably have to use the government-run

PLACES TO STAY
1	Le Vendôme InterContinental
4	Hotel Glayeul
6	Hotel Regis
24	Bristol Hotel

PLACES TO EAT
2	Hard Rock Café
17	Le Chef Restaurant
25	Weiner Keller
26	Henry J. Beans

OTHER
3	La Maison de l'Artisan
5	St George Yacht Club
7	Beirut Municipality Building
8	Grand Mosque
9	Old Parliament Building
10	St Louis Church
11	Old Palace of Justice
12	Grand Seraglio
13	Place Riad al-Solh
14	Main Post Office
15	St George & St Elie Churches
16	St George's Maronite Cathedral
18	Police Station
19	Sursock Museum
20	Maronite Cathedral
21	Hammam an-Nuzha al-Jadid
22	University of Lebanon
23	Sanayeh Public Garden
27	TV Station
28	Jordanian Embassy
29	Japanese Embassy
30	Mandarine Supermarket
31	Egyptian Embassy
32	UNESCO
33	Russian Embassy
34	Post & Telephone Office
35	Rida Travel
36	Cola Taxi & Bus Stand
37	Makassed Hospital
38	Hippodrome Entrance
39	Temporary Parliament Building
40	National Museum
41	Museum Taxi Stand
42	Hôtel-Dieu de France Hospital
43	Palais de Justice
44	General Security Office

telephone offices or one of the private telephone offices.

There are a couple of government-run places in Beirut. One is in Hamra near the Ministry of Tourism building on the junction of Rue Banque du Liban and Rue de Rome just behind the Glass Gallery. It is open from Monday to Saturday from 8 am to 2 pm (to 11 am on Friday). The other one is on Blvd Saeb Salam, not far from the Cola taxi stand, and has the same opening hours. To make a call, you go to the counter and fill in a slip of paper with the country and number you want and wait to be directed to a booth. You pay when you have finished your call.

The private offices are often located in shops and operate on a similar system, although their rates are a bit more than the government places. Their opening hours are usually longer, and because there are more of them, the extra expense is probably worth it. If you are stuck in the evening and need to make a call, your best bet is to use one of the larger hotels, but be warned – their charges can be expensive for international calls. The telephone code for Beirut is 01.

Fax
There are many private fax bureaux in Beirut (most double up as telephone offices as well). Many of these are on Rue Bliss, near to the AUB campus. An alternative is to use the larger hotels. Most have a business centre which you can use whether you are a guest or not. These tend to be more expensive than the private bureaux.

Internet
There is one place where you can access the Internet in Beirut – the News Café (☎ 602 384) in the Weavers Centre on Rue Clémenceau. You can't send or receive emails here, but you can get an inexpensive meal.

Travel Agencies
There are dozens of travel agencies all over Beirut. The following can provide all or most of these services: hotel bookings; car rental; tailor-made programmes; daily tours of the city or other parts of Lebanon; ski and scuba diving programmes; airport transfers; and ferry and flight bookings. You may need to shop around a bit to get the deal that best suits your budget.

Ghazi Travel Agency
　　Rue Bliss, Hamra (☎ 348555, 602087)
Habbal Travel
　　Rue Makdissi, Hamra (☎ 349213, 351237)

Jaber Travel
    Rue Verdun (near the Mandarine supermarket)
    (☎ 865695)
Nakhal & Cie
    Ghorayeb Building, Rue Sami Al-Solh (☎ 389507/8; fax 422302)
Nawas International
    Rue Sadat (☎ 740275/6/7/9)
Pan Asiatic Travel
    Gefinor Centre, Hamra (☎ 342708)
Rida Travel
    4th Floor, Amoudi Centre, Babir Square, Mazraa (☎ 640903, 643341; fax 630537; email ridatour @bignet.com.lb)
Saad Tours
    Achrafieh (☎ 423672)
    Pavillion Building, Rue Hamra (☎ 352194)
Skyways
    Rahme Centre, Sin El Fils (☎ 496012/3)
    Tajer Building, Clémenceau (☎ 367315)
    Bitar Building, Hazmieh (☎ 429899)
Tania Travel
    Rue Sidani, opposite the Jeanne d'Arc theatre, Hamra (☎ 739679, 739682/3/4; fax 340473; email taniatv@dm.net.lb; web site http://members.aol.com/TaniaTravl/ main.html)
    Rue Sodeco (☎ (03) 812375/6)

Bookshops

Beirut is well supplied with bookshops both in the east and the west. The main area to find bookshops, though, is in Hamra and around the AUB (not surprisingly). Apart from academic and specialist books, you can also buy novels, general interest books and books about Lebanon. Although there are very few current guidebooks on Lebanon, there are some beautifully produced coffee-table books with sumptuous photographs, although they are a bit on the expensive side.

The largest and best-stocked bookshop is the Librairie Antoine on Rue Hamra. It has a good selection of books and international newspapers and an encyclopaedic array of imported magazines in French, English and Arabic. Librairie Antoine also has a smaller branch in Achrafieh and four branches around the country.

Other recommended bookshops are Four Steps Down and Way In on Rue Hamra, both of which mainly stock English-language books. Another good bookshop is Librairie International on the ground floor of the Gefinor Centre in Hamra.

Campuses

The main campus in Beirut is the AUB. This is a good place to hang out. Non-students can visit the campus and use the post office, visit the museum, get a cheap lunch at the canteen and generally find out about events. There is a free English-language weekly newspaper, *Campus*, which lists various events at AUB and other campuses in Lebanon.

Cultural Centres

There are several cultural centres in Beirut including:

British Council
    Azzar Building, Rue Yamout (off Rue Sidani), Ras Beirut (☎ 740123/4/5)
Centro Cultural Hispanico
    Assaf Building, Rue Baalbeck (☎ 347755)
Goethe Institut
    Gideon Building, Rue Bliss, Manara (☎ 740524, 745058)
Institut Culturel Français
    Cité Bounnour, Rue de Damas (☎ 644850/1/2)
Italian Cultural Centre
    Najjar Building, Rue de Rome (☎ 346509)
Russian Cultural Centre
    Rue Verdun (☎ 864534)

These centres often have art exhibitions and film festivals, showing work from their respective countries. They are also a good place to drop by and catch up on the newspapers – most of them have a small library which you can use for a quiet read. You can check for details in the press or by calling them to see what's on.

Medical Services & Emergency

The following telephone numbers may be useful in case of emergency:

Civil Defence	125
Emergency Police	160
Fire Brigade	310105
Red Cross	145
Police	386440, 425250

Please bear in mind that all medical services, including ambulances, have to be paid for – there are no free medical services available. If you need an ambulance, call either the Red Cross or Civil Defence. If you have any sort

The Corniche Walk

One of the best walks to take around Beirut is the coastal walk along the Corniche on the western and northern shores. This is the favourite promenade of many Beirutis and is a great chance to mix with the locals at play. It doesn't really matter which end you start from and, taking it at a leisurely pace, you can do the walk in about half an hour, although you should allow longer for stops along the way and a walk down the rocks.

Starting from St George Yacht Club and following the road round to the west, you soon come to a rocky stretch of coast where the local amateur anglers cluster in huge numbers to fish from the railings or from the rocks below. They don't seem to catch very much, but every few feet there is some optimist with a line in the water. The whole of the northern coast is rocky, and moving further west, you come to a place where the anglers perch precariously on concrete bollards just offshore, casting their lines into the incoming surf. This is a scene pictured in many of the coffee-table books. The anglers stand for endless hours on a space the size of a chessboard in the hope of catching something. On the shore, a few simple cafés, covered in palm fronds, serve coffee and cold drinks to dry, passing spectators and wet anglers.

The entire length of this walk you see street vendors selling coffee, hot corn on the cob, roasted nuts, *kaak* (crisp bread with sesame seeds and thyme) and traditional flat breads looped together and strung from bicycles. You can easily snack your way from one end of the walk to the other.

The Corniche took a battering during the war and many of the palm trees, not to mention the buildings behind them, were destroyed, giving the effect of pulled teeth. Some of the older houses are still standing, hemmed in between the newer developments. There are now some desirable sea-front residences and a couple of swanky hotels along this stretch of the Corniche.

Further along you come to the **Bain Militaire** which is a sort of seaside playground for officers. If you are carrying a camera, you may be warned by the sentry not to point it at the complex. Just past the perimeter fence is a private bathing complex which has a pool and several cafés and restaurants. It is tucked away behind the funfair and is a pleasant enough place to sit and look out over the ocean.

The **Luna Park Funfair** is not very large, but is clearly popular with the local kids. It really comes alive in the late afternoon and early evening when it is packed with Lebanese families. The main ride at the fair is the enormous, creaking Ferris wheel from the top of which you can see the whole coast stretching away to Jounieh, north of Beirut. The ride is not for the nervous – there are no gates on the cars and the whole construction looks a bit too rusty for my liking, but if you're feeling adventurous give it a go.

From the funfair the road climbs steeply along the cliff edge. Behind you to your left, you can see a **lighthouse** on the hill above the road and a solitary, old, red-painted Lebanese mansion. The road which leads up past the lighthouse takes you back to Hamra.

This area is the headland of Beirut. Once you turn the corner onto the western Corniche, you are confronted with an array of cliff-top restaurants and cafés. These places have the best view in Beirut, overlooking the famous **Pigeon Rocks**. These enormous offshore rocks are the result of an ancient earthquake and the action of the sea has carved natural arches in them. The cliffs in front of the rocks are a sheer drop, but if you walk a little further, there are pathways leading down to the rocks. Down by the sea, the rocks have eroded into several inlets. Small boats use these as a harbour.  During the summer you can take a **boat ride** around the rocks and through some of the caves which pockmark the cliffs. Some of these boats are launched on a winch 6m above the waves and lowered gently into the swell. This whole area is a great place to get away from it all. Many people come down during the hour before sunset just to sit and look at the sea.

Back on the Corniche heading south towards Raouché, there are any number of small restaurants, juice bars and patisseries, but beyond that is a pretty dull stretch of uninteresting buildings. If you carry on walking, you pass the Merryland complex, which is a collection of restaurants overlooking the sea.

The road leads down from here and stretching out in front of you is the only real beach in Beirut, the public town beach, which leads away down to the Summerland resort in the south. ■

of accident that is not serious and you do not need an ambulance, it is better to get a taxi to take you to one of the hospitals. The general consensus is that the American University of Beirut Hospital (☎ 340460) on Rue du Caire is the best choice. The AUB also has a separate private clinic on Rue Ahmed Abdul Aziz (☎ 341898).

Other hospitals include:

Hôtel-Dieu de France, Rue Hôtel-Dieu (☎ 387000)
Makassed, Rue Tariq al-Jedide (☎ 646592)
Trad Hospital, Rue Mexique (☎ 361663)

There is a 24-hour/seven-day pharmacy, Mazen Pharmacy (☎ 343779), on Blvd Saeb Salam, almost opposite the large post office, It offers a delivery service up until 8 pm. You simply telephone your order through and pay on delivery. The pharmacist speaks English and French and can advise you on what drugs you may need.

Dangers & Annoyances

The most obvious hazard in Beirut is the traffic, especially when you are travelling on foot. Waiting for a gap in the traffic as you cross busy roads can take an age. Locals seem to take the fatalistic approach and saunter across the flow, trusting that cars will slow down. This technique is not recommended unless you have nerves of steel.

Another thing to watch out for when out walking, particularly at night, is potholes and uneven stones in the pavements. It is easy to twist your ankle or fall if you are not paying attention.

Theft is not a great problem, so don't be unduly paranoid, but it pays to be vigilant with your bags especially at busy places such as taxi stations. Keep your wallet or purse on your body – bum bags are a good idea. These also mean you can keep your passport handy for those on-the-road checks.

MUSEUMS
National Museum of Beirut

Lebanon's main archaeological museum couldn't have been in a worse position during the war – right on the Green Line, and

on one of the main crossing points from east to west. There were times when the crossing was closed for days at a time due to heavy shelling and gunfire. The building was closed for the duration of the war and the exhibits bricked up to avoid damage, but the fabric of the building itself suffered from the shelling and periodic occupation by the militias. Following the cease-fire, work began in earnest to restore the building.

The museum dates from 1942 and its facade and interior have an Egyptian style. The windows have been overlaid with black wrought-iron work in a lotus-bud design. The four pillars which flank the entrance hall are copies of those at Luxor and have lotus-head capitals. At the time of writing, teams of workers were slaving away, practically round the clock, to get the museum ready for reopening. There was no specific timetable for the work to be finished, but it seems likely that by the time you read this, the museum will be at least partly open.

Formerly the museum was open daily, except Monday, with a small entrance fee. The hours in winter, from 1 October until 31 March, were 9 am to 12 noon and from 2 pm to 5 pm. In summer the hours were the same in the mornings and 3 pm to 6 pm in the afternoon. It seems likely that once the museum reopens, these hours will resume. If you want to check if the museum is open, you can telephone the Department of Antiquities (☎ 426704). If you want to take photographs inside the museum, you have to obtain a written permit – enquire on the same number.

It has been difficult for the curators to properly assess the damage done to the artefacts as many of them are still in crates and bricked up in the basement of the building. It was said that they expected at least 60% of the exhibits to be undamaged. As one of only two archaeological museums in Lebanon, most of the important finds, which represent the cream of the national heritage, are housed here.

Following is a brief description of the collection and the layout of the museum as it was before the war.

The galleries were arranged over three

floors – the basement, ground floor and 1st floor. The ground floor **entrance hall** had a small collection of Phoenician pottery found at Tyre, dating from the 7th century BC. The first gallery on the left was the **Gallery of the Alphabet** which had several early *stelae* (inscribed stone slabs) representing various stages in the development of writing. Some of the earliest dated from the 10th century BC. One, dating from the Persian period, described the building of the temple at Byblos, which was dedicated to the goddess Balaat Gebal.

Following the gallery around, you would come to the **south alcove**, which used to house a collection of stone figures and stelae from Byblos.

The **Gallery of Rameses** was the next room. The pieces in this gallery came from a monument at Byblos which was built or restored by the great pharaoh Rameses II, who paid many visits to Phoenicia during his campaign against the Hittites in the 13th century BC. The pieces included statues and a portal with the cartouche of Rameses II and various stelae from the same period.

If you continued past the staircase which led to the 1st floor, you would come to the **Gallery of Echmoun** which used to house a collection of objects found at Sidon, Tyre and of course Echmoun itself. The exhibits included a set of four mutilated statues of children used to invoke the healing spirit of Echmoun.

The **Hygiea Gallery** was next on the circuit around the ground floor. This gallery housed mainly **statues** and **mosaics** from the Roman and Byzantine periods. The most notable of the mosaics was the one that depicted the life of Alexander the Great, and included a mythical scene from Olympus announcing his future birth.

The next room was the **Gallery of Jupiter** which had a beautiful 5th-century Byzantine mosaic at the entrance and some statues from the 2nd and 3rd centuries AD, including part of a colossal statue of Jupiter (or possibly Neptune). The gallery was flanked by two 2nd-century altars. From here, you would return to the entrance hall and to the main central hall. This space contained reconstructions of the **temples** at Baalbek and a piece of the capital showing the upper half of a bull. Behind the staircase leading up to the 1st floor were some **fresco fragments** from a Frankish chapel in Beirut.

The galleries on the 1st floor held the smaller objects and those dating from prehistory. Most of these exhibits came from the Byblos site where extensive digs have taken place. Many of the objects had some religious significance, but others were personal objects from everyday life including some exquisite jewellery.

The first thing you used to see going up the stairs was a frieze of **fossilised fish**, or *ichthyolites*. These came from two principal limestone sites in Lebanon: Haqel and Sahel Alma. Radioactive dating shows that the Haqel fossils date from 85 million years ago and the Sahel Alma fossils from million years ago. The fish fossils are all the more remarkable when you consider that the sites from which they come are now 1000m above sea level on a mountain top.

Turning to the left at the top of the stairs, the exhibit began with a collection of old and new **Stone Age weapons** and **tools** found at the sites of the later Phoenician settlements. There were also cases containing early pottery from this period and a couple of very early clay idols.

The next cases displayed the earliest **Phoenician artefacts** dating from the beginning of the 3rd millennium BC. There was an outstanding figure of Astarte, made of terracotta, showing the goddess holding her breasts, and also some jewellery dating from the 2nd millennium BC.

The next section of the upper gallery was devoted to the **treasures of Byblos** and contained an impressive collection of figurines and jewellery. Further along the gallery there were many objects found in the tombs of the kings of Byblos dating from the 18th century BC, including mirrors, vases and incense caskets. One of the most dazzling objects was a magnificent gold breastplate from the mid-19th century BC.

The collection continued with some Greek

pottery from the 5th century BC and later some fine Phoenician glassware from the 1st century BC onwards. The later part of the exhibits included some Byzantine jewellery and household artefacts and a collection of household objects from the Arab era.

The basement of the museum used to house a collection of **sarcophagi** and the **hypogeum of Tyre**, an underground vault whose walls were painted with mythological scenes. The **Ford Gallery** was on one side of the basement and contained a collection of sarcophagi in human shapes, mostly in white marble. Most of these had the tops of the tombs carved into a likeness of their former occupants. The faces would have originally been painted and you could still see traces of pigment on some of them. They were discovered near Sidon in 1901 and were mainly the coffins of wealthy Phoenician merchants.

American University of Beirut Museum

The museum on the AUB campus is small but well worth a look, especially as this is the only other archaeological museum in the city apart from the National Museum. It is housed in an attractive 19th-century building near the Main Gate on Rue Bliss. If you tell the guard on the gate that you want to visit the museum (or the post office or whatever), he will direct you to the visitors' desk. Once inside the campus, turn right and the museum is a large castellated building on your right past the church. The museum has a guidebook available to borrow while you walk around – ask at the desk as you go in. There are versions in English and French.

There is a good collection of Phoenician glassware and ceramics and some earlier artefacts. Some of the figurines are particularly interesting. There is no photography allowed inside the museum, but you can buy some rather overpriced postcards of the star exhibits at the desk. Entry is free and the museum's opening hours are Monday to Thursday from 10 am to 4 pm.

Sursock Museum

Just about the best thing to visit in east Beirut is the Sursock Museum near Achrafieh. It is

in a part of the city which still retains a fair amount of traditional architecture in the form of large 19th-century mansions. The Sursock Museum is the former home of the Sursock family and is a splendid example of 19th-century 'wedding cake' architecture – all-white, lacy stucco and sweeping staircases inspired by Italian villas.

The interior is suitably grand in style with heavy, wood panelling and marble floors. Some of the rooms are decorated in the oriental style and the main one has a collection of 19th-century Turkish silver. In the centre of the room is a gigantic 7th-century Abbasid jar. On the same floor is a small but interesting library, which is open by arrangement if you fancy doing some research. The former study of Nicholas Ibrahim Sursock features his portrait by Van Dongen. The room also houses a small collection of icons.

The museum's main function these days is to provide a venue for contemporary Lebanese artists. These exhibitions change periodically, but there is a permanent exhibition of Japanese prints and Islamic art.

The official name of the museum is Musée Nicholas Ibrahim Sursock and it at is Rue de l'Archevêché Grec-Orthodoxe, Achrafieh (☎ 334133, 201892). The museum is open only during exhibitions. It is a good idea to telephone before you visit as it is sometimes closed while new exhibitions are being installed.

THINGS TO SEE & DO
Hamra

Rue Hamra has become the main **shopping** street since the war. Close to the university campus and many of the hotels, it is the magnetic centre of the city with a huge selection of restaurants, fast-food joints, street vendors, bookshops, cinemas and so on. Other districts may be smarter, but Hamra has all the street life.

There are no important buildings or monuments in Hamra, but it is interesting to walk around the area, window-shopping and stopping occasionally in cafés to watch the world go by and soak up the atmosphere. The shops are mostly fashion boutiques (of the non-

moulds and other esoteric items which make good souvenirs.

If you start walking from the western end of the street, you can make a few detours down the side streets where some interesting small shops lurk – some selling traditional handicrafts and not so traditional pirated music tapes.

Further along on your right is the **Café de Paris**, a prewar survivor with a nice old-fashioned feel. There are some tables outside which, if you can stand the constant honking of car horns, are a good vantage point. You can pick up a newspaper on the way at Librairie Antoine. Around this part of Hamra are some second-hand book vendors. One or two have a pitch on the corner of Rue du Caire. It is well worth having a browse here; apart from picking up a cheap novel, they often have some rare out-of-print books on Lebanon.

Past Rue du Caire, there is a Roman Catholic church which, unfortunately, is kept locked except during services. This stretch of Rue Hamra is not especially interesting. A lot of banks and airline offices have their offices here. Near the junction with Rue de Rome is the tourist information office and, past that, is the campus of the **University of Lebanon** with its 19th-century buildings and attractive grounds. If you turn right into Rue Justinien, you come to the main gates of the university and just past that is an attractive **public garden** in the middle of a large square. On the north-east corner of the square, you can see a single, rather sad, Roman column which is covered with advertising posters. The garden square is quite pleasant and makes a good spot to sit and eat your felafels and recharge your batteries.

Downtown

The former heart of Beirut has seen some exceptionally hard times, especially during the war. This was the area where much of the fighting between rival militias took place. Before the war, this was the transport hub of the city and also the main shopping district with elegant arcades of shops and restaurants. The area also had many of the city's

PAUL DOYLE

Monument to Peace

If your idea of public art is 10 storeys of military weaponry squashed between layers of concrete and sandbags, then the new Lebanese monument to peace is the place to visit. Unveiled in 1996 outside the Ministry of Defence building on the outskirts of Beirut, this permanent sculpture was created by French artist Armand Fernandez. Many of Fernandez's earlier works of art were assemblages of everyday articles, including a rubbish sculpture made up of the contents of unsuspecting consumers' rubbish bins.

This 5000-ton structure contains real Soviet T-55 tanks, armoured vehicles and artillery. Fernandez believes the monument will become the symbol of continued peace in Lebanon by ensuring a constant reminder of the recent civil war's death and destruction.

There is no direct service taxi to visit the monument. Take a service taxi to the Museum area and change to one heading to the Ministry of Defence. The trip will cost LL 2000 one way.
Katrina Browning

designer variety), shoe shops and jewellers. Occasionally you come across household shops selling Lebanese coffee sets, felafel

administrative and religious buildings. Some of these are now undergoing restoration, but others are simply burnt-out shells.

The redevelopment of the area is in the hands of a company called **Solidere** (see the Rebuilding of Beirut section earlier). They have spent the time since the war ended deciding which of the damaged buildings could be saved and drawing up an elaborate plan for the rebuilding of the city centre. Many buildings were so damaged that whole blocks have gone under the bulldozer leaving behind a strange, end-of-the-world landscape. It is quite disconcerting to walk around this bombed-out ghost town and suddenly come across a pocket of commercial activity or a fully functioning building, but wherever people have been able to resume a normal life for themselves, they have.

The heart of the Downtown district is the **Place des Martyrs** (also known as the Place des Canons, but always called El Bourj by the locals). This huge, open space was named after the rebels who were executed by the Turks in 1915. The only feature of the Place des Martyrs still remaining is the bronze statue in the centre, known as the **Martyrs Statue**. Riddled with bullet holes, the statue has become a symbol of all that was destroyed during the fighting; the holes are now filled with flowers. If you want to see what the Place des Martyrs looked like before the war, there are street vendors hanging around the statue selling posters of prewar Beirut. They are rather poignant views of a lost world.

Nowadays the land has been cleared between the Bourj and the sea giving a fine view of, well, nothing at all. But in case your imagination needs some prompting, Solidere has erected an enormous billboard showing what the future development will be like, according to the architects. If you stand at the statue and squint, you will have a vision of the future. That vision may seem to your eyes a rather soulless version on what they are trying to replace, but bear in mind that what you are looking at is probably going to be one of the most expensive pieces of real estate in the Mediterranean.

There are still several buildings worth seeing in the Downtown area, even in their dilapidated state and, to be fair to the developers, they are trying to save what they can of the historical heritage of the area. On Rue Weygand, to the north and west of the Place des Martyrs, is the **Grand Mosque**, more properly called the Omari Mosque, which was quite badly damaged during the war. The mosque was originally built as the Church of John the Baptist of the Knights Hospitallers during the Byzantine era over a site previously occupied by a Roman Temple of Jupiter. Some parts of the original temple were reused in the construction of the church. The conversion to a mosque took place in the 1291 AD when Salah ad-Din retook Beirut. The building still contains traces of its former pagan and Christian origins, despite some quite drastic alterations.

Many of the streets around the Place

Currently under restoration by university students, the Martyrs Statue has pride of place in the Place des Martyrs.

d'Etoile were closed off at the time of writing due to the renovation works, but if you can, continue past the Grand Mosque heading west and then along Bab Edriss. You come to a turning on the left, Rue des Capucins. On your left is **St Louis Church** and a restored clock tower. Lower down to your left is an area being excavated in which some **Roman baths** have been uncovered. If you continue along Rue des Capucins, you come to a huge Ottoman building, the **Grand Seraglio**, whose structure has now been restored.

Following the road south, you come out in the Place Riad al-Solh, which is nothing more than a dusty space at a road junction. Turn left onto Rue Emir Bechir and you come to **St George's Maronite Cathedral** on the left. Despite its roofless state, the cathedral is still functioning on special occasions, such as Easter. The crypts of the church are being used as a store for archaeological finds. Behind the church a major dig, which has uncovered one of the main Roman streets, is underway. Archaeologists are hoping to discover the famous School of Law and the Cardo Maximus before time runs out and the site is built over.

Two further **churches**, St George and St Elie, lie to the north of the Maronite cathedral, but they are in a totally ruinous state. Next door to the Maronite cathedral are just about the only **Roman ruins** still standing in Beirut, at least in their original position. These consist of a few rather forlorn looking columns. But they have fared a lot better than many of the buildings of 20th-century Beirut.

Walking around this area, you cannot fail to be shocked by the extent of the destruction brought about by the war and the total disruption and chaos that such a conflict has brought about. What is even more shocking is that many of the wrecked buildings are still being lived in. A short walk away from the main area of reconstruction, you will see streets of houses, shops and apartments, which defy any definition of the word 'safe', in which families are still patching things together and making do. Their circumstances are many years away from any sort of normality and it is a sobering experience for a visitor to witness.

Pigeon Rocks

This is the most famous (in fact the only) natural feature of Beirut. For a first time visitor, the dramatic cliffs are a bit of a surprise. The offshore natural rock arches of the Pigeon Rocks are fairly spectacular and a natural magnet for city dwellers craving something beautiful to look at. Sunset is the favourite time for a visit to the rocks, or the hour or so before. The stretch of Corniche directly in front of the rocks faces a sheer drop of about a hundred metres and this is a good vantage point. But far more interesting is to take one the tracks down to the lower cliffs. One such track starts from the southern side of the rocks. After a steep 100m, you find yourself down on the lower level of chalk cliffs. These stretch out some considerable way and make a fine walk, especially if you are sick of the incessant traffic noise. Almost immediately, you can forget you are in the city.

The way across the rocks is quite rugged and sensible shoes are a good idea, although you see local women teetering precariously across the cliffs in high heels. Down on the lower levels you get a good side view of the Pigeon Rocks with the city behind. If you fancy sitting for a while to watch the waves crash through the rocks, there is probably the smallest café in the world (two chairs) overlooking the scene. Further down towards the open sea there is a larger café (four chairs), where you can sit and watch the sunset.

There are a number of inlets and caves in the cliffs. During the summer season small boats take people for a trip around the rocks and to the caves for a small fee.

Hammam

You can indulge yourself with a massage, sauna and bath at the *Hammam an-Nuzha al-Jadid* (☎ 641298) on Rue Kasti, off Ave du General Fouad Chehab. It is open all week, 24 hours a day, but women can only go on Monday from 9 am to 2 pm. The hammam provides the soap and towels.

Racecourse

Just behind the National Museum, the race-course, or Hippodrome, holds race meetings at the weekend and on public holidays. Horse racing has always been wildly popular with the Lebanese; in the old days the Hippodrome was *the* place to go at weekends. It is a great opportunity to soak up some local atmosphere and watch the thoroughbred Arabian horses go through their paces. There is betting at the track and if you are any judge of horses, you could end up with some winnings. The entrance to the grandstand is at the western end of the course, not far from Mazraa. See also Spectator Sport in the Facts for the Visitor chapter.

East Beirut

It has to be said that there is generally little in east Beirut to interest the visitor, unless you are shopping for designer clothes or looking for lunch in an expensive restaurant. This part of the city seems to consist mainly of rather characterless, well-heeled suburbs. Apart from the Sursock Museum (see Museums earlier), the only buildings of interest are a handful of churches. The one with the most interesting history is the **St George's Church** (now the Al-Khader Mosque) in the Khodr district. Everyone has heard the story about St George and the Dragon, well this is supposed to be where it all happened. The building itself is very small and tucked away near the junction of Ave Charles Helou and Rue Al-Khodr, just south of the highway. There is a supposed to be a healing power in the water from the nearby well, called the **Dragon's Well**.

A few kilometres further south in the district of Getawi is the **Armenian Catholic Archbishopric** on Rue Hôpital Libanais and nearby is the **Armenian Orthodox Cathedral**. Nearer the centre of town you can visit the **Maronite Cathedral** at Mar Maroun.

ACTIVITIES

One of the most popular activities throughout the summer months is **swimming**. The only free place to swim in Beirut is the public beach south of Raouché. This is a long sweep

St George & The Dragon

The legend of St George slaying the dragon is known the world over. The only varied point in the story is where it occurred. Some say that the event took place in Cappadocia, others point to Silene in Libya and still others to the eastern suburbs of Beirut. But wherever the event actually happened, the theme is always the same.

The story goes that a princess was held prisoner by a dragon and St George, dressed in armour and mounted on a horse, rescued the princess by slaying the dragon.

The dragon is seen as the symbol of evil, in particular, paganism. In the time of the Crusades, the Christians believed that a country could be converted to Christianity by the saint's killing of the evil – the dragon. The princess symbolises where this took place. So by killing the dragon, St George saved the city from the evil of pagan religion.

Katrina Browning

of sand without any shade and could be a recipe for instant heatstroke in mid-summer. As for cleanliness, the beach itself is not too bad, although there is some rubbish strewn about. There seems to be two camps of opinion about the safety of the water: those who wouldn't dream of swimming in the sea near Beirut on account of the pollution; and those who swim regularly and claim never to have had a problem with it. Let's put it this way, if you are desperate for a swim and don't mind rather murky water, you probably won't come to much harm.

If you can't face the briny, the only alternative is to pay for the privilege of swimming in one of the many privately run pools. Some of these are attached to hotels, others are just run as 'beach' resorts (although the beach in question is concrete). In either case, this is going to set you back about US$10 to US$12 per person. This will get you a changing cabin, sun lounger and access to refreshments.

One of the most popular places to swim is *Plage Long Beach*, which is behind the Luna Park Funfair just north of the Pigeon Rocks. There is an access road leading down to the resort between the funfair and a large, open-air restaurant. Entrance to the pool is US$10 and there are several cafés and restaurants, including a traditional Lebanese café with backgammon boards and nargileh pipes.

Many of the smarter places operate a members-only policy for people wanting to use their pool. The *Riviera Hotel* (☎ 602273/4/5) is in this category. It has a good location, facing north from the Corniche on the Ave de Paris, and has two pools and a snack bar on the sea side of the Corniche.

If you are going to be around Beirut for some time, it may be a good idea to ask about short-term membership. The same applies to the *St Georges Yacht Club* (☎ 360222, 365065) which has a lovely pool and bar alongside the marina. This is right next door to the old St Georges Hotel on Rue Minet al-Hosn, which has been closed since it was damaged during the war.

There are a few **sports clubs** opening up in Beirut and if you are missing your weekly game, there are **tennis** and **squash** courts at the *Escape Club* (☎ 812349, 806223) just along from the Hotel Mediterranée. They have three tennis and four squash courts, plus a gym. Nonmembers are welcome, but members are given priority when it comes to booking courts. From 7 am to 2 pm, a court costs US$14 per hour, and during peak times, from 3.30 to 8.30 pm, US$30 per hour. This includes free use of the gym and loan of racquets.

ORGANISED TOURS

Some of the local tour operators, such as Rida Travel, Nakhal & Cie and Saad Tours, have half-day tours of the city by coach. Depending on the number of people, the costs are about US$25 to US$30 per person. The itineraries are rather predictable: Pigeon Rocks, the Corniche, Hamra, the National Museum and the Downtown district to look at the excavations. Unless you really like being shepherded around, you would be better off just taking a taxi between these places and doing it at your own pace. See Travel Agencies earlier in this chapter and Organised Tours in the Getting Around chapter for more details.

PLACES TO STAY
Places to Stay – bottom end

There are lean pickings at the cheap end of the hotel range in Beirut. Most of the real cheapies from the old days were around the Place des Martyrs and are now under the bulldozer. Until independent travellers return to Lebanon in significant numbers, there isn't much demand for them anyway. Consequently there are no pensions, no youth hostels and only a handful of places that could really be described as cheap in the capital.

More of a hostel than a hotel is the *University Hotel* (☎ 347420) on Rue Bliss, opposite the main gate of the American University campus. The only snag is that you have to be a woman and have a letter of introduction from the university, but if you can manage it, then it is one of the cheapest places to stay in Beirut (about US$15 a night).

One of the cheapest hotels still up and running is the *Hotel Glayeul* (☎ 869690) on Rue Minet al-Hosn, near the St Georges Yacht Club. This is a tiny hotel on the sea front with a terrace restaurant overlooking the sea. It has only 11 rooms and is often full. The cost of a double room here is US$20. At the time of writing, the hotel was undergoing renovations, so it is likely that the price will change.

Nearby, down a small side street almost opposite the Hotel Glayeul is the *Hotel Regis* (☎ 361845). This hotel is slightly more comfortable with 20 rooms, all with private bath. Singles/doubles cost US$20/30, but no unmarried couples will be accommodated in the same room.

The *San Lorenzo Hotel* (☎ 348604/5) on Rue Hamra, near the junction with Rue Mahatma Gandhi, is a popular choice with budget travellers. The rooms are very simple and the hotel a bit run-down, but the location is superb, right in the heart of west Beirut. A reader reported some very dodgy wiring in the shower, so be warned. The entrance is easy to miss – look out for some stairs just past the Station 2000 shop. Rooms, including a bath, cost US$23 for a single, US$20

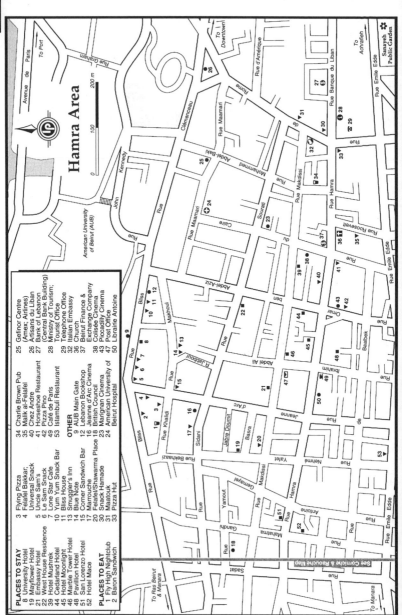

PLACES TO STAY
8 University Hotel
18 Mayflower Hotel
21 Embassy Hotel
39 West House Residence
44 Cedarland Hotel
45 Hotel Moonlight
46 Marble Tower Hotel
48 Pavillion Hotel
51 San Lorenzo Hotel
52 Hotel Mace

PLACES TO EAT
1 Fly High Nightclub
2 Baron Sandwich

3 Flying Pizza
4 Fayrid Bakkar;
   Universal Snack
5 Chez Andre
6 Uncle Sam's
7 Le Sam Snack
10 Lone Star Cafe
11 Yum Yum Snack Bar
13 Bliss House
14 Smugler's Inn
15 Blue Note
17 Corner Sandwich Bar
20 Marrouche
22 Falafel Shawarma Place
30 Snack Hamade
31 Maatouk
33 Pizza Hut

34 Charlie Brown Pub
35 Malirai Al-Freitai
40 Chez Andre
41 Horseshoe Restaurant
42 Pizza Pino
49 Café de Paris
53 Istambuli Restaurant

OTHER
9 AUB Main Gate
12 Lebanon Bookshop
16 Jeanne d'Arc Cinema
18 British Council
23 Magnian Cinema
24 American University of
   Beirut Hospital
25 Gefinor Centre
   (Amex; Airlines)
26 Artisans du Liban
27 Bank of Lebanon
   (Central Bank Building)
28 Ministry of Tourism;
   Tourist Office
29 Telephone Office
32 Italian Embassy
36 Church
37 Beirut Finance &
   Exchange Company
38 Polisseb Cinema
43 Piccadilly Cinema
47 Post Office
50 Librairie Antoine

per person for a double and US$11 per person for a triple. An odd feature of the hotel is the Swiss restaurant, *Taverne Suisse*, on the 1st floor (see under Foreign Restaurants in the Places to Eat section later in this chapter).

More highly recommended is the *Hotel Moonlight* (☎ 352308). It is off Rue Hamra, tucked down a side street between Rue Ibrahim Abdel Ali and Rue Omar ben Abdel-Aziz. Rooms here cost US$20/25/30 for a single/double/triple. The *Hotel Mushrek* (☎ 345773) also seems reasonable enough at US$22/29/43 for singles/doubles/triples. It is also in Hamra on Rue Makdissi.

Places to Stay – middle

There is a bit more choice if you are prepared to pay a little more. One of the best in this range is the unfortunately named *Hotel Mace* (☎/fax 344626/7, 340720). It is just off Rue Hamra on the south side towards the western end of the street. This is an older hotel which has had some recent refurbishment. It has a friendly atmosphere and is very clean. The rooms all have bathrooms, TV and air-con. The hotel has a roof restaurant, which, at the moment, is only open for breakfast. This is an all-round good deal at US$50/60 for singles/doubles (plus 16% service). You can pay a little more for a room with a kitchen if you want to be self-catering. Ask for the 'special price' and you should be offered a discount.

A brand new place which has only one floor open at the time of writing is the *Cedarland Hotel* (☎ 340234). It is just off Rue Hamra on Rue Omar ben Abdel-Aziz. It is immaculately clean and all rooms have private bath, air-con and TV. Singles/doubles cost US$30/45 and twin beds cost US$40. Breakfast is an extra US$5. They should be opening more rooms up shortly.

One of the most popular mid-range hotels, the *Embassy Hotel* (☎ 340814/5), is right in the heart of Hamra on Rue Makdissi, almost opposite the post office. The hotel charges US$34/47 for singles/doubles and lunch in their restaurant costs from US$5 to US$10. Dinner seems a remarkable bargain at US$3,

although it is probably pretty basic stuff. The Embassy claims to be the only hotel in Hamra with a garden and it is certainly a welcome added attraction. In the same area is the *Astra Hotel* (☎ 346600) on Rue Abdall Al-Tannoukhi. Singles/doubles cost US$40/50 including the service tax.

The *Mayflower Hotel* (☎ 340680; fax 342038), off Rue Hamra on Rue Nehmé Yafet, is a popular watering hole for expats (no doubt due to the English-style pub). It used to offer economy rooms at US$35/45 for singles/doubles. These may still be available, although the normal price is US$65/75.

The only hotel in this price range with a sea view is *Lord's Hotel* (☎ 740382/3) in Manara near the lighthouse. It was built in the 1950s. If you don't count the highway in between, this almost counts as a seaside hotel. It is across the Corniche from the Bain Militaire and very close to the Plage Long Beach and the Pigeon Rocks. The prices seem to be negotiable; the manager quoted US$45/60 (plus 16% service) for singles/doubles, which is much lower than their published tariff. Breakfast is extra and costs US$4. The hotel does a fixed-price lunch for US$8 but à la carte is about US$13 for lunch and dinner.

Places to Stay – top end

Not surprisingly, there is no shortage of very expensive hotels in Beirut, and more are being built all the time. If you can afford it, you are spoilt for choice – so this is just an edited highlight of the best of the best.

The two newest hotels are the *Marriott* (☎ 840540) and *Le Vendôme InterContinental* (☎ 369280). The 174-room Marriott, south of Beirut and not far from the airport, has singles/doubles for US$155 plus 16% service. It has the usual Marriott facilities – restaurants, pool, health club and shops. *Le Vendôme InterContinental* is a more boutique-style hotel on Rue Minet al-Hosn, near the Hard Rock Café. Singles/doubles with a city view cost US$190/210 and with a sea view US$230/250.

On Rue Makdissi, at the more modest end of the luxury class, is the *Marble Tower*

Hotel (☎ 354586, 346260; fax 346262). This is a very comfortable 60-room hotel and all rooms are air-conditioned. Singles/doubles cost US$60/75 including the service tax. There is a rooftop lounge and restaurant with live piano music. In the same sort of price bracket on the other side of Rue Hamra is the *Pavillion Hotel* (☎ 350160/1/2/3; fax 352 300). Singles/doubles cost US$65/90 plus 16% service. The hotel is clean and efficient but a bit lacking in style.

Trying to be smart is the *Concorde Hotel* (☎ 740664) on Rue Bliss, diagonally opposite the former Saudi Arabian embassy. It has all the usual features including a pub. Rooms here cost US$75/85 for singles/doubles. For the same money, you can stay at the *Grand Hotel Versailles* (☎ 739860/8; fax 739866), which has a lot more glamour and atmosphere. It is at the western end of Rue Hamra. Singles/doubles/triples cost US$65/75/105 plus 16% service. It has a restaurant serving Lebanese, Italian and Turkish food and a nightclub that seems pretty popular with the locals. The unique feature of this hotel is the full-size theatre which often holds performances of Lebanese folklore and music. The productions vary, so you have to check with the hotel about dates and times. Tickets for performances cost US$10.

Hotel Mediterranée (☎ 603015, 862812; fax 603014) has the advantage of a residents-only swimming pool on the roof and one of the best Lebanese restaurants in the area. It is on the Corniche near the Bain Militaire. Singles/doubles cost US$100/130 including breakfast and 16% service. The hotel does a good fixed-price lunch and dinner though for US$10 or US$15.

If you want to live in the lap of luxury, try the *Bristol Hotel* (☎ 351400, 346390; fax 602451), which is all tinkly chandeliers and silver service. One of the oldest and poshest hotels in Beirut, it has the prices to match. A basic single/double room costs US$110/115 plus 16% service. Needless to say your every whim is catered to. It is not far from Hamra on Rue Mme Curie, but of course your chauffeur will know the way.

Not quite as formal as the Bristol is the *Riviera Hotel* (☎ (03) 305565/6; fax (01) 602272) on the Ave de Paris. With sea views and a pool on the coast, this hotel is still very luxurious with lots of extras like a health club and Japanese restaurant. Singles/doubles cost US$125/145 plus 16% service.

A few kilometres south of Raouché are a couple of new and swanky beach resorts, *Summerland* and *Coral Beach*. These are really the only hotels designed as leisure resorts within the city limits. The better of the two is *Summerland* (☎ 313030; fax 319 213) which is a playground for the very well-off. The resort has an olympic-size swimming pool and a sea-water rock pool. There are also loads of sports facilities and a health club. It's very expensive at US$175/190 for singles/doubles including service. The *Coral Beach* (☎ 317200; fax 319500) has single/double rooms for US$156/198, which includes breakfast and the service tax.

Places to Stay – rented apartments

Beirut has a lot of seasonal visitors who come over for a few weeks or even months, and there is a good selection of serviced apartment buildings to cater for them. If you are staying some time, then it may be a good idea to consider a short-term rental. These places are really like hotels, but with studio flats instead of rooms. They vary from the so-so to the luxurious. You can often haggle and get a good price, especially if you are staying several weeks. It can often work out quite a bit cheaper than a hotel and you can save money on restaurant bills if you are not eating out every day.

In the heart of Hamra the *West House Residence* (☎ 351051/2/3; fax 352451) is recommended. It is near the junction of Rue Sourati and Rue Omar ben Abdel-Aziz. It has 24 self-contained studio apartments with a choice of double or twin beds, a small sitting room, coffee and tea-making equipment, TV, air-con and a bathroom with 24-hour hot water. It isn't luxurious, but it's OK. The nightly charge is around US$35, but if you stay for a week it is about US$200 or US$350 for a fortnight. If you stay for a month, the price ranges from US$500 to

US$950 depending on the size of the room. The same company owns a similar apartment hotel building on Rue Artois called *West House Residence II* (☎ 350450).

At the same price is another apartment hotel, *Residence Haddad* (☎ 342313), which has just opened up on Rue Sidani off Rue Hamra and has similar facilities.

Imperial Suites (☎ 860986, 862781; fax 603687) on Rue de l'Australie in Raouché is a short walk from the Corniche and Pigeon Rocks and is very comfortable, friendly and well run. The clientele seems to be a mixture of business and holiday guests. It has its own supermarket on the ground floor and is convenient to local shops and takeaways. The daily rate for a small apartment with a small but well-equipped kitchen, luxury bathroom, TV and air-con is US$120. Doubles/triples cost US$165/200 including service tax – reductions are available for long-stay guests.

PLACES TO EAT

Beirut is a food paradise with all kinds of cuisine on offer. Eating out is a very important part of the social life of many Beirutis who linger over very lengthy lunches and dinners. Not all the Lebanese restaurants are expensive and it is possible to eat well on the cheap if your budget is limited.

It is quite common to visit one restaurant for mezze, then move on to another for a main course and end up in a café for sweets and coffee, so don't feel obliged to order a three-course meal in a restaurant. The starters are often so delicious and filling that a main course is often unnecessary.

The number of restaurants in Beirut is so huge that this section is just a recommended few – some tested personally, some recommended by locals, but the Lebanese take such care with their food that I don't know of a *bad* restaurant – just some that are better value than others.

Cafés

There are many cafés dotted around Beirut which serve excellent Arabic coffee and sweet pastries. In some of the older establishments you can even smoke a nargileh pipe.

European-style cafés are also popular; the *Café de Paris* on Rue Hamra has a 'watch the world go by' feel to it. In most cafés Arabic coffee costs between LL 1000 and LL 1500. Pastries and sweets vary in price between LL 1000 and LL 2000. If you are on a budget, avoid ordering Nescafé as it is invariably expensive.

Cheap Eats

Almost every street in the city has at least one fast-food takeaway. The usual system in these places is to order your food and pay at the till and then take your receipt to the food counter.

The fast-food joints tend to fall into a few distinct types. The most common type is the felafel and shawarma sandwich shop. These are pretty substantial and usually cost about LL 2000 each. An alternative is the Lebanese pizza which is flat bread with either a za'atar (thyme and sumak) or cheese topping. They come rolled up in paper and are even cheaper than a felafel or shawarma at about LL 750 to LL 1200 depending on the topping. Also at these bakery shops you can get a flat triangular pastry that is stuffed with spinach and lemon – quite delicious – for about LL 1000. Western chains such as Pizza Hut and burger joints are becoming increasingly popular.

In Hamra and around the American University there are many of these places plus some good cheap restaurants mostly catering for students. On Rue Hamra one of the best felafel/shawarma places is between Rue Jeanne d'Arc and Rue Antoine Gemayel near the Strand cinema, although the sign is in Arabic only. The place is very popular so the food is always fresh. Felafels cost LL 1000 and a shawarma (chicken or lamb) costs LL 1500. Another good felafel place is *Malik al-Felafel* (King of Felafel) on Rue Roosevelt.

The *Corner Sandwich Bar* at the intersection of Rue Makhoul and Rue Jeanne d'Arc makes chicken, meat, cheese and labneh sandwiches for LL 2000. It also has a wide variety of fresh juices for LL 1000 to LL 2500, depending on the mix of fruit. Opposite the AUB main gate is *Le Sam Snack*, where you can get a hamburger for LL 2500 and french fries for LL 1000.

Snack Hamade on Rue de Rome, just off Rue Hamra, has Lebanese pizzas starting from LL 750 for za'atar to LL 1250 for cheese or meat. One block further, on Rue de Rome, is *Maatouk* takeaway, which has chicken and meat shawarma for LL 2000 and a wide variety of Lebanese rice dishes.

In the same area, on the corner of Rue Hamra and Rue de Rome is a *Pizza Hut* (☎ 343640) set back from the road in a kind of precinct. Simple Italian-style pizzas here cost about LL 10,000. A bit cheaper is the popular *Horseshoe Restaurant* (☎ 310664) on the corner of Rue Hamra and Rue du Caire. It is a fast-food joint selling chicken, fish, and meat burgers for around LL 2000.

A few metres down the opposite side of Rue Hamra, inside an arcade is *Chez Andre* (☎ 345662), one of the nicer sandwich bars that survived the war. They have excellent lahm bi ajin and sandwiches for LL 1500 to LL 3000, plus draught beer (LL 3000) and wines or spirits (LL 5000). Don't be put off by the dingy arcade; Chez Andre is the third shop on the left-hand side. It is open from 8 am to midnight, Monday to Saturday.

Another cheap takeaway/restaurant is the *Pizza Pino* (☎ 345005/6), near the Piccadilly cinema on Rue Omar ben Abdel-Aziz, where a pizza or steak costs LL 7500.

There are several cheap places down Rue Jeanne d'Arc and on Rue Bliss near the main gate of the university. If you are very hungry, a good choice is *Universal Snack* (☎ 342 209), near the junction of Rue Jeanne d'Arc and Rue Bliss which, apart from the usual Lebanese dishes, serves a variety of grills and breakfasts, including a full bacon and egg English breakfast (LL 7500). It serves a very filling hamburger, salad and chips (LL 5500) and traditional Lebanese breakfast (fuul, labneh, bread etc) for LL 6500. Other items worth trying are the chicken club sandwich (LL 7500) and a real bargain, an omelette sandwich (LL 2500).

Next door is a good felafel and shawarma place, *Felafel Bakkar*, where a felafel sandwich costs LL 1500 (LL 2000 for an extra felafel) and shawarma sandwiches are LL 3000. In Rue Sidani, on the same side as the Jeanne d'Arc theatre, is *Marrouche*, which has excellent chicken sandwiches with a special garlic sauce for LL 2000.

On Rue Bliss opposite the campus is *Yum Yum*, a grocery store-cum-sandwich bar. It has a variety of fillings ranging from LL 2000 (cheese, aubergine, labneh, potato) to LL 2500 (meat or chicken). It also sells mineral water LL 750 for a bottle (LL 500 for half a bottle), soft drinks (LL 750) and canned fruit juices (LL 500 to LL 1750). You can also use the phone in the shop for LL 500 per local call. It is open all week from 7 am to midnight.

If you prefer freshly squeezed juice, go to *Bliss House* a few doors further east. It charges LL 2000 for a small glass and LL 3500 for a large one.

Further west on Rue Bliss is *Baron Sandwich* which specialises in spicy Armenian sausages (soujouk and pasterma) for LL 2500 which goes down well with ayran (a salty yoghurt drink) for LL 1000.

One very cheap eating option is to use the *AUB campus dining room*. You go through the main gate on Rue Bliss and turn left. The dining room is a few metres to the left, in the same building as the post office. It serves lunch from noon to 3 pm daily and coffee and sandwiches all day. Lunch dishes cost about LL 3000 and look very fresh. It typically has a selection of salads and maybe lasagne or some other hot savoury dishes, including vegetarian, plus fruit and pudding.

On the Corniche there are many budget places worth checking out. A good Lebanese place is *Al-Halwani* (☎ 869816, 812881), formerly the Al-Wali, near the Pigeon Rocks. A selection of fast food and mezze dishes will cost about US$6.

At Ras Beirut there are several fast-food places and there is little to choose between them. A new one, *Delight*, across the road from the funfair, has the novelty of English fish and chips (LL 9500) as well as the usual chicken and burgers. It's worth noting that right in front of the fair is a 24-hour pub called *Lena's* which has pool tables.

In the same area is a reasonable Lebanese place overlooking the sea. It is between the Bain Militaire and the funfair and is called *Arous al-Bahr*. It has a pleasant open-air eating area with trees. A mixed mezze is LL 9000 (one dish is LL 3000) and various kebabs are LL 7500. Half a bottle of arak is LL 10,000, but a bottle of house wine will set you back LL 20,000.

Round the Corniche at Raouché there are a few simple sandwich and snack places dotted here and there between the swankier places. Near Merryland on the other side of the street is a row of cafés and juice bars. *Hakim* is a cheap but good place which sells a variety of sandwiches and kebabs. The meat varieties (chicken, shawarma, liver etc) are LL 2000. Further south on the other side of the road is an excellent new chicken place called *Poulco*. It sells about a dozen varieties of chicken sandwiches plus whole roast chicken on a spit. Sandwiches cost about LL 2000 and a whole chicken is LL 9000. There are a couple of vegetarian alternatives such as cheese and spinach in filo pastry (LL 2000 for two pieces) and a selection of cold drinks. The best feature of this place is the terrace which overlooks the whole beach to the south.

Mid-Range

For US$10 to US$15 per head, you can enjoy quite a wide range of restaurants. You can stay within that price range so long as you steer clear of fish and seafood dishes and take it easy on the wine. Many restaurants, even quite smart ones, offer a fixed-price lunch menu and these can be very good value.

Around the AUB campus there are several good but modest restaurants. *Uncle Sam's* (☎ 353500, 354475), on the corner of Rue Jeanne d'Arc and Rue Bliss, is very popular with the campus crowd and has main courses for between US$6 and US$9 and you can have a beer at the bar for US$2. There's a US$1 cover charge and a 16% service charge as well. It is open 7 am to midnight from Monday to Friday and to 3 pm Saturday, closed Sunday.

Nearby on Rue Khalidi is the *Flying Pizza*

(☎ 353975), a reasonably priced pizzeria which also does takeaways. It charges LL 9750 for a small pizza, LL 19,000 for a large pizza, LL 2000 for a soft drink and LL 3000 for a beer. Wine is about LL 10,000 a bottle. There are no additional charges and it is open from 11 am to midnight, daily.

The *Blue Note* pub/restaurant (☎ 743857) is on Rue Makhoul, a continuation of Rue Khalidi. It's a pleasant restaurant offering mezze dishes that start from LL 4000 for a hummus or aubergine dip and main courses that start at LL 8500. Or you can have a drink at the bar – LL 4000 for a local beer or LL 6000 for imported brands or spirits. Other drinks cost LL 6200. It has live jazz music on Friday and Saturday nights, but there is a cover charge of LL 6000. It is open all week, except Sunday, from noon until late.

Next door, offering international cuisine and live music, is the *Smuggler's Inn* (☎ 354 941). It's on the expensive side, but a plat de jour with salad, coffee and dessert will cost US$8 plus US$1 cover charge and 14% service charge. It is open all week, except Sunday, from noon to 4 pm and from 7 pm until late.

At the eastern end of the Hamra district is *Charlie Brown Pub*. It is popular with British expats and has a traditional pub ambience. It has a full range of beers and serves bar snacks and light meals.

On Rue Emile Edde, near Hamra, is the *Istambuli Restaurant* (☎ 352049, 353029) which is a reasonable place serving Lebanese and Turkish food. It has the usual selection of mezze and salads starting from LL 3000 and grills of various kinds for LL 8000. Local beer costs LL 2000 and a bottle of wine is LL 15,000. It is open from 11 am to 11.30 pm daily.

On the coast side of the Corniche are two restaurants with the same owners, the *Laterasse Dbaibo* and the *Bouzouki Dancing Club* (☎ 812893/4). They are superbly situated overlooking the Pigeon Rocks and have various outdoor and indoor eating areas. Because of the view, they are favourite spots for a 'sundowner'. A beer from the bar costs US$2. If you are eating a full meal with a

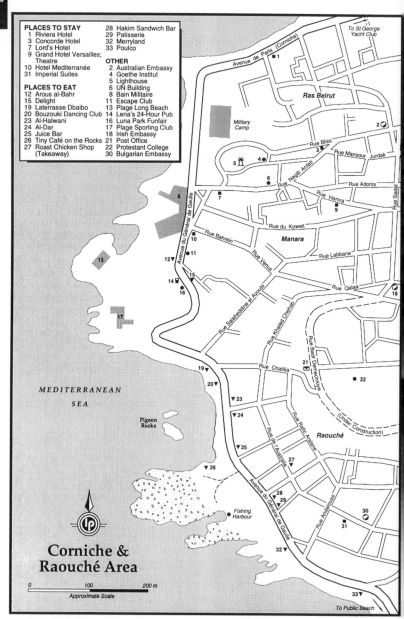

PLACES TO STAY
1 Riviera Hotel
3 Concorde Hotel
7 Lord's Hotel
9 Grand Hotel Versailles;
  Theatre
10 Hotel Mediterranée
31 Imperial Suites

PLACES TO EAT
12 Arous al-Bahr
15 Delight
19 Laterrasse Dbaibo
20 Bouzouki Dancing Club
23 Al-Halwani
24 Al-Dar
25 Juice Bar
26 Tiny Café on the Rocks
27 Roast Chicken Shop
  (Takeaway)
28 Hakim Sandwich Bar
29 Patisserie
32 Merryland
33 Poulco

OTHER
2 Australian Embassy
4 Goethe Institut
5 Lighthouse
6 UN Building
8 Bain Militaire
11 Escape Club
13 Plage Long Beach
14 Lena's 24-Hour Pub
16 Luna Park Funfair
17 Plage Sporting Club
18 Irish Embassy
21 Post Office
22 Protestant College
30 Bulgarian Embassy

To St George Yacht Club

Avenue de Paris (Corniche)

Ras Beirut

Military Camp

Rue Bliss

Rue Mansour Jurdak

Rue Negib Ardati

Rue Adonis

Rue Hamra

Avenue du Général de Gaulle

Rue Bahrein

Rue du Koweit

Manara

Rue Labbane

Rue Venus

Rue Qalaa

Rue Sadat

Rue Salaheddine el Ayoubi

Rue Khaled Chehab

MEDITERRANEAN SEA

Pigeon Rocks

Rue Chatila

Rue Badr Demachkie

(Under Construction)

Rue Rafic Arslane

Rue de l'Australie

Raouché

Rue Andalouss

Avenue du Général de Gaulle

Fishing Harbour

To Public Beach

Corniche & Raouché Area

0   100   200 m
Approximate Scale

couple of drinks, it will cost you between US$12 and US$20.

Expensive

Near the Pigeon Rocks is the *Al-Dar* (☎ 863173) which many Beirutis reckon is one of the best restaurants for mezze. It is all smoked glass and white linen and the clientele seems to be mainly business people, but if you want to sample the best Lebanese food it may be worth a try. The average cost of dinner with drinks is about US$30 to US$40.

In Achrafieh there are number of fine, and expensive, restaurants. The *Beirut Cellar* (☎ 216990, 338185) serves Lebanese and international cuisine. The average price of a meal and drinks is US$30. On Rue Abdel Wahab al-Inglizi *Al Mijana* (☎ 328082, 333112) serves Lebanese food with a meal and drinks priced from about US$40.

Foreign Restaurants

Beirut is a very cosmopolitan city and has many different foreign restaurants. Italian food is very popular and usually very reasonably priced. French cuisine is also popular, but tends to come with a high price tag. Far eastern food is fast gaining in popularity and there are several Chinese, Japanese, Thai and Indian places opening up. If you are fed up with Lebanese food, here is a selection of foreign restaurants.

One of the most well-known is the *Hard Rock Café* (☎ 373023/4), on the northern coast of the Corniche in Ain al-Mreisse. Part of the American restaurant chain and popular with young people, it has meals for about US$16 per person. Similar is the *Lone Star Cafe* on Rue Bliss, one of an international chain, which serves the standard Tex-Mex fare. It is popular with the young crowd and a meal costs about US$15.

Also in Ain al-Mreisse is one of the most popular Italian restaurants, *La Spaghetteria Italiana* (☎ 868298, 363487). It specialises in pasta dishes and is often very crowded. Open for lunch and dinner daily, a meal costs from US$20 to US$25 per person with drinks. It is worth visiting for the good views across the ocean.

Taverne Suisse on the 1st floor of the San Lorenzo Hotel (see Places to Stay – bottom end, earlier in this chapter) serves both Swiss and Lebanese food. A full lunch or dinner will cost you about US$10.

A good Japanese restaurant is *Tokyo* (☎ 800303) on the Corniche at Manara. All the classic Japanese dishes are available here such as sushi, sashimi, fish tempura and a variety of yakitori (kebabs). The prices are not cheap but, compared to Japanese restaurants in Europe, are quite a bargain at US$30 to US$35 per head.

Also in Manara, on Rue Arditi, is *Sirena* (☎ 804640/2), an Indian restaurant specialising in tandoori dishes. It has quite a smart decor and the food is good and not too expensive at US$20 to US$25 for a main course and a few side dishes with drinks. It is only open in the evenings.

In Achrafieh, east Beirut, there are a few places worth trying. A recommended French place is *L'Entrecôte* (☎ 334048) on Rue Fassouh. It has a fixed-price menu which is quite a bargain at LL 17,500. A typical menu features tender entrecôte steak, walnut salad, french fries and dessert. This place can get very full so it is best to book.

A simpler and cheaper place is *Le Chef* (☎ 445373, 446769) on Rue Gouraud. This place is small and cosy and not very expensive. Expect to pay from US$10 to US$15.

ENTERTAINMENT

There are quite a few nightclubs and discos catering for different tastes and pockets in Beirut. Many of the nightclubs are in hotels, but these tend to be quite pricey. Hamra and Achrafieh have a good selection of cinemas often showing recent films from the US and Europe, mostly with Arabic subtitles. There is a good serious Lebanese film industry and if you are a film buff, you should seek out some of the new wave Lebanese films. There are also music and comedy revue shows at the theatres as well as more serious contemporary drama. Unless you have a good understanding of Arabic, these are unlikely to be of great interest.

Cinemas

The best way to check what's on is to look in the French-language daily *L'Orient-Le Jour*. Failing that here is a list of the most convenient cinemas. Cinema tickets cost LL 10,000, except on Monday, when they cost LL 5000.

Broadway, Rue Hamra (☎ 345294)
Clémenceau, Rue Hamra (☎ 366540)
Colisée, Rue du Caire, Hamra (☎ 342962)
Concorde, Rue Dunant (☎ 347144)
Eldorado, Rue Hamra (☎ 341723)
Elysée, Rue Hamra (☎ 861748)
Empire 2 & 3, Achrafieh (☎ 328806)
Étoile, Rue Hamra (☎ 342616)
Hamra, Rue Hamra (☎ 342044)
Monte Carlo, Rue Omar ben Abdel-Aziz, Hamra (☎ 340520)
Piccadilly, Rue Omar ben Abdel-Aziz, Hamra (☎ 340078)
Sagesse, Rue Sagesse, Achrafieh (☎ 201494)
Saroulla, Rue Hamra (☎ 242867)
Vendôme, Achrafieh (☎ 443992)

In addition, the foreign cultural centres often have film seasons featuring work from their respective countries.

Theatres

Once again the listings for individual theatres can be found in *L'Orient-Le Jour*. Not all of the theatres have productions on all the time, but here is a list of the main theatres in Beirut.

Beirut Theatre, Ain al-Mreisse (☎ 343988)
Concorde, Rue Hamra (☎ 352347)
Elysée, Achrafieh (☎ 581970)
Estral, Rue Hamra (☎ 349455)
Jeanne d'Arc, Rue Jeanne d'Arc, Hamra (☎ 354932)
Piccadilly, Rue Hamra (☎ 340078)
Versailles, Hamra (☎ 862561)

Nightclubs

Clubs in Beirut can range from the cool and smart to the tacky. They are not all expensive and many of them offer live music.

One popular and very reasonable club is *Jimmy's* (☎ 867240) on Rue Verdun, which also serves Middle Eastern food. Quieter but more expensive is *Le Rétro* (☎ 334667) on Rue Sursock, Achrafieh. You don't have to eat here and it is a good place to see and be seen.

Also on Rue Sursock is the *Music Box* (☎ 216487, 446570) which has a young crowd and is very popular. Just down the road is another *Le Retro* (☎ 202118). All of these clubs have a smart dress code.

If you like jazz, there is the *Blue Note* (☎ 743857) on Rue Makhoul (see the Mid-Range Places to Eat section earlier in this chapter). It has live jazz on Friday and Saturday and you don't have to eat. In the same street is *Fly High* which is a popular place near the AUB campus. It has a happy hour between 5 and 7 pm, where you get two drinks for the price of one. It is open till very late, seven days a week.

Of the hotel clubs, one of the most popular is the *Weiner Keller* (☎ 350050), which is in the Weiner House Hotel, a few blocks south of Rue Hamra. It has belly dancing and live Lebanese music. Also popular is *Excalibur* at the Grand Hotel Versailles at the western end of Rue Hamra. A bit more expensive is the *Beachcomber* (☎ 317200/4) at the Coral Beach Resort in Jnah.

THINGS TO BUY

There are few things to buy which are exclusive to Beirut, but some craft shops sell traditional Lebanese bits and pieces. Blue glass is popular and you often see sellers of worry beads on the streets. Some of these beads are made from semiprecious stones and are quite expensive. The best places for local crafts in Beirut include the Artisans du Liban shop on Rue Clémenceau in Hamra, La Maison de l'Artisan on Rue Minet al-Hosn in Ain al-Mreisse and L'Artisanale near the Bristol Hotel.

Around Hamra there are some shops which sells kitchen items. Lebanese coffee sets are a good souvenir if you're not travelling light. The glass flasks which contain water in cafés are also a good buy. They have a narrow spout which you hold away from your mouth and pour the water in a narrow stream – hopefully not down your shirt.

GETTING THERE & AWAY
Air
Beirut international airport is served by the local carrier, Middle East Airlines (MEA), and several Arab, Asian and European airlines. For details of airlines and routes, see the Getting There & Away chapter.

Several airlines have their offices in the Gefinor Centre in Hamra, including Aeroflot (☎ 739596), Air Canada (☎ 811690), British Airways (☎ 3738794), Cathay Pacific Airways (☎ 741391), Gulf Air (☎ 353367), KLM-Royal Dutch Airlines (☎ 483299), Malaysia Airlines (☎ 741343/4), and MEA (☎ 737000). Elsewhere are the following:

Air France
    Rue Bliss (☎ 200704/5/6)
Alitalia
    Rue Hamra (☎ 353051)
Austrian Airlines
    Rue Hamra (☎ 343620)
Balkan Airlines
    Rue Hamra (☎ 343260)
Cyprus Airways
    Rue Sursock (☎ 200886)
Emirates
    (☎ 739040/2/3)
Lufthansa Airlines
    Rue Hamra (☎ 347006/7)
MEA
    Airport Office (☎ 822780)
Royal Jordanian Airlines
    Blvd Saeb Salam (☎ 493320)
TAROM
    Khayat, Martinez Building (☎ 342898/776)

Bus
There are regular bus services between Beirut and Damascus and Aleppo in Syria. From Beirut, the buses leave from the eastern side of the Cola taxi stand at roughly two hour intervals for Damascus (9 am, 11 am etc), except for the first bus which leaves at 7.30 am. The last bus leaves at 3.30 pm. The fare is LL 6500 for a one-way ticket. The journey takes about three hours. If you are going to Aleppo (ask for Halab), the buses are even more frequent, leaving at 1 ½ hour intervals from 8 am until 6 pm, then at 7 pm, 9 pm and a late bus leaves at 11 pm. The one-way fare is LL 12,000 and the journey takes about seven hours.

If you are coming from Syria, the main Karnak bus station is about a 15-minute walk to the west of Martyrs Square in Damascus, although not all the buses running this route are Karnak buses (the Syrian-owned government buses). See also Land in the Getting There & Away chapter for more details.

Taxi & Service Taxi
To and from Syria, these all depart from the Cola taxi stand and operate on the usual system of waiting until the car fills up before leaving. They have an advantage over the buses in that you don't have to wait around too long to depart, but the disadvantages are that they can be a bit of a squash, especially on a long journey. If you want the taxi to yourself, you will have to pay for all five passenger seats. See under Land in the Getting There & Away chapter for more details.

Car & Motorcycle
For information on the problems involved in bringing a private vehicle into Lebanon and a list of car rental agencies, see under Land in the Getting There & Away chapter and under Car & Motorcycle in the Getting Around chapter.

GETTING AROUND
The Airport
Beirut international airport is approximately 5km south of Beirut. Taxis to and from the airport are the biggest rip-off in Lebanon. It is not uncommon to be charged US$25 for the 15-minute run into the centre. One way round this is to walk about 200m to the main road when you leave the airport building and hail a service taxi heading north into Beirut. Ask to go to Cola where you can pick up another service taxi to your destination. A service taxi from the airport highway to Cola shouldn't cost more than US$5 and from there the local fare is a fixed rate of LL 1000.

There is now a bus service (No 5), operated by the Lebanese Commuting Company, to and from the airport into the port area. The fare is only LL 500 and from the port you can catch another bus (No 1) to Hamra for another LL 500.

BEIRUT

Bus

There are now several regular bus services operated by the new Lebanese Commuting Company. It operates a 'hail and ride' system. Short hops cost LL 250 and longer journeys LL 500. The No 2 runs from Hamra to Dawra via the port and Achrafieh. The No 3 goes from Cola to Hamra and the No 4 goes from Dawra to Jounieh. There are also several buses which run along the Corniche starting at the junction of Ave de Paris and Rue Minet al-Hosn and running around to Blvd Saeb Salam.

Service Taxi

Service taxis are plentiful and cheap in Beirut. Most routes around the capital are covered and you can hail one at any point on the route. The only way to find out if the driver is going where you want is to hail him and ask. They will drop you off at any point along their route. Official taxis are usually Mercedes and have a taxi sign on the roof, but there are many pirate operators plying the routes. Mostly these are OK, but obviously you take a chance if you get into an unlicensed taxi. The fixed fare for all routes in central Beirut is LL 1000. You can pay the driver at any point in the journey. The fare to outlying suburbs is LL 2000.

Taxi

Taxis are not metered and it is a good idea to agree on the fare with the driver before you set off. Official taxis have red licence plates but again there are pirate taxis touting for trade. These just have the regular black plates and can be anything from a full-time driver who hasn't got a licence, to private individuals on their way somewhere and looking for a paying fare. Women should be careful about using unlicensed taxis, especially at night and if there are no other passengers.

The fares within Beirut should be between LL 5000 and LL 10,000 to the outlying suburbs, which is basically five times the service taxi rate. If you think the taxi driver is asking too much, don't get in and wait for another taxi.

You can also telephone for a taxi from a number of private hire firms. They charge a bit more, but are safer at night. Remember to ask the fare over the phone. Some of the better known companies include:

Beirut Taxi, Chourane (☎ 805418)
City Taxi, Achrafieh (☎ 397903)
Dora Taxi, Dawra (☎ 888316)
Lebanon Taxi, Hamra (☎ 865556)
Radio Taxi, Hamra (☎ 804026, 352250)
Sultan Taxi, Hamra (☎ 868432, 867021)
TV Taxi, Ras Beirut (☎ 862489, 862490)

Around Beirut

The mountains rise steeply around Beirut to the east and this is where people come to escape the city heat and enjoy the dramatic scenery. Many families take apartments for the whole summer season, commuting only when necessary to the humid sauna of the city below. Many of these resorts have grown from simple mountain villages into smart and sophisticated playgrounds for the middle class. The distance to the most accessible of the mountain resorts is amazingly short – 20 minutes from the centre of Beirut and you are in a different, almost alpine, country.

Also within a short drive north of Beirut, on the coast road, are some interesting places which make a good day trip.

BEIT MERI

This popular resort is 17km from Beirut centre and 800m above sea level. The views from the town are very good in both directions: on one side, you see Ras Beirut jutting out into the sea and on the other, the deep valley of Nahr al-Jamani blocked to the east by the Sannine massif. The original village has grown into a small town, with many villas built in strategic positions to take advantage of the views. To cater for summer visitors there are also a few hotels, including the Al Bustan (one of the most luxurious in Lebanon), but most of the hotels are for long-term guests only.

Beit Meri has been occupied since Phoenician times and some ruins from the Roman and Byzantine periods still exist. At the time of writing the ruins were occupied as a lookout post for the Syrian army and could not be visited. This situation will hopefully change in the future. The ruins are found at the end of the road leading to the right from the town's main roundabout junction, about 1km in the direction of the Hotel Al Bustan. Worth seeing in particular are the fine **mosaics** on the floor of the Byzantine church dating from the 5th century AD. There are also the remains of a number of

PETER JOUSIFFE

HIGHLIGHTS

- Take the Téléphérique (above) up to the outstretched arms of the Virgin of Lebanon in Harissa
- Immerse yourself in Lebanese culture at the annual international music festival in Beit Meri
- Ascend Jebel Sannine for breathtaking views of Lebanon
- Soak away your cares at the Ain Fawar hot spring in Bikfaya
- Wander along the banks of the meandering Nahr al-Kalb and read the ancient stelae inscriptions
- Explore the depths of the magnificent Jeita Grotto
- Party hard in the Jounieh nightclubs or gamble at the reopened Casino de Liban
- Visit the Faraya Natural Bridge and the ancient Faqra ruins
- View the modern sculptures of the Basbous brothers in Rachana

137

small **temples**, including one dedicated to Juno which was built in the reign of Trajan (98-117 AD). Nearby is the Maronite **monastery of Deir al-Qalaa**, which was built in the 17th century on the remains of a Roman temple, which in turn was probably built on an earlier Phoenician temple. As at Baalbek, this was dedicated to Baal, known here as Baal Marqod.

On this same road there is an old church, the **Marsassine Church**, which is worth seeing. It is unlocked and there is an unusual internal staircase leading up to the bell tower.

In the absence of ruins to visit, there is little to do in Beit Meri except walk around and enjoy the views, which is a pleasant enough way to pass a few hours. Every year, in February and March, there is an **international music festival** at the Hotel Al Bustan. The festival is a mixture of classical recitals and traditional Lebanese music and attracts major artists such as Maria Ewing and Evelyn Glennie. For more details, see under Arts in the Facts about Lebanon chapter.

Places to Stay & Eat

The only hotel, apart from long-stay apartments, is the ultra-posh *Hotel Al Bustan* (☎ (04) 972980/1/2). It is the last word in luxury and set in a very attractive location. The rooms, service and food are first rate, but the place is as expensive as it looks. Singles/doubles cost US$210/230 per night and that doesn't include breakfast or the 16% service charge. Still, it's worth dropping into the Scottish bar for a drink; it has a rather British, clubby feel to it and a beer will set you back US$3.

If you want something more simple, there is a good snack bar-cum-restaurant on the main roundabout called *Hakim's Fast Food* (☎ (04) 971278). It has a wide range of drinks and simple meals which are fairly cheap.

Getting There & Away

You can get a service taxi from the Cola stand in Beirut for LL 4000 to Beit Meri. The taxis stop on the main roundabout in the town and you can easily walk round the whole town from there. If you have difficulty getting a taxi direct from the centre, take a service taxi to Mkalles, which is to the east of Beirut, and pick up another taxi from there.

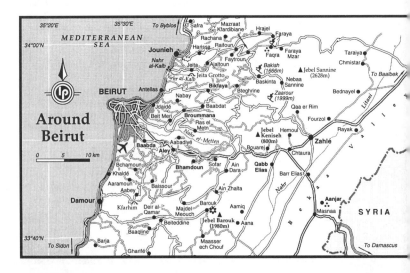

In the evening the number of taxis leaving from Beit Meri drops considerably, but even so, you should not have to wait more than 15 minutes to catch one back to Beirut. Either flag down a taxi on the road heading west to Beirut or wait at the roundabout.

BROUMMANA

Six kilometres north-east of Beit Meri is the resort town of Broummana. It is quite an interesting walk from Beit Meri, although slightly uphill. The road runs along the crest overlooking the Nahr al-Jamani. Whereas Beit Meri is sedate and quiet, Broummana is a bustling little town heaving with hotels, cafés, shops and night life. As a consequence, the place can be crowded to bursting point at weekends and the traffic congestion horrendous.

The views down to Beirut and the Mediterranean are even better than at Beit Meri, and there are pleasant **walks** you can take down the hill side which is dense with pine trees. Broummana is situated perfectly to catch the breeze and has a pleasant climate, even during the height of summer. The town has nothing as serious as ancient monuments to distract you from the pleasures of eating, drinking and all-round partying, which are the main attractions.

At night the revelries continue at several discos, all strung out along the main road which loops around like a horseshoe. There is also a cinema if you prefer. Needless to say, if you visit Broummana out of season, things are a lot quieter – and cheaper – but most of the fun has gone out of the place, unless scenic walks are really your thing.

One special event is worth noting: in August, Broummana hosts a national tennis tournament.

Places to Stay

The problem with any of the Mount Lebanon resorts is the shortage of cheap, or even mid-range, accommodation. The whole place is geared to well-off middle-class tourists. If you are prepared to visit during the low season, the prices drop dramatically – often by half or more, which is why the cheaper places tend to shut up shop altogether, opening only in the high season.

One of the nicest hotels which is open all year is the *Kanaan Hotel* (☎ (04) 960084, 961649; fax 961213), an old family-run place with bags of character and friendly owners. It is right on the main road with views overlooking the Mediterranean. The lounge is decorated with old Lebanese objets d'art, oil paintings and chandeliers. A large terrace overlooks the road where you can watch the world go by. Singles/doubles/triples cost US$50/75/90 for B&B in the high season and US$35/50/65 in low season. The hotel has a coffee bar and mini-market downstairs.

The *Grace Hotel* (☎ (04) 961065, 960751) is further along the main road away from Beirut. The entrance is round the hairpin corner. It has 24 clean and comfortable suites. Expensive in summer at US$125 per night, it offers a bargain rate in the low season of only US$50 per night or US$400 per month. The suites are all doubles.

Almost opposite the Grace Hotel and down a tiny side street is the small *Capri Hotel* (☎ (04) 961781) which looks as though it has lots of character. It only caters for long-term (three months) summer guests. Prices range from US$850 to US$1800 per month, depending on the size, number of rooms and the view.

Further up the hill, past the Grace Hotel, is the *Belvedere Hnoud* (☎ (04) 961103), a moderate two-star place with 33 rooms. Singles/doubles cost US$30/50. Beyond it, the four-star *Primotel* (☎ (04) 963142, 963087) is more upmarket with rooms from US$125 to US$275 plus 16% service charge. The other top-end hotel is at the opposite end of town. *The Printania Palace* (☎ (04) 960416/7/8/9; fax 960415) is generally reckoned to be the best hotel in town and is predictably expensive. Singles/doubles here cost US$150/160 plus 16% service. The price varies according to the season.

Places to Eat

If you are looking for a restaurant, there are dozens to choose from, in all price brackets.

Near the Printania Cinema is a good *pizza restaurant* where you can eat for between US\$5 and US\$10. There is also a *pizza/Italian restaurant* on the ground level of the Grace Hotel which has a terrace with a view towards Beirut.

If you want a cheap snack, there is a crêperie stand about halfway along the main road called *Tonnino Broummana*. Sweet or savoury French-style crêpes cost from LL 2000 (cheese) to LL 5000 (house special).

Along the same stretch there is the *Safari Restaurant*, a new-looking place which sells an array of snacks and drinks. Down past the Kanaan Hotel, on the same side of the road, is *Tom Well's Pub & Restaurant*, which specialises in steaks, or you can just have a drink at the bar.

Getting There & Away

The same service taxis which serve Beit Meri often go on to Broummana; they will drop you anywhere along the main road through the town. It is a good idea to take the taxi to the far end of town and then stroll back down to the lower end if you are just making a day trip. That way you can flag a taxi quite easily on the road back to Beit Meri. The fare to and from Beirut is LL 5000.

BIKFAYA

The road from Broummana to Bikfaya runs along the valley of Nahr Antelias and passes through the village of Baabdat. As you leave the village, there is a good view of **Jebel Keniseh** (880m), part of the Mount Lebanon range. A small detour down a road on the right, which leads to Choueir, passes the **monastery of Mar Musa**.

Bikfaya is a village which has grown into a summer resort. The area is famous for its fruits and the **Ain Fawar hot spring**, which is reputed to be good for liver ailments – just the thing if you have been partying too much.

Bikfaya suffered quite a lot of damage during the war: it is the home town of the Gemayel family, the founders of the Phalangist party and militia, and it got caught up in the fighting between rival Maronite militias. Historically the village made its

money from the silk trade, but these days Bikfaya relies on the beauty of its surroundings to attract tourists, and also, to an extent, on agriculture. Every August there is a **flower festival**, which attracts a great number of visitors.

Getting There & Away

You should have no trouble getting a service taxi from either Beit Meri or Broummana, which is about 15km away. If you are coming direct from Beirut, you can get a service taxi to Antelias (which is on the coast road on the way to Jounieh) and then pick up another service taxi to Bikfaya at the turnoff. A service taxi from Broummana should cost about LL 3000.

JEBEL SANNINE

This impressive mountain (2628m) is worth climbing in the summer for the unparalleled views of Lebanon from its summit. Actually it has two summits: the higher one is less interesting and it is the slightly lower peak which affords the spectacular views. To make the climb, head for the village of **Baskinta**, which is east of Bikfaya. From there, continue 6km to the hamlet of **Nebaa Sannine**, where there is a *nebaa* (spring) which feeds the **Wadi Sellet ash-Shakroub**, the starting point for the climb. It is best to make the climb from the most southerly slopes rather than tackling the slopes which overlook the hamlet. It is a moderately steep climb which should not take more than three hours. The last part of the climb is easier; there is a path which runs like a ledge around the mountain top.

From the top, you can see Qornet as-Sawda, Lebanon's highest peak at 3090m, to the north and Jebel ash-Sheikh (2814m) to the south. The Bekaa Valley and the Anti-Lebanon range are clearly visible to the east and in the foreground is Jebel Keniseh and Jebel Barouk (1980m). To the west you can see the foothills of the Mount Lebanon range slope all the way down to Beirut. A clear, fine day is a good choice for this ascent and you need to be well shod and reasonably fit.

Getting There & Away

If you do not have your own transport, the only practical solution would be to take a taxi to the hamlet of Nebaa Sannine and arrange to be picked up at a specific time and place. Failing that, you would have to make the walk back to Baskinta, about 6km, and pick up a service taxi from there. It would be a wise idea to inform someone (your hotel or friends) of your plans and what time you expect to return.

NAHR AL-KALB

The mouth of Nahr al-Kalb, or Dog River (the Lycus river of antiquity), is on the coast road heading north between Beirut and Jounieh. Here, conquering armies down the millennia have left some plaque or memorial carved into the sides of the gorge. It is a tradition which has persisted into this century. Apart from the earlier Assyrian carvings, there are **stelae** (carved inscriptions) in Latin, Greek, Arabic, French and English. All of these, except for the stele of Nebuchadnezzar II, are on the left bank, following the ancient courses of the steep roads carved along the slopes of the gorge.

Some of the oldest stelae have eroded to almost nothing, but some of the later inscriptions are still clear and sharp. If you ignore the nearby motorway with its constant roar of traffic, the Nahr al-Kalb is an interesting place to visit. Apart from the inscriptions, the walk along the left bank of the river is quite pleasant and there are some river-side places to stop for lunch or a drink.

River-side Inscriptions

Starting from the motorway, the first bridge is the old 'modern' road. A hundred metres past that you see the charming old **Arab bridge** which now serves as a crossing point to a restaurant. The restaurant has rather ruined the view by putting up a tunnel of polythene over the bridge to keep their customers dry.

The inscriptions are helpfully numbered and run as follows:

. Engraved by **Nebuchadnezzar II** on the rocky wall

> ### Howling Wolf
> Nahr-al Kalb got its name from the large statue of a wolf which used to guard the entrance to the river. The terms for wolf and dog are the same in Arabic, although the Latin name for the river was *Lycus* (wolf).
>
> Legend has it that the statue used to howl as a warning against invaders. How this worked nobody has been able to work out, but it may have been due to some kind of wind trap causing an acoustic effect. In 1942 Australian soldiers, who were working on the nearby railway, apparently uncovered a large, but badly damaged, wolf statue. This has since disappeared. ■

on the right (north) bank near the junction of the motorway and the old 'modern' road is a cuneiform inscription from the 6th century BC. This is very overgrown and hard to see.

All the other inscriptions are on the left bank starting near the Arab bridge and following the bank of the river to the main road, then continuing up the side of the gorge. Follow the stairs up until you are on top of the motorway tunnel. The ancient Egyptian and Roman roads continue and there are further inscriptions.

2. This is an Arabic inscription lying almost at water level opposite the Arab bridge and commemorating its construction. It dates from the 14th century and was inscribed on behalf of Sultan Seif ad-Din Barquq by the builder of the bridge, Saifi Itmish.

3. A few metres down river there is a Latin inscription from the Roman emperor **Caracalla** (Marcus Aurelius Antonius; 198-217 AD). This describes the achievements of the 3rd Gallic Legion.

4. Above the Roman inscription is a modern obelisk which marks the French and Allied armies' arrival in Lebanon in 1942.

5. Another modern inscription opposite the Arab bridge commemorates the 1941 liberation of Lebanon and Syria.

6. A French inscription marks the French invasion of Damascus on 25 July 1920 under General Gouraud.

7. The original stele showing an Egyptian Pharaoh and the god Ptah has been covered by the later inscription by the French army commemorating their 1860 expedition in the Chouf Mountains.

8. An Assyrian king is depicted wearing a crown with his right hand raised, but this is badly preserved.

9. This inscription commemorates the British army invasion of 1918.

10. An Assyrian figure, presumably a king, is depicted here but it is very weather-beaten.

11. This is an Assyrian stele which again is in a very bad state of preservation.

12. A British commemorative plaque dating from 1918 marks the achievements of the British 21st Battalion and the French Palestine Corps.

13. A Greek inscription.

14. This is another Greek inscription, but it is very worn. Just past this and to the right is the white rock plinth where the wolf statue once stood.

15. About 30m further on, a stony path climbs sharply. This next stele shows an Assyrian king in an attitude of prayer.

16. Next along is a rectangular tablet showing **Pharaoh Rameses II** of Egypt (1292-1225 BC) sacrificing a prisoner to the god Harmakhis. This is the oldest inscription.

17. A little higher and only a few metres away is another Assyrian king.

18. About 25m further up the slope, you come to the road at the top. There you'll see a rectangular stele which shows Rameses II again, this time sacrificing a prisoner to the sun god Amon by burning him to death.

19. The last stele is Assyrian and shows **Prince Assarhaddon** with cuneiform text describing his victory against Egypt in 671 BC.

Also worth seeing is the nearby Catholic retreat of **Deir Luwaizeh** on the north side of the gorge. It has a huge statue of Christ, which stands on top of the building, with arms outstretched.

Places to Stay & Eat

There are no places to stay in the immediate vicinity, but Nahr al-Kalb is very close to the amenities of Jounieh. As for eating, there is one really good restaurant, *Tazka* (☎ (09) 216830/1), just across the old Arab bridge. You can sit out on the river terrace and have just a few mezze or the full works. It is open for lunch and dinner every day except Monday. An average meal will cost around US$10, an open buffet meal US$15 and an à la carte meal around US$25; extra for drinks. The food is well above average. The restaurant sometimes has an oriental night with belly-dancing entertainment.

On the left bank there is a new complex of bars, restaurants and an adventure playground for kids called *Happy Valley*, which obviously caters for families on a day trip. You can get pizzas and burgers there quite cheaply or just have a drink at the *Best Seller Pub*.

Getting There & Away

Nahr al-Kalb is simple to get to – just take a service taxi from the Cola stand in Beirut that is going to Jounieh and get it to drop you off. The river mouth is just past the long tunnel on the highway and is easy to spot. The fare from Beirut is LL 2500 and you have to change service taxi at Dawra. When you leave, it is easy to flag down a service taxi going in either direction on the highway.

JEITA GROTTO

It would be a pity to visit Nahr al-Kalb and not see the Jeita Grotto (☎ (09) 220840/1/2/3), which is a stunning series of caves with stalactites and stalagmites in profusion. The road to the caves is the first turning on the right past Nahr al-Kalb if you are facing north. It is about 5km up a winding road and is possible to walk but a bit arduous. During the war, the caves were used as an ammunitions store. They have now been restored and reopened to the public. The water which pours from the grotto is the source of the Nahr al-Kalb and in winter the levels rise so high that the lower caverns are flooded.

Part of the trip into the caves involves a

AROUND BEIRUT

The naturally formed stalagmites and stalactites in the Jeita Grotto have been named according to their resemblance to ancient classical statues found in Lebanon.

A Shot of Discovery

The Jeita Grotto caves were originally discovered in 1836 by an American named Thompson who was out on a hunting trip. He fired a shot into the blackness to judge the size of his find and realised that the cavern was enormous. He reported his discovery, but it was not until 1873 that the authorities sent a team from the Beirut Water Supply Company to investigate. They discovered a vast honeycomb of galleries and ravines with an astonishing natural spectacle of rock formations. This first survey did not go very far into the system and it was the later expeditions – in 1902, 1927 and two further explorations in the 1950s – which managed to chart over 10km into the system. In 1958 a new, dry upper chamber was discovered, large enough to seat an audience of 1000. Many concerts were given here including some by Stockhausen in 1969. ■

boat ride through some of the more magnificent caverns. This eerie experience cannot help but bring to mind the image of crossing the River Styx into the underworld.

The extraordinary series of caverns now houses a wonderful **son et lumière** show. The boat ride through the lower cavern is only operated during summer when the water is lower, but the upper galleries are open all year. Entrance is LL 16,500 (adults) and LL 9250 (children). The caves are open Tuesday to Thursday from 9 am to 6 pm and Friday to Sunday from 9 am to 7 pm. The caves are closed on Monday, unless it is a public holiday. There is strictly no photography allowed inside the caves, and all cameras must be handed in at the door.

Getting There & Away

You can catch a service taxi to Nahr al-Kalb and either walk from there (a stiff half-hour uphill climb), or catch a taxi to take you up from the highway – not many service taxis go up this road. A return trip to the caves will set you back at least US$10 from Nahr al-Kalb. The turnoff is clearly signposted on the highway.

JOUNIEH

Jounieh is only 21km north of Beirut and has become the capital's playground. Although it lacks anything in the way of historical monuments, Jounieh is worth visiting if you want to spend a day swimming and relaxing. At night during the summer, the place is buzzing with night life. It is set on a wide, attractive bay with the mountains rising steeply behind. Many Lebanese visiting home for the summer prefer to stay in Jounieh rather than Beirut.

Orientation & Information

Jounieh's growth from a small village to a built-up playground was partly the result of the war. The Christian community in Beirut decamped en masse to Jounieh, which became the unofficial capital of Christian

Lebanon. As a result, there is little left of the small-town charm that used to characterise the bay. Now it is a modern town full of high-rise apartments, restaurants, shops, night clubs and beach resorts stretching the whole 2km along the bay. Actually the northern end of the bay was a separate village called Maameltein, but the development of the bay has blended the two seamlessly together.

At the southern end of the bay is the port where you catch the ferry to Cyprus when it is operating. The old road hugs the bay and still retains some charm, including a few examples of old buildings that have survived the developers. The new four-lane highway slashes through the upper part of town lined with businesses, shops and eateries. In between and stretching up into the hills above the town is a sea of new apartments and hotels.

Most of the amenities such as banks, the post office and the municipality building are in the lower part of town on or around Rue Mina, as is the taxi stand. It is easy to change money here if the banks are closed; most shops and hotels will only be too happy to change US dollars.

The telephone code for Jounieh is 09.

Tourist Office The tourist office in the municipality building, opposite the British Bank building, is expected to reopen soon. At the time of writing, it was closed.

Things to See & Do
Bearing in mind that this is a leisure town, there is very little to do that does not involve expenses. The **walk** along the bay from the port to Maameltein is a good way to spend an hour or so, stopping for a cooling drink on the way.

Towards the southern end of the bay along Rue Mina, you can see some good remaining examples of **traditional Lebanese houses**. Some of these have been restored and their ground floors have become designer boutiques or trendy cafés; others are empty and in need of urgent repair.

Further along the bay, the hotel developers

have gobbled up the plots of land which face the sea and there is barely a centimetre of sea front which is not now a private resort of some kind. All of which means that in order to **swim**, you have to pay. Charges vary from US$5 to US$10 depending on the place. In order to maximise their piece of the bay, all these resorts have built out over the sea, so swimming is usually from a concrete pier.

Once you have exhausted the swimming, eating and drinking possibilities, the most fun thing to do in Jounieh is to take the **Téléphérique** (cable car) from the centre of town up to the dizzying heights of Harissa. This ride was dubbed the Terrorifique by my companion and I think this just about sums it up. Needless to say this is not for you if you suffer from vertigo. The ascent is at a very steep angle and the cars are tiny, taking four people at a push. The ride takes about nine minutes and leaves from near the Aquarium Hotel.

The cable car (☎ (09) 914324) operates from 10 am until midnight. It is closed on Christmas Day and Good Friday. Return tickets cost LL 7500/4500/3500 for adults/students/children.

The **Casino de Liban** (☎ (09) 832097, 930067, 830097) was the most famous of all the casinos in the Mediterranean, and after years in mothballs during the war, has reopened with great fanfare. It is on the northern end of Jounieh bay in Maameltein. In the old days, it was the scene of beauty pageants, outrageous floor shows with girls wearing chandeliers on their heads, live animals and a whiff of James Bond-style glamour. The gaming rooms were always packed with sheikhs, sultans and spies, playing baccarat, roulette and blackjack.

The new incarnation may be a bit of a disappointment. It was described in one magazine as looking like 'it was based on the design of a video arcade in a multiplex cinema'. Dinner and dance-cum-casino entertainment with showgirls is a very dated concept, but it may be worth a look for nostalgia's sake. The casino has three gambling rooms, one room for slot and poker machines, five restaurants, a nightclub and eight bars. There are also two show rooms. You can dine and watch the show or just have drinks.

Places to Stay – bottom end

The *Hotel St Joseph* (☎ (09) 931189) is in the old part of town on Rue Mina, about 50m north of the municipality building. It is more of a pension than a hotel with only 15 rooms in a lovely 300-year-old house. The main rooms have high vaulted ceilings and there is a lovely roof terrace with views over the street on one side and the sea on the other. The hotel attracts long-stay guests and it is difficult to get a room in summer. It charges US$20 per person for a room with shower and toilet (maybe a bit more for the very large rooms).

Further north on the sea front is the *Middle Beach Pension* (☎ (09) 910651; fax 910650). It has chalets, which can sleep two or more people, for US$50 per night.

Places to Stay – middle & top end

One of the nicest seaside hotels is the *Arcada Marina* (☎ (09) 915546, 832250; fax 935 956), at the beginning of Rue Maameltein (the extension of Rue Mina heading north). The hotel is a converted and extended old building. It has a bar and nightclub downstairs with brick-vaulted ceilings. There are 70 rooms with air-con, bathrooms and TV. There is a swimming pool and a terrace built out into the bay for sea bathing. Singles/doubles cost US$70/80 including breakfast and service.

Further north along Rue Maameltein is the *Aquarium Hotel* (☎ (09) 936858, 911467; fax 935098) on the right-hand side, close to the Téléphérique. This is a fairly modern hotel which is due for some renovations but is quite clean and comfortable. The hotel faces the sea and has a private pool across the road. The 60 rooms all have satellite TV, air-con etc. The single/double rooms cost US$106 plus 16% service or a suite costs US$180 plus 16% service. The hotel restaurant serves Lebanese and western dishes and lunch or dinner will cost about US$15.

Further along Rue Maameltein, there is the *Dallas Hotel* (☎ (09) 937720/1; fax 914301) which is set off the main road up a short hill. This is a four-star hotel with rooms at US$75/95 for singles/doubles. It has a good fixed-price menu for lunch and dinner; lunch is US$7 and dinner US$10 or US$12. There is an annexe which houses a health club.

At the far end of the bay, at the Maameltein end, is the *Montemar Hotel* (☎ (09) 912803, 918134; fax 936206), which has great views across the bay. Built in 1968 it was the first hotel in Jounieh, next to what was the train station. It has a swimming pool, an English-style pub and a nightclub downstairs. The rooms are quite reasonable at US$45/60 for singles/doubles including service. Meals cost from about US$12 to US$17 and breakfast costs US$5.

Places to Eat

There are so many places where you can eat in Jounieh that your best bet is to look around until you find one that suits you and your budget. There are plenty of snack and fast-food places along Rue Mina and further north on Rue Maameltein.

A good eatery is *La Crêperie* (☎ (09) 912491) where you can have a selection of savoury and sweet crêpes at reasonable prices (US$6 on average). It's in an old Lebanese house set on a cliff with a magnificent view of Jounieh's bay. It is just before the centre of town on the old Jounieh road.

The *restaurant* at the Al Medina Hotel (☎ (09) 918484) is reputed to be the best in town, at least according to some locals I spoke to. The hotel is for long-term guests only. It is a sea-front place specialising in Lebanese mezze and a full blow-out will cost around US$20 with drinks. It is right on the shore about halfway around the bay. Across the road is *Le Beyrouth* (☎ (09) 830730), a supper nightclub which has a nightly show with Lebanese music and dancing. If you are going to eat, expect to pay about US$20.

Entertainment

Jounieh is famous for the amazing extent of its night entertainment. There are many nightclubs, discos and nightly shows for those who want to kick up their heels and enjoy the Lebanese night life. The shows tend to start about 10.30 pm and go on until the small hours. Some of the more popular clubs include:

Alecco's (☎ (09) 220900, 220669), Kaslik, has a nightly show with oriental and international music. The average price of a meal and drinks is US$35.

Al Layali (☎ (09) 930418, (03) 753045), Maameltein, has oriental and belly-dancing shows. A meal with drinks costs around US$40.

Bermuda (☎ (09) 936138/531), Jounieh, has oriental and international music. The average price of a meal plus one drink is US$20.

Duplexe (☎ (09) 831058, 344200/2), Kaslik, has oriental and international music. The average price of food and drink is US$35.

Epsilon (☎ (09) 936127, 918489) offers a nightly show, including food and drink, for around US$20.

Oliver's Club (☎ (09) 934616), Maameltein, has food, drink and music for around US$20. This club is popular with the young local crowd.

Opera (☎ (09) 911140, 900296), Kaslik, offers oriental and international music, food and drinks for around US$35.

Picolo Padre (☎ (09) 934616), Maameltein, offers a nightly show, a meal and drinks for around US$22.

Shangai (☎ (09) 916615, 930793), Maameltein, has a nightly show with a meal and drinks for around US$20.

Getting There & Away

The service taxis to Jounieh leave from the Cola stand in Beirut or from Dawra in east Beirut. They are very frequent and you should not have to wait too long. If you get a taxi which is going further north, you will get dropped off on the highway. Ask to be let out near the Téléphérique and there is a pedestrian bridge across the highway which leads to the centre of town (about five minutes walk). The fare from Beirut is LL 4000.

HARISSA

High above Jounieh bay is the gigantic white **statue of the Virgin of Lebanon** with her arms outstretched, where she has stood since the end of the last century. Around her are the

The monumental statue of the Virgin of Lebanon, weighing 13 tons, was built in France and moved to Harissa in the late 19th century.

churches and cathedrals of various denominations, the latest being the modernist Maronite cathedral whose outline can be seen from Jounieh below.

There is an impressive Orthodox church and a chapel beneath the Virgin statue. During religious festivals, such as Easter, there are often rather colourful **religious parades** which attract the crowds. At other times, people come just to enjoy the fantastic view from the top and enjoy lunch in the restaurant at the top of the cable car ride.

Places to Stay & Eat

Since the Hotel Harissa closed down, there are no places to stay in Harissa for short-term visitors. The *Azurama Hotel*, about 50m above the Nahr al-Kalb, rents rooms by the month. A two-person room costs US$275 per month, a two-room suite US$375 and a three-room suite US$450.

The *Téléphérique Restaurant* has nightly entertainment, mezze and grills for about US$15 per person. It is also open for lunch, minus the entertainment.

The main street of Harissa village has a selection of shops, snack places and restaurants where you can get a burger or a pizza for a few dollars.

Getting There & Away

From Jounieh you have two death-defying options: either you take the cable car or you go by road. If you want a taxi, you can pick one up at the main taxi stand just off Rue Mina, not far from the Hotel St Joseph. The road to Harissa redefines the term 'hairpin bend'. The road twists alarmingly with sheer drops along part of the route, but the ride takes only 15 minutes. The fare is about US$5. For details about the cable car, see the earlier Jounieh section.

FARAYA

There are two routes up to the ski resorts of Faraya and nearby Faqra; one from Jounieh via Harissa and the other on the road just north of the Nahr al-Kalb – the one to Jeita Grotto. The second route goes through a couple of villages-turned-resorts.

The first few kilometres along this route are solidly developed with shops, restaurants and apartments. Past that there is a small place called **Aintoura** which has a large college run by the Lazarist fathers (the first French establishment to be founded in Lebanon). Unfortunately the old building was destroyed by the Turks who occupied it between 1914 and 1918 and the buildings are now modern.

Further on, at **Ajaltoun**, the views of the coast and Beirut in the distance are lovely. There are a number of restaurants, such as the *Nakhoul Restaurant*, along the way which are good stopovers. There are also a number of pottery sellers by the road side if you feel like shopping for souvenirs.

When you reach **Raifoun**, you come to a roundabout; take the left exit which leads up to **Faytroun**. There is nothing much of interest in the village, but there are some ski shops where you can buy or hire equipment. Past Faytroun there are some dramatic rock formations. These are dolomite limestone formations, known by the locals as the 'House of Ghosts'. They are **rock tombs** which seem to be cut in the side of these hills and are visible from the road.

In Faraya there are several places to stay which are open all year and ski shops which are open during the winter season. It's a small village with little or nothing in the way of formal entertainment outside of the hotels. It is very pretty in a Swiss-alpine kind of way. The **Christian cemetery** is atmospheric and worth a look. The main attraction of the area is its natural beauty. If you're not there for the skiing, then there are some beautiful **walks**; you could walk to Faqra (6km) and back in a couple of hours. The ski station is 7km up the mountain road which is above the village. See the Ski Facts boxed story in the Facts for the Visitor chapter for details on skiing in Faraya. Tour Vacances organises reasonably priced package tours to Faraya (for details see Organised Tours in the Getting Around chapter).

One of the most famous natural features of the area is the **Faraya Natural Bridge** just off the road between Faraya and Faqra. It is easy to spot from the road if you look to the right. There is a parking place just off the road. It is an interesting but steep walk down to the bridge itself. Centuries ago the bridge was thought to be a work of human construction, but it is in fact entirely a freak of nature.

Places to Stay & Eat

The *Coin Vert Hotel* (☎ (09) 321260/1; fax 720812) is right on the main road in the village. It is a simple but clean one-star hotel which is open all year. It has only 24 rooms and singles/doubles/triples cost US$25/35/45. It has a restaurant which serves European and Lebanese dishes with an average cost of US$8 for lunch or dinner.

The *Old Bridge Hotel* (☎ (09) 720206) is in a lovely setting down by a river, close to the old church. It is a small place, again open all year, with 20 rooms. The price of singles/doubles is US$38. The most attractive thing about the hotel is the terrace overlooking the river and old bridge. The restaurant is good but a bit pricey at US$30 to US$50 per person for a full three-course lunch or dinner with drinks.

Another recommended place is the *Tamerland Hotel* (☎ (09) 321268), in the centre of the village. This family-run hotel is friendly and informal with a choice of regular rooms or suites. The regular rooms cost between US$40 and US$60 per night with private bathroom and ·satellite TV. Breakfast is an extra US$5 for two people. The restaurant specialises in fresh fish (straight from the tank), but you can have a more simple meal of steak, fries and salad for US$5.

Above the village, about 5km on the road to the ski station, is the excellent *Chateau d'Eau* (☎ (09) 951602). It has recently been done up and is very comfortable with a nice clubby atmosphere. Reputedly in the winter it has a lively après-ski scene with plenty of partying. The hotel gets its name from the crashing cascade nearby which adds an interesting sound effect. Singles/doubles/triples cost US$45/50/70 in the low season and US$50/55/75 in the high season. Breakfast is included in the price. The restaurant serves French and Lebanese food at mid-range prices plus chef's specials.

Getting There & Away

You may be able to pick up a service taxi all the way to Faraya from the Cola stand in Beirut, but only in the busy winter season when there are plenty of people coming and going. Unfortunately Faraya is not on the main route to anywhere else. More likely you will have to go by service taxi to Jounieh and get a taxi from there. If you haggle, you will probably get a taxi to take you for US$15 (it is about a half-hour ride). When you leave, you will either need to get the hotel to call a taxi for you or, if you are lucky, find one in the main street in the Faraya village on its way back to Jounieh or Beirut.

FAQRA

Faqra is only 6km from Faraya and is also a ski resort. It is even smaller than Faraya and there are very few facilities, such as shops etc, in the village. The main reason to go there, apart from skiing, is to see the **ruins** which date from the Greek era and which lie very picturesquely on the side of a hill overlooking the valley below. These look especially attractive and romantic when there is snow and they feature on several postcard scenes of Lebanon.

There is a large temple which is dedicated to Adonis, the 'very great god', and nearby a couple of altars, one dedicated to Astarte, the other to Baal Qalach. The large temple is in the middle of a labyrinth of rocks and is preceded by a rectangular court cut out of the rock. The main temple portico had six Corinthian columns. Surrounding the temple are some rock-cut tombs and to the north is a ruined tower monument from a later period. It originally had a pyramid-shaped top rather like the one at Amor, near Hermel.

See the Ski Facts boxed story in the Facts for the Visitor chapter for details on skiing in Faqra.

Places to Stay & Eat

The only place to stay in Faqra is the ultra-smart *L'Auberge de Faqra* (☎ (01) 339220, 885591/2/3; fax (09) 710293). This hotel is very much in the upper price bracket and is part of a large sports and leisure development. Hotel guests can use the facilities such as the swimming pool, tennis and squash courts, although there is a small extra charge for these facilities. The hotel also has its own ski lifts up to the pistes. Double rooms cost US$212 (high season) and from US$122 in the low season (May/June and October/November). All prices include breakfast and the service charge.

On the road above the village, next to a petrol station, there is a small restaurant called *Highland Snack* which offers about the only cheap meals in the area. Further down near the ruins is *Restaurant Faqra*, which is a bit more expensive, and about

1km past the village is *Restaurant Kanater*, also reckoned to be quite good.

RACHANA

In the same area, about 5km north of the village of Aachqout, is Rachana – the 'Museum Village'. This place is worth visiting for the family of artists who have their homes and studios there. You know you are in the right place when you come across great **modern sculptures** lining the road side.

The Basbous brothers have created an extraordinary artistic community in the village. Of the three brothers, Michel, Alfred and Yusuf, only two are still alive; Michel died some years ago. Both of the surviving brothers are still working prolifically in stone, wood and metal, creating striking and sometimes bizarre figures. They are very welcoming to visitors and will happily show you around. They have become something of a tourist attraction in their own right and at the weekend many visitors pass by their studios to look or buy.

When Michel was alive, he built an amazing house in organic shapes, reminiscent of Gaudi. He used all manner of found materials such as the curved windscreen used as a window. The tiny house is now used as a workshop by Yusuf who works in an instinctive primitive style. His brother Alfred has a house and large studio down the road. He has been sculpting for 37 years and has exhibited internationally.

To find their studios, turn left at the junction of the main street in Rachana, by a small shop selling cold drinks. A few hundred metres along the road you will come to a bend and this is where Yusuf's house is. Alfred's is a short distance around the corner.

Getting There & Away

If you do not have your own transport, you will need to get a taxi from Jounieh and get it to wait for you while you visit the studios. The return trip from Jounieh and back will cost about US$20. Alternatively you could try hitching from Aachqout on the main road.

North of Beirut

BYBLOS (JBAIL)

The name of Byblos is known the world over (to anyone who paid attention in class) as the world's oldest continually inhabited town. Byblos was old before the great civilisations of the Middle East were even thought of. Archaeologists believe that the site has been occupied for at least seven thousand years and probably more. None of the capital cities of the world today can boast such an ancient lineage.

The historic harbour and old town of Byblos, (called Gebal in the Bible, Giblet by the Crusaders and Jbail in Arabic), is still unspoiled and very picturesque. In its tourist heyday before the war, it was a favourite watering hole for the crews of visiting private yachts, international celebrities and the beautiful people of the Mediterranean jet set. It still retains the rather chic air of a place to see and be seen in, although the new generation of locals has grown up without the benefit of a tourist economy and the original town has spilled over its historic boundaries in an unlovely jumble of modern styles. There is a buzz of anticipation for the arrival of the well-heeled postwar tourists who will breathe new life into the resort.

History

To describe Byblos' history requires a trip back into prehistoric times. The earliest occupation dates from the 5th millennium BC when the first settlers fished and tended their animals. This was also the era of early agriculture, and the remains of cultivated grains have been found at a site that has been partially excavated on the promontory. This Neolithic community lived in houses of a single room with crushed limestone floors. Many tools and primitive weapons have been discovered at the site, some of which are on display at the National Museum in Beirut. By the Chalcolithic period (around the 4th millennium BC), the use of metals and ceramics had become commonplace.

HIGHLIGHTS

PETER JOUSIFFE

- Explore Byblos' fascinating Phoenician, Roman (above), Greek and Crusader archaeological ruins
- Spend a few hours wandering around Byblos' historic harbour and have a drink with Pepe Abed
- Stay a few nights at the excellent Amchit cliff-top camping ground of Les Colombes
- Visit the place of legend where Adonis was gored by a wild boar
- See the river run red at the Afqa Grotto
- Descend on foot to the extraordinary rock formation of Bala Gorge
- Take one of eight hiking trails from the scorpion-shaped village of Douma
- Marvel at the splendid natural sea wall enclosing Batroun's harbour
- Taste freshly made lemonade – a specialty of Batroun
- Picnic in view of the fairytale Moussalayha Castle

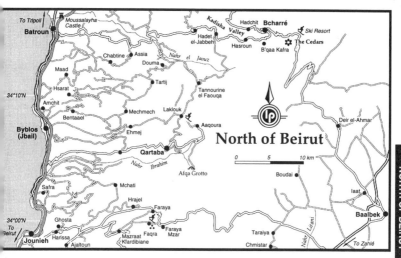

These early inhabitants of Byblos buried their dead in distinctive terracotta storage jars which have been found in great numbers at the archaeological site.

By the mid-3rd millennium BC, Byblos, as well as other areas along the coast, was colonised by the Phoenicians. The city-state of Byblos became a significant religious centre in the area. The temple of Baalat Gebal was famous in antiquity. It was probably built on the site of an early sacred grotto, and it underwent several rebuildings during the course of time due to both natural and military catastrophes.

Close links with Egypt encouraged the development of Byblos, both culturally and religiously. The temple received generous offerings from several Pharaohs during this prosperous era and Byblos evolved its hybrid style of art and architecture: part Egyptian, part Mesopotamian, and later showing some Mycenaean influences.

Around 2150 BC the Amorites invaded and took the city. Culturally they were a less developed people who ruined much of the city's well-ordered layout as well as its settled and prosperous wellbeing. This is the period of the underground royal tombs and of the Obelisk Temple dedicated to Resheph, god of burning and destructive fire. Amorite rule lasted until 1725 BC, but the people of Byblos were resilient enough to keep something of their own identity throughout this occupation and a continuity of their art can be seen throughout this and subsequent periods.

The Amorite occupation was ended by another invasion, this time by the warlike Hyksos. The Amorites were shocked into a quick submission by the Hyksos army who arrived with horses and chariots, hurling javelins and carrying lances; all new to the people of this region. The Egyptians, also suffering from the Hyksos' invasion of their country, soon retaliated and, from 1580 BC, claimed the coast of Phoenicia as their own.

A long period of good trade and development followed, during which time the kings of Byblos were the subservient partners of their Egyptian masters. Many Egyptian customs were adopted, with temples and burial chambers being decorated in the Egyptian manner. The cult of Isis was very strong during this time.

The linear alphabet, perhaps the most significant achievement of the Phoenicians that has been handed down to us, was also developed during this period. It is thought that the alphabet may have originated in Byblos, and was invented as a more practical way of recording trading transactions than the cuneiform script that was previously used. This new system of writing quickly spread throughout the civilised world.

The Greeks called Gebal 'Byblos' after the Greek word for papyrus, *bublos*, because papyrus was shipped from Egypt to Greece via this Phoenician port. A collection of sheets were called *biblion*, or book, and from the Greek *ta b blia*, or 'the books', the English word 'Bible' was derived.

This period of prosperity did not last and between 1100 and 725 BC Byblos was eclipsed by Tyre as the most important Phoenician city-state. Byblos became a pawn in the power struggle between the Greeks and the Assyrians between 725 and 612 BC, eventually being ruled by the Assyrians and then the Neo-Babylonians.

Following the conquest of Babylon by Cyrus the Great in 539 BC, Byblos was regenerated as a trading link to the east under the Persian empire. During the Hellenistic period, Byblos, unlike Tyre, voluntarily became an ally of Alexander and continued to flourish under its own royal dynasty.

When the Greek Empire waned and the Roman Empire waxed, Byblos concentrated its trading efforts to the west. From 63 BC onwards, the Roman Empire became a market for Phoenician goods. Byblos had long ago burst its original confines and now the city boasted lavish public architecture and suburban farming developments.

Unfortunately, Byblos had sowed the seeds of its own downfall by not regulating the pace of deforestation – the very resource that had made this boom town wealthy was in a dwindling supply. When the Roman Empire split into east and west in 395 AD, Byblos allied itself to Constantinople and became increasingly important as a religious centre. Pagan religion gradually gave way to Christianity and the city became the seat of a bishopric under Emperor Diocletian. The

city was protected by the Eastern Roman Empire until the Islamic invasion in 636 AD.

The focus turned eastwards under the Muslims and Byblos' sea port dwindled into insignificance along with the city's defences. Damascus and Baghdad were not interested in cultivating trade with Europe, and Byblos now called Jbail, was left vulnerable. During the Crusader offensive, which began in 1098, Jbail fell to the Count of Tripoli Raymond de Saint Gilles. Despite resuming trade with Europe, the city never regained its former power. The subsequent power struggles between the Crusaders and the Muslim forces continued until August 1266 when Emir Najibi, lieutenant of Sultan Baibars laid siege to the town. The defenders withdrew to Tripoli under the cover of night.

The next few centuries were relatively uneventful; the Turks took control of the city in 1516 and Byblos passed into insignificance until Ernest Renan, a French historian and philosopher, began to excavate the site during his stay in Lebanon from 1860 to 1861. It wasn't until the 1920s that a proper survey of the site was carried out; work that is still going on today. Excavations at Byblos came to a standstill during the civil war and have yet to resume.

Orientation

The town radiates uphill to the east of the harbour and is flanked on the south by a promontory which is the site of the Crusader castle and ancient ruins. The older part of the inhabited town stops at the medieval ramparts at the top of the hill, and from there to the main highway is the modern part of town where most of the usual amenities can be found. At the end of the promontory is a defensive tower which you can climb for a good view of the harbour and castle.

Information

Tourist Office The tourist information office (☎ (09) 540325) is near the main entrance to the Crusader castle site.

Money The main road in and out of the town Rue Jbail, has several banks including the

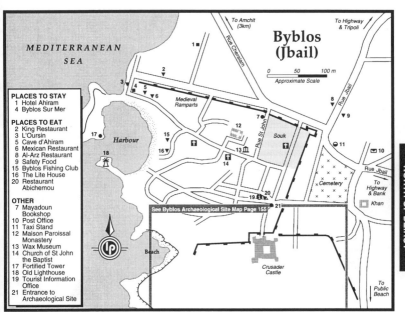

PLACES TO STAY
1 Hotel Ahiram
4 Byblos Sur Mer

PLACES TO EAT
2 King Restaurant
3 L'Oursin
5 Cave d'Ahiram
6 Mexican Restaurant
8 Al-Arz Restaurant
9 Safety Food
15 Byblos Fishing Club
16 The Lite House
20 Restaurant
   Abichemou

OTHER
7 Mayadoun
  Bookshop
10 Post Office
11 Taxi Stand
12 Maison Paroissal
   Monastery
13 Wax Museum
14 Church of St John
   the Baptist
17 Fortified Tower
18 Old Lighthouse
19 Tourist Information
   Office
21 Entrance to
   Archaeological Site

Byblos (Jbail)

To Amchit (3km)
To Highway & Tripoli
MEDITERRANEAN SEA
Medieval Ramparts
Harbour
Souk
Cemetery
Khan
Crusader Castle
Beach
To Highway & Bank
To Public Beach

See Byblos Archaeological Site Map Page 155

NORTH OF BEIRUT

Metropolitan Bank and the Banque du Liban. Both are on the left as you face the direction of the highway. There are some bureaux de change as well – look out for signs in the shop windows. You can also change money in the hotels.

Post & Communications There is a post office tucked way on the first floor of a building just off Rue Jbail. Look for a large, modern building with the sign 'Diab Brothers' on the corner of Rue Jbail. The entrance to the post office is a few metres along this road on the right. It is open Monday to Saturday from 8 am to 1.30 pm. The telephone code for Byblos is 09.

Bookshop There is a bookshop in the old town, on Rue St John, called Mayadoun Bookshop, which sells a good selection of books in English and French. They have a guide to Byblos in English, French and German, which sells for US$5. The guides

have obviously been in mothballs since they were published in the 1960s.

The shop also sells international magazines and newspapers. It is open from Monday to Saturday.

Walking Tour
Byblos is ideal to explore on foot. Starting at the taxi stand on Rue Jbail, head north and take the road leading down on your left to the **harbour**. This road curves around to the left and you come out by the Byblos Sur Mer hotel. A quiet stroll around the harbour brings you to a turn on your left leading uphill. Take this road, which leads up to the **Church of St John the Baptist**. Opposite the church is the **Wax Museum** with its tableaux of Lebanese culture. Continue further up the hill, past Rue St John, and turn right. This brings you to the entrance to the **archaeological site**. Allow plenty of time to explore the site. When you leave by the same entrance, continue straight ahead and

this road leads you to the **souk** area with rows of medieval shops. Once you have finished exploring the souks, head west back down to the harbour and end up (hopefully around sunset) at the **Byblos Fishing Club** for a well-earned drink and a look at the private collection of antiquities.

The Ruins
The site is open daily from 8 am to sunset and entrance costs LL 6000. Guides who speak English, French, German, Italian or Japanese are available. They seem to rely on gratuities, but figure on paying at least LL 10,000 (more if there are several of you).

Crusader Castle The most dominant monument at the archaeological site is the castle built by the Franks in the 12th century and constructed out of monumental blocks, no doubt pillaged from the classical ruins. Some of the blocks are the largest used in any construction in the Middle East (apart from one or two at Baalbek). The castle measures 49.5m by 44m with a deep moat around it. You can see the nearby Phoenician ramparts on either side of the entrance. The structure is far from elegant but has some points of interest. The whole of the basement area is a huge water cistern which is largely intact. The best part of the castle (unless you are passionate about Frankish architecture) is to climb to the ramparts and see the whole of Byblos spread out with the sea behind. Apart from a glorious view, it gives you a very clear idea of the layout of the ancient city. Access to the roof is via a staircase. A word of warning: there are no safety rails on either the staircase or the roof and there are some sheer drops. See also The Architecture of Lebanon section in the Facts about Lebanon chapter.

Ramparts The defences of Byblos have been maintained and added to since the foundation of the city. They date from the 2nd and 3rd millennium BC. Six different constructions have been discovered forming a 25m thick wall. The ramparts curve around from the castle to the shore and on the other side of the castle curve west and then south,

Now in the National Museum in Beirut, this pectoral set was buried in King Ibshemuabi's tomb in Byblos more than 3800 years ago.

blocking access to the promontory where the original city was confined.

Temple of Resheph This 3rd-millennium temple was burned and rebuilt during the Amorite occupation. The later temple (known as the Obelisk Temple) was removed to a nearby site so that Dunand, an archaeologist, could excavate the original structure. It consists of a sacred enclosure. In the middle is a three-part sanctuary facing east.

Temple of Baalat Gebal This is the oldest temple at Byblos with parts dating back to the 4th millennium BC. The temple underwent major rebuilding after being destroyed by fire during the Amorite period. A few centuries later the site was levelled and a new sanctuary was built. A Roman colonnade of six standing columns from around 300 AD line the route to this temple.

Obelisk Temple Despite being rebuilt on this new site, the Obelisk Temple is one of the more interesting places to visit at Byblos. The temple consists of a forecourt and a courtyard which houses the slightly raised sanctuary. The collection of standing obelisks was discovered in the courtyard, including one built at the command of Abichemou, king of Byblos at the end of the

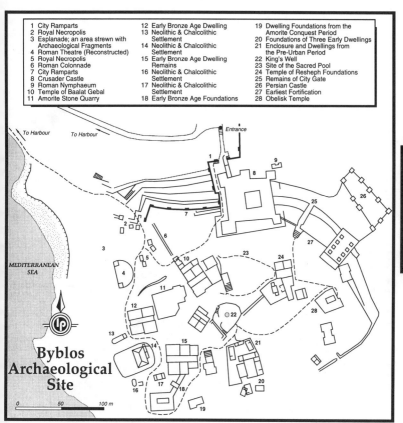

1 City Ramparts	12 Early Bronze Age Dwelling	19 Dwelling Foundations from the
2 Royal Necropolis	13 Neolithic & Chalcolithic	Amorite Conquest Period
3 Esplanade; an area strewn with	Settlement	20 Foundations of Three Early Dwellings
Archaeological Fragments	14 Neolithic & Chalcolithic	21 Enclosure and Dwellings from
4 Roman Theatre (Reconstructed)	Settlement	the Pre-Urban Period
5 Royal Necropolis	15 Early Bronze Age Dwelling	22 King's Well
6 Roman Colonnade	Remains	23 Site of the Sacred Pool
7 City Ramparts	16 Neolithic & Chalcolithic	24 Temple of Resheph Foundations
8 Crusader Castle	Settlement	25 Remains of City Gate
9 Roman Nymphaeum	17 Neolithic & Chalcolithic	26 Persian Castle
10 Temple of Baalat Gebal	Settlement	27 Earliest Fortification
11 Amorite Stone Quarry	18 Early Bronze Age Foundations	28 Obelisk Temple

Byblos Archaeological Site

19th century BC. They were thought to have been originally **God boxes** where the gods would live and be worshipped. Several votive offerings have been found here. Other schools of thought suggest that they may be connected to the rites of Adonis and Astarte.

King's Well In the centre of the promontory is a deep depression which is the site of the King's Well (Bir al-Malik). This supplied the city with water until the end of the Hellenistic era. Access was via steep steps which have been rebuilt many times over the course of the centuries.

Roman Theatre This charming reconstruction of the theatre is only one-third its original size and has been sited near the cliff edge, which gives it marvellous views across the ocean. The fine mosaic floor, discovered in the orchestra, has been removed to the National Museum in Beirut. One notable feature is the series of miniature porticos in front of the stage.

Royal Necropolis This series of nine royal tombs are cut in vertical shafts deep down into the rock and date from the 2nd millennium BC. These **well tombs** are not found elsewhere and attempts to protect the tombs from plunder proved fruitless – all of them have been raided for treasure. The most important tomb is that of King Hiram (1200 BC) who was a contemporary of Rameses II of Egypt. The shaft containing his grave was inscribed with early Phoenician script and said *Warning here. Thy death is below.* Hiram's sarcophagus has been removed to the National Museum in Beirut.

Early Settlements To the south of the site is the Neolithic (5th millennium BC) and Chalcolithic (4th millennium BC) enclosures. The crushed limestone floors and low retaining walls can still be seen, although this part of the site is quite overgrown. Throughout the site, large burial jars were found in which the bodies were curled up in a foetal position. In the earlier period the dead were buried beneath the floors of the houses.

The Medieval Town

Church of St John the Baptist In the centre of this Crusader town is the Romanesque-style Church of St John, which was begun in 1115 AD. The church has an unusual layout; the apses are facing north-east, but a sharp change in direction brings the northern half of the church back into its more conventional east-west alignment. Apparently this is because a mistake in orientation was only discovered after the apses had been built and was corrected halfway through construction. The south portal is purely Romanesque, but the north doorway is of an 18th-century Arab design.

Wax Museum (☎ (09) 540463) Almost opposite the Church of St John is a small museum containing wax figures in various tableaux representing the history of Byblos from earliest times. Some of these are a bit bizarre to say the least. But the traditional costumes are well worth seeing. It is open daily from 9 am to 6 pm and entrance costs LL 5000.

Souk Area The medieval part of the city still has a lively souk area. To the north and east of the castle, the streets are crammed with all manner of small shops selling everything from clothes to pirated tapes, from household goods to snacks and drinks. The souk is geared towards local trade rather than tourists, so if it's exotica you're looking for, you would do better elsewhere.

Beach

Near the promontory is a great beach. It is about a kilometre south of the centre of town. Follow the road which runs parallel to the coast and a small road leads down to the beach on the right. This is one of the better beaches in Lebanon and has soft sand. If you are lucky, you may spot some underwater ruins, so bring a snorkel. The taxi fare from the centre of town is about LL 3000.

Boat Rides

Down by the old port the anglers take visitors on 15-minute rides in their small boats for LL 4000 per person from spring until autumn.

Places to Stay

There are only two hotels in town. The cheaper of the two is the *Hotel Ahiram* (☎ (09) 540440), which is a five-minute walk from the harbour heading north (signposts point the way). This is a mid-range hotel with 25 rooms and is just above a stretch of beach belonging to the hotel. It also has a pool, a bar and a small restaurant, but it is not exactly a bargain at US$45/65/75 for singles/doubles/triples. The rooms are small and the bathrooms need attention, but it is adequate for a night or two. All the rooms have TV, air-con and room service. The price includes the service charge and a basic breakfast. If you order juice or eggs, you will be charged extra. Lunch or dinner costs about US$10. There is a small display of antiquities in the lobby which are for sale and not very expensive.

The other hotel, *Byblos Sur Mer* (☎ (09) 540356, 548000, 942983; fax 944859), is right on the harbour and has wonderful views both across the sea and the harbour. This is an expensive place to stay, but it has a great deal of style and, of course, the rooms are very comfortable with all the usual luxuries associated with a hotel of this class. There are two restaurants, including one, *L'Oursin*, which specialises in fish, right across the road on a private jetty next to the hotel swimming pool. The hotel has 33 rooms and five suites. Singles/doubles cost US$95/115 including the service charge. Breakfast is an extra US$7. There is a fixed-price lunch available for around US$20 and dinner costs between US$20 and US$50.

Places to Eat – cheap

There is no shortage of small places selling shawarma sandwiches and felafels, as well as the usual pizza and burger joints along the main street, Rue Jbail. A good place to try, near the junction with the road down to the harbour, is the reassuringly named *Safety Food* (☎ (09) 943017), where you can get a filling sandwich or a variety of burgers for about US$2. There are also some stalls which sell a selection of hot or cold snacks on the approach road down to the harbour.

Along the same stretch of road are three small restaurants next to each other: one sells burgers, one is an ice-cream parlour, and one, *King Restaurant*, specialises in chicken. The filleted, fried chicken with garlic sauce is very good. Dinner with a couple of beers costs about US$9.

Down by the port is *El Molino*, which has meals ranging from US$5 to US$10, including hamburgers for US$5. It is closed on Monday.

Places to Eat – mid-range

Restaurant Abichemou (☎ (09) 540484) has been running for 25 years and commands an impressive view over the castle from its 1st-floor terrace. It is right outside the entrance to the ruins. The menu is Lebanese and there is a special fixed-price menu at lunchtime, which is a pretty good deal. A selection of mezze dishes and a main course grill, plus fruit and coffee costs US$10. If you want fish instead of meat, the price is US$15. In the evening an à-la-carte dinner will cost around US$20.

There is another Lebanese restaurant in the mid-price range opposite Safety Food on Rue Jbail called *Al-Arz Restaurant* (09) 540278), which also has a selection of mezze plus grills and is a similar price. If you crave something different, there is a *Mexican restaurant* a few doors up from the Byblos Sur Mer hotel on the harbour. It has tacos, tortilla dishes and Mexican dips and salsas. Expect to spend US$15 per head (a lot more if you have a taste for margaritas!).

Places to Eat – expensive

Byblos has no shortage of smarter places to eat, especially around the harbour area. If you are only going to splurge once during your stay, go to the famous *Byblos Fishing Club* (☎ (09) 540213). Even if you don't want the full works, do drop in for a drink and watch the sun go down over the harbour. This is the place which was once described as the most fashionable restaurant in the Middle East, and the framed photos of celebrity diners (hundreds of them) tell their own story. Frank Sinatra, Marlon Brando, Brigitte Bardot – anyone who was anyone in the world of showbiz or politics in the 1960s seems to have passed through here and sat at the bar made from an old fishing boat. The bar is still here, but the celebrities are a bit thin on the ground these days. Never mind, owner Pepe Abed (see the Pepe the Pirate boxed story on the next page) still keeps his amazing collection of antiquities on display in a museum-cum-bar downstairs. Open from 11 am to midnight, lunch or dinner will cost from US$20 to US$30 plus drinks.

Next door is *The Lite House*, a smart, new French restaurant which specialises in seafood. The prices are high, with salads at US$5 and fishy starters (such as smoked salmon) at US$12. Main courses are about US$10 on average, but much more if you order seafood.

If you are looking for entertainment as well as food, the *Cave d'Ahiram Restaurant* (☎ (09) 540206), next door to the Byblos Sur Mer hotel, has live music in the evening (from 10 pm onwards) and features the usual mezze and grill menu. Starters here cost from

Pepe the Pirate

Known as the Pirate of Byblos, Pepe Abed is a tourist attraction in his own right. Restaurateur, jewellery designer, marine archaeologist – these are just some of the things which have brought the beautiful people of the prewar jet set to his bar, the *Fishing Club*, at Byblos.

Born in Mexico of Lebanese parents, he took off around the world with his playboy cousin and, having mixed with the glitterati of the day, he ended up in Byblos. He opened the Fishing Club in 1963 and it soon became one of the most fashionable restaurants in the Mediterranean. His regular visitors included Marlon Brando, David Niven, Brigitte Bardot and Anita Ekberg, and their pictures, along with those of dozens of other celebrities, line the walls of the bar.

Pepe, now in his 80s, lives in an apartment at the Fishing Club, where he houses an impressive collection of antiquities that he has found over the years on diving expeditions. A marble knight's head sits across his table. 'He is my best friend – he never speaks,' says Pepe.

Visitors can see his collection as some of it is housed in the basement museum, but his collection of stunning ethnic-inspired jewellery, designed and made by himself, is a more private matter. He never sells his work, but he may be persuaded to let you have look – if he is in the mood. Otherwise, content yourself with a look around the 'hall of fame' and have a cool beer. ■

US$2 to US$3 and main courses about US$9. There is both a harbour view and a terrace overlooking the sea.

Getting There & Away

Bus The Lebanese Commuting Company operates a bus service from Beirut to Byblos. The bus leaves from the Corniche area in Mazraa and the trip costs LL 500 one way.

Service Taxi You can easily catch a service taxi from Beirut (from the Cola taxi stand or Dawra) for LL 4000. Ask for Jbail, which is the Arabic name for the town. If Byblos is not the final destination of the service taxi and it is going further north, then you will be dropped at the side of the highway, but it is only a five or 10-minute walk into town. Beware if you have heavy luggage though.

Taxi A private taxi to Byblos will cost around US$20 from the centre of Beirut. A return journey will cost the same again and taxis can be found near the centre of Byblos.

Getting Around

Everywhere in Byblos is easily reached on foot, but if you need to use a taxi, they congregate at the junction of Rue Jbail and the road down to the harbour, and also at a point halfway along Rue Jbail heading east toward the highway. A short ride of up to 5km will cost around US$5 (to destinations within the town US$2). The local service taxis, which leave from the same places, charge from LL 1000 to LL 2000, depending on your destination, or you can flag one down on the highway, which is five minutes walk from the centre of town.

AMCHIT

The town of Amchit, 3km north of Byblos, is a well-preserved relic of Lebanon's past. The collection of **traditional townhouses** were built originally by wealthy silk merchants in the 19th century. They are now nearly all privately owned – some are fully restored, others need funds for restoration.

There are 88 old houses in total, which are now under a preservation order. The houses were constructed using the old stones of the area and you can often spot an ancient piece of carving being used as a lintel. The architecture is influenced by both the oriental and Venetian styles, with double-arched mandolin windows and covered courtyards. This Italian influence was due to the trade agreement between the Duke of Tuscany and Lebanon.

The houses are not officially open to the public, but if you ask around, often the owners are happy to show visitors inside.

It was in Amchit that Ernest Renan lived for a while; it was also here that he lost his sister, Henriette, whose tomb can still be seen outside the small church at the top of the village. The church here was built on the site of an earlier temple of which some remains are still visible.

A more up-to-date celebrity in Amchit is **Bechara Karan** who is a well-known artist and herbalist with his own very popular TV show. Ask for directions to his house and he may treat you to a glass of his herbal elixir.

Places to Stay

Les Colombes (☎ (09) 943782, 940332), known locally as Camping Amchit, is just off the old coast road in the lower part of Amchit. It is the only camp site in Lebanon and is run by the owner, François Matta, and his wife Pascale. François' mother started the camp in the grounds around the family house back in the 1960s. The camp is on a cliff-top site overlooking a beautiful stretch of coast and is planted with trees and shrubs which have now reached maturity and provide abundant shade. It really is a most attractive location. If you don't have your own tent you can hire one, as well as sleeping bags. There are also small 'tungalows' – bungalows in the shape of a tent with two beds and a shower, which are a slightly more comfortable alternative to camping.

It also has some chalets, but these tend to be booked for long-term summer visitors. There are quite a few facilities on the site. There is a private pathway down to the sea where you can bathe from the rocks (with excellent snorkelling!) and there are plans to create a sea-water pool from a natural rock formation at the foot of the cliffs.

This place is highly recommended. There are a lot of thoughtful touches such as a bread

Ernest Renan (1823-92)
The name of Ernest Renan turns up frequently in Lebanon. His early life in France prepared him for a career as a Roman Catholic priest, but he later broke away from the church. He is famous as a theological writer and critic. His best known work, *Vie de Jesus* (Life of Jesus), was published in 1863 and formed part of an eight-volume work *History of the Origins of Christianity*.

He lived in Amchit with his beloved sister, Henriette, during his research of the site at Byblos. She died after an illness and is buried in the churchyard in Amchit, where you can still see her mausoleum. Renan described the spot in his preface to *Vie de Jesus*: 'beneath the palms of Amchit near sacred Byblos, not far from the river Adonis to which the women of the ancient mysteries came to mingle their tears...' ■

oven for baking your own pizza, facilities for the disabled and a small chapel which holds Sunday mass. There is a kitchen with gas burners, electrical points (220V) for caravans, telephone, mail and a poste restante service. There is even a weekly beach party for guests thrown in free. The owner speaks English and French and is very helpful.

Prices for camping are US$3 per person (half price for children), US$1 to rent a tent, and US$0.50c to rent a sleeping bag. The tungalows are US$20 per night for two people. The two-person chalets are US$20 and the four-person chalets are US$30. Meals are available cheaply during the summer season (May to October). A fixed-price menu lunch or dinner costs only US$2.50.

Getting There and Away
A local taxi from Byblos costs US$5 or you can catch a service taxi from Beirut heading north (past Byblos) and get them to drop you at the Amchit turnoff. The highway dissects the town and it is about a five-minute walk to the upper part of town and 10 minutes to the lower part (to the sea and the camping ground).

QARTABA
The road heading east from Byblos leads up through the mountains towards Afqa and Laklouk. The village of Qartaba is worth a stop en route to explore. It is 35km from Byblos and is built on the south slope of the Jebel Wardiye, overlooking the Nahr Ibrahim (also known as the Adonis River).

On a small plateau to the south you can see the remains of a **ruined village** including the remnants of a fairly large monument. Slightly higher up, there is a small temple which was converted to a church in the Byzantine era. This is called locally **Mar Jurios Azraq**, meaning St George the Blue.

AFQA GROTTO
Ernest Renan thought Afqa Grotto was one the most beautiful sights in the world. It is the sacred source of the Nahr Ibrahim, 45km east of Byblos, and, according to legend, it was the place where Adonis (or Tammuz to give him his Phoenician name) met his death; he was gored by a wild boar while out hunting. The legendary love story between Tammuz and Astarte (or Adonis and Aphrodite, if you prefer) has persisted through the millennia.

The area near Afqa Grotto is riddled with ancient shrines and grottos dedicated to the tragic youth and his story has come to symbolise life, death and rebirth. Each spring the river runs red, which in antiquity was supposed to be the blood of Tammuz. In reality, the torrent picks up ferruginous minerals

from the soil and stains the water the colour of red wine.

> Thammuz came next behind
> Whose annual wound in Lebanon allured
> The Syrian damsels to lament his fate
> In amorous ditties all a summer's day
> While smooth Adonis from his native rock
> Ran purple to the sea, supposed with blood
> Of Thammuz yearly wounded
> (Milton, *Paradise Lost*)

Afqa today is a very popular excursion for Lebanese families at the weekend. The roaring torrent rages down from the grotto 200m above. You can walk up a flight of steps on the left bank of the river (steep but not too difficult). When you reach the top, the cave is enormous. The freezing water surges out of an unseen underground source.

At the foot of the main fall is a bridge. If you walk down beneath the bridge, there are a couple of cafés on a terrace with soothing views as the water crashes and tumbles over the rocks to the river below.

On a raised plateau nearby, above the left bank, are the ruinous remains of a **Roman temple** which is dedicated to Astarte (Venus). In the foundations, on the river side, is the entrance to a sort of tunnel which is thought to have carried water into a sacred pool in the temple into which offerings may have been thrown or devotees carried out their ablutions. Constantine destroyed the temple on account of its licentious rites, but the power of legend has stayed with the place. Both Christians and Shiites attribute healing powers to the place and strips of cloth are still tied to the nearby fig tree in a ritual which dates back to antiquity.

Places to Eat
The café/restaurant, *Ashshalal*, beneath the bridge, is the only place to eat in the vicinity. It serves tea, coffee and cold drinks. Light meals and snacks of the kebab and chips variety are available quite cheaply. It is only open during the spring and summer months. Lunch costs from US$6 to US$8.

ANN JOUSIFFE

ANN JOUSIFFE

ANN JOUSIFFE

PETER JOUSIFFE

Top: Six Roman columns lead the way to the Phoenician Temple of Baalat Gebal at Byblos.
Left: Water roars from Afqa Grotto – a popular weekend day trip from Beirut.
Middle Right: Phoenician, Roman and Crusader ruins feature in the seaside village of Batroun.
Bottom Right: Moussalayha Castle was once a coastal stronghold of Ayyubid princes.

PETER JOUSIFFE

PETER JOUSIFFE

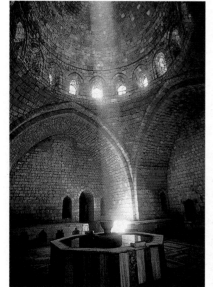

ANN JOUSIFFE

PETER JOUSIFFE

Top Left: Picturesque Bcharré perches on the northern edge of the Kadisha Valley.
Top Right: For traditional souvenirs and a lively atmosphere, Tripoli's souks are a must.
Bottom Left: A shaft of light highlights a tiled fountain in one of Tripoli's Mameluke buildings
Bottom Right: The most intriguing aspect of Tripoli's hammams are the domes.

Getting There & Away

Without a private car, the only way to get to Afqa is by taxi. It is not on a service taxi route, so this will cost around US$20 from Byblos. Hitching would be OK at the weekend when there was enough traffic on the road, but during the week, you could easily get stuck for quite a while waiting for a lift.

LAKLOUK

Laklouk is one of the main ski resorts in Lebanon during the winter season. (For skiing details, see the Ski Facts boxed story in the Facts about Lebanon chapter.) It is set in an attractive rocky location high in Mount Lebanon, 28km east of Byblos. It is also a pleasant summer resort. The place consists of a few hotels and restaurants – there isn't a village as such.

Apart from enjoying the scenery, there are a few places of interest nearby. A couple of kilometres from the resort on the Chatin-Bala road is an unusual **rock formation**, which has several houses or chapels carved into the rock. This is known as the 'bishop's house'. The landscape here is reminiscent of that at Cappadocia in Turkey.

Further along the same road, about 6km from Laklouk, is the **Bala Gorge**. There is a small turning on the left if you are coming from Laklouk and, after about 400m, the road ends. This is the beginning of the descent on foot to the gorge. The walk down is easy and takes about 15 minutes. At the bottom is an extraordinary natural rock formation – a rock bridge spans the chasm and a waterfall crashes down into a deep hole behind. It is really worth the effort to visit, but be warned there are no fences or barriers and the drops are sheer. The return walk takes between 20 and 25 minutes.

Places to Stay & Eat

The *Shangrila Hotel* (☎ (09) 945521, (01) 200019; fax (01) 336007) is a pleasant, old-world place, built in the 1950s, right in the centre of the resort and close to the ski lifts. It is open all year and in summer has a sun room and pool. Staff at the hotel can organise horse-riding excursions and mountain bikes

for hire. Singles/doubles/triples cost US$70/100/135. If you want to sleep four in a room, the cost is US$170. All prices include breakfast. The restaurant has a daily menu for a fixed price of US$20 with a range of European and Lebanese dishes.

A bit cheaper is the *Nirvana Hotel* (☎ (09) 945521), which is an annexe of the Shangrila Hotel and only open when the Shangrila is fully booked.

The *Motel Lavalade* (☎ (09) 904140, 904257) is the first hotel on the left as you enter Laklouk. It is open all year and has a swimming pool and tennis courts open in the summer. A double room costs US$50 all year.

For cheap eats, there are a couple of simple snack places. The *Auberge* and *Terra E* both do the usual sandwiches and snacks for between LL 4000 and LL 5000 per person.

Getting There & Away

Laklouk is not on any bus or service taxi route, so you will need your own transport or spring for a taxi from Byblos. A one-way trip will cost in the region of US$20.

DOUMA

This is another traditional red-roofed village, famous for being in the shape of a scorpion – this can be seen from the hillside overlooking the village. It is about 22km north-east of Byblos and is a quiet and peaceful place where nothing much happens; it makes a good base for country walks.

Apart from wandering around, there is not a lot to see: the main square has a **Roman sarcophagus** and there are two churches. Above the village there are some Roman inscriptions from the reign of Hadrian (about 300 AD). There is also a small souk and some local cafés clustered around the main village square from which you can watch the world go by.

The Douma Hotel arranges hiking expeditions – there are eight different walks from Douma of varying difficulty.

Places to Stay & Eat

There is one, pretty good hotel in Douma, 1km from the main square along the main road. The *Douma Hotel* (☎ (09) 520106, 520202; fax (01) 351598) is a pleasant enough place of 36 rooms with TV and bath. It is open all year and prices are US$40/55 for singles/doubles including breakfast. A suite costs US$70. There is no pool, but there is a billiards room and a good restaurant where a Lebanese, Italian or French dinner will cost from US$10 to US$15 per head.

Apart from the hotel, there are a number of small, cheaper places around the village square which serves felafels and Lebanese pizzas.

Getting There & Away

There are no buses to Douma and very few service taxis from Byblos. You can take a service taxi to Batroun on the coast and pick up a taxi from there, which would cost about US$15, or get a taxi from Byblos, which would cost about US$20.

BATROUN

Batroun is a small Maronite town on the coast about 56km north of Beirut. This was the Graeco-Roman town of Botrys, but its foundation was much earlier than this. It is mentioned in the Tell al-Amarna tablets as a dependency of the king of Byblos. Called Butron in medieval times, it fell under the diocese of the County of Tripoli. It was famous for its vineyards during the Crusader period.

Today the town has a small fishing port with a couple of interesting **old churches**. St Georges Orthodox Church was built in the late 18th century and has 21 fine, painted panels and carved, wooden doves above the altar screen. Across the square is St Estaphan Church, also known as the fisherman's church. These are both near the old harbour.

The old harbour has an extraordinary natural sea wall creating a pool on the landside. This natural feature was reinforced by the Phoenicians and the remains of their harbour are visible. To the north-east of town is the remnants of a **Roman theatre**. This is now in the garden of a private house and can be seen over the wall, or, you can ask to be allowed to see the ruin if you want a closer

look. To find it, head north along the main street, Rue Principe, and walk 200m past the Badawni Restaurant and turn right by the pharmacy. The Roman theatre is about 50m along on your right near a restaurant called Studio Jamal.

A local speciality of Batroun is freshly made lemonade. There are several juice shops and cafés along the main street which serve this. Also the souks are worth a visit for their traditional architecture – there is a fanlight design over each shop which is typically Lebanese. There is also a rocky bathing beach on the south side of town.

If you are in Batroun in August, there are plans to revive the 'Saidat al-Bahr' (Lady of the Sea) Festival which should take place on the 15th of the month.

Places to Stay

The main hotel in Batroun is the *San Stephano Beach* (☎ (06) 640366, 642366), which is on the south side of town. It is a whole resort complex with a large swimming pool, restaurant and beach snack bar. Double rooms cost US$70.

A bit further along to the south is the *Sawrai Hotel* (☎ (06) 642100), which used to have regular rooms, but now only has chalets. Prices are US$75/125 for a one/two-room chalet with kitchen and bathroom. The pool and restaurant only operate during the summer – guests have to eat out or self-cater during the low season.

Places to Eat

A good place to eat is the *Badawni Restaurant* (☎ (06) 640156) on Rue Principe, not far from the clock tower, which serves well-cooked, fresh mezze for LL 1000 each and shawarma for LL 2000. They also do pizzas (LL 5000) and hamburgers (LL 2500). A good fruit juice place is *Mango's Cocktail*, also on Rue Principe. For the traditional lemonade, try *Hilmi Sweets* further north along Rue Principe, close to the souk area.

Getting There & Away

As Batroun is a coastal town just off the highway, you could easily get a service taxi from Beirut or Byblos heading for Tripoli to drop you at the turnoff and walk the short way into town. The cost from Beirut should be LL 4000. Alternatively take the Tripoli bus from Beirut and get the driver to drop you off. The price will be the full fare to Tripoli, LL 5000.

MOUSSALAYHA CASTLE

About 3km beyond Batroun off the Tripoli highway is this fairytale castle which you should not miss. It is visible from the highway and there is a short approach road leading to the east. Moussalayha is a legacy of Lebanon's Ayyubid princes of the 16th century. It used to defend the only land route between Beirut and Tripoli.

It stands on a rocky outcrop and is built on the summit in such a way as to look like part of the living rock itself. Beneath the castle runs a small river with an ancient stone bridge crossing it. The whole scene is incredibly picturesque and makes an ideal picnic spot or stopping off place. You can climb up a rock stairway to the summit and enter the tiny castle through a door at the top.

Although the site is very ancient (it is probably the ancient Gigarta mentioned by Pliny), the castle is not. There is no mention of it during Crusader times, so it seems likely that the site was abandoned until the present castle was constructed.

Getting There & Away

If you are using a service taxi heading for Tripoli, simply get them to drop you off at Moussalayha and then flag down another service taxi when you want to continue your journey (there are plenty of service taxis serving this route). The castle is within easy walking distance from the highway. If you have a taxi to yourself, it is probably better to get it to wait for you. Cars can only approach as far as the old bridge.

QUBBA

This is a small village built in tiers on a hill 56km north of Beirut. Its name probably derives from the Italian family Qobba, who settled there in the time of the Crusaders. The main reason for visiting this village is to see the Crusader church, called the **Holy Church of the Saviour**, which is perched high on the east and south faces of the hill. There are also some **hand-cut grottoes** and **burial places** nearby, one of which was used by a hermit as a dwelling. The church is still used occasionally – on saint's days for instance – for services.

There is another Crusader monument in the village. High on the headland is a **Crusader watchtower**, the Bourj as-Salla, from which fires were lit as warnings, and sometimes for celebrations as well.

Getting There & Away

Qubba is set back from the old coast road to the east, but is visible from the road if you keep your eyes open. If you are travelling by service taxi, it is walkable from the highway turnoff. Otherwise you can drive up to the village and then walk up to the church. Access is by a winding pathway.

NORTH OF BEIRUT

Tripoli & The Cedars

The northern part of Lebanon around Tripoli does not attract as many visitors as some of the more famous places, which is a shame because Tripoli is a fascinating city and the villages of the north are still very traditional and unspoilt. On the whole, the north has a slightly more Middle Eastern flavour than the rest of the country. Many traditional crafts that one associates with the souks of the Middle East are found here. The north is also home to the famous Cedars of Lebanon, situated high in the mountains. The scenery in this area is probably the most beautiful in the whole of Lebanon.

Tripoli (Trablous)

Tripoli, or Trablous in Arabic, is the second-largest city in Lebanon, and has a long and distinguished history. Many of its souks, mosques and other monuments are medieval, including the huge Crusader castle which dominates the city. Many of the monuments are now being restored after years of neglect and war damage.

Tripoli has two main parts: the port area of Al-Mina, and the Old City on the land side. Both are well worth visiting. The port area offers the opportunity for boat rides and swimming, and the souk areas of the Old City are unspoilt and fascinating. Despite the obvious attractions of Tripoli, it is still overlooked by most tourism programmes, which may be a good or a bad thing depending which way you look at it.

Tripoli is also famous as the sweets capital of Lebanon, and any trip to the city is not complete without a visit to one of its Arabic sweet shops. The main speciality is *halawet el-jibn*, a delicious sweet made from cheese and served with syrup.

History
Although much of its early history is lost to

HIGHLIGHTS

PETER JOUSIFFE

- Visit the only museum dedicated to Khalil Gibran – Bcharré's most famous citizen (above)
- Explore the Crusader castle and experience the commercial hustle and bustle of Tripoli's Old City
- Hire a boat from Al-Mina and visit the wildlife sanctuary of Palm Islands Park
- Hear a recital in the great hall of Balamand's Greek Orthodox abbey
- Spend a few days whizzing down the snow-covered slopes high above the Cedars
- Witness a festival in celebration of the unique and ancient Cedars of Lebanon
- Hike through the Kadisha Valley with its waterfalls, rock-carved tombs and stunning scenery
- Marvel at incredible Maronite monasteries built into the Kadisha cliffs
- Drive around the traditional and unspoilt villages of Akkar

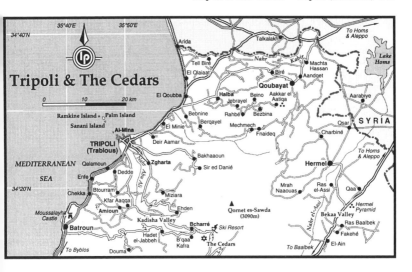

Tripoli & The Cedars

us, Tripoli is thought to be the Kadytis of Phoenician times. The original city, founded probably around 800 BC, was situated in the area now called Al-Mina, but virtually nothing remains of it. The Greeks named the city, Tripolis, as it was divided into three walled quarters, each being the federal seat of Phoenicia's other city-states: Byblos, Sidon and Aradus. Prior to this federation, the town was only a small trading port.

During the rule of the Seleucids and, later, the Romans, Tripoli was embellished with many sumptuous temples and other buildings. A huge earthquake in 543 AD changed the geography of the port area completely and destroyed most of the town. It was quickly rebuilt but, by 635 AD, a general of Mu'awiyah, the governor of Syria who founded the Umayyad dynasty (661-750 AD), beseiged the city. He attempted to starve the town into submission, but the inhabitants of Tripoli escaped by sea with the help of the Byzantine emperor. When the general entered the town, he found it deserted. To repopulate the town, he brought in a military garrison and a Jewish colony. The garrison was often away and a Byzantine notable took advantage of the situation

to seize the town. It was then in Christian hands, until it was recaptured by the Umayyads and then by the Abbasid caliphs. Tripoli remained under Abbasid control until the middle of the 11th century and the coming of the Crusaders.

The Crusaders took the town in 1109 after a long and difficult siege, during which a magnificent Arabic library of 100,000 volumes was destroyed by fire. Raymond de Saint-Gilles began the siege which was completed after his death by his French cousin, Guillaume Jourdain. The final victory was brought about with the help of a Genoese squadron. Italian influences can still be seen in Tripoli.

The Crusaders managed to hang on to Tripoli for 180 years, during which time the castle of Raymond de Saint-Gilles was built and a prosperous economy, based on weaving, was established.

The Mameluke sultan Qala'un took the city of Tripoli in 1289 and made territorial concessions to the Muslims who built a town at the foot of the castle mount and on the banks of the river. This is the present-day Old City. The Muslims also built a series of defensive towers at Al-Mina. The Turkish

Ottomans took over the town in 1516 under the ruling sultan Selim I.

The 'old' part of Tripoli today is about 3km inland from the port and is mostly medieval in design, with modern areas spreading out from the old centre. During the last few decades, the orange orchards between the Old City and port area have gradually been developed as residential districts and nowadays the city is one homogeneous whole.

Since independence in 1946 Tripoli has become the administrative capital of northern Lebanon. It was the centre of an insurrection in 1958 where rebels defended themselves for several weeks against the forces of the central government within the labyrinth of the Old City.

Tripoli suffered some damage during the civil war but not nearly as much as the south of the country. Today it is concentrating on rebuilding its industry and business sectors; there is a large trade pavilion which hosts an annual business fair. It is also looking to tourism as a source of future income.

Orientation
There are two main parts to Tripoli: the city proper and Al-Mina. The main part of Tripoli is set slightly inland from the sea. The dominant feature of the city is the Citadel of Raymond de Saint-Gilles, set on a hill overlooking the Old City and the Kadisha River (also called the Nahr Abu Ali). A maze of souks cluster at the foot of the hill, and further afield are the modern shopping and residential districts. The centre is at Sahet et-Tall (pronounced et-tahl), a large square by the clock tower and municipality building where you'll find the service taxi and bus stands, cheap eateries and hotels. The Old City sprawls east of Sahet et-Tall, while the modern centre is west of the square.

Three main avenues lead to Al-Mina, 3km to the west. This is a promontory which has the port area and fishing harbours. There are beaches around Al-Mina and some nearby islands which can be reached by boat from the northern shore of the promontory. Al-Mina is a separate little town and has some hotels and restaurants.

Information
Tourist Office The Tripoli tourism office (☎ (06) 433590) is right on the first major roundabout as you enter Tripoli from the south. The roundabout has a large 'Allah' sign in Arabic in the middle and the office is on the right as you face north. It has a few brochures and a map of the city which lists the various monuments. The staff can advise you about visiting the Palm Islands conservation area, for which you need a permit.

Money Most of the banks are on the main road which runs north to south through Tripoli, Rue Fouad Chehab. There are also some moneychangers on Rue Tall, which is where you will be dropped off if you are coming by service taxi or bus. Many of the moneychangers are open in the evening.

Post & Communications There are two post offices in Tripoli. The main one is on Rue Fouad Chehab near the Bank of Lebanon building, just south of the 'Allah' roundabout, and the other is in Al-Mina on Rue ibn Sina. There are also public telephone offices at these places.

The telephone code for Tripoli is 06.

Emergency The following Tripoli telephone numbers may be useful in the event of an emergency:

Police	430754, 614011
Ambulance	610861
Red Cross	602510

Old City
The Old City mostly dates from the Mameluke era (14th and 15th centuries) and is a maze of narrow alleyways, colourful souks, hammams, khans, mosques and theological schools (*madrassah*). As some parts were damaged during the war, there is a lot of renovation work being carried out. It is a very lively place where artisans, including jewellers, tailors and coppersmiths, continue to work as they have done for centuries.

The monuments of Tripoli, of which there are 30 altogether, are numbered with small

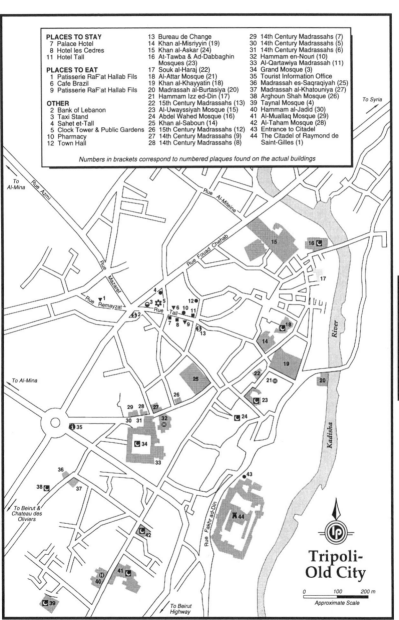

PLACES TO STAY
7 Palace Hotel
8 Hotel les Cedres
11 Hotel Tall

PLACES TO EAT
1 Patisserie RaF'at Hallab Fils
6 Cafe Brazil
9 Patisserie RaF'at Hallab Fils

OTHER
2 Bank of Lebanon
3 Taxi Stand
4 Sahet et-Tall
5 Clock Tower & Public Gardens
10 Pharmacy
12 Town Hall

13 Bureau de Change
14 Khan al-Misriyyin (19)
15 Khan al-Askar (24)
16 At-Tawba & Ad-Dabbaghin
   Mosques (23)
17 Souk al-Haraj (22)
18 Al-Attar Mosque (21)
19 Khan al-Khayyatin (18)
20 Madrassah al-Burtasiya (20)
21 Hammam Izz ed-Din (17)
22 15th Century Madrassahs (13)
23 Al-Uwayssiyah Mosque (15)
24 Abdel Wahed Mosque (16)
25 Khan al-Saboun (14)
26 15th Century Madrassahs (12)
27 14th Century Madrassahs (9)
28 14th Century Madrassahs (8)

29 14th Century Madrassahs (7)
30 14th Century Madrassahs (5)
31 14th Century Madrassahs (6)
32 Hammam en-Nouri (10)
33 Al-Qartawiya Madrassah (11)
34 Grand Mosque (3)
35 Tourist Information Office
36 Madrassah es-Saqraqiyah (25)
37 Madrassah al-Khatouniya (27)
38 Arghoun Shah Mosque (26)
39 Taynal Mosque (4)
40 Hammam al-Jadid (30)
41 Al-Muallaq Mosque (29)
42 Al-Taham Mosque (28)
43 Entrance to Citadel
44 The Citadel of Raymond de
   Saint-Gilles (1)

Numbers in brackets correspond to numbered plaques found on the actual buildings

To Syria

Rue Azmi

To Al-Mina

Rue Al-Mieine

Rue Fouad Chehab

Rue Mazaret

Rue Remayzat

Rue Tall

To Al-Mina

River

Kadisha

To Beirut &
Chateau des
Oliviers

Rue Fakhr ad-Din

To Beirut
Highway

0   100   200 m

Approximate Scale

Tripoli-
Old City

TRIPOLI & THE CEDARS

plaques. Most are within the Old City and also within easy walking distance of each other.

The **Grand Mosque** was converted from an earlier cathedral, probably St Mary of the Tower. The present-day *minaret* (tower) still looks rather like a bell tower of the Lombard style. Parts of the baptistery have been reused in the adjacent **Al-Qartawiya Madrassah** (1316-1326). This madrassah has a lovely facade of black-and-white facings and a honeycomb pattern above the portal. The **Al-Burtasiya Mosque and Madrassah** (1310), near the Kadisha River, is also worth a visit to see the intricately decorated and inlaid *mihrab* (prayer niche).

One of the most outstanding examples of Islamic architecture is the **Taynal Mosque** (1336) with its magnificent inner portal. It still has a partially preserved Carmelite nave, although the rest of the building is typical of 14th-century Arab architecture. This building has been recently restored.

As well as the religious buildings there are a couple of ancient hammams. The **Hammam en-Nouri** (1333) and the **Hammam al-Jadid** are both in the Old City. The former is a palatial ruin of a bathhouse with numerous cupolas studded with glass which cast shafts of light down into the rooms. In the main room is a marble pool with an intriguing optical illusion as you walk around it. The latter is called the 'new bath' as it was built much later in 1740. It was a gift to the city by Asaad Pasha al-Azem of Damascus. The portal of the Hammam al-Jadid has a 14-link chain draped over it which is carved from a single block of stone. These two old hammams are not in use. If you want a steam bath and massage, go to **Hamman al-Abd** just off the gold souk (Rue Bijouterie). It is only open to men – if you are female, you have to hire the whole building! A two-hour Turkish bath and massage costs LL 14,000. In the Old City there's also the 500-year-old **Nuzha Hammam** which is again only open to men.

Other commercial buildings are the *khans*, or caravanserais, where merchants brought their goods for sale and storage. Several of these are still in use as workshops and storage areas. The **Khan al-Khayyatin** is in the process of restoration. Tailors have worked here and in the nearby **Souk al-Haraj** since the 14th century. Another khan, the 14th-century **Khan al-Misriyyin**, was used by the Egyptian traders in Tripoli. The whole of the Old City has the authentic air of a medieval town and is certainly not touristy. See also The Architecture of Lebanon section in the Facts about Lebanon chapter.

Citadel of Raymond de Saint-Gilles

The city is dominated by the vast citadel, known as Qalaat Sanjil in Arabic. In 1100 Raymond de Saint-Gilles of Toulouse occupied the hill which overlooks the valley, the town and the coast. He decided to transform this position, which he called Mont Pelerin (Mount Pilgrim), into a fortress. The original castle was burnt down in 1287 and then on several subsequent occasions. It was rebuilt by Emir Essendemir Kurgi in 1307-8, and it has been added to piecemeal over the centuries. As a result, the only really early parts are the foundation stones; some of the wings of the citadel were built as late as the 16th century. Even so, it is an impressive building which charts the stormy history of the city.

Engraved above the Frankish gateway is an edict of the Mameluke Sultan Sha'aban about the military budget. Over the first doorway of the castle is another engraving, this time from Süleyman the Magnificent, who ordered the restoration (yet again) of 'this blessed tower, that it may serve as a fortified position until the end of time'.

The castle is open daily. The entrance is up a steep road on the western approach to the castle mount. There is not always someone to collect the entrance fee, but the official charge for entry is LL 5000. Students can enter for LL 2500. A word of warning when exploring the castle: there are some sheer drops which are not protected by barriers or warnings, so take care.

When you have explored the castle, walk down to the bridge and cross the river. The view from the east bank is the best one of the castle with its sheer walls and picturesque

The Tragedy of Melisinda

One of the most romantic and tragic figures who lived in the Saint-Gilles citadel was the beautiful sister of Raymond de Saint-Gilles, Melisinda. Hearing about her charm and beauty, the emperor of Constantinople asked for her hand and Raymond delightedly accepted. It was to be a very advantageous alliance. A splendid dowry was prepared and 12 galleys made ready to conduct Melisinda to Byzantium in a manner fitting for a future empress.

At the last minute the emperor decided it was more politically fitting to ally himself with the house of Antioch and asked Maria, sister of Prince Bohemond I, to marry him instead. Raymond was furious at the insult to him and his sister. He loaded the 12 galleys with thugs who were sent to pillage the emperor's territories.

Meanwhile, Melisinda was heartbroken and died soon afterwards of grief. Her tragic story is remembered in the sad songs of the wandering troubadours. ■

Arab buildings nestling at the foot of the mount.

Al-Mina

Al-Mina is situated on a headland and three main avenues run from the old part of Tripoli down to the port. Until a few decades ago the avenues ran between orange groves, but these have now been built over, mostly with unexciting residential developments and modern shops. There are a few hotels and restaurants overlooking the fishing port and it is a relaxing place to hang out, eat fish and perhaps take a boat trip to the nearby islands.

Start at the northern coast of the headland; there is little of interest on the southern part which is mostly apartment buildings and also houses the trade fair pavilion. The only monument of real interest is the **Lion Tower**, so-called because of the bas-relief decorations on the facade. The tower, which is called Bourj es-Sba in Arabic, is a miniature fortress dating from the end of the 15th century and probably built by the Sultan Qait Bey to protect the coastline against attack from the Turks. It is an exceptional example

of Muslim military architecture with a striking black and white striped portico. The whole of the ground floor is one vast chamber which used to be decorated with paintings and armorial carvings, traces of which you can still see. The upper floor has eight rooms opening onto a central hall. At the top there is a terrace which has views over the city and the harbour area.

The Lion Tower is at the eastern end of the harbour, separated from Al-Mina proper by the old railway sidings. The **railway and old station** are now disused and dilapidated, the rusting tracks are overgrown, and the old steam locomotives are still there, rusting away as well. Railway buffs should not miss a rather poignant wander among the old locomotives. In the middle of the desolation is a café right next to the station. There is a second tower, **Bourj Ras al-Nahr**, about 1km to the east by the mouth of the Kadisha River. However, it is very ruined, with only the ground floor surviving.

Along the sea front of Al-Mina there are many **boats** plying for hire to take people to the nearby islands. A return trip takes about two hours (with time for a swim) and is a relaxing change from rambling around ruins. The fare for a return trip is LL 5000 or, if there is a group, you can hire the entire boat (10 to 12 persons) for LL 50,000 and make an expedition of it.

If you want to visit the **Palm Islands Park**, which consists of the three far islands of Palm Island, Sanani Island and Ramkine Island, you need a permit. This area has been recently protected as a wildlife sanctuary. Permits are available to bona fide birdwatchers, photographers etc, and can be obtained from the Ministry of Tourism offices in Beirut or Tripoli. Obviously you will have to negotiate with one of the boat owners to take you there and back and it will be more expensive than a trip to the closer islands. (Also see the Nature Reserves section in the Facts about Lebanon chapter.)

Places to Stay – bottom end

Compared to other parts of Lebanon, Tripoli has quite a few cheap hotels. There are a few

TRIPOLI & THE CEDARS

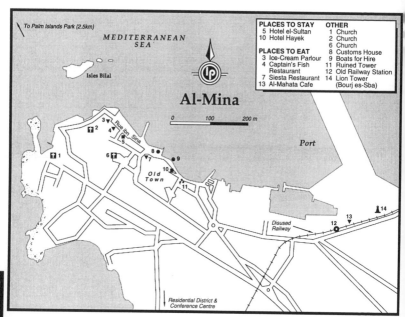

To Palm Islands Park (2.5km)

MEDITERRANEAN
SEA

Isles Bilal

Al-Mina

Rue Ibn Sina

Port

Old
Town

Disused
Railway

Residential District &
Conference Centre

0   100   200 m

PLACES TO STAY
5 Hotel el-Sultan
10 Hotel Hayek

PLACES TO EAT
3 Ice-Cream Parlour
4 Captain's Fish
   Restaurant
7 Siesta Restaurant
13 Al-Mahata Cafe

OTHER
1 Church
2 Church
6 Church
8 Customs House
9 Boats for Hire
11 Ruined Tower
12 Old Railway Station
14 Lion Tower
   (Bourj es-Sba)

TRIPOLI & THE CEDARS

along Rue Tall. The rather basic, family-run *Hotel les Cedres* has rooms with shared bath from US$6 to US$7 per person.

In a beautiful old building with high ceilings and stained glass windows is the *Palace Hotel* (☎ (06) 432257). It charges US$10 per person for doubles with shared bath and US$25/30 in doubles/triples with private bathroom and air-con.

Best of the lot is the *Hotel Koura* (☎ (06) 628407), also known as the Hotel Tall. It is a very nice, converted old house off Rue Tall, near the Palace Hotel. The road is called Rue Izz ed-Dine – look for a sign on the corner for Chaptini Travel. It is run by a couple who speak French, but not English. Singles/doubles cost US$10/20. A double room with bath and air-con costs US$30; without air-con US$25.

The *Hotel Hayek* (☎ (06) 601311) in Al-Mina has 12 rooms with sea views at US$18/25 for doubles/triples with shared bath and complimentary tea and coffee. It's

a pink building on Rue ibn Sina (opposite the post office), and there's a supermarket Hayek on the ground floor. The hotel entrance is round the back; if the door is shut, ask at the supermarket.

Places to Stay – middle

There are a few mid-range hotels in Al-Mina. The best is the *Hotel el-Sultan* (☎ (06) 601627, 611640). It is right on the corniche, on the corner of Rue ibn Sina and Rue al-Meshti. All the rooms have a TV, minibar and air-con. Singles/doubles cost US$36/46 including breakfast. There is also a restaurant on the 1st floor where lunch or dinner costs around US$10 to US$15.

Places to Stay – top end

There is one really extraordinary place to stay in Tripoli and that is *Chateau des Oliviers*, also known as *Villa Nadia* (☎ (06) 423513, 629271; fax 610222, 615024). This is really a private mansion converted into a hotel by the owner Nadia Dibo. It is set a few kilometres south of the city in the Haykalieh region high on a hill and has a 'country house' feel to it. Madame Nadia built the chateau to house her wonderful collection of oriental antiques and the ground floor rooms all have a theme: French, Chinese, Spanish and oriental. It is like stepping into the *Arabian Nights*. The chateau has a garden and a swimming pool and there is even a small nightclub. The chateau has only 22 rooms and 6 suites, so it's advisable to book in advance. A night of luxury will cost you between US$90 and US$300, but discounts are available so it's always worth asking. Fixed-price lunch or dinner is available from US$20.

Places to Eat

On and around Rue Tall there are several simple restaurants serving shawarma sandwiches for LL 1500 and felafels for only LL 750. You can also get a plate of fuul or hummus for LL 1500. Just along from the clock tower is the *Cafe Brazil* serving light snacks, and further along on the other side of the road is the famous sweet shop *RaF'at Hallab Fils*, which should be visited for its local specialities. It is reputed to be the best patisserie in Lebanon. There is another RaF'at Hallab Fils on Rue Remayzat.

In Al-Mina there is a good restaurant called *Siesta*, which serves everything from light snacks to full meals. It is right on the corniche opposite the fishing harbour. You can get a pizza or burger and fries for about LL 6000 as well as ice creams and shakes for about LL 4000. A little further north along the corniche is the *Captain's Fish Restaurant* (☎ (06) 613013), where a three-course lunch or dinner costs US$15 plus drinks. It is open daily until 10 pm. Next door is an ice-cream parlour which sells all sorts of goodies. A fresh fruit sundae will cost about LL 5000.

If you feel like a full Lebanese meal, try the *restaurant* in the Hotel el-Sultan. It has a good selection of mezze for LL 2000 to LL 2500 each, and a steak will cost around LL 10,000.

Things to Buy

Exploring the old souks is the best way to shop in Tripoli. If you are looking for jewellery, there is a whole souk devoted to gold. If you are looking for a more modest souvenir, then head for the brass souk. You can pick up a really well-made piece for much less than in Beirut and the choice is enormous. Even if you don't want to buy, it is well worth a visit just to see the metal workers making pieces by hand in the same way that they have done for centuries.

Getting There & Away

Bus & Service Taxi The service taxi stand is on Rue Tall by the clock tower and public gardens. Service taxis from Beirut charge LL 5000. Tripoli is a good place from which to visit Bcharré, the Cedars and the Kadisha Valley. Service taxis to Bcharré charge LL 6000 and to the Cedars LL 10,000. There is also a bus several times a day between Tripoli and Beirut. The fare is LL 2000.

From Tripoli you can also get service taxis to Syria. They leave when full from the Rue Tall stand. They charge LL 8000 to Homs and the same to Lattakia in northern Syria.

Getting Around

Taxi Local taxis can be flagged on the street and charge LL 500 for a short hop within the city (LL 1000 to Al-Mina).

Around Tripoli

QUBBET AL-BEDDAWI

This sanctuary, built upon the site of the Crusader Priory of St Anthony of Padua, is only 3km east of Tripoli near the main Lattakia highway. It is famous as a small **monastery of dervishes** (that's right, the whirling variety), but people visit mainly to see the **sacred pool** of fish which is thought to originate in antiquity as a pool sacred to Astarte. The crescent-shaped pool has thousands of carp which have been worshipped since ancient times. A nearby spring keeps the water clear. Fish were considered sacred by the Phoenicians, being connected to the idea of the egg from which Tanit, the chief goddess of Carthage, hatched. These carp, some of which live to be 200 years old, are often fed with chickpeas by visitors.

Getting There & Away
It is a short ride by taxi from central Tripoli – only about 10 minutes. The fare should be about LL 3000.

ENFE
On the coast 15km south of Tripoli is the village of Enfe (the name means 'nose' in honour of the shape of the coastline). This was the town of Nephim, a fief of the County of Tripoli during the Crusades. The lords of Nephim played an important role here and later moved to Cyprus in the 13th century. There is very little left of the Crusader castle, except for a few ruined stone walls. Several vaults carved into the rock remain, and the most interesting relics are two **Crusader moats**, one of which is over 40m long.

The castle had a sadistic history: the lord of Nephim, Count Bohemond VII, walled up his rivals, the Embiaci, in the castle. This grisly scene was later recalled in Edgar Allan Poe's story, *The Cask of Amontillado*.

There are also four **churches**, one of which is Byzantine with the remains of painted murals. It is romantically named 'Our Lady of the Wind'. The Church of the Holy Sepulchre dates from the time of Bohemond and is still in use.

Places to Stay & Eat
As the coast is clean and attractive in this part of Lebanon, it attracts a lot of day-trippers and holiday makers. The newish *Marina del Sol* (☎ (06) 541301, (03) 331466/77) is not so much a hotel as a complete resort. Many Lebanese have leases on the resort's apartments or rent for the whole season. For short-term guests, there is a selection of suites available. A family apartment costs from US$125 per night without breakfast and US$150 with breakfast. If you are staying a week or longer, you can probably negotiate the price. This place has a huge

The Marina Grotto
Just 4km north of Enfe, past the village of Qalamoun, is the Marina Grotto. It is about a 20-minute walk to the east of the village over stony slopes (you may need to ask directions). The grotto, with its orange-coloured rear wall, stands out against the grey rock of the rest of the escarpment.

The grotto was a sanctuary and has **painted murals** from two periods; the older inscriptions are in Greek. The pictures show scenes from the life of Saint Marina, whose story is a curious one.

Saint Marina was raised as a boy in a Maronite monastery where her father, a widower, became a monk. She grew up with the name Marinos and only her father and the abbot knew that she was female. When they died, she remained in the monastery as a monk. When a local girl bore a child (fathered by one of the monks), Marinos was accused of being responsible and banished from the monastery. She kept silent and took the abandoned child to live in the grotto where she miraculously nursed the child with her own milk. When she died, the truth of her sex became known and she was canonised. Her body was taken for burial in Constantinople where it lies in the Saint Marina Chapel.

The grotto became a place of pilgrimage for women who could not nurse their children and it is known locally as the Milk Grotto. ■

sea-water pool and many sports and health facilities. It works out cheaper than paying Beirut prices for the same facilities. It even has its own working fishing harbour.

Worth trying in Enfe is the *Abou Ghassan* fish restaurant on the main street. People come from all over Lebanon to eat here. It's not cheap, but the food is very good.

Getting There & Away
Enfe is on the service taxi route between Tripoli, Byblos and Beirut, so it is easy to get to; simply ask the driver to drop you at the turnoff. You will probably be charged the full service taxi fare to Tripoli (LL 5000). Alternatively, a taxi from Tripoli will cost about LL 8000.

CHEKKA
A coastal town just south of Enfe, Chekka

seems at first glance to be a place to be avoided at all costs. The town is dominated by a hideous cement works which does nothing for its ambience. Amazingly enough, there are a few quite upmarket hotels here. The reason is a fairly splendid, sandy **beach** and good, safe bathing. Along the coast in this region are also many salt pans where sea water evaporates in shallow pools by the sea to leave behind salt crystals.

A road climbs to a wooded headland to the south of Chekka, where an old **monastery** nestles at the top. The views from here are great.

QALAMOUN

Yet another small village on the northern coast road, this one is worth mentioning for one reason: the stretch of shops selling really good copper and brass ware. You can't miss them as they are all together on the main road which runs through the village. There are old and new pieces on sale and the prices are reasonable. This is the place to practise your haggling skills.

BALAMAND

High above the village of Qalamoun, over-looking the old Tripoli to Beirut road, is the **Greek Orthodox abbey** of Balamand (or Belmont). This started out as a Cistercian abbey founded in 1157. It is possibly even older than this, as it was built on the site of a Byzantine monastery. The Cistercians either abandoned it or were driven out, possibly in 1289 when Qala'un took Tripoli.

The monastery underwent major restoration work several centuries ago and the Crusader buildings are all but lost to later designs. The Church of Our Lady of Balamand is very pretty with its bell tower intact (rare in the Middle East where bell towers were usually demolished by the Muslims or by earthquakes). The church interior has been carefully restored and is worth seeing for the fine icons set into a carved screen behind the altar. The great hall of the abbey with its vaulted ceiling is now used for concerts and recitals.

These days the abbey is a university. It is the principal seat of learning in the north of Lebanon as well as a cultural and religious centre. If you want information about concerts or about visiting the abbey, call ☎ (06) 400740, 400742.

Getting There & Away

Balamand is 12km by road south of Tripoli. You can get a taxi there from the main stand on Rue Tall in Tripoli.

Bcharré & The Cedars

The drive to Bcharré takes you through some of the most beautiful mountain landscape in Lebanon. There are several routes from the coast and all take you along winding roads, continually gaining in altitude and offering spectacular views of peaks and gorges. Villages with red-tiled roofs perch atop hills or cling precariously to the mountain sides. Olive groves and vineyards, lush valleys and mountain peaks rise higher and higher with every turn of the road. The area is that of the Kadisha Valley, also known as the Holy Valley, where the early Maronite Christian community established itself. The valley is steep-sided with numerous waterfalls and makes a great place for trekking as well as visiting the ancient monasteries and tombs that are dotted around the valley (see later in this chapter).

BCHARRÉ

The main town in the Kadisha Valley is Bcharré, a red-roofed town perched on the side of the valley and dominated by three large churches. These were built and subsequently rebuilt by the leading families of the town in ever more imposing styles and the largest, St Saba Church, is more like a small cathedral perched on the edge of the gorge. In Phoenician times the town was known as Beit Chari, and later during the Crusades as Buissera, when it was one of the fiefs of the County of Tripoli.

There is a post office and public telephone bureau on Rue Gibran in the centre of town,

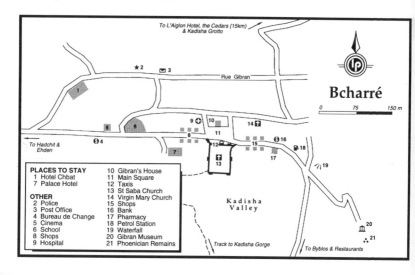

Bcharré

0   75   150 m

To L'Aiglon Hotel, the Cedars (15km)
& Kadisha Grotto

Rue Gibran

To Hadchit &
Ehden

Kadisha
Valley

Track to Kadisha Gorge

To Byblos & Restaurants

PLACES TO STAY
1 Hotel Chbat
7 Palace Hotel

OTHER
2 Police
3 Post Office
4 Bureau de Change
5 Cinema
6 School
8 Shops
9 Hospital
10 Gibran's House
11 Main Square
12 Taxis
13 St Saba Church
14 Virgin Mary Church
15 Shops
16 Bank
17 Pharmacy
18 Petrol Station
19 Waterfall
20 Gibran Museum
21 Phoenician Remains

north of the main square. It is open daily from 8 am to 1 pm.

Gibran Museum

Bcharré's most famous citizen is Khalil Gibran (see boxed story), the late 19th-century poet and artist whose tomb is in the town together with a museum dedicated to his works. The museum contains hundreds of his paintings and drawings as well as his personal effects. These things have been gathered and housed in an old monastery building on the edge of town.

The museum is about 10 minutes walk from the centre of town up a steep hill and is open every day, except Monday, from 9 am to 5 pm. Entrance costs LL 2000 and there are booklets available in English and French.

Places to Stay & Eat

In the centre of town is the *Palace Hotel* (☎ (06) 671460), a smallish place with 24 rooms, all with bath and air-con. Singles/doubles/triples cost US$25/35/45 including service tax. Breakfast is an extra LL 5000. Lunch and dinner in the restaurant is à la carte only and costs around US$10 to US$20. There is a new annexe attached to

the hotel where singles/doubles cost US$40 and triples cost US$60.

A little way out of town on the road to the Kadisha Grotto is *L'Aiglon Hotel* (☎ (06) 671529). It only has eight rooms, all with bath. A double room costs US$30 (no reduction for singles) and includes breakfast. The hotel has spectacular views from the restaurant, which has an outside terrace open during the summer. In the busy season there is also a nightclub in the basement.

The best hotel in town is *Hotel Chbat* (☎ (06) 671237, 671270), which was built in 1955 on the side of a hill in the upper part of Bcharré with views across the Kadisha Valley. It has a relaxed homely atmosphere with big open fires and a Lebanese cook who has been with the hotel since it opened. Singles/doubles/triples cost US$65/78/88 plus 14% service, but you should ask for a discount. The price includes breakfast. Unusually, the hotel also has a couple of dormitories for groups and students who want budget accommodation. To qualify, there needs to be at least 10 people in your party and you need to book in advance. This is popular with school skiing groups in winter. In summer there is a swimming pool.

Khalil Gibran (1883-1931)

Gibran Khalil Gibran is Lebanon's most famous and celebrated literary figure. He was a philosophical essayist, novelist, mystic poet and painter whose influences were the Bible, Nietzsche and William Blake. He's mostly known in the west as Khalil Gibran, author of *The Prophet*.

He was born in Bcharré in the high mountains of Lebanon on 6 January 1883. Having received his primary education in Beirut, he emigrated with his parents to the US where he lived in Boston. Returning to Beirut in 1898 he continued his studies with an emphasis on classical Arabic. On his return to Boston in 1903 he published his first literary essays and met Mary Haskell. She became his benefactor and remained so for the rest of his life.

His artistic tutelage came under Auguste Rodin during a stay in Paris in 1909, and it was during this period that he developed his visual art skills. In 1912 he went to New York and continued to write literary essays and short stories. He began painting in a highly romanticised, mystical style strongly reminiscent of William Blake.

When he died in 1931, his body was returned to Lebanon and he now lies in a casket at the Gibran Museum in Bcharré. Some of his personal possessions are with him in the former monastery building, including an ancient Armenian tapestry portraying the crucifixion scene in which Christ is smiling. ∎

Lunch or dinner in the restaurant costs from US$10 to US$15.

Along the road at the head of the valley, just outside Bcharré, are several restaurants which take advantage of the views along the gorge. *River Roc* is a restaurant/nightclub, but quite expensive. On the same stretch are *Mississippi* and *Kadisha* (the sign in Arabic only) which both sell snacks and full meals. Another 100m away from town on the other side of the road is *Saba*. All of these are in the mid-price range.

THE CEDARS

'The Cedars' is a name used for both the small grove of trees which stands at an altitude of more than 2000m on the slopes of Jebel Makmal and the ski resort a couple of kilometres further up the road. The famous trees, about 4km from Bcharré, are the remnant of a vast forest of cedar which once covered the mountains of Lebanon (see The Cedar Tree boxed story on the next page).

A few of the trees are very old, and it's thought that some reach an age of 1500 years. Not all of the trees are that old but all are at least 200 years old. Three centuries ago there were more trees: in 1550 there were 28 trees over 1000 years old; in 1660, 22; and in 1696, only 16. Today there are 12. These days it is strictly forbidden to cut the trees, which are known locally as *arz ar-rab* (God's cedars). They are under the protection of the Patriarch of Lebanon, who built a chapel in the cedar grove in 1848. Each year in August there is a festival here presided over by the patriarch himself.

The grove of cedars is protected by a fence and you can visit every day all year. They look particularly dramatic against a backdrop of snow. Occasionally, access to the grove is restricted, for example when the snow is melting, so as not to cause damage to the roots from people walking on them when the ground is too soft.

Two kilometres further up the road is the ski station which has a small village of shops and hotels around the ski lifts. There are also equipment-hire shops. See the Ski Facts at a Glance boxed story in the Facts for the Visitor chapter for details about skiing in the Cedars. The road which continues beyond this point leads to the Bekaa Valley. It is only open during the summer months.

Places to Stay & Eat

Almost all the places at the Cedars are only open during the ski season. At other times the nearest hotels and restaurants are in Bcharré.

On the road between Bcharré and the Cedars is the *Alpine Hotel* (☎ (06) 671517), which is cosy and quite simple and, unlike the others, is open all year. Bed and breakfast costs US$30 per person. If you are staying a few days, the Alpine offers half board for US$35 per day. Lunch or dinner costs from US$10 to US$15.

The *St Bernard Hotel* (☎ (03) 289600) is right by the forest grove and rooms cost

The Cedar Tree – *Cedrus Libani*

There are three or four species of cedar tree throughout North Africa and Asia. The most famous of these is the Cedar of Lebanon, which was mentioned in the Old Testament, although today only a few of the original groves still exist. In antiquity the cedar forests covered great swathes of the Mount Lebanon range and provided a source of wealth for the Phoenicians who exported the fragrant and durable wood to Egypt and Palestine.

The original Temple of Solomon in Jerusalem was built of this wood, as were many sarcophagi discovered in Egypt. A slow but sure process of deforestation took place over the millennia, and although new trees are now being planted, it will be centuries before they mature.

Of the few remaining ancient trees, most are in the grove at the Cedars, above Bcharré, and in Barouk, south of Beirut. Some of the trees at the Cedars are thought to be well over 1000 years old. Their trunks have a huge girth and their height can reach 30m. Naturally, there are strict rules about taking any timber from these remaining trees and the souvenirs for sale nearby are made from fallen branches. ■

US$50 per person. It is closed outside the ski season. Handy for the slopes is *Hotel La Cabane* (☎ (03) 321575) which has a restaurant and bar. Rooms start from US$23 per person. Also nearby is the *Baghdadi Café* which offers ski hire. A slightly smarter

eatery is *Le Pichet Restaurant*, 100m down the hill.

A cheap option recommended by a reader is *Tony's Ski Shop*. There is no hotel sign, but Tony will fix you up with a simple room for US$5.

Getting There & Away

There are service taxis to Bcharré and the Cedars from the Rue Tall stand in Tripoli. They charge LL 6000 to Bcharré and LL 10,000 to the Cedars. Outside the ski season there are only a few service taxis to Bcharré and you will have to take a regular taxi from there to the Cedars. The fare is about US$80, but you may be able to haggle the price down.

THE KADISHA VALLEY

Down in the gorge itself and in the surrounding villages is the cultural legacy of the early Maronite community in Lebanon. This rugged and remote mountain area was the perfect natural protection for the sect which was persecuted at various times through the centuries. For a detailed history of the Maronites, see under Religion in the Facts about Lebanon chapter.

The valley starts in the west near coastal Batroun and rises dramatically to the head just beyond Bcharré. It is nearly 50km long, but the main area of interest is the higher 20km-section from Tourza up to the Kadisha Grotto. This is a hiker's paradise with numerous waterfalls, rock-carved tombs and monasteries, and stunning scenery. The Kadisha River, also called the Nahr Abu Ali, runs along the bottom of the valley and meets the sea at Tripoli.

Some parts of the valley are accessible by road, although a 4WD is needed for the western stretch past Deir as-Salib. Other parts are only accessible on foot via a series of paths running down the side of the gorge.

The road, which runs around the top of the valley (on both sides), is punctuated with villages. There are frequent shops and restaurants along the route and there is a restaurant, *D'Oliviers*, down in the valley itself near the bottom.

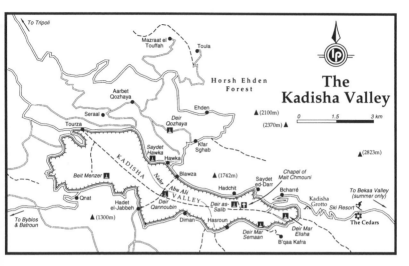

If you are going for a hike in the valley, it is important to take an adequate water supply with you especially during the high summer. Beware of drinking from the mountain streams as they often have rubbish dumped in them upstream.

Chapel of Mart Chmouni

Built under a rocky ledge in the Middle Ages, this chapel has two constructed naves, one in a natural rock formation. Sadly the 13th-century paintings which adorn the walls have been covered with a layer of plaster.

The chapel is at the eastern end of the valley at the point where Wadi Houla and Wadi Qannoubin meet. You can follow a steep path down from Hadchit or you can get there along a path on the valley floor.

Chapel of Saydet Hawka

This is a small monastery consisting of a chapel and few monks' cells within a cave. It is thought to date from the 13th century. This monastery is associated with the attack by armed Mamelukes against the natural fortress of Aassi Hawka, which is in a cave high above the monastery. The cave is only accessible to experienced rock climbers.

The monastery is deserted for most of the year and is used to celebrate the Feast of the Assumption of the Virgin with a high mass on the evening of 14 August. You can get there via a path from Hawka (about 30 minutes one way) or via the valley-floor path.

Deir as-Salib

This monastery is built beneath a large natural rock ledge and has a double chapel. Several caves in the cliff were used as hermits' cells.

The monastery is now in a state of ruin and deserted. You can still see some fragments of the original 13th-century frescoes, reminiscent of the Byzantines, which would have originally covered all the walls. Arabic inscriptions commemorate the life of a hermit who lived there. You can descend by a steep path from Hadchit (30 minutes) or you can take the path along the valley floor.

Deir Qozhaya

Also known as Der Mar Antonias Qozhaya, this hermitage is the largest in the valley. It has been continually in use since it was founded in the 12th century. A new museum, which opened in 1995, houses a collection of religious and ethnographic objects as well as an old printing press which was used to publish the Psalms in Syriac, a language still used by the Maronites in their services. The monastery has been printing texts since the 16th century. There is also a souvenir shop which sells all manner of kitsch religious knick-knacks.

To see the museum you need to knock at the main building and get one of the monks to open it up for you. Near the entrance to the monastery is the **Grotto of St Anthony**, known locally as the 'Cave of the Mad', where you can see the chains used to constrain the insane or possessed who were left at the monastery. You can drive down from Aarbet Qozhaya or walk along the path on the floor of the valley.

Deir Mar Elisha

It was here that the Lebanese Maronite Order was founded in 1695. The monastery and church are built into the side of the cliff. It has four small chapels fitted into the natural rock. This hermitage was known to travellers in the 17th and 18th centuries, although it is thought to have been founded much earlier in the 14th century. The Anchorite of Lebanon, François de Chasteuil (1588-1644) is buried here. You can get to the monastery from a steep winding road down from near the head of the valley on the south side.

Deir Qannoubin

The name Qannoubin is derived from the Greek *kenobion*, which means 'monastery'. This is a very ancient site and was the Maronite patriarchal seat from the 15th to the 19th centuries. The church is half-built into the rock face and is decorated with frescoes dating from the 18th century.

Near the entrance is a vault containing the naturally mummified body thought to be that of Patriarch Yousef Tyan. Nearby is the chapel-cave of St Marina where the remains of 17 Maronite patriarchs are buried. To get there you can walk down from Blawza and then up to Qannoubin. It takes about one hour each way.

Deir Mar Semaan

This is a very early hermitage founded in 1112 by Takla, the daughter of a local priest called Basil. This is a spartan four-room hermitage carved into the rocks. There are a few traces of frescoes, and remains of water cisterns. You can walk down a steep path from the road on the south side of the valley. The walk takes about 15 minutes one way.

B'qaa Kafra

This is the highest village in Lebanon and the birthplace of St Charbel. It is above the valley road on the south side between Bcharré and Hasroun. The main reason for visiting B'qaa Kafra is to see the **museum** which commemorates the saint's life in paintings. It is open daily, except Monday, and there is a shop and café at the entrance. The village now has a new convent named after St Charbel and there is a church, Notre Dame, across the way from the museum. St Charbel's Feast is celebrated on the third Sunday of July.

Hasroun

Hasroun is a very traditional small village with red-tiled roofs. It is 2km from B'qaa Kafra on the south road along the valley. There is a path leading down into the valley from Hasroun which leads past the old church of Mar Mikhail and the monastery of Mar Yaaqoub.

Diman

In Diman on the south side of the valley is the Maronite Patriarchy which took over from Deir Qannoubin in the 19th century. It is the summer residence of the patriarch. You can't miss it – it is a large building on the valley side of the road. The church is not very old but is well worth looking at for the panoramic **paintings** of the Kadisha Valley around the walls as well as religious scenes by the Lebanese painter, Saliba Doueihy. These seem to date from the 1930s or 1940s when the spire of the church was built. The grounds behind the building lead to the edge of the gorge with a good view across the valley.

Hadchit

This village is 3km west of Bcharré, about 1km off the main valley road on the north side. The **church** is once again the dominant feature. This one has a headless Roman statue which sits outside at the corner of the church. It used to be inside until it was recognised as a pagan statue and its arms broken off. The church interior is quite grand with painted panels everywhere. There are no restaurants in the village, only a sandwich bar near the top.

Ehden

This village on the north side of the Kadisha Valley dates back to the Middle Ages. It is a popular summer resort and is known for its old souk and traditional main square where the whole village gathers on summer evenings. St Joseph's Church is on the main road and has a **statue** of Yousef Bey Karam, a national hero of the 19th century, on horseback outside. He was killed by the Turks near Ehden. There is also an older church, St George's, which is in ruins. To the north-west of the village on a hill is the tiny **chapel** of Our Lady of the Castle, which was probably a Roman look-out post originally. The village has a number of springs nearby which are pleasant to visit by foot.

Horsh Ehden

Just above the village is the nature reserve of Horsh Ehden (see Nature Reserves in the Facts about Lebanon chapter for more information). This is a large area of wilderness and natural beauty which is perfect for mountain treks and nature watching.

Places to Stay & Eat

Most people who visit the Kadisha Valley stay in either Bcharré or the Cedars, but there are alternatives. In Ehden the *Grand Hotel Abchi* (☎ (06) 560001) is a largish, modern hotel which overlooks the village from the west. A double room costs US$50 and a suite costs US$75. *Hotel La Mairie* (☎ (06) 560108) is on the main road of the village. Singles/doubles with breakfast cost US$50/

60. A two-room suite/apartment costs US$120/250.

In Ehden there is a famous eatery, *Nabaa Mar Sarkis*, which serves outstanding mezze and local specialities. It is not cheap – expect to pay about US$20 per head. There are several other cheaper restaurants in Ehden: *Restaurant Père Joup* and *Restaurant Rabia* which are both on the main road. On the western outskirts of Ehden is *Restaurant Mortier*. All of these serve typical Lebanese food.

Getting There & Away

If you are taking a service taxi from Tripoli to Bcharré, you can ask the driver to drop you at Ehden or any other point en route along the north side of the valley. If you want to get to the south side of the valley, you will have to go to Bcharré and get a taxi from there. A service taxi to any point from Ehden to Bcharré will cost LL 6000.

You would be better off with your own transport to explore this part of Lebanon. If you don't have a car, it might be worth hiring a car and driver for the day to take you round. Your hotel can arrange this. Expect to pay from US$80 to US$100 for a whole day, which is not too bad if there are a few of you to share the costs.

Akkar

Akkar, the area at the extreme northern part of Lebanon beyond Tripoli, is usually only visited if you are driving to Syria. The coastal plain here widens out; inland the landscape is still mountainous, but more rounded than jagged. This is the end of the Mount Lebanon range.

In this area there is only one town of any size, Qoubayat, with little there for tourists to see. The main reason for visiting the north is to drive around the unspoilt villages where a more traditional agricultural life still exists. Once you leave the main highway there are virtually no restaurants, apart from simple cafés in the villages, and no hotels.

Qoubayat

Built at the foot of wooded mountains, Qoubayat was on the overland route from Tripoli to Homs in Syria before the new highway was built. It is a typical small northern town whose main industry is silk manufacture.

Qoubayat has an old shrine called the **Lady of Shahlo** and a large old church, **St Georges**. The town has a number of traditional houses with mullioned windows and is pleasant enough to wander around.

Three kilometres further along the road is the village of **Aandqet**, which also has silk spinning mills. A further 1km down a track is the tiny village of **Aaidamoun** where Akkar carpets are traditionally made by the local women. Nearby is the Roman temple of **Maqam** which is constructed in a simple style.

Getting There & Away Service taxis leave from the Rue Tall stand in Tripoli. The fare to Qoubayat is LL 4000.

Castle of Akkar

The castle stands at an altitude of 700m on a rocky spur from which you can see the Crac des Chevaliers in Syria. It is in a pretty remote spot, about 45km from Tripoli, off the highway heading north. The castle was named after its supposed founder Muhriz ibn Akkar, whose family owned the castle until 1019. It was conquered by the Fatimid caliphs of Egypt and then by the Seljuk Turks. When the Frankish Crusaders took Tripoli in 1109, they were given Akkar by treaty. There followed the usual tug of war between the Crusaders and the Arabs. It is easy to see why it was such a prize; from such a position the castle dwellers could make raids on the main highway between Homs and Baalbek and then retire to an impenetrable lair.

At the time of the Ottoman sultans Akkar was governed by the emirs of Beit Safa, but Fakhr ad-Din seized it and destroyed the fortress. The walls are still standing but the interior is a heap of rubble.

Getting There & Away

Reaching Akkar is tricky without your own transport. Apart from a few small villages en route the road leads nowhere, so hitching is out. The nearest transport point is Halba on the Tripoli to Qoubayat road. A service taxi will drop you off at Halba and from there you will need a taxi to take you to the Castle of Akkar and back again.

The Bekaa Valley

The Bekaa Valley is a high plateau between the Mount Lebanon and the Anti-Lebanon ranges. The climate is drier than elsewhere in Lebanon, as the valley falls in a rain shadow, and it is very hot here in the summer months. This makes it ideal for Lebanon's wine production, as the valley is fed by the waters of two major rivers, the Nahr al-Aasi (Orontes River) and the Nahr Litani. Large areas of the valley are covered with vines belonging to the main vineyards in Lebanon – Ksara and Kefraya.

In history the Bekaa was an important grain-producing region, and was one of Rome's 'breadbaskets'. Today the Bekaa, while still producing a couple of crops a year, is nowhere near as productive. Deforestation and long-term neglect have reduced the fertility of the land. One crop flourished exceptionally well before and during the war – cannabis. Until quite recently 'Red Leb' was the country's most famous (or infamous) product. These days the farmers of the Bekaa have cleaned up their act and the cannabis plantations, which once covered the whole of the northern Bekaa, have ceased production in favour of less exciting crops.

There are two major sites to visit in the Bekaa: Baalbek (ancient Heliopolis), with its world-famous temples and Aanjar, a well-preserved Umayyad city. The whole valley is dotted with small Roman sites, isolated temples or tombs which are rewarding if you have the time, but are often quite a hike from the road.

CHTAURA

Chtaura (50km from Beirut) is the transport hub of the Bekaa, with roads heading north to Baalbek and Homs (Syria), south to Lake Qaraoun and on to Marjayoun, and east to Damascus and Jordan. The town itself is nothing special to look at, although there are some pleasant orchards and small parks in the outlying areas; its function as a stopover is clear from the many cheap eateries which

HIGHLIGHTS

ANN JOUSIFFE

- Visit the ruins of Aanjar – the only significant Umayyad archaeological find in the Middle East (above)
- Enjoy a traditional Lebanese meal in one of Zahlé's alfresco river-side restaurants
- Try the local firewater, arak, a specialty of Zahlé
- Tour the Ksara Winery and savour the wines of this well-known vineyard
- Explore the impressive Phoenician, Roman and Greek temple ruins of the famous Baalbek site
- Wander around Baalbek's quarry where the world's largest cut stone lies partially under ground
- Inspect Amor, the strange and fascinating 27m-high pyramid tomb near Hermel
- Walk along the banks of the Nahr al-Aasi and see the tumbling waterfalls of Shilal Heira, Dedawra and Shilman
- Climb the spiral staircases connecting the monks' cells in Deir Mar Maroun

line the main road. But the small restaurants are friendly and traditional, often serving local produce such as cheese and yoghurt or the locally made fruit or nut syrups which are to be found in speciality stores all over the world. Try the almond syrup with iced milk for something different.

Chtaura is also the main banking centre for the Bekaa and you will find many banks and bureaux de change along the main road, as well as shops selling eastern souvenirs. One of the old hotels is now a barracks for Syrian soldiers and the presence of a large, international-class hotel gives away its role

as a meeting point for Lebanese and Syrian political conferences. Chtaura is also known as a health resort for asthma and rheumatism sufferers.

Places to Stay

The only up-and-running cheap option is the *Hotel Khater* (☎ (08) 840133), which is on the main road above a shop-cum-café. The rooms are simple and fairly clean, but there is no restaurant (even for breakfast) and you will have to wander down to a nearby café. Singles/doubles/triples cost US$10/20/30. If you want a quiet night's rest, ask for a room at the back which overlooks trees rather than the busy main road.

The other hotel in Chtaura is at the opposite end of the scale. The *Chtaura Park Hotel* (☎ (08) 540011, 540997; fax 542686) is a super luxury hotel with prices to match. Singles/doubles with breakfast cost from US$118/144 plus 16% service. The hotel has a sauna and all mod-cons.

Places to Eat

The best place in town is the *Akl Restaurant* with its two venues, one indoors and the other outdoors, close together on the main road. This long-established restaurant specialises in mezze dishes and can serve 27 different saucer-sized appetisers if you're feeling hungry. Expect to spend US$10 to US$20 depending on what you order.

Also worth trying are the *Restaurant Moutran* and *Restaurant Habre*, both on the main road near the Hotel Khater. These are also traditional Lebanese restaurants but not as fancy as the Akl.

There are a number of snack places in Chtaura. Downstairs from the Hotel Khater is a *café/shop* selling a bizarre combination of alcohol and ammunition. If you're not in the market for that, you can also get a half-decent sandwich and coffee.

Getting There & Away

There are frequent service taxis to and from Beirut which cost LL 5000. They congregate on the main street and you can easily get connections onward to Zahlé, Baalbek,

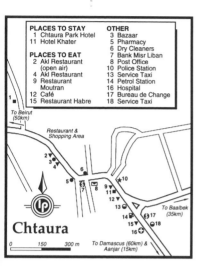

PLACES TO STAY	OTHER
1 Chtaura Park Hotel	3 Bazaar
11 Hotel Khater	5 Pharmacy
	6 Dry Cleaners
PLACES TO EAT	7 Bank Misr Liban
2 Akl Restaurant	8 Post Office
(open air)	10 Police Station
4 Akl Restaurant	13 Service Taxi
9 Restaurant	14 Petrol Station
Moutran	16 Hospital
12 Café	17 Bureau de Change
15 Restaurant Habre	18 Service Taxi

Restaurant & Shopping Area

To Beirut (50km)

Chtaura

0   150   300 m

To Baalbek (35km)

To Damascus (60km) & Aanjar (15km)

Damascus and Homs, as well as to some of the smaller places along the Bekaa Valley.

ZAHLÉ

Zahlé, an attractive town 7km north-east of Chtaura, is quite a contrast to its neighbour. Set along the steep banks of the Birdawni River which tumbles through a gorge from Jebel Sannine, it has lots of character. Zahlé is traditionally a Roman Catholic town and has long exploited its attractions as a resort. There are literally dozens of open-air restaurants packed along the river's edge in the upper part of the town. During summer weekends and evenings, these are usually full of locals and Beirutis enjoying some of the finest Lebanese cooking to be found in the whole country, washed down with the local firewater, arak (see the Arak boxed story).

Zahlé is a good place to explore on foot. Its large, traditional, red-roofed houses lend an air of faded grandeur to the place.

Information

Zahlé is a medium-size town with all the basic amenities near the centre. The main road which runs through town is Rue Brazil

Arak

If there is a national drink of Lebanon, or indeed the rest of the Middle East, then this is it. An acquired taste for some westerners, this aniseed-flavoured drink has become a universal favourite in the eastern Mediterranean under several guises – ouzo in Greece, raki in Turkey – but are all fundamentally the same thing. It is a drink that doesn't travel well. Somehow it just doesn't taste the same when drunk in London, New York or Sydney. It is very much a drink of the Mediterranean.

It is also curiously classless, sipped at both the smartest dinner or the humblest café. It manages this by being both cheap and expensive but, unlike wine, the difference between the US$4 bottle and the US$20 fancy ceramic flask is nonexistent to the untutored palate.

It comes as a bit of a surprise that arak is a by-product of wine-making, not having the least hint of 'grapiness' to its flavour. In fact it is a brandy, made from the bits left over from the wine press – the red grape skins, pips and so forth, much like the Italian grappa, but with the additional flavour of aniseed. After the first wine fermentation, the skins and solids rise to the top of the vat. These are separated and fermented into a potent but evil-smelling brew, the result of which is distilled into a lethal spirit of 92 to 94% alcohol.

One glass of this would probably kill you (or at least make you very ill). The toxins have to be carefully filtered out and the liquor refined until what you end up with is a clear and very pure form of alcohol. The methanol is separated from the brew by a further distillation and the result is a very refined product.

The distinctive flavour is added next with macerated green aniseeds from Syria, and water added to dilute it to a drinkable level of potency. After this the poisonous 'head' of the brew is removed; what remains is pure arak. The result is left to mature for six to 10 months, in the case of the finer araks, and considerably less time for the cheapo varieties.

With all the refining processes that it goes through it is not surprising that arak has the reputation for not giving you a hangover. But even so, it is surprisingly potent and even diluted can get you drunk very quickly.

Anise is not everyone's favourite flavour but diluted with ice and water arak makes a better partner for Lebanese cuisine than you would imagine. Arak, and indeed all aniseed-flavoured drinks, develops a milk opacity with the addition of water. It has a cooling and palate-cleansing effect which becomes more pleasant as you get used to the taste. So overcome any 'araknaphobia' and try it with your next mezze – you could easily become converted. ■

BEKAA VALLEY

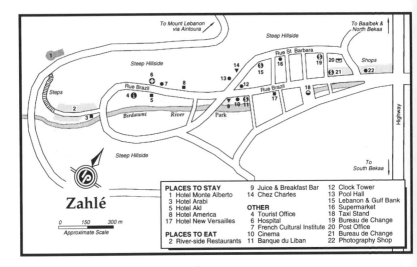

To Mount Lebanon
via Aintoura

To Baalbek &
North Bekaa

Steep Hillside

Rue St Barbara

Steep Hillside

Steep Hillside

Shops

Rue Brazil

Steps

Rue Brazil

Birdawni   River   Park

Highway

Steep Hillside

To
South Bekaa

Zahlé

0   150   300 m
Approximate Scale

PLACES TO STAY	9 Juice & Breakfast Bar	12 Clock Tower
1 Hotel Monte Alberto	14 Chez Charles	13 Pool Hall
3 Hotel Arabi		15 Lebanon & Gulf Bank
5 Hotel Akl	**OTHER**	16 Supermarket
8 Hotel America	4 Tourist Office	18 Taxi Stand
17 Hotel New Versailles	6 Hospital	19 Bureau de Change
	7 French Cultural Institute	20 Post Office
PLACES TO EAT	10 Cinema	21 Bureau de Change
2 River-side Restaurants	11 Banque du Liban	22 Photography Shop

with Rue St Barbara running parallel. This is where the banks, bureaux de change and the post office can be found. The tourist information office (☎ (08) 802566; fax 803595) is in the Chamber of Commerce building on Rue Brazil.

There is a hospital on Rue Brazil towards the head of the valley. In case of emergency, call the Red Cross (☎ (08) 824892). The police can be contacted at (☎ (08) 803521, 824110).

Places to Stay

Most of the hotels are on the main road , Rue Brazil. *Hotel America* (☎ (08) 820536) is just about the cheapest place in town. It is run by a Muslim family and no English is spoken, but it is friendly and adequate, if a bit grubby and run-down. There are 21 rooms with bath and singles/doubles cost US$10/20.

Just along the street on the other side is the lovely *Hotel Akl* (☎ (08) 820701), a well-run hotel in a 150-year-old house. Spotlessly clean and friendly rooms at this highly recommended place cost US$20 with private bath and US$17 without. There is a lounge downstairs with a TV and piano.

Another cheapie at the other end of Rue Brazil is the *Hotel New Versailles*, which has singles/doubles for US$20 and breakfast for US$10.

At the head of the valley on the river bank is the *Hotel Arabi* (☎ (08) 821214; fax 800144), a small, very smart hotel with only 16 rooms. It is quite expensive at US$60 for singles or doubles including service. Breakfast will cost an extra US$5. It has two restaurants: the open-air one (in summer only) is very popular with affluent Beirutis at the weekend.

If views are what you're after, then *Hotel Monte Alberto* (☎ (08) 800342, 822365) is the place to head. Situated high above the town, but only a five-minute walk down to the river, it is very clean and comfortable. Singles/twins cost US$40 and rooms with a double bed cost US$55. Be sure to ask for a room with a view when you book. Breakfast is an extra US$5. One of the features of the hotel is its circular panoramic restaurant overlooking the gorge. Dinner costs about US$15.

Places to Eat

There is no shortage of places to eat at all levels of spending, but one of the great treats is dinner by the river along the walkway at the head of the valley. To get there, walk right through town until the road curves round the end of the valley. You will see a pedestrian street which follows the course of the river. Facing the water are shoulder-to-shoulder restaurants all with a good reputation. On the land side of the walkway are various fast-food places, juice bars and entertainment arcades. There is not much to choose price-wise between the river-side restaurants. Budget for US$15 per head for a full mezze. Recommended is the outside *restaurant* at the Hotel Arabi, but it is just a question of wandering along and making your choice.

Back in the centre of town, near the clock tower, *Chez Charles* is a good eating option. Not as expensive as the river-side places, it is cosy and the food is good. Expect to pay about US$8 to US$10 for a good lunch or dinner with a few drinks. Along Rue Brazil are a number of good juice bars and snack places which serve a good breakfast for a few dollars.

Getting There & Away

A service taxi from Chtaura will cost LL 1500. If it is serving Baalbek and dropping you off, then there is an eight-minute walk from the roundabout to the centre of town, so it is better to get one that is going only to Zahlé. The main taxi stand in town is a square on Rue Brazil, where you can pick up a service taxi to various points in the Bekaa.

AROUND ZAHLÉ
Ksara Winery

A visit to the winery at Ksara, a couple of kilometres south of Zahlé, is an interesting way to pass a morning. It is especially pleasant to wander around the cool caves on a hot day and there is always a tasting session at the end of the visit. There is a multilingual guide to show you around the various processes of wine and arak production and a chance to try some of the more unusual products.

The winery is open to visitors from 10 am to 2 pm daily. It is more geared up for receiving groups, so if you are an independent

traveller it would be prudent to call first (☎ (08) 801662).

Getting There & Away A service taxi from Zahlé heading south will drop you in Ksara village (LL 1000), a five-minute walk from the winery. Otherwise a taxi will take you there and back for US$10 and wait for you. If you are driving yourself, head south along the main highway for about 2km until you come to Ksara, then look for a turning on the right to the winery.

AANJAR

Aanjar is the only significant Umayyad site in Lebanon. It is only 15km from Chtaura (58km from Beirut) in the southern part of the Bekaa Valley. It was a late discovery; archaeologists did not discover the site until the 1940s and serious excavation work only began there in the 1950s.

At first the site seemed painfully modest in comparison to the other sites in Lebanon, and early guidebooks hardly gave it a mention. However, as the excavations progressed, things became more exciting. Almost all periods of Arab history have been preserved in other sites in Lebanon – only the Umayyad period was missing (apart from the ruined mosque at Baalbek). The site began to reveal information about this epoch of Middle Eastern history in which these warlike caliphs held sway over a region that stretched from the Indus Valley to the south of France during the 7th and 8th centuries AD.

The Umayyad City

Aanjar was a walled and fortified city built along symmetrical Roman lines. The layout is rectangular – almost square – with two major avenues, each 20m wide, bisecting it. The city walls each have a gate at the mid-point of each side which were protected by towers. It its heyday, the main streets, the *cardo maximus* and *documanus maximus*, were flanked by palaces, baths, mosques and shops, as well as extensive dwellings. About 600 shops have been uncovered, which strongly indicates that the city was a major trading place. This makes sense as it is positioned right on the east-west trade route.

Unlike the other ancient cities of Lebanon, this town was built from scratch and flourished briefly, then fell, abandoned in the face of defeat at the hands of the Abbasids. So what we see here is uniquely of one era. The most beautiful building at Aanjar is the reconstructed **great palace**, which has graceful tiers of arches that betray a Byzantine touch here and there. See also The Architecture of Lebanon section in the Facts about Lebanon chapter.

Only one gate is open – Aanjar is still partly occupied by the Syrian army. You can see their bunkers and mess huts on the northern side of the site. The site is open daily from 8 am until sunset. The entrance fee is LL 4000.

Majdel Aanjar

The village of Majdel Aanjar is 1km from the Aanjar site. Above the village on a hill are the remains of some **Roman ruins**, includ-

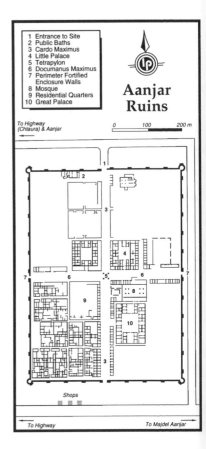

1 Entrance to Site
2 Public Baths
3 Cardo Maximus
4 Little Palace
5 Tetrapylon
6 Documanus Maximus
7 Perimeter Fortified
  Enclosure Walls
8 Mosque
9 Residential Quarters
10 Great Palace

Aanjar Ruins

To Highway (Chtaura) & Aanjar

0   100   200 m

Shops

To Highway   To Majdel Aanjar

Stone torsos are all that remain of the ancient statues that once watched over the Umayyad city of Aanjar.

ing a temple and some fortifications. Not many people go to this site partly because it is not well known and because of the uphill walk to get there. Go through the village and right up the hill. The road turns to track halfway up and the last part is quite steep. The views are worth the effort.

Back in the village below, it's worth taking a look at the **13th-century minaret** which was restored in 1959. It is square with decorative cornices and four windows.

Dakweh

Three kilometres from Majdel Aanjar is

another site of interest at Dakweh, or rather on the hill just behind the village. It is a 10 to 15-minute walk up to a lovely **Roman necropolis**. There is a small temple in good condition and several cave-tombs.

Places to Eat

There is a good place called *Restaurant Soleil*, off the main Damascus highway on the road to Aanjar at about the 500m point. It specialises in fresh fish. Near the site itself are a few shops where you can buy water and snacks.

Getting There & Away

If you are taking a service taxi from Chtaura heading south or to the Syrian border, you will have to get out at Aanjar town (Haouch Moussa) to the site. If you don't have your own car, the best way is to negotiate a return trip with a taxi driver who will wait for you (allow one hour for a visit – two if you are very thorough). This should cost about US$10 for a one-hour stay.

To visit the other sites you need either a strong constitution and some walking boots or a taxi driver hired by the hour who can wait for you while you explore.

LAKE QARAOUN & THE LITANI DAM

Way down south in the Bekaa Valley is the Litani Dam. This was built in 1959 and has created a lake of 11 sq km. The Litani is the longest river in Lebanon – it rises in the north of the Bekaa near Baalbek and flows into the sea near Tyre. Although the dam was built for the practical reason of producing electricity and providing irrigation, it is an attractive spot to visit and several restaurants have sprung up along the lake's edge.

There is a visitor centre at the southern end of the lake (the dam end) on the eastern side.

Getting There & Away

It is difficult to get a service taxi to the far south of the Bekaa; you will probably have to negotiate hard with a taxi driver to take you. Hitching is a possibility but really you need your own car in order not to get stuck in the back of beyond.

BAALBEK

Baalbek, in the northern Bekaa Valley, 86km from Beirut, had until the mid-1990s been a no-go zone for tourists. The fame of the Roman temples was eclipsed by its fame as the seat of Hezbollah, or Party of God, and its association with hostage-taking and radical anti-western politics. There are still numerous reminders of Hezbollah's supremacy here, including the 10m-high posters of Ayatollah Khomeini and the difficulty in getting a drink. But the world turns even for Hezbollah and now the official policy is to welcome tourists back to Baalbek. The dress code for visitors has become more relaxed and rumour has it that a few cafés have started to serve alcohol again.

Baalbek, the 'Sun City' of the ancient world, is the most impressive ancient site in Lebanon. It is arguably the most important Roman site in the Middle East. It once enjoyed a reputation as one of the wonders of the world and mystics still attribute special powers to the courtyard complex. Its temples were built on an extravagant scale on the site of earlier temples. Baalbek grew a culture around it which drew people from far and wide for religious festivals.

It is also notable for its misnomers: the Temple of Bacchus was not dedicated to Bacchus, nor was the Temple of Venus dedicated to Venus. Even the main hotel is rather curiously called the Palmyra, not the Baalbek.

An international **festival** has been revived at the Baalbek site. See Arts in the Facts about Lebanon chapter for more details.

History

The site was originally Phoenician and was dedicated to the God Baal (later Hadad), hence its name. The site was no doubt chosen for its nearby springs and favoured situation between the Litani and al-Aasi rivers, and also because of its position on the trade route.

The Greeks and Romans called the city 'Heliopolis', literally the 'City of the Sun', and dedicated the main temple to Jupiter

Heliopolitan, who was associated with Baal/Hadad, the father of all gods and god of the sun. However, this Baal of Heliopolis was actually a triad of gods – his partners being Venus and Mercury. Venus was associated with Astarte or Atargatis, the chief female deity, but it is not known for certain who Mercury was associated with in the Phoenician pantheon (current thought finds Simios to be the most likely candidate). This triad of gods was extraordinarily popular and altars dedicated to them have been found not only in the east but in the Balkans, Spain, France and even Scotland.

It was originally a cult of nature worship and sacrifice – possibly even human sacrifice – and the temples were a focus for all manner of sexual and licentious forms of worship. Sacred prostitution coupled with an insatiable blood-lust seem to have featured in the cult. According to ancient tablets from Ugarit, which describe the practices of the Phoenician gods in a gruesome way, Anath, the sister and wife of Baal,

'... waded up to the knees, up to the neck in human blood. Human heads lay at her feet, human hands flew over her like locusts. She tied the heads of her victims as ornaments on her back, their hands she tied upon her belt ... When she was satisfied she washed her hands in streams of blood before turning again to other things.'

Following the conquest of Alexander the Great, Baalbek became known as Heliopolis, a name which was kept by the subsequent Roman conquerors. In 64 BC Pompey the Great passed through Baalbek and was intrigued by its gods. A few years later in 47 BC Julius Caesar founded a Roman colony there because of its strategic position between Palmyra, in the Syrian desert, and the coastal cities. He named the new colony after his daughter Julia. The town became occupied by Roman soldiers and building works were begun. Baalbek was soon recognised as the premier city in Roman Syria.

The reconstruction of the temples was a huge undertaking. It is known that the great Temple of Jupiter was nearing completion in 60 AD during the reign of Nero. The building

of such extravagant temples was as much, if not more, a political act than a spiritual one. The Romans made efforts to integrate the peoples of the orient by looking favourably on their cults and building beautiful monuments to celebrate them. Even so, the deciding factor in building on such a massive and expansive scale at Baalbek was probably the threat of Christianity which was beginning to pose a real threat to the old order. So, up went the temples in an attempt to 'fix' the religious orientation of the people in favour of pagan worship. By this time there were no human sacrifices, but still the temple prostitution remained and probably bulls were sacrificed – a persistent theme all over the Middle East.

Several emperors had a hand in the building of the temples: Hadrian (117-38), Antoninus Pius (138-61), Septimius Severus (193-211) and his son Caracalla (211-17) who completed the main constructions. The first known picture of the temple appeared on a coin from Severus' reign. The works were partly paid for by dignitaries, heroes and notables of the region, who would pledge money for columns and gold decorations (no doubt in return for civic recognition).

When Constantine became emperor, the pagan world was under threat and building work was suspended. But when Julian the Apostate became emperor, he reverted to paganism and tried to reinstate it throughout the empire. There was a terrible backlash against Christians which resulted in mass martyrdom for the Christian population. By the time the Christian emperor, Theodosius, took the throne, Christianity reasserted itself and the temples of Baalbek were converted to a Christian basilica using the stones of the temples. So Baalbek's great pagan monuments were partially demolished even before they had been finished.

After the death of Theodosius, Baalbek faded in grandeur and importance. A chronicler of Justinian reports the dispatching of eight rose-granite columns to Constantinople for the construction of the Hagia Sofia.

When the Moslem Arabs invaded Syria,

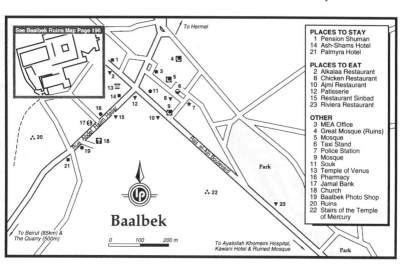

Baalbek

To Hermel

PLACES TO STAY
1 Pension Shuman
14 Ash-Shams Hotel
21 Palmyra Hotel

PLACES TO EAT
2 Alkalaa Restaurant
8 Chicken Restaurant
10 Ajmi Restaurant
12 Patisserie
15 Restaurant Sinbad
23 Riviera Restaurant

OTHER
3 MEA Office
4 Great Mosque (Ruins)
5 Mosque
6 Taxi Stand
7 Police Station
9 Mosque
11 Souk
13 Temple of Venus
16 Pharmacy
17 Jamal Bank
18 Church
19 Baalbek Photo Shop
20 Ruins
22 Stairs of the Temple of Mercury

See Baalbek Ruins Map Page 190.

To Beirut (85km) & The Quarry (500m)

0   100   200 m

To Ayatollah Khomeini Hospital, Kawani Hotel & Ruined Mosque

Park

they converted the Baalbek temples into a citadel and restored its Syriac name. For several centuries it came under the rule of Damascus. It went through a period of regular invasions, sackings, lootings and devastation. The city was sacked by the Arabs in 748 and by the Mongol chieftain, Tamerlane, in 1400. It became almost unrecognisable.

In addition to the ravages caused by humans, there was also a succession of earthquakes in 1158, 1203, 1664 and most spectacularly in 1759, which caused the fall of the ramparts and three of the huge pillars of the Temple of Jupiter and the departure of most of the population. Most of what remains today lies within the area of the Arab fortifications; the Temple of Mercury further out is virtually gone. By erecting walls around some of the buildings, the Arabs unwittingly preserved the temples inside the sanctuary.

Towards the end of the 19th century the European powers became interested in the ruins and their conservation. When Kaiser Wilhelm II visited Baalbek on a tour of the Middle East, he was immediately concerned that something should be done to excavate

the site. He obtained the permission of the Sultan of Turkey to send a team of archaeologists to begin work. For the next seven years the team recorded the site in detail. By this time Baalbek was frequently visited by tourists who helped themselves to sculptures and inscriptions. They also carved their names on the temple walls.

After the defeat of Turkey and Germany in WWI, Baalbek's German scholars were replaced by French ones. Over a period of decades all the later masonry was removed and the temples restored as near as possible to their 1st-century splendour.

Orientation

The town of Baalbek is small with around 12,000 inhabitants. It is easy to tour the whole town on foot and the ruins are close to the centre of town. Ras el-Ain is about 10 minutes on foot from the centre.

Information

Money There is a branch of the Jamal Bank on the main road into town on the left. You can also change currency at the Palmyra Hotel or in various shops around the central shopping area.

BEKAA VALLEY

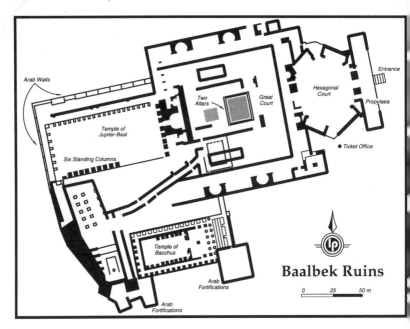

Baalbek Ruins

0   25   50 m

Dangers & Annoyances

Visiting Baalbek these days is perfectly safe for tourists, although it is prudent and considerate not to wander around in shorts (men and women) or any other kind of revealing clothes. This is a Hezbollah area whose Shiite Muslim population has close allegiance with Iran (you will no doubt notice pictures of Ayatollah Khomeini around the place) and is therefore more conservative in its dress and behaviour. Alcohol is not openly on sale in shops, although if you ask, they often have an 'under-the-counter' supply. Rumour has it that things are becoming more relaxed and that a few cafés are serving alcohol openly. The Palmyra Hotel is the exception and has always served alcohol.

The Main Temples

Entrance to the main site is at the south-east end of the temple complex. You enter the ruins via the monumental staircase leading up to the **Propylaea** which has a portico flanked by two towers and a colonnade along the facade. The column bases bear the inscription 'For the safety and victories of our lord, Caracalla'. Through a central door you move into the **Hexagonal Court**. There is a threshold which marks the limit of the sacred enclosure. This first courtyard is about 50m deep. It used to be surrounded by a columned portico and to the north and south four exedrae opened symmetrically onto the portico, each with four columns. These rooms were decorated with niches with either triangular or round pediments. To the north of the court is a famous bas-relief of Jupiter Heliopolitan which was found near the Lejuj spring, 5km from Baalbek.

The **Great Court**, or Sacrificial Courtyard, is beyond the first court. It was richly decorated on three sides and had a double row of niches surmounted with pediments. There are a number of exedra: four semicircular and eight rectangular. Between the exedrae there are niches which also held

dismantled. The foundations of a huge **altar** stand where the basilica used to be.

The **Temple of Jupiter-Baal** was built on an immense substructure over 300m long, and the approach to the temple was up another monumental staircase which rose high above the surrounding buildings. It consisted of a cella in which the statue of the god was housed and a surrounding portico of 10 columns along the facade and 19 columns along the side, making for 54 columns in all. These columns are the largest in the world – 22.9m high with a girth of 2.2m in diameter. Today only six of these remain standing with the architrave still in position. Their immensity has to be seen to be believed. It was thought in the old days that Baalbek had been constructed by giants and a quick look over the side of the temple to the foundation stones beneath reveals some of the largest building blocks to be found anywhere on earth. One of these megalithic blocks measures 19.5m by 4.3m and is estimated to weigh over 1000 tons – how it was moved and positioned so precisely remains a mystery. See also The Architecture of Lebanon section in the Facts about Lebanon chapter.

From the south side of the temple is a wonderful view of the so-called **Temple of Bacchus**. This is in fact dedicated not to Bacchus but to Venus/Astarte and is the most wonderfully decorated temple in the Roman world. It is also in a great state of preservation and was completed around 150 AD. It is not built on the scale of the Temple of Jupiter but more than makes up for it in style and decoration. Ironically it was called 'the small temple' in antiquity, although it is larger than the Parthenon in Athens. The entrance is up a flight of 30 stairs with three landings. It has a portico running around it with eight columns along the facade and 15 along the sides. They support a rich entablature; the frieze is decorated with lions and bulls. This supports a ceiling of curved stone which is decorated with vivid scenes: Mars, a winged Victory, Diana taking an arrow from her quiver, a Tyche with a cornucopia, Vulcan with his hammer, Bacchus, and Ceres holding a sheaf of corn.

Bronze statue of Jupiter Heliopolitan, now in the Musée de Louvre in Paris. He would usually have held a whip in his right hand and a thunderbolt in his left. A winged sun disc lies on his chest and below are reliefs depicting the seven planets of Roman astrology.

statues. All these porticoes and exedrae would have once been covered by a wooden roof to protect visitors from the sun and rain. To either side of the courtyard were two pools which still have some highly decorative carving on their sides showing Trions and Nereids, Medusas and Cupids riding dragons. In the centre of the courtyard stood the Christian basilica which has now been

The highlight of the temple is the doorway, which has been drawn and painted by many artists, its half fallen keystone forever a symbol of Baalbek. See the Sketches of Baalbek boxed story in The Architecture of Lebanon section. Inside, the cella is richly decorated with fluted columns. The 'holy place' was at the back of the cella, which is reached by another staircase with two ramps. When the temple was in use this would have been a dark and mysterious place, probably lit dramatically by oil lamps with piercing shafts of daylight falling on the image of the god or goddess.

The site is open daily from 8.30 am to sunset. Admission for adults/students is LL 10,000/4000. For Lebanese adults/students, the entrance fee is LL 4000/2000. Guided tours are available in several languages, including English and French. There is no set fee so it is best to negotiate beforehand – around US$10. Numerous souvenir sellers and peddlers congregate around the entrance. You can take a short camel ride for LL 2000.

Other Places of Interest

Near the main ruins about 300m from the acropolis is the exquisite, tiny **Temple of Venus** (probably dedicated to Fortuna rather than Venus), a circular building with many fluted columns. Inside, it was decorated with tiers of tabernacles and covered with a cupola. During the early Christian era it was turned into a basilica and dedicated to St Barbara. A copy of this gem of a temple was reconstructed in the 18th century in the grounds of Stourhead in Wiltshire, England, where it now stands by the lake.

To the east of the Propylaea stands the ruined **Great Mosque** which was built from the stones of the temples using many different styles of columns and capitals. At the north-west corner are the ruins of a great octagonal minaret on a square base.

To the south-east of the centre of Baalbek is the source of the **Ras el-Ain** spring. The area has pleasant shady parks along the spring and is the site of occasional festivities with horses and camels and side stalls. At the head of the spring is a ruined early **mosque**,

> ### The Quarry
> About 1km south of the centre of Baalbek, on Sheikh Abdullah Hill, is the quarry where the huge temple stones originated. Here you can see the largest cut stone in the world lying on its side, partially submerged in the earth. The Arabs call this stone *hajar al-hubla* which means 'Stone of the Pregnant Woman'. This came about as a corruption of its original name, *hajar al-qubla*, or 'Stone of the South'. Even so, local folklore has it that women can touch the stone to increase their fertility.
>
> It is 21.5m by 4m by 4.5m and is thought to weigh 2000 tons. It was no doubt destined to take its place with the other outsized blocks of stone which form the foundations of the Temple of Jupiter, or perhaps some planned but unbuilt temple of which we know nothing. In any case it is so huge as to defy the imagination about the skills of the engineers who cut and moved these huge stones. Even today with all our technology it would be nigh on impossible to move and position such a monster. Also dotted around the quarry are some simple **rock-cut tombs**, some of which are used as sheep pens by local shepherds. ∎

which at some point was thought to be the Temple of Neptune.

South-west of the Ras el-Ain Blvd is the site of the **Temple of Mercury**. All that remains today are the three flights of steps which would have led up to the portal.

Places to Stay – bottom end

The *Ash-Shams Hotel* (08) 373284) is a clean little place run by a tailor on Rue Abdel Halim Hajjar up on the 1st floor. It has four rooms (with washbasins) that sleep up to four people for US$6 per person. The toilet and shower are shared. The only other cheapie is the *Pension Shuman* (☎ (08) 370160), near the temple ruins. It has four rooms of varying size which cost LL 10,000 per person.

Places to Stay – top end

The *Palmyra Hotel* (☎ (08) 370230) is one of those great old survivors from the days of Victorian tourism. The over 120-year-old building is right by the ruins and the former train station. It still has the air of faded

Many civilisations left their mark while crossing the caravan route of the Bekaa Valley. At Baalbek, the Romans built on an extravagant scale (top) as well as with incredible detail (bottom middle). Aanjar's Umayyad ruins are a rare example of the days of the first Muslim rulers (bottom left), while the builders of the Hermel Pyramid are unknown (bottom right).

Top: Tyre's part-restored Corinthian colonnade was once a long avenue of marble columns
Middle: This patisserie is one of many treats to be found within the vaulted souks in Sidon
Bottom: The late 19th-century lavish interiors of the Palace of Beiteddine give an insight
into the lives of Emir Bashir II and his sons.

grandeur which hints at its former luxury. The staff are of the 'old retainer' school and are very friendly and helpful. The hotel lacks any mod-cons; heating in winter is by paraffin stove and there is no air-con. Even so it is an experience to stay here. The hotel has a lovely garden terrace dotted with antique bits of masonry and shaded with jasmine trellises, so it's worth stopping by for a drink even if you aren't staying. Like most hotels of this age it has a bit of a history. During WWI it was used by the German army and during WWII it was the British army headquarters in the area. General de Gaulle stayed there as well as General Allenby, Alfonso of Spain, the Empress of Abyssinia and the writer Jean Cocteau.

Rooms here cost US$33/46 plus 15% service for singles/doubles with bath. The hotel has a bar and restaurant where lunch/dinner will cost around US$10. Perhaps the chef was having an off day, but the lunch we had there was not great.

Places to Eat

There are a lot of cheap eateries on the Rue Abdel Halim Hajjar which serve good, fresh felafels and sandwiches for around LL 1250. Baalbek specialises in Lebanese meat pizzas, lahm bi ajin, which can be bought for LL 1200.

There are several adequate restaurants in town, none are very glamorous. The *Restaurant Sinbad*, near the Palmyra Hotel, has simple meals. Close to the ruins opposite the Pension Shuman is the *Alkalaa Restaurant*, which is quite good. Probably your best bet is to explore the Ras el-Ain Blvd where several restaurants look very promising with attractive eating areas outside. One of the nicest is the *Riviera Restaurant* (☎ (08) 370296) towards the Ras el-Ain end of the boulevard. It backs onto the spring where you can enjoy soft drinks for LL 1500 or coffee for LL 1000 and choose from a good selection of mezze dishes for about LL 1000 each.

Closer to the centre of Baalbek is the *Ajmi Restaurant*, also on Ras el-Ain Blvd. This is close to the souk area where there are a number of 'hole-in-the-wall' eateries but the Ajmi is the only one with indoor seating. On the corner near the Ajmi is a good-looking *patisserie* serving cakes and coffee.

Getting There & Away

Some service taxis go directly from Beirut to Baalbek and charge LL 8000. From Chtaura the fare is LL 4000 and from Zahlé, LL 3000. It is also possible to pick up a service taxi to Damascus or Homs. These are quite frequent and charge LL 8000 (LL 5000 to the border). The driver will ask to see a visa for Syria before taking you. Travellers have reported that, despite the official ruling to the contrary, visas will be issued at the border, and if you can persuade the driver to take you, it should be OK.

During the summer months there is also a road across the mountains to the Cedars and Bcharré. Service taxis do not run on this route, but a taxi in either direction should cost about US$33. The trip takes about 1½ hours and offers spectacular scenery.

HERMEL

Hermel is the northernmost town in the Bekaa. It is a small Shiite town whose main economy is agriculture. It is not very interesting for the casual visitor, but there are several places of interest in the locality. If you do not have your own vehicle, it would be the place to pick up a taxi to take you around the district. This is a painless way to see some out of the way monuments if you only have a short time.

If Hermel ever gets properly excavated, it could turn out to be quite an important historical site; ancient remains have been found, the most interesting being an altar dedicated to Jupiter Heliopolitan which is now (hopefully) in the National Museum in Beirut.

Places to Stay & Eat

There are no hotels in Hermel; the nearest place to stay is on the Nahr al-Aasi. Along the main road, just past the taxi stand, you can find a few cafés and shawarma stands selling snacks and sandwiches. There are also one or two grocery stores selling cold

BEKAA VALLEY

drinks etc. There are no proper restaurants in Hermel.

Getting There & Away
Service taxis run north from Baalbek to Hermel and cost LL 4000.

AROUND HERMEL
Amor: the Hermel Pyramid
Ten kilometres south of the town of Hermel is a 27m-high monument in the middle of nowhere sitting on the crest of a small hill. It can be seen for miles away and, although there is no signpost from the main road, you really can't miss it. It is a solid square construction with a pyramid on top and no one is quite sure what it is or why it is standing alone. It is definitely not Graeco-Roman and looks a bit like some of the tower tombs at Palmyra (in Syria) to the east. Its age is estimated at around 2000 years and it is probably a Syrian royal tomb, although some writers have suggested it may have been a hunting lodge (very unlikely). The sides of the building are decorated with hunting scenes showing stags and boars being attacked by mastiffs. One side shows a bull being attacked by wolves or bears. Unfortunately the inscriptions are gone, so the pyramid remains an enigma.

Getting There & Away If you are travelling to or from Hermel by service taxi, you could get the driver to drop you by the turnoff. It is about 1km from the main road to the monument along a track which is easy to spot. If you are driving, the track is OK for a car to drive along.

Nahr al-Aasi
Near a bridge that crosses the Nahr al-Aasi, or Orontes River, are several restaurants specialising in trout and a couple of hotels. This bridge is about 7km from Hermel and is near the only accommodation in the area. It is a good base to begin a walk along the river to the pools and waterfalls which lie about 5 or 6km to the north (ie downstream). These **waterfalls** are called Shilal Heira, Dedawra and Shilman. It is about a one-hour walk in the other direction to the source of the river; a large basin called **Ain ez-Zerqa** (the Blue Spring). This is only 200m from the Mar Maroun monastery.

Places to Stay & Eat There is a good and not too expensive hotel right by the river, about 100m from the bridge. This is the *Hotel Asamaka* (03) 883024) with 25 clean rooms which cost US$25 for doubles/triples. The hotel has a restaurant right by the water under awnings and serves mezze and trout (fresh from a pool) for about US$10. It also serves alcohol. Just by the bridge is another restaurant, the *Casino Restaurant*, serving much the same sort of menu at similar prices.

Offering similar standards as the Asamaka is the recently built *Al-Fardos Hotel* (☎ (03) 670138). Singles/doubles cost US$15/20.

Deir Mar Maroun
To get to this small, ancient monastery cut into the rock overlooking the Nahr al-Aasi, you can either take a 3km hike or a 12km drive. Inside the monastery are several tiers of cells connected with spiral staircases.

The monastery was established in the 5th century by St Maron, the founder of the Maronite church and was destroyed by Justinian II in the 7th century – hundreds were put to death as heretics. The survivors of this persecution fled up to the mountains and across to the Kadisha Valley (see the Tripoli & The Cedars chapter). Later on it was fortified by the Arabs for military use.

Round the corner from the monastery is the source of Nahr al-Aasi, the Ain ez-Zerqa.

Getting There & Away If you don't have your own car, then you can hire a taxi in Hermel to take you there and back. A short tour of Deir Mar Maroun and the Hermel Pyramid and back to Hermel should cost about US$10.

South of Beirut

The southern part of Lebanon is less developed than rest of the country. It was the scene of heavy fighting during the civil war, and the extreme south continues to be periodically subjected to cross-border attacks from Israel. There is a UN-controlled buffer zone along the southern and south-eastern border areas which is closed to visitors. Unless there is a particular security alert it is possible to travel quite easily as far as Tyre (Sour) and Nabatiyeh.

The Chouf Mountains are wild and beautiful. Most people travel there to see the Palace of Beiteddine, but it is also pleasant to wander among the mountain villages of the area. All of the places in the south are easily visited on a day trip from Beirut. There are comparatively few places to stay and, apart from Beiteddine, little or no tourism.

The Chouf Mountains

The Druze stronghold of the Chouf Mountains lies south-east of Beirut and forms the southern part of the Mount Lebanon range. Peppered with small villages, the mountains are mostly terraced for easy cultivation. Olives, apples and grapes are the main crops fed by numerous springs and wells. There are several rivers which run from east to west and divide the land into steep canyons.

The main road runs from Damour on the coast, almost parallel to the Nahr ad-Damour, and up into the mountains. The whole area is very scenic whether you are travelling by car or hiking. Along with the Kadisha Valley in the north, this is probably the best area to explore on foot.

Historically the Chouf Mountains had a mixed Maronite and Druze population, both of whom lived there since the Middle Ages. From time to time violent struggles between the two communities erupted. A particularly severe massacre took place in 1860 in which

hundreds of Maronites at Deir al-Qamar were killed by the Druze after which the Maronites left the Chouf in large numbers to live in Beirut or emigrate. The Chouf Mountains are still dominated by the Druze today.

During the civil war, the Chouf was occupied by the Israeli army which in turn brought in members of the Lebanese Forces, the militia of the Christian Phalangist Party. When the Israelis withdrew in 1983, fierce fighting broke out between the Christian militias and the Druze. The Druze eventually won the 'Mountain War' and drove out the militias.

DEIR AL-QAMAR

In the Middle Ages Lebanon was divided into fiefs, each ruled by an emir. By the early 17th century Fakhr ad-Din had extended his power throughout the territory, which roughly corresponds to modern Lebanon, and united the small fiefdoms into one. His first capital was at nearby Baaqline, but because of water shortages, he moved to Deir al-Qamar which is fed by numerous springs. It is a Maronite village of great charm, sitting 850m above sea level and overlooking the valley, with Beiteddine visible in the background.

Things to See

The words *deir al-qamar* mean 'monastery of the moon', and the lunar motif can be seen carved in stone on a figure of the Madonna in the **abbey** which sits on the lower slopes of the town. The crescent moon was a symbol of Phoenicia's pagan cult and the Madonna standing on it could be taken as a symbol of Christianity superseding the pagan religion; on the other hand it could simply be incorporating the old religion into the new.

The whole town is preserved as a national monument and its numerous historic buildings are in the process of restoration. The fountain square is the focal point of the town with many of the historic buildings around it. On the lower (south) side of the square is the **serail**, which is built on the hill side on several levels. It is the local municipal office and not open to visitors, but the exterior is interesting enough.

On the north side of the square are the huge **barracks** built by Fakhr ad-Din for his troops and horses. Next to them is the old **silk khan** and the **Palace of Emir Yunis Ma'an**, dating originally from 1590. On the corner of the square is an 18th-century **Ottoman house**, still a private residence with a wonderful polychrome portal. The original barracks and palace were destroyed by Yusef, Pasha of Tripoli, in 1614. Fakhr ad-Din vowed his revenge and took Yusef's castle at Akkar near Tripoli. He tore down the castle and brought the stones back to Deir al-Qamar to make his restorations. See also the Castle of Akkar section in the Tripoli & The Cedars chapter.

About 1km out of the town in the direction of Beiteddine is the extraordinary **Castle Moussa** (☎ (05) 500106, 501660), the dream-child of Mr Moussa who built this fantasy castle and filled it with waxwork tableaux depicting everything from traditional Lebanese life to Santa's Grotto. There is a shop at the end of the tour and a man who makes Arabic coffee on a brazier for guests. This definitely deserves a visit. The castle is open daily from 9 am to 5 pm and the entrance fee is LL 5000.

Places to Stay & Eat

There are no places to stay in Deir al-Qamar, but there are several cheap restaurants and snack bars along the main road through town. The *Paradise Cafe* sells simple meals and snacks and there is another *café/restaurant* at the fork in the road.

There is a good restaurant next door to the Castle Moussa called *Restaurant Farah* (☎ (05) 500509) which serves mezze and has spectacular views. Lunch or dinner will cost about US$15.

Getting There & Away

Service taxis en route to Beiteddine go through Deir al-Qamar and can drop you off there. If you are planning to visit both places in the same day, it would be better to continue to Beiteddine and then walk back (5km) to Deir al-Qamar, a pleasant, downhill walk. Fares from Beirut are LL 4000.

BEITEDDINE

Some 50km south-east of Beirut, Beiteddine is the name of both a village and a magnificent palace complex which lies within it. The palace can be seen from across the valley as you approach and looks almost like a vision from a fairy tale. The style is a cross between traditional Arab and Italian baroque (the architects were, in fact, Italian) with its grounds descending over several terraces planted with poplars and flowering shrubs.

The village is quite picturesque. Many of the houses are built in the traditional stone style with graceful arches. Quite a lot of buildings appear to be abandoned and are waiting to be reclaimed and restored; the whole area was the scene of fierce fighting during the civil war.

There were three other palaces in the vicinity, built for the emir's sons. Of these only one, the **Emir Amine Palace**, still stands and is now a luxury hotel above the main part of the village. Nearby is Emir Bashir's **country house**, which now houses the archbishopric. There are still some remains of the original building including a beautiful stone doorway which leads onto a roof shaped like a Chinese pagoda.

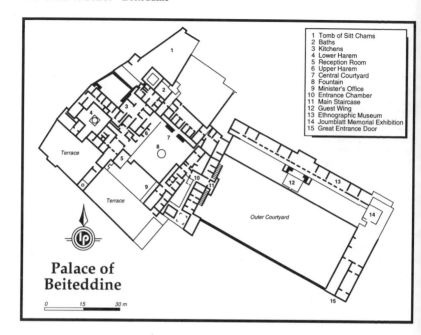

1 Tomb of Sitt Chams
2 Baths
3 Kitchens
4 Lower Harem
5 Reception Room
6 Upper Harem
7 Central Courtyard
8 Fountain
9 Minister's Office
10 Entrance Chamber
11 Main Staircase
12 Guest Wing
13 Ethnographic Museum
14 Joumblatt Memorial Exhibition
15 Great Entrance Door

Palace of Beiteddine

0   15   30 m

A **festival** is held in Beiteddine every summer in July and August. It features international and Arab musicians, singers, dancers and actors. Contact the tourist office in Beirut for more details.

Palace of Beiteddine

This 19th-century palace complex was built over a period of 30 years, starting in 1788, and became the stronghold of Emir Bashir, the leading member at the time of the Shihab family. It is the greatest surviving achievement of 19th-century Lebanese architecture and skilled artisans were given free rein to try out new ideas. Purists might say that the end result is vulgar and over the top, but whatever your taste the palace is certainly impressive. It is built high on a mountain overlooking a ravine. The grounds below the palace are terraced into well-kept gardens and orchards.

The original site was a Druze hermitage which has been incorporated into the complex. The palace came to be built after the Shihab family took over from the Ma'an dynasty when it died out. Partly due to family disagreements, Emir Bashir decided to move from Deir al-Qamar and build his own palace which would reflect the increasing power and glory of his reign. The final edifice measures over 300m in length.

After WWI the palace was used for local administration by the French, but after 1930, it was declared a historic monument and placed under the care of the Department of Antiquities which set about restoring it. In 1943 Lebanon's first president after independence, Bishara al-Khuri, made it the official summer residence and brought back the remains of Emir Bashir from Istanbul where he'd died in 1850.

The palace suffered tremendous losses following the Israeli invasion. It is reckoned about 90% of the contents were lost. After the end of the fighting in the mountains in 1983, the Druze leader Walid Joumblatt ordered the restoration of the palace. He declared its new role to be a 'Palace of the People' and, as such, it contains several museums housing various collections. Most of the items now on display are there courtesy of the Joumblatt family.

The palace consists of three main courts: **Dar al-Baraniyyeh** (the outer court to which passing visitors were admitted freely), **Dar al-Wousta** (the central court which housed the palace guards and offices of the ministers) and **Dar al-Harim** (the private family quarters). Beneath Dar al-Wousta and Dar al-Harim are huge vaulted **stables** which held 500 horses and their riders in addition to the 600 infantry which formed the emir's guard.

From the entrance to the palace, you pass through zigzag passages which lead to a 60m-long courtyard where public festivals and gatherings would take place. It was from here that the emir would leave for his hunting expeditions or to fight wars. Along the north side of this courtyard are the guest apartments. It was the custom of noble houses to offer hospitality for three days to visitors before asking their business or their identity. The French poet, Lamartine, who was a guest at the palace, wrote the following description:

Magnificently dressed black slaves armed with silver-plated pistols and glittering finely-chased gold Damascus sabres stood on either side of a door carved in woods of various colours with marble all around and Arabic inscriptions above. The vast courtyards facing the palace swarmed with a host of servants, courtiers, priests and soldiers wearing all the variety of picturesque costumes characteristic of the five peoples of the Lebanon ... Five or six hundred Arab steeds were saddled and bridled, covered in brilliant drapery of every hue ...

The restored upper floor of this wing is used as museum space to exhibit the **Rachid Karami Ethnographic Collection**. This large collection includes pottery from the Bronze and Iron ages, Roman glass, Islamic pottery, lead sarcophagi and gold jewellery. There is also a scale model of the palace and, in other rooms, a collection of weapons and costumes. In the far corner of the ground floor of the court is a building now used to commemorate the life of the late Druze leader, **Kemal Joumblatt**. The exhibition includes a reproduction of his private room in his early life.

At the far end of the first courtyard is a double staircase leading up to the entrance of the second court. This is known as the 'tumbling staircase' on account of the tale of a sheep which escaped the butcher's knife and head-butted an eminent pasha down the stairs. These days the head of the stairs is decorated with a bust of Kemal Joumblatt.

Through an arched passageway is the second court. The entrance is decorated with an inscription of welcome and a decorative **marble portal**. Inside is a charming courtyard with a fountain; the open side overlooks the valley. The apartments and offices off the courtyard are set along graceful arcades. The rooms are luxurious and richly decorated with marble, mosaics and marquetry. The furnishings are in a traditional oriental style. The walls and ceilings are of painted, carved wood embellished with Arabic calligraphy.

The entrance to the third court is a beautiful facade which leads through to the lower court (the kitchens and famous bathhouse) and the upper court (the reception rooms). The rooms are lavishly decorated. On the ground floor is the *salaamlik* (main reception room).

The huge kitchens are well worth a look. In their heyday they catered for 500 people a day. Endless trays of food would have been carried on vast trays to set before the divans and sofas of the court and their visitors. The bathhouse, or *hammam*, is a series of domed rooms fitted out in marble with basins and fountains. Nearby is the tomb of Sitt Chams, the emir's first wife.

In the lower part of the palace, the former stables house another museum, this time of **Byzantine mosaics**. These were mostly excavated from a former church at Jiyyeh, the ancient city of Porphyrion. The mosaics were brought to Beiteddine, at the request of Walid Joumblatt, to protect them from looting during the Mountain War. It is a pretty impressive collection. See also The Architecture of Lebanon section in the Facts about Lebanon chapter.

The palace (☎ (05) 500045/78) is open every day except Monday from 8.30 am to 6 pm. Admission is LL 4000 and there are multilingual brochures available.

Places to Stay & Eat

The cheapest hotel option in the area is the nondescript *Rif Hotel* (☎ (05) 501680), about 3km south of Beiteddine in a small village called Samqaniye, on the road to Moukhtara. Here a double room with bath costs US$15 per person plus 15% service tax. Lunch or dinner costs US$8.

The only hotel in Beiteddine itself is the very swanky and expensive *Mir Amin Place* (☎ (05) 501315/6/7/8). Set on the hill above Beiteddine and overlooking the palace below, this is the restored home of the emir's eldest son. With singles/doubles starting from US$133/167, it is not an option for Moses travellers. Even so it is well worth dropping by for a drink on the terrace where the pool is decorated like an oriental carpet. The hotel has three restaurants: *Al-Diwan* (oriental food), *Arcadia* (European food) and *Le Jardin*. If you need to ask how much it costs, you can't afford it.

Down in the town there are several simple restaurants and snack places. Near the main square is *Hatemia Restaurant* which is OK but a bit overpriced. On the road above the palace there are a couple of good places next to each other. The first is *Al Wasr Restaurant & Snacks* where you can have a good lunch for about US$8. The other, *Nasr Khan Al-Mir*, is a bit more upmarket, but both have good views across to the palace. On the road which curves down opposite the palace there is a waterfall and a lovely eatery called *Le Moulin*. Further down still overlooking the valley is a café, called *Al-Shalalat*, which sells tea, coffee and snacks.

Getting There & Away

The route to Beiteddine is south from Beirut along the coast to Damour and then east.

Service taxis serve the route and the fare to Beiteddine is LL 4000.

It is quite feasible to visit several places and get dropped off along the way, hailing a passing service taxi when you want to move on. Along the quieter stretches you may have a bit of a wait. The service taxi stand in Beiteddine is close to the palace on the main square.

AROUND THE CHOUF
The Cedars of Barouk

On the road between Beiteddine and Sofar, to the north-west, is the small village of Barouk. High above the village is a grove of cedar trees, not as ancient as the ones above Bcharré, but more numerous; it is thought that 400 trees remain on Jebel Barouk. Access is tricky and involves a 40-minute stiff uphill walk from the village. At this high altitude it can get pretty cold, so be prepared.

Getting There & Away Barouk village is 10km from Beiteddine on a very quiet road. If you don't have your own vehicle, the only way to get here would be by taxi from Beiteddine, in which case you would need to book a return journey or risk hitching. You should allow three hours for the walk to the cedars and back.

Kfarhim Grotto

About halfway between Damour and Deir al-Qamar is the village of Kfarhim where a small, natural cave was discovered over 80 years ago. The grotto has stalagmites and stalactites, but is nowhere as large or impressive as the Jeita Grotto. It is open to the public daily from 7 am to 7 pm and admission is LL 2500. There's a souvenir shop here where you can buy slide film.

The South

SIDON (SAIDA)
History

The ancient town of Sidon, or Saida, is the largest town in southern Lebanon and lies

Saladin (1138-93)
The figure of Saladin, a Muslim leader during the Crusades, has come down to us through numerous books, films and poems. He figured most notably in Sir Walter Scott's book *The Talisman* as a chivalrous warrior. In many ways he epitomised the idea of a paragon of princely virtue. Rather fittingly his name in Arabic, Salah ad-Din, means 'Righteousness of the Faith'.

Saladin was born in Tikrit in modern Iraq to Kurdish parents. At the young age of 14 he joined other members of his family (the Ayyubids) in the service of Nur ad-Din. He went to fight with the Fatimids of Egypt against the Crusaders based in Palestine and distinguished himself in three expeditions. He then revitalised the Egyptian economy and reorganised the military.

After Nur ad-Din's death in 1174, Saladin expanded his power throughout the Middle East and allied the armies of Damascus, Mosul and Aleppo under his command. He turned his attentions to routing the Crusaders from Jerusalem and other parts of the Holy Land. In response the Europeans launched the Third Crusade to win back Jerusalem.

Saladin eventually concluded an armistice with King Richard I of England that allowed the Crusaders to reconstitute their kingdom but left Jerusalem in Muslim hands. ■

next page), and from glass manufacture which, at the time, was the best in the world. Like many Phoenician cities, Sidon was built on a promontory with an offshore island. The island sheltered the harbour from storms and provided a safe haven during times of war.

The Phoenician period of the city began around the 12th to 10th centuries BC and reached its golden age during the Persian empire (550-333 BC). The people of Sidon became great shipbuilders and provided experienced sailors for the Persian fleet. It was during this period that the Temple of Echmoun was built about 2km to the north-east of the city. Inscriptions found there reveal that Phoenician Sidon was built in two sections; the maritime city (Sidon Yam), and the upper part (Sidon Sadeh) which was built on the lower spurs of the Mount Lebanon range.

In common with the other Phoenician city-states, Sidon suffered from conquest and invasion numerous times during its history. At the end of the Persian era, the Sidonians locked the city gates and set fire to the city rather than hand it over to Artaxerxes III. More than 40,000 people died in the fire. This weakened the city to such an extent that when Alexander the Great marched through the Middle East in 333 BC, the Sidonians were in no position to resist him. Sidon handed over power to the Greeks without a struggle.

Under the Greeks Sidon enjoyed relative freedom and an advanced cultural life. Later the city came successively under the control of the Seleucids and the Ptolemies. In the early days of the Roman Empire it formed a kind of republic with its own senate and its own minted coins. Augustus put an end to its independence and brought it under direct Roman rule. When St Paul visited Sidon on his journey from Caesarea to Rome in the 1st century AD, it had fallen into a decline although it was still commercially important.

During the Byzantine period it became the seat of a bishopric. It was during this time that the strong earthquake of 551 AD destroyed most of the cities in Phoenicia. Sidon came out of it better than most and

45km south of Beirut. There is evidence that Sidon was settled as early as 4000 BC. It was one of the most important Phoenician cities. Much of its wealth came from the murex trade, which produced a highly valued purple dye (see the Murex boxed story on the

Murex

The famous purple dye of Phoenicia comes from the murex, a kind of mollusc which grew in abundance in the coastal waters off Sidon and Tyre. There were in fact two kinds of mollusc used in the dye process: the *Murex* and the *Buccinum*. They both have a long sac or vein filled with a yellowish fluid that turns purple when exposed to light. The discovery of this natural source of purple dye made the fortunes of many merchants in Sidon and Tyre.

The origins of the discovery are lost, but a myth remains that Melkart, the god, was walking on the beach one day with his lover, a nymph called Tyrus, and his dog. The dog bit into one of the murex shells and its muzzle became stained with a purple dye. When she saw the beautiful colour, Tyrus demanded that Melkart make her a garment of purple. So Melkart gathered a quantity of the shellfish to dye a gown which he presented to her.

This romantic tale hides the fact that the production of dye was a smelly, messy business which involved a great deal of hard work. The molluscs were gathered in deep water by dropping narrow-necked baskets baited with mussels and frog meat. Once harvested the shellfish were hauled off to dye pits where their sacs were removed, pulped and heated in huge lead vessels. All the extraneous matter was skimmed off and the resulting dye fixed.

The dye pits were placed downwind of the residential areas to avoid the noxious smell. With practice the dyers could produce a variety of colours from pale pink to deep violet by mixing the *Murex* and *Buccinum* fluids in different quantities. The dye industry was on such a large scale that the farming of the molluscs caused them to become almost extinct even until the present day. ■

became the home of Beirut's famous School of Law when that city was badly damaged. The following century was uneventful until the invasion and conquest by the Arabs in 667. The city took the Arabic name, Saida, and was administered from Damascus.

In 1111 the city was besieged by Baldwin I, King of Jerusalem, and the Sidonians gave up after 47 days of resistance. Under the Franks the city was ruled by Jerusalem. In 1187 Saladin took the city and razed the ramparts to the ground. After a period of changing hands and numerous rebuildings, it finally fell to the Mamelukes after the fall of Acre in 1291.

In the 15th century Sidon's fortunes rose as one of the trading ports of Damascus. It flourished again in the 17th century under the rule of Fakhr ad-Din. He rebuilt and modernised parts of the city, including the Khan al-Franj which was used by the French traders, revitalising the economy which had fallen into a decline. The prosperity was only temporary and by the 19th century the city had fallen back into obscurity.

In the early part of this century the area around Sidon was developed for agriculture, and fruit in particular remains the main crop. There are huge olive and orange groves and the occasional banana plantation swaying exotically on either side of the main road. The oranges are delicious and are said to be the original 'Jaffa' variety which is now grown extensively in Israel for export. Sidon is also the main port and administrative centre for the south of Lebanon.

Orientation

There is a main highway which runs north-south through Sidon. Near the northern end of the city is a square where the taxis gather, Sahet en-Nejmeh. The main road through town, Rue Riad al-Solh, is lined with shops, cafés and banks. The old part of the city with the port, Sea Castle and souks are to the west of the main road, while the modern shopping centres and residential buildings are on the eastern side. If you are arriving from the north, you can easily spot the Sea Castle which is the dominant feature of the city.

Information

Money The many banks are mainly clustered together on or near the main road, Rue Riad ıl-Solh, south of the taxi stand. In the old souks are several moneychangers whose rates are not too bad.

Post & Communications The main post office and telephone bureau is a large white building across the road and slightly west of the Government Rest House. You can easily spot the building by the huge antenna on the roof. The telephone code for Sidon is 07.

Bookshop There is a small bookshop and stationers, Librairie Saida, on the road which runs west of the main square where the taxis stop. The books are mostly in Arabic, but it also has a fair selection of French and German magazines and local postcards on sale.

Sea Castle

This was originally the site of a Phoenician temple to Melkart but later became a fortification; the castle which remains today is from the 12th century and uses many of the columns and stones from earlier structures.

The Sea Castle (Qasr al-Bahr) is reached on foot across a causeway which encloses the old fishing harbour. The Franks built the castle as a defence from both sea and inland invaders. It was constructed hastily from previous masonry (which you can still see sticking out from the foundations) when it was learned that the emperor of Germany, Frederic II, would be arriving.

The main walls surrounding the fortress are now broken in many places but two towers are still intact. The rooms are vast and gloomy and scattered with old carved capitals and rusting cannonballs. Each floor is connected by a winding staircase which leads up to the roof (it is useful to have a torch here). From both of the roofs there is a great view across the old city and fishing harbour. The water is clear and shallow and you can see many broken columns of rose granite lying on the sea floor.

The castle is open daily from 9 am to 6 pm and entrance costs LL 2000.

Khan al-Franj

This is one of the many khans built by Fakhr ad-Din during his reign in the 17th century. The khans were designed to store goods and house the travelling merchants. They nearly all follow the same basic design of a large central courtyard with a fountain and covered arcades with a galleried 2nd storey providing accommodation.

The Khan al-Franj (Inn of the Foreigners) was the principal khan in the 19th century and was the centre of economic activity in the city. It also housed the French consulate. Today it is being restored and will provide Sidon with a cultural centre.

Great Mosque

Towards the southern end of the old town facing the Egyptian (southern) harbour is the Great Mosque. This was originally the Church of St John of the Hospitallers and was turned into a mosque after the Crusaders were driven out of the Holy Land. The entrance to the mosque is down a maze of covered streets in the old part of town. An old courtyard is now a whitewashed entrance square which is used for ritual ablutions with an old fountain in the centre. This fountain is decorated with Corinthian columns which have been whitewashed over, as has the interior of the main prayer hall. See also The Architecture of Lebanon section in the Facts about Lebanon chapter.

To the east of the mosque is the site of the palace built by Fakhr ad-Din which is now demolished. To the west is a sheer stone wall which overlooks the Egyptian harbour. Visitors are not exactly encouraged, but it is worth asking at the gate whether you can look around. Be sure to avoid prayer times.

Castle of St Louis

This castle, the ruins of which stand on a hill to the south of town, was built by the Frankish Crusaders on what is thought to have been the ancient acropolis of Sidon. Remains of a theatre have been uncovered here by archaeologists, but the site remains largely unexcavated. It was named after King Louis IX, better known as St Louis, who stayed at the castle for some time. After the Arab conquest, it was modified and rebuilt. There

Sidon (Saida)

0   150   300 m
Approximate Scale

MEDITERRANEAN
SEA

Port

EGYPTIAN
PORT

To Nahr el-Awali,
Fun Fair, Temple
of Echmoun
& Beirut

Rue Shakrieh

Rue Riad al-Solh

Sahet en-
Nejmeh

Rue Fakhr ad-Din

To Tyre

PLACES TO STAY
3   Government Rest House
21 Hotel d'Orient

PLACES TO EAT
5   Café
8   Café
16 Patisserie Canaan

OTHER
1   Lighthouse
2   Sea Castle
4   Fish Market
6   Khan al-Franj
7   Souk Area
9   Mosque
10 Church
11 Librairie Saida
12 Post Office
13 Green Mosque
14 Municipal Office
15 Taxis
17 Bank
18 Bank
19 Bank
20 Shops
22 Great Mosque
23 Castle of St Louis
24 Murex Hill

is a low wall around the base of the hill and a locked gate. The site is usually unattended.

Souks

The old part of town lies between the Sea Castle and the Castle of St Louis. The old covered souk of Sidon is near the Sea Castle and the open-air fish market. Here shopkeepers have their workshops and ply their trades in the same way they have done for centuries.

Nearby are the coffee houses where men meet to smoke water pipes and pass the afternoon. There is a huge number of pastry

shops in the souks where you can buy all manner of cakes and biscuits. The utterly delicious *sanioura* is a speciality of Sidon and is a light crumbly biscuit. The souks are also famous for producing orange-blossom water.

It is a bit difficult to find your way around the souks. However, you'll be surrounded by young people who will tag along and they're quite helpful in showing you around (they'll expect a small tip though).

Khan al-Saboun

This khan is rather run-down at the moment.

although there is talk of restoring it. You can find it if you walk along the old harbour north of the Sea Castle causeway. It follows the same design as the other khans, but has been used as a makeshift residence and workshop for the last few decades.

Places to Stay

There is only one hotel in Sidon, the small *Nazel esh-Sharq* or *Hotel d'Orient* (☎ (07) 720364) on Rue Shakrieh in the old town. It is tricky to find – above a tiny baggage shop not far from the Muslim cemetery. If you look above the street to the 1st floor, there is an old sign with the words 'Hotel d'Orient'. It is really basic with only six rooms and one shared bathroom with cold water, although you can pay extra if you want a hot shower. The price for singles/doubles is US$10/13. If you want to sleep four people per room, the price is US$5 per person.

Places to Eat

There are lots of cheap cafés and shawarma stalls around Sahet en-Nejmeh as well as plenty of patisseries. Particularly recommended is the *Patisserie Canaan*; the *Patisserie Abou Nawas* and *Patisserie Ramla* are also good. There are also cheap places for lunch around the northern harbour and the fish market. You can get a filling sandwich and salad for a few thousand lira.

There is very little in the way of proper restaurants in town (local people dining out tend to head for places up the coast), but there is the splendid *Government Rest House* which is in a restored medieval building, former seraglio, almost opposite the Sea Castle. It is a bit more expensive and you can expect to pay US$10 for a decent lunch of a few dips and a grill and salad. You don't have to eat though, and it is well worth dropping by for a drink or coffee, sitting out on the lovely terrace which overlooks the gardens and the sea.

Getting There & Away

The bus and service taxi stands are on Sahet en-Nejmeh. Service taxis charge LL 2500 to Beirut (Cola stand) and LL 3000 to Tyre. The buses are cheaper at LL 1750, but they do not leave until full. Service taxis tend to be quicker having only five places to fill. A private taxi to Echmoun and back will cost around US$6. Alternatively, a one-way ride will cost US$2 to US$3 and you can walk back along the Nahr el-Awali.

AROUND SIDON
Temple of Echmoun

This Phoenician temple is about 2km north-east of Sidon on the Nahr el-Awali. The whole area is filled with citrus orchards and the river side is a favourite picnic spot with locals. The region has long been a fruit-growing area and the site of the temple is known as Boustan al-Sheikh (Garden of the Sheikh).

Echmoun was the principal god of the city of Sidon and was associated with healing. This is the only Phoenician site in Lebanon which has retained more than just its foundation walls. The temple complex was begun in the 7th century BC and the following centuries saw numerous additions to the basic building. Some of the buildings are far later than the original Phoenician temple, such as the Roman colonnade and the Byzantine church and mosaics. This shows how important the site was as a place of pilgrimage for a very long period of time.

The legendary story of Echmoun closely follows that of Tammuz and Adonis. Echmoun began as a mortal youth from Berytus (Beirut). The goddess Astarte fell in love with him, but to escape from her, he mutilated himself and died. Not to be thwarted she brought him back to life in the form of a god, hence his story linked to fertility and rebirth. He was still primarily a god of healing and is identified with the Greek Asklepios, the god of medicine, and the Roman Aesculapius. It is from the snake motif of Echmoun that we get the serpentine symbol of the medical profession. The idea of a serpent coiled around a staff was found on a gold plaque at Echmoun.

The look of the temple complex is reminiscent of the terraced Persian site at Persepolis, an open-air sanctuary rather than

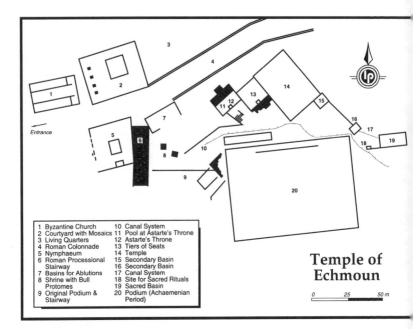

1 Byzantine Church
2 Courtyard with Mosaics
3 Living Quarters
4 Roman Colonnade
5 Nymphaeum
6 Roman Processional
  Stairway
7 Basins for Ablutions
8 Shrine with Bull
  Protomes
9 Original Podium &
  Stairway
10 Canal System
11 Pool at Astarte's Throne
12 Astarte's Throne
13 Tiers of Seats
14 Temple
15 Secondary Basin
16 Secondary Basin
17 Canal System
18 Site for Sacred Rituals
19 Sacred Basin
20 Podium (Achaemenian
   Period)

**Temple of
Echmoun**

0   25   50 m

enclosed in the Greek style. It has a nearby water source for the ritual ablutions. It was customary for people coming to the temple to ask for the god's help to bring a small statue with the name of the person who needed healing. Many of these votive statues depicted children.

Between the 6th and 4th centuries BC Sidon was known for its opulence, culture and industry. During this era one of the rulers of Sidon was Echmounazar II . His sarcophagus was discovered in 1858 and it had inscriptions on it relating that he and his mother, Amashtarte, built temples to the gods at Sidon including the Temple of Echmoun. His sarcophagus is now in the Louvre museum in Paris.

The temple built by Echmounazar II was rediscovered earlier this century by archaeologists during the excavation of Boustan al-Sheikh. It had been destroyed by an earthquake around the middle of the 4th century BC. Although the temple was never rebuilt,

the site retained its reputation as a place o healing and some of the smaller building were restored and the later church built. I was used by both pagan and Christian pil grims. The site remained popular until th 3rd century AD even though it was by tha time in ruins.

Temple Layout As you enter the site, ther is a colonnade of shops on the right whic probably did a roaring trade selling souvenir to pilgrims. On the left is a **Byzantine Churc** with a mosaic floor. Just past that is a larg **courtyard with mosaics** from the 3r century BC. The fine mosaics show the fou seasons. On the right is a Roman proces sional stairway, which leads to the uppe levels of the site. The stairway was added i the 1st century AD. Also on the right is **Nymphaeum** with a fountain and niche containing statues of the nymphs.

Further along on the right is one of th most interesting artefacts, the **Throne o**

Detail of the sarcophagus of Echmounazar II. Ordered by Echmounazar from Egypt and engraved with Phoenician inscriptions, it was discovered in 1858 on the outskirts of Sidon. His father's sarcophagus was found nearby.

Astarte flanked by two sphinxes. The throne is carved from a solid block of granite in the Egyptian style. There is also a very worn frieze depicting a hunting scene.

The site has no formal opening times and there is no charge for entry. There is usually a soldier at the entrance taking care of the site. If you turn up on your own (not in a tour bus), don't be surprised if he accompanies you around the site. Independent visitors are a bit of a rarity.

Getting There & Away The site is within walking distance (about 30 minutes) of Sidon. Take the main road heading north and turn right at the small fair ground. This road follows the river bank and the site is about 10 minutes walk on your left. If you want to take a taxi there, you can catch one from the main taxi rank in Sidon. The fare should be about LL 3000 one way. To return by taxi, you will have to arrange to be picked up or ask the driver to wait.

Joun
Joun is a large village in the midst of olive plantations above the Nahr el-Awali. Its main claim to fame is that it was the home for many years of the famous woman travel-

ler Lady Hester Stanhope. Before the war there was even a café named after her in the main square.

Today it is a quiet place which is pleasant to wander around. A 20-minute walk to the north of the village brings you to a farm which used to belong to the monastery of St Saviour. This was the home in which Lady Hester lived. Fifty metres to the south-west of the house is her tomb which lies in the shade of an olive grove. See the Lady Hester Stanhope boxed story on the next page.

Getting There & Away Joun is about 15km north-east of Sidon and can be reached by taxi. The fare is around US$12 one way. You will need to arrange to be collected or have the taxi wait as there is little traffic on this road.

Sarafand
Sarafand is the biblical Zarephath (also later known as Sarepta) which is famous for the miracle of Elijah who raised the widow's son from the dead and multiplied her olive oil and grain supplies. The story is in 1 Kings 17. It is also thought that this was the place where glass-making was discovered (the word *seraph* means 'to melt' in Hebrew).

Sarafand is 19km south of Sidon and is no longer a vital trading town, but rather a sleepy village with a few restaurants. The modern village is built on the inland side of the main coastal road. You can see the ruined Phoenician masonry of houses and cisterns visible on the shore. There are even the remains of ancient slipways used by Phoenician vessels. The original port extended for over 1km and enclosed three small bays which are still used by the local anglers as anchorages. The site had some excavation work carried out in 1969 but this was stopped during the war.

During the Crusades, Sarepta, as it was then called, was a fairly large, fortified town. It was the seat of a bishopric and home to a Carmelite order. There was a church commemorating St Elijah in the centre of town, probably beneath the site of the Wadi al-Khader.

SOUTH OF BEIRUT

Lady Hester Stanhope (1776-1839)

The Middle East has always attracted intrepid women explorers and adventurers and Lady Hester Stanhope was one of the most extreme examples of the breed. She was born to an affluent but eccentric life in London in 1776, the daughter of the domineering Earl of Stanhope and Hester Pitt, sister of William Pitt, the future prime minister of England. The Earl of Stanhope was a strong believer in the French Revolution and forced his family to adopt socialist principles, such as making do without a horse and carriage. Hester stood up to him and argued against his unconventional ideas.

She grew up without a governess and later on a tutor engaged by her father was charged with high treason. She became close to her uncle, William Pitt, and when he became prime minister, she moved into 10 Downing Street and played political hostess. Her first love was Sir John Moore who took her favourite brother, James, to serve with him in Salamanca. They were both killed and when her uncle also died, Hester was homeless and brokenhearted.

Hester decided to travel abroad and took her personal physician, Dr Meryon, with her. He remained in her service for 28 years, even during her notorious affair with Michael Bruce. She and her retinue travelled the Middle East and were treated like royalty. Her greatest moment of glory was riding into Palmyra in Syria on an Arab stallion at the head of her travelling procession.

Her name was famous all over the Arab world by the time she came to Joun (north-east of Sidon) and it was here that she was to remain for the rest of her life. Having installed herself as a guest in the house of a Christian merchant, she announced that she liked the house so much that she would stay for the remainder of her days. The merchant took this as a figure of speech, and after a few weeks asked when she was planning to return to Europe. 'But I do not intend to return,' she replied. When he asked if she intended to build a house nearby, she replied, 'No! This house suits me very well'. When the merchant argued that he could not let or sell the house to her, she simply stated, 'I do not wish to hire it or to buy it, but I intend to keep it'. The merchant protested to the local emir, but Hester wrote directly to the sultan in Constantinople who wrote back 'Obey the Princess of Europe in everything'.

So that was how Hester came to possess the house at Joun. Her affair with Michael Bruce was over, but she still had Dr Meryon for company. She gradually became a recluse, only receiving a few visitors who would wait at Sidon for word of whether she would see them. The poet Lamartine was a visitor as was the son of a childhood friend, Kinglake. He reported that she was wearing a large turban of cashmere shawls and a flowing white robe and seemed to be quite alone in her oriental sitting rooms.

When she died, she was totally alone and the British consul had to be sent for to take care of her burial. Her simple tomb is built like a step pyramid among the olive groves at Joun with the simple inscription: 'Lady Hester Lucy Stanhope, born 12 March 1776, died 23 June 1839'. ∎

Places to Stay & Eat One of the few hotels in the south is in Sarafand. The *Mounis Hotel* (☎ (07) 724932) is built out on the ocean and is connected to the mainland by a causeway. It is clean and modern with double rooms costing US$50. Lunch and dinner are available in the hotel restaurant for about US$12.

Sarafand has spawned a collection of fish restaurants along the coast road, supplied by the local fishing industry. They tend to be on the expensive side with fish being chosen by the customer and sold by weight. Allow from US$15 to US$20 per person for grilled fish and side dishes. One of the most highly recommended is *Fouad Ville*, on the Sidon side of town.

Getting There & Away Sarafand is on the main north-south highway and service taxis can drop you here from either Beirut or Sidon. The service taxi fare from Sidon is LL 2000.

TYRE (SOUR)
History

Tyre was arguably the greatest of the Phoenician city-states whose rise and fall was spectacular. It was from here that Phoenician sailors set out for Carthage and founded a new empire. Even in biblical times it was famed for its splendour and antiquity.

Tyre's origins are lost to us; according to Herodotus, the city was already 2300 years old when he wrote his histories, which dates it back to approximately 2750 BC, around the time of the founding of the temple of Melkart (Heracles) and the Canaanite invasions. The original founders are believed to have come from Sidon to establish a new city port.

Under the 18th (Egyptian) dynasty, Tyre fell under the supremacy of the Pharaohs and, like the other Phoenician cities of Sidon, Byblos and Ugarit, paid tribute to their Egyptian masters until after the reign of Rameses II. During this period (17th to 13th centuries BC), Tyre benefited from the protection of Egypt and prospered commercially.

Toward the end of the 2nd millennium BC, Tyre became a kingdom ruled at first by Abibaal. His son Hiram I ascended the throne and forged very close relations with the Hebrew kings Solomon and David. Hiram sent cedar wood and skilled workers to help construct the famed temple in Jerusalem, as well as large amounts of gold. In return he received a district in Galilee with 20 towns in it.

The original layout of Tyre was in two parts; an offshore island which was the older part of the city and the overspill on the mainland. Hiram developed the island-city and connected it to other small islands nearby by landfill, and to the mainland by a narrow causeway. During his reign, the Phoenicians colonised Sicily and North Africa, which later became the off-shoot Carthaginian empire. At this time the Mediterranean Sea was called 'the Tyrian Sea' and Tyre was the most important city on it.

After Hiram's 34-year reign ended, Tyre fell into bloody revolution. A succession of kings followed Hiram, most notably Ithobaal I, a high priest of Astarte, who reigned for 32 years. His daughter was the infamous Jezebel of the Bible who married King Ahab of Israel and met a sticky end. Perhaps the most famous woman of ancient Tyrian legend was Princess Alissar, also known as Dido. She was embroiled in a power plot and, it having failed, seized a fleet of ships and sailed for North Africa. She founded a new port on the ruins of Kambeh. This became known in time as Carthage and became the seat of the Carthaginian empire.

The rise of Carthage gradually saw the corresponding fall in Tyre's fortunes. Weakened as a power, the Tyrians sued for peace when the Assyrians conquered the Levant and became their vassal state. When the Assyrians lost some of their power, Tyre ceased to pay tribute or recognise their authority.

Tyre went through many wars, including a 13-year siege by the Babylonian king, Nebuchadnezzar, in the early 6th century BC. The inhabitants stood firm behind the high walls of the island-city and the siege failed. In the 4th century BC Tyre was not to be so lucky. This time the conqueror was Alexander the Great.

Following his defeat of the Persian army, Alexander set about conquering the known world. One of his early targets was Tyre. The city was thought to be impregnable, but Alexander built a mole in the sea to reach the city. This impressive feat was carried out under a constant hail of missiles. At the same time on the mainland, Alexander's engineers were constructing huge mobile towers called *helepoleis* which, at 20-storeys high, were the tallest siege towers ever used in the history of war. After seven months these great war machines lumbered across the mole and lowered the drawbridge, unleashing the archers and artillery on the city.

Tyre fell in 332 BC and Alexander, enraged at the dogged resistance of the Tyrians which had caused heavy Greek losses, destroyed half the city. The city's 30,000 citizens were massacred or sold into slavery. This destruction heralded the domination of the Greeks in the Mediterranean.

In 64 BC Tyre came under Roman rule and

Alexander the Great

Alexander was one of history's greatest military leaders. He was born in Pella, an ancient city of Macedonia in northern Greece in 356 BC. His father was Philip II of Macedonia and his mother was Olympia, a princess of Epirus. Alexander had an extraordinary and privileged upbringing; his tutor was Aristotle who gave him a knowledge of rhetoric and literature and a grounding in science, medicine and philosophy.

With the assassination of his father in 336 BC, Alexander became king of Macedonia. He set about disposing of his enemies and quelling rebellions. He razed Thebes to the ground as punishment for disloyalty, sparing only the temples and the house of the poet Pindar. Thebes' 30,000 citizens were enslaved. This immediately brought the other Greek states into submission.

After restoring order at home, Alexander turned his attention to the threat from Persia. When he was elected commander of all the Greek forces at the congress of Corinth, he set out with 40,000 men in 334 BC. His three chief officers were Antigonus, Ptolemy and Seleucus; all became rulers of the empire after Alexander's death.

Alexander's first great victory against the Persians was near Troy where he attacked 40,000 Persian and Greek mercenaries. Alexander, according to tradition, only lost 110 men. After this, all of Asia submitted to him. When he encountered the main Persian army, led by Darius III, at Issus in northern Syria, he was greatly outnumbered but still scored a decisive victory. King Darius fled north, abandoning his family who Alexander treated with the respect due to a royal family.

After this turning point in his career, Alexander swept south conquering the Phoenician sea ports. Only Tyre was a real obstacle. The city was heavily defended and only submitted after a lengthy siege. Gaza was captured next and Alexander passed into Egypt where he was greeted as a deliverer. In 332 BC he founded the city of Alexandria at the mouth of the Nile which would later develop into the literary, scientific and commercial centre of the Greek world.

In 331 BC Alexander made his celebrated pilgrimage to the oracle at the Temple of Amon Ra, the Egyptian equivalent of Zeus. This is in the remote oasis of Siwa in the western desert. His quest was to be recognised as a son of Amon Ra and therefore a true ruler of Egypt. He came away satisfied, and the seeds of the idea of his own divinity were sown. Then he turned northwards, reorganised his troops at Tyre, and headed for Babylon. Crossing the Tigris and Euphrates rivers, he met Darius again and once again Alexander defeated the Persians at the battle of Gaugamela in 331 BC. Darius fled once again, but was slain by two of his own generals.

Alexander plundered the treasuries of the Persians and burned their towns, finishing the destruction of the Persian empire forever. He did not stop there and carried on eastwards, eventually conquering most of central Asia and even parts of northern India. He achieved all this in just three years. He had grandiose plans for his new empire and dreamed of uniting the world. He founded many cities, often named after him, and his veteran troops colonised them, spreading Greek language and culture far and wide.

Shortly before his untimely death, he issued an order that he should be worshipped as a god in the Greek cities, an order which was ignored after his death. He died of a fever in Babylon in the spring of 323 BC, leaving no clear instructions for the administration of the empire. His generals fought over the spoils and ended up by dividing the empire into three. Although his dream of a 'one world empire' died with him, he paved the way for the later Hellenistic Greek kingdoms and subsequently the Roman Empire. ■

many important monuments were built in the city including an aqueduct, a triumphal arch and the largest hippodrome yet discovered. Later in the Roman era Tyre became Christian and under the Byzantine rule was the seat of an archbishopric with 14 bishoprics under its control.

By the 4th century AD it had recovered some of its former splendour and a basilica was built on the site of the former temple of

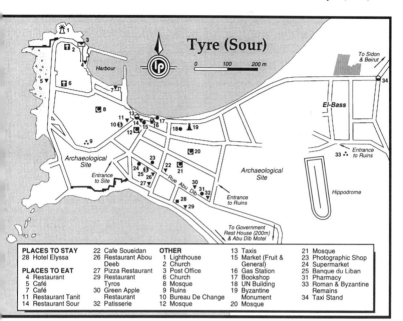

Tyre (Sour)

PLACES TO STAY	22 Cafe Soueidan	OTHER	13 Taxis	21 Mosque
28 Hotel Elyssa	26 Restaurant Abou	1 Lighthouse	15 Market (Fruit &	23 Photographic Shop
	Deeb	2 Church	General)	24 Supermarket
PLACES TO EAT	27 Pizza Restaurant	3 Post Office	16 Gas Station	25 Banque du Liban
4 Restaurant	29 Restaurant	6 Church	17 Bookshop	31 Pharmacy
5 Café	Tyros	8 Mosque	18 UN Building	33 Roman & Byzantine
7 Café	30 Green Apple	9 Ruins	19 Byzantine	Remains
11 Restaurant Tanit	Restaurant	10 Bureau De Change	Monument	34 Taxi Stand
14 Restaurant Sour	32 Patisserie	12 Mosque	20 Mosque	

Melkart, probably using the much older stone in its construction. The city was taken by the Arabs in 636 under whose rule it remained until the Crusades.

People from other coastal cities had fled to Tyre when the Crusaders started to take the Middle East in 1124. They felt safe behind Tyre's 'impregnable' walls. After a siege of five and a half months, Tyre's defences collapsed and the Christian army occupied the city and the surrounding fertile land. The Crusaders rebuilt the defensive walls and constructed a cathedral to replace the earlier basilica which had been demolished in 303 on the orders of Diocletian. The new cathedral was begun by the Venetians. It was finished by the beginning of the 12th century. According to tradition, it contains the tomb of Frederick Barbarossa.

Tyre remained in Crusader hands for 167 years, until the Muslim Mameluke army retook the city in 1291. Over time the classical and early Christian remains were demol-ished and the worked stone reused in later buildings. The ports silted up and the mole which connected the island to the main land became a sand bar; the city of Tyre became a peninsula which is now covered in modern buildings.

At the beginning of the 17th century Fakhr ad-Din attempted to rebuild and revitalise Tyre but without much success. In 1766 the city fell into the hands of the Metwalis. Under Jezzar Pasha many building materials were shipped south to Acre and sands gradually covered the remaining ruins in Tyre. Following the fall of the Ottoman Empire, Tyre became part of the Lebanese Republic.

Orientation

Tyre lies on the coast with the former island part of the city jutting out into the sea to the west. To the north of the headland is the old 'Sidonian' harbour, so-called because it faces Sidon. It is still used by a few shallow-bottomed fishing boats. To the south is the

SOUTH OF BEIRUT

Detail of a sarcophagus found at Tyre, carved with a scene from Homer's *Illiad*. Here Achilles has killed Hector and the body is dragged behind a chariot to the Achaean camp. Hector's father, Priam, kneels before Achilles and begs for the return of his son's body.

'Egyptian' harbour where fleets once set sail for Alexandria. The 'neck' of the peninsula is the wide sand bar which covers the old causeway. The modern shopping streets and residential district of Tyre are built over this land. On the eastern side of Tyre is the residential suburb of El-Bass and the excavated Roman site.

Information

Money The main shopping street, Rue Abu Dib, runs from east to west through the centre of Tyre. About halfway along is a Banque du Liban branch. There is also a bureau de change near the north harbour, next door to the Restaurant Tanit on the road which leads to the taxi stand.

Post & Communications The main post office and telephone bureau is at the western end of the north harbour, not far from the lighthouse. Tyre's telephone code is 07.

Dangers & Annoyances Tyre is the southernmost town in Lebanon before the Israeli border and as such comes into the firing line during times of unrest. Unless there is a particularly tense episode between the Hezbollah and Israel, you can regard a visit to Tyre as relatively safe. Try to be as up-to-date as possible with any political or military developments, and if you are advised to stay away from Tyre, then don't go.

Things to See & Do

The main reason for visiting Tyre is to look at the **excavated ruins**. Since 1979 Tyre has been declared a World Heritage Site. These are in three parts; the first is to the south side of the old Phoenician island-city. It is a large site of colonnades, public baths, mosaic streets and an unusual rectangular arena. Most of the buildings on this site date from the Greek and Roman periods with some later Byzantine monuments. If you look out from the shore, you will see what look like islands breaking the surface. These are in fact the remains of Phoenician jetties and the breakwater from the Egyptian port. The site is open daily and admission is LL 2000.

The second site is about a five-minute walk to the north of the first site. It is fenced off and not open to the public, but you can see the ruins from the road, including the remains of the **Crusader cathedral**. There is not much left of this building except the foundations and a few re-erected granite columns. Beneath this is a network of Roman and Byzantine roads and other buildings.

The third area is on the landward side to the east, about 20 minutes on foot from the other sites. It has some of the most impressive archaeological remains of Tyre. A vast **Roman necropolis** of highly decorated tombs was uncovered during the 1960s. A three-bay monumental arch stands across the main Roman road which led into the ancient city. Alongside the road are the remains of an **aqueduct** which brought water from Ras Al-Ain, 6km south of Tyre.

South of the necropolis is the huge, partly reconstructed **Roman hippodrome**. The structure is 480m long and seated 20,000 spectators. The hippodrome was used for the very popular and dangerous chariot races as seen in the movie *Ben Hur*. Each end of the long, narrow course was marked by a turning stone, called a *metae*, which you can still see. The tight, high-speed turns at the metae were the most exciting part of the race and often produced dramatic spills and collisions. Today, local Tyrians use the hippodrome as a jogging course.

The site is open daily and the admission price is LL 2000. The main entrance is near El-Bass, but there is another gate near the end of Rue Abu Dib, which is unstaffed but often open.

The inaugural **Tyre Festival** was held at the hippodrome site in 1997. The festival, to be held annually in late July/early August, includes a mix of local and international singers, artists and musicians. A highlight of the festival is a spectacular laser display which illuminates the entire site. For more specific details, contact the tourist office in Beirut.

Places to Stay

There are only three hotels in Tyre. The cheaper of the two is *Hotel Elyssa* (☎ (07) 287855), which is on the south side of the peninsula facing the sea. It has 40 rooms, all with bath, and a restaurant. Rooms cost US$35/55 for singles/doubles which includes breakfast and service. Lunch and dinner are a good deal at around LL 10,000; a beer is LL 3000.

If you follow the road south, the old *Government Rest House* (☎ (07) 740 677) has been turned into a four-star, rather expensive beach hotel. Of the 30 rooms and 110 cabins being built, most are for long-term stay but some are held back for overnighters. There is a restaurant, bar, tearoom and shop as well as a good bathing beach. During the week, singles/doubles cost US$70/80 plus 16%

service. At the weekend, singles/doubles cost US$200 with doubles only attracting the 16% service tax. All prices include breakfast and beach entrance. Beach entrance only costs US$10.

Just outside the southern entrance to Tyre is the *Abu Dib Motel* (☎ (03) 234630). Room rates range from US$50 to US$100, depending on the size of the room. The price includes breakfast.

Places to Eat

Eating in Tyre is no problem. A number of Lebanese and fast food-type restaurants have recently opened and there are a few good fish restaurants. In the north harbour area is the *Pub/Restaurant Tanit*, a small, friendly place open during the summer season. A grill and salad costs around US$10 and a beer is US$3. It is decorated with a lot of old pictures of Lebanon.

Along the harbour front there are a few cafés. On the west-facing headland there is a pleasant *outdoor café* which overlooks the sea. Most of the cheap eateries are on or around Rue Abu Dib. At the eastern end of the street is a *patisserie* where you can buy delicious cakes and coffee. Further along the same side of the street is the *Green Apple Restaurant*, and further along still is *Cafe Soueidan*; both serve light meals and snacks. Almost opposite is the *Restaurant Abou Deeb*, which serves mezze and grills. Overlooking the square with the taxi stand on the north side of the peninsula is *Restaurant Sour*, which also sells snacks and drinks.

On the south side of the peninsula near Hotel Elyssa are *Restaurant Tyros*, which serves Lebanese food, and a *pizza restaurant* where you can eat in or buy takeaways. In all these places expect to pay around US$5 for a lunch of salad plus grill or pizza and a soft drink. Fish is much more expensive.

Getting There & Away

The service taxi stand in Tyre is about 50m before the port on the northern coastal road. Service taxis to and from Beirut cost LL 5000; to Sidon, LL 3000.

AROUND TYRE
Tomb of Hiram
On the road to Qana at the 6km mark is a Persian period tomb (550-330 BC). This has traditionally been associated with Hiram, the famous King of Tyre. It is called 'Qabr Hiram' in Arabic. There is some doubt as to whether this is in fact his tomb, but it certainly dates from the Phoenician period. It is about 4m long, 3m wide and 2m high, and has a 2m-high pyramidal cover.

When Renan, the French theologian and historian, started excavations at the foot of the tomb in the mid-19th century, he found an even earlier staircase which connected to the mausoleum's foundations. There are other signs of tombs in the area as well as a sanctuary, but there have been no further excavations.

Qana
Qana is a small Shiite village 14km southeast of Tyre. The discovery of **early Christian carvings** on the rocks outside the village and a grotto nearby give evidence that this is the **Cana of Galilee** where Jesus performed his first miracle at a wedding, turning water into wine. At another site in the village large wine presses, thought to date from the 1st century AD, have been uncovered. The Holy Land has, to be fair, other claimants to being the authentic Cana of the Bible, notably a village named Kefr Kenna in Israel. The 4th-century historian, Eusabius, seems to support the idea that Cana was near Sidon, as does St Jerome in the 3rd century. In any case the site is of great interest.

The site is on the edge of the village down a steep path. The turning is marked by a modern, white marble stone with black Arabic script. The turning leads to a small car park from where it is a five-minute walk down to the grotto and carvings. To see inside the grotto you will need a torch. The site is not supervised so you can visit any time.

To see the wine presses is bit more tricky as they are between two back gardens of village houses. You will need to ask locally for directions (or get your taxi driver to show you). People are very helpful in the village about giving directions or taking you along to the place.

In 1996 Qana was the site of a massacre in which 107 Lebanese civilians were killed by Israeli shells at a UN base. An official day of mourning is now held annually throughout Lebanon on April 18.

Getting There & Away Qana is not on the service taxi route so you will need to hire a taxi both ways from Tyre. The return trip costs about US$10, but this is negotiable.

Beaufort Castle
At the time of writing you cannot visit Beaufort Castle (in Arabic 'Qalaat ash-Shaqif') as it is occupied by the Israeli military. The situation may change so ask around for the latest information. If it is open, this is one of the most impressive medieval castles in the Middle East to visit. It is near the town of Nabatiyeh (which is as far as you can get by service taxi).

The castle sits on a hill 710m above sea level. From the summit, you can see Tyre and the coast to the west, Israel and Syria to the south and east, and the mountains to the north. Because of its strategic position, it is still a military prize 1000 years after it was built.

It was captured from Chehab ed-Dine in 1139 by the Crusader Fulk of Anjou, King of Jerusalem, who gave it back to the lords of Sayette. William of Tyre relates that after the defeat of the Crusaders in Banyas (in Syria) in 1192, many of the knights took refuge in the castle. It was then besieged by Saladin who, to speed up the process, resorted to a ruse. He persuaded Renaud, Prince of Sayette, to have a meeting, but when Renaud left the fortress, Saladin overpowered him and tortured him in front of the castle walls. Renaud's men did not give in and it took two years to starve them out.

The castle changed sides several times before the Crusaders were finally driven out of the Holy Land. In the 17th century Fakhr ad-Din, from the House of Ma'an, saw the advantage of such a fortress in his revolt against the Sublime Porte when the pashas of Acre and Damascus sent forces against him.

During the recent civil war, Beaufort Castle suffered quite a bit of damage and is still a significant military look-out post for the Israelis.

Getting There & Away The nearest you can get to the castle at the moment is the small town of Nabatiyeh. A service taxi from Beirut costs LL 4000; from Sidon LL 2000. You can catch a glimpse of the castle from a distance but venturing any nearer, even on foot, would be extremely foolhardy.

Glossary

Abbasids – Baghdad-based successor dynasty to the *Umayyads*; ruled from 750 AD until the sack of Baghdad by the Mongols in 1258

acropolis – hilltop citadel and temples of a classical Hellenistic city

amn al-aam – General Security office

Amorites – Western Semitic people who emerged from the Syrian deserts around 2000 BC and influenced life in the cities of Mesopotamia and Phoenicia until 1600 BC

apse – semicircular recess for the altar in a church

Arab League – a league of 22 independent Arab states, formed in 1945, to further cultural, economic, military, political and social cooperation between the states

Aramaic – an ancient Semitic language, still spoken in parts of Syria and Lebanon

AUB – American University of Beirut

Ayyubids – Egyptian-based dynasty founded by *Saladin* (1169-1250)

bourj – tower

bureau de téléphone – private telephone kiosk

caliph – Islamic ruler; originally known as the Companion of Mohammed or the successor of the prophet Mohammad; an Arabic word meaning 'successor' or 'lieutenant'

capital – the uppermost part of a column, supporting the *entablature* or arch

Capuchin – a strict branch of the Franciscan religious order

caravanserai – see *khan*

cella – inner part of temple which houses the statue of a god or goddess

Chalcolithic – period between the *Neolithic* and Bronze ages in which there was an increase in urbanisation and trade and the ~~occa~~sional use of copper

~~cuneiform~~ – wedge-shaped characters of ~~ancie~~nt languages, including Baby-

dabke – an energetic folk dance that is the national Lebanese dance

deir – monastery

donjon – dungeon

Druze – a religious sect based on Islamic teachings; followers are found in Lebanon, Syria and Israel

Eid al-Adha – Feast of Sacrifice marking the pilgrimage to Mecca

Eid al-Fitr – Festival of Breaking the Fast; celebrated at the end of *Ramadan*

emir – an independent ruler or chieftain; military commander or governor; also spelt amir

entablature – the part of a temple above the column, having an architrave, a frieze and a cornice

exedra – a room or outdoor area with seats used for discussions

ezan – call to prayer; also spelt izan

Fatimids – a Shiite dynasty from North Africa who claimed to be descended from Fatima, daughter of the prophet Mohammed, and her husband Ali ibn-abi Talib, the fourth *caliph*

felafel – deep-fried spicy, ground chickpea balls, usually served wrapped in flat bread with salad and sauce

fuul – paste made from fava beans, garlic and lemon

GCC – Gulf Cooperation Council

Green Line – line which divided Beirut's eastern (Christian) half from its western (Muslim) half

hajj – annual pilgrimage to Mecca

halloumi – salty, rubbery cheese

hammam – Turkish-style bathhouse with sauna and massage

haram – the sacred area inside a mosque

hieroglyphics – ancient form of writing, which used pictures and symbols to represent objects, words or sounds

hijra – migration; usually refers to Mohammed's flight from Mecca in 622 AD; also name of Islamic calendar

IDP – International Driving Permit

iftar – breaking of the day's fast during *Ramadan*

imam – prayer leader in a mosque; Muslim cleric

iwan – vaulted hall, opening onto a central court, usually in the *madrassah* of a mosque

jebel – mountain

jihad – literally 'striving in the way of the faith'; holy war

Kaaba – the rectangular structure at the centre of the Grand Mosque in Mecca (containing the black stone) around which *hajj* pilgrims walk

khan – large inn enclosing a courtyard, providing accommodation for caravans; also known as caravanserai

kibbe – finely minced paste of lamb and bulgur wheat

kursi – a wooden stand for holding the *Qur'an*

lahm bi ajin – lamb-filled pastry rolls similar to a pizza

Levant – literally 'where the sun rises'; region of the eastern Mediterranean from Egypt to Greece

madrassah – theological college that is part of a non-congregational mosque; also a school

Mameluke – Turkish slave-soldier dynasty that ruled Egypt from 1250 to 1517

MEA – Middle East Airlines

medina – old walled centre of any Islamic city

metae – turning stone in ancient hippodrome

mezze – appetisers

mihrab – prayer niche in the wall of a mosque which indicates the direction of Mecca

minaret – tower of a mosque from which the call to prayer is made

minbar – pulpit in a mosque

muezzin – mosque official who, from the *minaret*, sings the *ezan* five times a day

murex – a kind of mollusc from which the famous purple dye of Tyre comes

mutasarrif – Christian governor-general in Lebanon during the Ottoman Empire

nahr – river

nargileh – water pipe used to smoke tobacco

nave – the central part of a church

nebaa – spring

necropolis – city of the dead; cemetery

Neolithic – literally 'new stone' age; period based on the use of stone tools which witnessed the development of domestication and the beginnings of urbanisation

obelisk – monolithic stone pillar, with square sides tapering to a pyramidal, often gilded, top; used as a monument in ancient Egypt

pasha – a provincial governor or other high official of the Ottoman Empire

Pax Romana – the Roman peace; the long period of stability under the Roman Empire

Phalangist – member of a Lebanese Christian paramilitary organisation, founded in 1936

PLO – Palestine Liberation Organization

qa'im maqamiyats – administrative regions of Mount Lebanon in the mid-19th century

Qur'an – the holy book of Islam; also spelt Koran

rakats – cycles of prayer during which the *Qur'an* is read and bows and prostrations are performed in different series

Ramadan – the Muslim month of fasting

salaamlik – main reception room

Saladin – warlord who retook Jerusalem from the Crusaders; founder of the *Ayyubid* dynasty; also spelt Salah ad-Din

sarcophagus – a stone or marble coffin or tomb, especially one with an inscription

serail – Ottoman palace; also spelt seraglio

shari'a – Islamic law

shawarma – seasoned and spit-roasted meat

Shiism – a main branch of Islam which regards the prophet Mohammed's cousin Ali and his successors as the true leaders

SLA – South Lebanese Army

souk – market

stele – inscribed stone slab; plural stelae

Sublime Porte – the government of the Ottoman Empire; also called the Porte

sultan – the absolute ruler of a Muslim state

sumak – tangy herb

Sunni – a main branch of Islam based on the words and acts of the prophet Mohammed, with the caliph seen as the true successor

Syriac – a dialect of Aramaic spoken in Syria until about the 13th century and still used as a liturgical language

tabouleh – salad of parsley, onions, tomatoes and soaked bulgur wheat, dressed with lemon and oil

Umayyads – first great dynasty of Arab Muslim rulers, based in Damascus (661-750 AD); also spelt Omayyad

UN – United Nations

UNRWA – United Nations Relief and Work Agency

vizier – high official in Muslim countries; usually provincial governor or chief minister to the *sultan*

za'atar – mixture of thyme and *sumak*

zajal – popular form of poetry in which a group of poets enters into a witty dialogue by improvising verses

Index

Abbreviations

AB – Around Beirut
B – Beirut

BK – The Bekaa Valley
NB – North of Beirut

T – Tripoli & The Cedars
SB – South of Beirut

Maps

Aanjar Ruins (BK) 186
Around Beirut (AB) 138

Baalbek (BK) 189
  Baalbek Ruins 190
Bcharré (T) 174
Beirut (B) 114
  Corniche & Raouché Area 132
  Hamra Area 126
Bekaa Valley (BK) 182
Byblos (Jbail) (NB) 153
  Byblos Archaeological Site 155

Chtaura (BK) 183

Kadisha Valley, The (T) 177

Lebanon
  between 16 & 17

North of Beirut (NB) 151

Palace of Beiteddine (SB) 198
Phoenician World, The 13

Sidon (Saida) (SB) 204
South of Beirut (SB) 196

Temple of Echmoun (SB) 206
Tripoli & The Cedars (T) 165
  Tripoli – Old City 167
  Al-Mina 170
Tyre (Sour) (SB) 211

Zahlé (BK) 184

Boxed Stories

Approximate Science of Trans-
  literation, The 50
Air Travel Glossary 98-9
Alexander the Great (SB) 210
Arabic Music 36
Arak (BK) 183
Bus & Service Taxi Fares 102,
  104
Cedar Tree – *Cedrus Libani*, The
  (T) 176
Corniche Walk, The (B) 117
Ernest Renan (1823-92) (NB)
  159
Everyday Health 75
Fairouz 38
Highlights 58-9

Hiram versus Solomon 15
Howling Wolf (AB) 141
Islamic Holidays 81
Lady Hester Stanhope (1776-
  1839) (SB) 208
Lebanese Wine 95
Lebanon's Grand Prix Ambi-
  tions 85
Marina Grotto, The (T) 172
Medical Kit Check List 71
Monument to Peace (B) 121
Murex (SB) 202
Mythology 45
Nutrition 73
Oriental Dancing 35
Pepe the Pirate (NB) 158

Phoenician Alphabet 14
Quarry, The (BK) 192
Recipes of Lebanon 91-2
Saladin (1138-92) (SB) 201
Shipwreck at Cape Gelidonya, A
  15
Shot of Discovery, A (AB) 143
Sketches of Baalbek 47
Ski Resorts at a Glance 83
St George & the Dragon (B) 124
Süleyman the Magnificent 22
Tragedy of Melisinda, The (T)
  169
Time Line 12

Text

Map references are in **bold** type.

Aaidamoun (T) 180
Aandqet (T) 180
Aanjar (Haouch Moussa)
  (BK) 185-7, **186**
  architecture 48
Abbasids 19-20
Abed, Pepe (NB) 157, 158
accommodation 84

activities, *see* individual entries
Adonis, *see* Tammuz
Afqa Grotto (NB) 160-1
Ain Fawar Hot Spring (AB) 140
Aintoura (AB) 147
air travel 96-101
  airports 96
  air travel glossary 98-9
  departure tax 102
  tickets 96-7

Australia 100
Canada 99
Europe 100-1
Middle East 101
New Zealand 100
UK 100
USA 99
Ajaltoun (AB) 147
Akkar (T) 179-80
Al-Khuri, Bishara 25, (SB) 198

Al-Mina (T) 169, **170**
Al-Shaykh, Hanan 37
Alexander the Great 16-17,
  (SB) 209-10
Amchit (NB) 158-60
Amor, *see* Hermel Pyramid
Antiochus III 17
Aoun, General Michel 29
Arab League 26, 27
Arabic (language) 50-3, 90-1
Arabs 18-21
Arak (BK) 183
archaeological sites
  Aanjar (BK) 185-6, **186**
  Baalbek (BK) 187-92, **190**
  Batroun (NB) 162
  Beaufort Castle (SB) 214-15
  Beirut Downtown (B) 121-3
  Beit Meri (AB) 137
  Byblos (NB) 154-6, **155**
  Castle of St Louis (SB) 203-4
  Citadel of Raymond de Saint-
    Gilles (T) 168-9
  Deir al-Qamar (SB) 196
  Douma (NB) 161
  Enfe (T) 172
  Faqra (AB) 148
  Hermel (BK) 193-4
  Nahr al-Kalb (AB) 141-2
  Palace of Beiteddine (SB)
    198-200, **198**
  Qana (SB) 214
  Sea Castle (SB) 203
  Temple of Echmoun (SB) 205-7,
    206
  Tomb of Hiram (SB) 214
  Tyre (SB) 212, **211**
architecture 37, 44-9, *see also*
  individual entries
  1300 AD to the French Mandate
    49
  Byzantines, Arabs & Crusaders
    48-9
  Greeks & Romans 44-8
  Neolithic to Iron Age 44
  Phoenicians 44
arts 35-8, (AB) 149, (T) 175
Ashurnasirpal II 16
Ashtoreth, *see* Astarte
Astarte (Ashtoreth) 45,
  (SB) 205, (SB) 207
Ayyubids 21

B'qaa Kafra (T) 178
Baal 45
Baalbek 47, (BK) 187-93, **189, 190**
  architecture 48
  festival 35
  getting there & away 193

Great Court 190-1
history 17, 187-9
information 189-90
places to eat 193
places to stay 192-3
Temple of Bacchus 191-2
Temple of Jupiter-Baal 191
Temple of Venus 192
Bakish 83
Bala Gorge (NB) 161
Balamand (T) 173
bargaining, *see* money
Barouk (SB) 200
Bashir II 23, (B) 110, (SB) 197-8
Baskinta (AB) 140
Batroun (NB) 162-3
Bcharré (T) 173-6, **174**
  Gibran Museum 174
Beaufort Castle (SB) 214-15
Beirut 108-36, **114, 126, 132**
  activities 124-5
  American University of Beirut
    Museum 120
  architecture 46
  bookshops 116
  Corniche 117, **132**
  cultural centres 116
  Downtown 112, 121-3
  East Beirut 124
  entertainment 133-4
  getting around 135-6
  getting there & away 135
  Grand Mosque 122
  Grand Seraglio 123
  Hamra 120-1, **126**
  history 109-11
  information 113-18
  medical services 116-18
  museums 118-20
  National Museum 118-20
  orientation 111
  Pigeon Rocks 123
  Place des Martyrs 122
  places to eat 129-33
  places to stay 125-9
  postal services 113
  shopping 134
  Sursock Museum 120
  things to see & do 120-4
  tourist office 113
  tours 125
  travel agencies 115-16
  walking tour 117
Beiteddine (SB) 197-200
  festival 198
  Palace of Beiteddine 49,
    198-200, **198**
Beit Meri (AB) 137-9
  Bustan festival 35

Berytus, *see* Beirut
Bekaa Valley 31, 181-94, **182**
bicycle 102, 106
Bikfaya (AB) 140
birds, *see* fauna
boat travel 102
books 66-7, *see also* literature
Broummana (AB) 139-40
Bustan, *see* Beit Meri
bus travel 101, 102, 104, 106
  to/from Syria 101
business hours 81
Byblos (Jbail) (NB) 150-8, **153,
  155**
  architecture 44, 48
  getting around 158
  getting there & away 158
  history 150-2
  information 152-3
  places to eat 157-8
  places to stay 156-7
  walking tour 153-4
  Wax Museum 156
Byzantines 18
  architecture 48

car travel 102, 105-6
  driving permits 61
  motoring organisation 80
  rental 105-6
  road rules 105
  Syria 102
Caracalla 38
Casino de Liban (AB) 144
castles, *see* individual entries
Castle Moussa (SB) 197
Castle of Akkar (T) 180
cedar, *see* flora
Cedars, The 83, (T) 175-6
  festival 175
Chamoun, Camille 25-6
Chapel of Mart Chmouni (T) 177
Chapel of Saydet Hawka (T) 177
Chapel-Cave of St Marina
  (T) 178
Castle of St Louis 203-4
Chehab, Fouad 26
Chekka (T) 172-3
children, travel with 80
Chouf Mountains (SB) 195-200
Christianity 18, 23-4, 26, 27, 29,
  42
  Catholic 42
  Eastern Orthodox 42
  Maronites 18, 19, 20-1, 42,
    (T) 178
Chtaura (BK) 181-3, **183**
Church of St John the Baptist
  (NB) 156

churches, *see* individual entries
cinema 37, 84-5
Citadel of Raymond de Saint-
    Gilles (T) 168-9
civil war, *see* history
climate 31-2
conduct, *see* cultural considera-
    tions
conservation, *see* environmental
    issues
Corniche, *see* Beirut
costs, *see* money
Crusader Castle (NB) 154
Crusader Cathedral (SB) 212
Crusaders 20-1, (T) 165, (SB)
    211
    architecture 48
cultural considerations 38-9
cultural events (festivals) 35-7
    Baalbek 35
    Beiteddine (SB) 198
    Beir Meri 35, (AB) 138
    Bikfaya (AB) 140
    Cedars, The 175
    Tyre (SB) 213
currency, *see* money
customs 63
cycling, *see* bicycle

dabke 35
Dagon 45
Dakweh (BK) 186-7
dance 35
Debbas, Charles 24
Deir al-Qalaa (AB) 138
Deir al-Qamar (SB) 196-7
Deir as-Salib (T) 177
Deir Mar Elisha (T) 178
Deir Mar Maroun (BK) 194
Deir Mar Semaan (T) 178
Deir Qannoubin (T) 178
Deir Qozhaya (T) 177-8
departure tax, *see* air travel
Diman (T) 178
disabled travellers 80
discos 85
Douma (NB) 161-2
Downtown, *see* Beirut
Dragon's Well (B) 124
drinks 94-5, (BK) 183, (BK) 185
driving, *see* car travel, motor-
    cycle travel
Druze 20, 22-4, 26, 29, 41-2,
    (SB) 195
duty-free, *see* customs

Echmoun, Temple of 45,
    (SB) 205-7, **206**
Echmounazar II (SB) 206

ecology, *see* environmental
    issues
economy 34
education 35
Ehden (T) 179
electricity 70
email services 65-6
embassies 61-3
Enfe (T) 172
entertainment, *see* individual
    entries
environmental issues 32-3
etiquette, *see* cultural considera-
    tions

Fairouz 37, 38
Fakhr ad-Din 22-3, (B) 110,
    (SB) 202, (SB) 211
Faqra 83, (AB) 148-9
Faraya 83, (AB) 147-8
    Natural Bridge (AB) 147
Fatimids 20
fauna 32-3
fax services 65-6
Faytroun (AB) 147
ferry travel, *see* boat travel
festivals, *see* cultural events
films 37, 68, *see* also cinema
flora 32, 33
    cedar 32, (T) 175-6, (SB) 200
food 88-94
Franjieh, Suleiman 26
French (language) 53-5
French Colonial Rule 24-5
    architecture 49

gay & lesbian travellers 80
Gebal, *see* Byblos
Gemayel, Amin 28
Gemayel, Bashir 28
geography 30-1
Gibran, Khalil 37, (T) 174-5
government 33-4
Grand Mosque (B) 122, (T) 168
Grand Seraglio (B) 123
Great Mosque (SB) 203
Greek Orthodox Abbey (T) 173
Greeks 17
    architecture 44
Green Line 27
Grotto of St Anthony (T) 178

Hadchit (T) 179
hammam (B) 123
Hamra, *see* Beirut
Haouch Moussa, *see* Aanjar
Hariri, Rafiq 29, 33-4
Harissa (AB) 146-7
Harun ar-Rashid 19

Hasroun (T) 178
health 70-9
    cuts, bites & stings 77-8
    environmental hazards 73-5
    immunisations 70-1
    infectious diseases 75-7
    women's health 78
health insurance 60-1
Helou, Charles 26
Heracles, *see* Melkart
Hermel (BK) 193-4
    Pyramid (Amor) 194
Herod the Great 17
Hezbollah 28-30
hiking, *see* trekking
Hiram, King of Tyre 15-16,
    (SB) 209
    Tomb of (SB) 214
history 11-30
    Abbasids 19-20
    Alexander the Great 16-17,
        (SB) 209-10
    Arabs 18-21
    Ayyubids 21
    Byzantines 18
    civil war 27-30, (B) 110
    Crusaders 20-1, (T) 165,
        (SB) 211
    Fatimids 20
    French Colonial Rule 24-5
    Greeks 17
    Hiram, King of Tyre 15-16,
        (SB) 209, (SB) 214
    independence 25-7
    Israel 26-30
    Ma'an, House of 22-3
    Mamelukes 21-2
    Mongols 21
    Ottomans 22-4
    Palestine 27-30
    Phoenicians 11-16, (NB) 151-2,
        (SB) 201-2, (SB) 209, **13**
    Reconstruction of Lebanon 30
    Romans 17-18, (BK) 188
    Shihabs 23
    Syria 25, 27, 29
    time line 12
    Umayyads 19, (BK) 185-6
    USA 28
    WWI 24
hitching 106
holidays, *see* public holidays
Holy Church of the Saviour
    (NB) 163
Horsh Ehden 33, (T) 179
Hrawi, Elias 29

immunisations 70-1
insurance, travel 60-1

Internet, *see* online services
Islam 18-21, 22-4, 26, 27, 29,
    39-42, 81
    architecture 49
    Druze 20, 22-4, 26, 29, 41-2,
        (SB) 195
    holidays 40-1, 81
    Shiites 39-40
    Sunnis 39-40
Israel 26-30

Jbail, *see* Byblos
Jebel ash-Sheikh 31
Jebel Kenishe (AB) 140
Jebel Sannine 31, (AB) 140-1
Jeita Grotto (AB) 142-3
Joumblatt, Kemal (SB) 199
Joumblatt, Walid 29, (SB) 199
Joun (SB) 207, 208
Jounieh (AB) 143-6
    Casino de Liban 144
    entertainment 145-6
    getting there & away 146
    places to eat 145
    places to stay 145
    Téléphérique 144
    things to see & do 144-5

Kadisha Valley, The (T) 176-9,
    177
Karan, Bechara (NB) 159
Kfarhim Grotto (SB) 200
Ksara Winery (BK) 185

Lake Qaraoun (BK) 187
Laklouk 83, (NB) 161
language 50-5, 90-1
    Arabic 50-3, 90-1
    French 53-5
laundry 70
Litani Dam (BK) 187
literature 37, (T) 175, *see also*
    books

Ma'an, Ahmad 23
Ma'an, House of 22-3
Majdel Aanjar (BK) 186
Mamelukes 21-2
maps 56, (B) 111
Maqam (T) 180
Marina Grotto (T) 172
Mar Jurios Azraq (NB) 160
Maronite Cathedral (B) 124
Maronites 18, 19, 20-1, 24, 42,
    (T) 178
measures 70
media 68-9
medical services, *see* Beirut
medical treatment, *see* health

Melkart (Heracles) 45, (SB) 202
Moawwad, René 29
Mohammed 18, 39-40
monasteries, *see also* Deir
    Monastery of Mar Musa
        (AB) 140
money 63-5
    ATMs 64
    bargaining 64-5
    changing money 64
    costs 63
    currency 64
    tipping 64-5
Mongols 21
mosques 49, *see also* individual
    entries
motorcycle travel 105-6
    driving permits 61
    motoring organisation 80
mountains
    Jebel ash-Sheikh 31
    Jebel Kenishe (AB) 140
    Jebel Sannine 31, (AB) 140-1
    Qornet as-Sawda 31
Moussalayha Castle (NB) 163
Mu'awiyah 19, 40
murex 15, (SB) 201
museums, *see* individual city
    entries
music 35-8
Muslim, *see* Islam
mythology 45, *see also* individ-
    ual entries

Nahr al-Aasi (BK) 194
Nahr al-Kalb (AB) 141-2
National Pact 25
nature reserves 33
    Horsh Ehden 33, (T) 179
    Palm Islands Park 33, (T) 169
Nebaa Sannine (AB) 140
nightclubs, *see* discos
Nur ad-Din 21, (SB) 201

Obelisk Temple (NB) 154
online services 67-8
Ottomans 22-4
    architecture 49

painting 38
Palace of Beiteddine
    (SB) 198-200, **198**
    architecture 49
Palestine 27-30
    Palestine Liberation Organiza-
        tion (PLO) 27-30
Palm Islands Park 33, (T) 169
passport 57
Phalangists 27-8

Phoenicians 11-16, (NB) 151-2,
    (SB) 201-2, (SB) 209, **13**
    architecture 44
photography 69-70
Pigeon Rocks (B) 117
Place des Martyrs (B) 122
planning 56-7
politics, *see* government
population 34-5
postal services 65
Ptolemy I 17
public holidays 81-2, *see also*
    Islam

Qalamoun (T) 173
Qana 30, (SB) 214
Qartaba (NB) 160
Qornet as-Sawda 31
Qoubayat (T) 180
Qubba (NB) 163
Qubbet al-Beddawi (T) 171-2

Rachana (AB) 149
Raifoun (AB) 147
Raymond de Saint-Gilles
    (NB) 152, (T) 165, (T) 168,
    (T) 169
religion, *see* individual entries
Renan, Ernest (NB) 152,
    (NB) 159, (SB) 214
rental, *see* car travel, motorcycle
    travel
Roberts, David 47
Romans 17-18, (BK) 188
    architecture 44

safety 80-1, (B) 118
Saida, *see* Sidon
Saladin (Salah ad-Din) 20, 21,
    (SB) 201
Sarafand (SB) 207-8
Sargon of Akkad 11
sculpture 38, (AB) 149
Sea Castle (SB) 203
senior travellers 80
service taxi travel, *see* taxi travel
Shihabs 23
Shiites, *see* Islam
shopping 85-6
    Beirut 134
    Tripoli 171
Sidon (Saida) (SB) 200-5, **204**
    architecture 49
    Castle of St Louis 203-4
    getting there & away 205
    Great Mosque 203
    history 200-2
    information 202-3
    Khan al-Franj 203

places to eat 205
places to stay 205
Sea Castle 203
skiing 82-3, (AB) 147-8,
    (NB) 161, (T) 175
Solidere 30, (B) 112, (B) 122
Solomon, King 15
Sour, see Tyre
South Lebanese Army (SLA)
    28-9
sport, spectator 85
Stanhope, Lady Hester
    (SB) 207, (SB) 208
St George's Church (B) 124
St George's Maronite Cathedral
    (B) 123
St Louis Church (B) 123
St Maron, John 18, 42
Süleyman the Magnificent 22
Sunnis, see Islam
swimming 82, (B) 124-5,
    (AB) 144
Syria 25, 27, 29

Taif Agreement 29
Tammuz (Adonis) 45, (NB) 160,
    (SB) 205
taxi travel 102, 104-5, 106
    Syria 102
Téléphérique (AB) 144
telephone services 65
temples

Baalat Gebal (NB) 154
Bacchus (BK) 191-2
Echmoun 45, (SB) 205-7, **206**
Jupiter-Baal (BK) 191
Obelisk (NB) 154
Venus (BK) 192
theatre 37-8, 84-5
time 70, see also business hours
tipping, see money
toilets 79
Tomb of Hiram (SB) 214
tourist offices 57, (B) 113
tours 102-3, 106-7
Trablous, see Tripoli
train travel 104
travel preparations, see planning
travel with children, see children
trekking 82-3, 106, (AB) 139,
    (NB) 161, (T) 176-7
Tripoli (Trablous) (T) 164-71,
    167, 170
    Al-Mina 169, **170**
    architecture 49
    Citadel of Raymond de Saint-
        Gilles 168-9
    getting there & away 171
    history 164-6
    information 166
    Old City 166-8
    orientation 166
    places to eat 171
    places to stay 169-71

shopping 171
Tyre (Sour) (SB) 209-13, **211**
    architecture 48
    Crusader Cathedral 212
    festival 213
    getting there & away 213
    history 209-11
    information 212
    places to eat 213
    places to stay 213
    Roman Hippodrome 213
    Roman Necropolis 212

Umayyads 19, (BK) 185-6

video 69-70
visas 57-60

walking, see trekking
weights 70
wild life, see fauna
wine 95, (BK) 185
    see also drinks
women travellers 79-80
    health 78
work 83-4
WWI 24

Zaarour 83
Zahlé (BK) 183-5, **184**

LONELY PLANET PHRASEBOOKS

Nepali phrasebook

Ethiopian Amharic phrasebook

Latin American Spanish phrasebook

Ukrainian phrasebook

Greek phrasebook

Vietnamese phrasebook

Building bridges,
Breaking barriers,
Beyond babble-on

Listen for the gems

Speak your own words

Ask your own questions

Master of your own image

- handy pocket-sized books
- easy to understand Pronunciation chapter
- clear and comprehensive Grammar chapter
- romanisation alongside script to allow ease of pronunciation
- script throughout so users can point to phrases
- extensive vocabulary sections, words and phrases for every situations
- full of cultural information and tips for the traveller

'...vital for a real DIY spirit and attitude in language learning' – Backpacker

'the phrasebooks have good cultural backgrounders and offer solid advice for challenging situations in remote locations' – San Francisco Examiner

'...they are unbeatable for their coverage of the world's more obscure languages' – The Geographical Magazine

---

Arabic (Egyptian)
Arabic (Moroccan)
Australia
  Australian English, Aboriginal and Torres Strait languages
Baltic States
  Estonian, Latvian, Lithuanian
Bengali
Burmese
Brazilian
Cantonese
Central Europe
  Czech, French, German, Hungarian, Italian and Slovak
Eastern Europe
  Bulgarian, Czech, Hungarian, Polish, Romanian and Slovak
Egyptian Arabic
Ethiopian (Amharic)
Fijian
French
German
Greek

Hindi/Urdu
Indonesian
Italian
Japanese
Korean
Lao
Latin American Spanish
Malay
Mandarin
Mediterranean Europe
  Albanian, Croatian, Greek, Italian, Macedonian, Maltese, Serbian, Slovene
Mongolian
Moroccan Arabic
Nepali
Papua New Guinea
Pilipino (Tagalog)
Quechua
Russian
Scandinavian Europe
  Danish, Finnish, Icelandic, Norwegian and Swedish

South-East Asia
  Burmese, Indonesian, Khmer, Lao, Malay, Tagalog (Pilipino), Thai and Vietnamese
Spanish
Sri Lanka
Swahili
Thai
Thai Hill Tribes
Tibetan
Turkish
Ukrainian
USA
  US English, Vernacular Talk, Native American languages and Hawaiian
Vietnamese
Western Europe
  Basque, Catalan, Dutch, French, German, Irish, Italian, Portuguese, Scottish Gaelic, Spanish (Castilian) and Welsh

---

LONELY PLANET JOURNEYS

JOURNEYS is a unique collection of travel writing – published by the company that understands travel better than anyone else. It is a series for anyone who has ever experienced – or dreamed of – the magical moment when they encountered a strange culture or saw a place for the first time. They are tales to read while you're planning a trip, while you're on the road or while you're in an armchair, in front of a fire.

JOURNEYS books catch the spirit of a place, illuminate a culture, recount a crazy adventure, or introduce a fascinating way of life. They always entertain, and always enrich the experience of travel.

THE GATES OF DAMASCUS
Lieve Joris
Translated by Sam Garrett

This best-selling book is a beautifully drawn portrait of day-to-day life in modern Syria. Through her intimate contact with local people, Lieve Joris draws us into the fascinating world that lies behind the gates of Damascus. Hala's husband is a political prisoner, jailed for his opposition to the Assad regime; through the author's friendship with Hala we see how Syrian politics impacts on the lives of ordinary people.

Lieve Joris, who was born in Belgium, is one of Europe's leading travel writers. In addition to an award-winning book on Hungary, she has published widely acclaimed accounts of her journeys to the Middle East and Africa. *The Gates of Damascus* is her fifth book.

'Expands the boundaries of travel writing' – Times Literary Supplement

---

KINGDOM OF THE FILM STARS
Journey into Jordan
Annie Caulfield

Kingdom of the Film Stars is a travel book and a love story. With honesty and humour, Annie Caulfield writes of travelling in Jordan and falling in love with a Bedouin. Her book offers fascinating insights into the country – from the traditional tent life of nomadic tribes to the first woman MP's battle with fundamentalist colleagues. *Kingdom of the Film Stars* unpicks some of the tight-woven Western myths about the Arab world, presenting cultural and political issues within the intimate framework of a compelling love story.

Annie Caulfield, who was born in Ireland and currently lives in London, is an award-winning playwright and journalist. She has travelled widely in the Middle East.

'Annie Caulfield is a remarkable traveller. Her story is fresh, courageous, moving, witty and sexy!' – Dawn French

LONELY PLANET TRAVEL ATLASES

Lonely Planet has long been famous for the number and quality of its guidebook maps. Now we've gone one step further and in conjunction with Steinhart Katzir Publishers produced a handy companion series: Lonely Planet travel atlases – maps of a country produced in book form.

Unlike other maps, which look good but lead travellers astray, our travel atlases have been researched on the road by Lonely Planet's experienced team of writers. All details are carefully checked to ensure the atlas corresponds with the equivalent Lonely Planet guidebook.

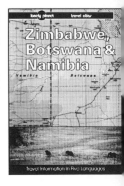

The handy atlas format means no holes, wrinkles, torn sections or constant folding and unfolding. These atlases can survive long periods on the road, unlike cumbersome fold-out maps. The comprehensive index ensures easy reference.

- full-colour throughout
- maps researched and checked by Lonely Planet authors
- place names correspond with Lonely Planet guidebooks
  – no confusing spelling differences
- legend and travelling information in English, French, German, Japanese and Spanish
- size: 230 x 160 mm

Available now:
Chile & Easter Island • Egypt • India & Bangladesh • Israel & the Palestinian Territories •Jordan, Syria & Lebanon • Kenya • Laos • Portugal • South Africa, Lesotho & Swaziland • Thailand • Turkey • Vietnam • Zimbabwe, Botswana & Namibia

---

LONELY PLANET TV SERIES & VIDEOS

Lonely Planet travel guides have been brought to life on television screens around the world. Like our guides, the programmes are based on the joy of independent travel, and look honestly at some of the most exciting, picturesque and frustrating places in the world. Each show is presented by one of three travellers from Australia, England or the USA and combines an innovative mixture of video, Super-8 film, atmospheric soundscapes and original music.

Videos of each episode – containing additional footage not shown on television – are available from good book and video shops, but the availability of individual videos varies with regional screening schedules.

Video destinations include: Alaska • American Rockies • Australia – The South-East • Baja California & the Copper Canyon • Brazil • Central Asia • Chile & Easter Island • Corsica, Sicily & Sardinia – The Mediterranean Islands • East Africa (Tanzania & Zanzibar) • Ecuador & the Galapagos Islands • Greenland & Iceland • Indonesia • Israel & the Sinai Desert • Jamaica • Japan • La Ruta Maya • Morocco • New York • North India • Pacific Islands (Fiji, Solomon Islands & Vanuatu) • South India • South West China • Turkey • Vietnam • West Africa • Zimbabwe, Botswana & Namibia

The Lonely Planet TV series is produced by:
Pilot Productions
The Old Studio
18 Middle Row
London W10 5AT UK

For video availability and ordering information contact your nearest Lonely Planet office.

Music from the TV series is available on CD & cassette.

PLANET TALK

Lonely Planet's FREE quarterly newsletter

We love hearing from you and think you'd like to hear from us.

When...is the right time to see reindeer in Finland?
Where...can you hear the best palm-wine music in Ghana?
How...do you get from Asunción to Areguá by steam train?
What...is the best way to see India?

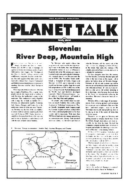

For the answer to these and many other questions read PLANET TALK.

Every issue is packed with up-to-date travel news and advice including:

* a letter from Lonely Planet co-founders Tony and Maureen Wheeler
* go behind the scenes on the road with a Lonely Planet author
* feature article on an important and topical travel issue
* a selection of recent letters from travellers
* details on forthcoming Lonely Planet promotions
* complete list of Lonely Planet products

To join our mailing list contact any Lonely Planet office.

Also available: Lonely Planet T-shirts. 100% heavyweight cotton.

LONELY PLANET ONLINE

Get the latest travel information before you leave or while you're on the road

Whether you've just begun planning your next trip, or you're chasing down specific info on currency regulations or visa requirements, check out Lonely Planet Online for up-to-the minute travel information.

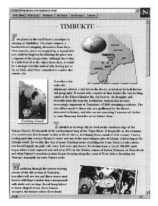

As well as travel profiles of your favourite destinations (including maps and photos), you'll find current reports from our researchers and other travellers, updates on health and visas, travel advisories, and discussion of the ecological and political issues you need to be aware of as you travel.

There's also an online travellers' forum where you can share your experience of life on the road, meet travel companions and ask other travellers for their recommendations and advice. We also have plenty of links to other online sites useful to independent travellers.

And of course we have a complete and up-to-date list of all Lonely Planet travel products including guides, phrasebooks, atlases, Journeys and videos and a simple online ordering facility if you can't find the book you want elsewhere.

www.lonelyplanet.com
or
AOL keyword: lp

LONELY PLANET PRODUCTS

Lonely Planet is known worldwide for publishing practical, reliable and no-nonsense travel information in our guides and on our web site. The Lonely Planet list covers just about every accessible part of the world. Currently there are eight series: *travel guides*, *shoestring guides*, *walking guides*, *city guides*, *phrasebooks*, *audio packs*, *travel atlases* and *Journeys* – a unique collection of travel writing.

EUROPE

Amsterdam • Austria • Baltic States phrasebook • Britain • Central Europe on a shoestring • Central Europe phrasebook • Czech & Slovak Republics • Denmark • Dublin • Eastern Europe on a shoestring • Eastern Europe phrasebook • Estonia, Latvia & Lithuania • Finland • France • French phrasebook • German phrasebook • Greece • Greek phrasebook • Hungary • Iceland, Greenland & the Faroe Islands • Ireland • Italian phrasebook • Italy • Mediterranean Europe on a shoestring • Mediterranean Europe phrasebook • Paris • Poland • Portugal • Portugal travel atlas • Prague • Russia, Ukraine & Belarus • Russian phrasebook • Scandinavian & Baltic Europe on a shoestring • Scandinavian Europe phrasebook • Slovenia • Spain • Spanish phrasebook • St Petersburg • Switzerland • Trekking in Greece • Trekking in Spain • Ukrainian phrasebook • Vienna • Walking in Britain • Walking in Switzerland • Western Europe on a shoestring • Western Europe phrasebook

Travel Literature: The Olive Grove: Travels in Greece

NORTH AMERICA

Alaska • Backpacking in Alaska • Baja California • California & Nevada • Canada • Florida • Hawaii • Honolulu • Los Angeles • Mexico • Miami • New England • New Orleans • New York City • New York, New Jersey & Pennsylvania • Pacific Northwest USA • Rocky Mountain States • San Francisco • Southwest USA • USA phrasebook • Washington, DC & the Capital Region

CENTRAL AMERICA & THE CARIBBEAN

Bermuda • Central America on a shoestring • Costa Rica • Cuba • Eastern Caribbean • Guatemala, Belize & Yucatán: La Ruta Maya • Jamaica

SOUTH AMERICA

Argentina, Uruguay & Paraguay • Bolivia • Brazil • Brazilian phrasebook • Buenos Aires • Chile & Easter Island • Chile & Easter Island travel atlas • Colombia • Ecuador & the Galápagos Islands • Latin American Spanish phrasebook • Peru • Quechua phrasebook • Rio de Janeiro • South America on a shoestring • Trekking in the Patagonian Andes • Venezuela

Travel Literature: Full Circle: A South American Journey

ANTARCTICA

Antarctica

ISLANDS OF THE INDIAN OCEAN

Madagascar & Comoros • Maldives • Mauritius, Réunion & Seychelles

AFRICA

Africa - the South • Africa on a shoestring • Arabic (Moroccan) phrasebook • Cape Town • Central Africa • East Africa • Egypt • Egypt travel atlas • Ethiopian (Amharic) phrasebook • Kenya • Kenya travel atlas • Malawi, Mozambique & Zambia • Morocco • North Africa • South Africa, Lesotho & Swaziland • South Africa, Lesotho & Swaziland travel atlas • Swahili phrasebook • Trekking in East Africa • West Africa • Zimbabwe, Botswana & Namibia • Zimbabwe, Botswana & Namibia travel atlas

Travel Literature: The Rainbird: A Central African Journey • Songs to an African Sunset: A Zimbabwean Story

MAIL ORDER

Lonely Planet products are distributed worldwide.They are also available by mail order from Lonely Planet, so if you have difficulty finding a title please write to us. North American and South American residents should write to Embarcadero West, 155 Filbert St, Suite 251, Oakland CA 94607, USA; European and African residents should write to 10 Barley Mow Passage, Chiswick, London W4 4PH; and residents of other countries to PO Box 617, Hawthorn, Victoria 3122, Australia.

NORTH-EAST ASIA

Beijing • Cantonese phrasebook • China • Hong Kong • Hong Kong, Macau & Guangzhou • Japan • Japanese phrasebook • Japanese audio pack • Korea • Korean phrasebook • Mandarin phrasebook • Mongolia • Mongolian phrasebook • North-East Asia on a shoestring • Seoul • Taiwan • Tibet • Tibet phrasebook • Tokyo

Travel Literature: Lost Japan

MIDDLE EAST & CENTRAL ASIA

Arab Gulf States • Arabic (Egyptian) phrasebook • Central Asia • Iran • Israel & the Palestinian Territories • Israel & the Palestinian Territories travel atlas • Istanbul • Jerusalem • Jordan & Syria • Jordan, Syria & Lebanon travel atlas • Lebanon • Middle East • Turkey • Turkish phrasebook • Turkey travel atlas • Yemen

Travel Literature: The Gates of Damascus • Kingdom of the Film Stars: Journey into Jordan

ALSO AVAILABLE:

Travel with Children • Traveller's Tales

INDIAN SUBCONTINENT

Bangladesh • Bengali phrasebook • Delhi • Hindi/Urdu phrasebook • India • India & Bangladesh travel atlas • Indian Himalaya • Karakoram Highway • Nepal • Nepali phrasebook • Pakistan • Rajasthan • Sri Lanka • Sri Lanka phrasebook • Trekking in the Indian Himalaya • Trekking in the Karakoram & Hindukush • Trekking in the Nepal Himalaya

Travel Literature: In Rajasthan • Shopping for Buddhas

SOUTH-EAST ASIA

Bali & Lombok • Bangkok • Burmese phrasebook • Cambodia • Ho Chi Minh City • Indonesia • Indonesian phrasebook • Indonesian audio pack • Jakarta • Java • Laos • Lao phrasebook • Laos travel atlas • Malay phrasebook • Malaysia, Singapore & Brunei • Myanmar (Burma) • Philippines • Pilipino phrasebook • Singapore • South-East Asia on a shoestring • South-East Asia phrasebook • Thailand • Thailand's Islands & Beaches • Thailand travel atlas • Thai phrasebook • Thai audio pack • Thai Hill Tribes phrasebook • Vietnam • Vietnamese phrasebook • Vietnam travel atlas

AUSTRALIA & THE PACIFIC

Australia • Australian phrasebook • Bushwalking in Australia • Bushwalking in Papua New Guinea • Fiji • Fijian phrasebook • Islands of Australia's Great Barrier Reef • Melbourne • Micronesia • New Caledonia • New South Wales & the ACT • New Zealand • Northern Territory • Outback Australia • Papua New Guinea • Papua New Guinea phrasebook • Queensland • Rarotonga & the Cook Islands • Samoa • Solomon Islands • South Australia • Sydney • Tahiti & French Polynesia • Tasmania • Tonga • Tramping in New Zealand • Vanuatu • Victoria • Western Australia

Travel Literature: Islands in the Clouds • Sean & David's Long Drive

THE LONELY PLANET STORY

Lonely Planet published its first book in 1973 in response to the numerous 'How did you do it?' questions Maureen and Tony Wheeler were asked after driving, bussing, hitching, sailing and railing their way from England to Australia.

Written at a kitchen table and hand collated, trimmed and stapled, *Across Asia on the Cheap* became an instant local bestseller, inspiring thoughts of another book.

Eighteen months in South-East Asia resulted in their second guide, *South-East Asia on a shoestring*, which they put together in a backstreet Chinese hotel in Singapore in 1975. The 'yellow bible', as it quickly became known to backpackers around the world, soon became *the* guide to the region. It has sold well over half a million copies and is now in its 9th edition, still retaining its familiar yellow cover.

Today there are over 240 titles, including travel guides, walking guides, language kits & phrasebooks, travel atlases and travel literature. The company is the largest independent travel publisher in the world. Although Lonely Planet initially specialised in guides to Asia, today there are few corners of the globe that have not been covered.

The emphasis continues to be on travel for independent travellers. Tony and Maureen still travel for several months of each year and play an active part in the writing, updating and quality control of Lonely Planet's guides.

They have been joined by over 70 authors and 170 staff at our offices in Melbourne (Australia), Oakland (USA), London (UK) and Paris (France). Travellers themselves also make a valuable contribution to the guides through the feedback we receive in thousands of letters each year and on our web site.

The people at Lonely Planet strongly believe that travellers can make a positive contribution to the countries they visit, both through their appreciation of the countries' culture, wildlife and natural features, and through the money they spend. In addition, the company makes a direct contribution to the countries and regions it covers. Since 1986 a percentage of the income from each book has been donated to ventures such as famine relief in Africa; aid projects in India; agricultural projects in Central America; Greenpeace's efforts to halt French nuclear testing in the Pacific; and Amnesty International.

'I hope we send people out with the right attitude about travel. You realise when you travel that there are so many different perspectives about the world, so we hope these books will make people more interested in what they see. Guidebooks can't really guide people. All you can do is point them in the right direction.'

– Tony Wheeler

LONELY PLANET PUBLICATIONS

Australia
PO Box 617, Hawthorn 3122, Victoria
tel: (03) 9819 1877 fax: (03) 9819 6459
e-mail: talk2us@lonelyplanet.com.au

USA
Embarcadero West, 155 Filbert St, Suite 251,
Oakland, CA 94607
tel: (510) 893 8555 TOLL FREE: 800 275-8555
fax: (510) 893 8563
e-mail: info@lonelyplanet.com

UK
10 Barley Mow Passage, Chiswick,
London W4 4PH
tel: (0181) 742 3161 fax: (0181) 742 2772
e-mail: lonelyplanetuk@compuserve.com

France:
71 bis rue du Cardinal Lemoine, 75005 Paris
tel: 1 44 32 06 20 fax: 1 46 34 72 55
e-mail: 100560.415@compuserve.com

World Wide Web: http://www.lonelyplanet.com
or *AOL* keyword: lp